PEIRCE, SIGNS, AND MEANING

C.S. Peirce was the founder of pragmatism and a pioneer in the field of semiotics. His work investigated the problem of meaning, which is the core aspect of semiosis as well as a significant issue in many academic fields. Floyd Merrell demonstrates throughout *Pierce, Signs, and Meaning* that Peirce's views remain dynamically relevant to the analysis of subsequent work in the philosophy of language.

Merrell discusses Peirce's thought in relation to that of early-twentieth-century philosophers such as Frege, Russell, and Quine, and contemporaries such as Goodman, Putnam, Davidson, and Rorty. In doing so, Merrell demonstrates how quests for meaning inevitably fall victim to vagueness in pursuit of generality, and how vagueness manifests an inevitable tinge of inconsistency, just as generalities always remain incomplete. He suggests that vagueness and incompleteness/generality, overdetermination and underdetermination, and Peirce's phenomenological categories of Firstness, Secondness, and Thirdness must be incorporated into notions of sign structure for a proper treatment of meaning. He also argues that the twentieth-century search for meaning has placed overbearing stress on language while ignoring nonlinguistic sign modes and means.

Peirce, Signs, and Meaning is an important sequel to Merrell's trilogy, *Signs Becoming Signs*, *Semiosis in the Postmodern Age*, and *Signs Grow*. This book is not only a significant contribution to the field of semiotics, it has much to offer scholars in literature, philosophy, linguistics, cultural studies, and other academic disciplines in which meaning is a central concern.

FLOYD MERRELL is Professor of Semiotics and Spanish-American Literature at Purdue University.

FLOYD MERRELL

Peirce, Signs, and Meaning

UNVERSITY OF TORONTO PRESS
Toronto Buffalo London

Toronto Buffalo London
Printed in Canada

ISBN 0-8020-4135-3 (cloth)
ISBN 0-8020-7982-2 (paper)

♾

Toronto Studies in Semiotics
Editors: Marcel Danesi, Umberto Eco, Paul Perron, Thomas A. Sebeok

---

Canadian Cataloguing in Publication Data

Merrell. Floyd, 1937–
Pierce, signs, and meaning

(Toronto studies in semiotics)
Includes bibliographical references and index.
ISBN 0-8020-4135-3 (bound) ISBN 0-8020-7982-2 (pbk.)

1. Meaning (Philosophy). 2. Semiotics. 3. Peirce, Charles S. (Charles Sanders), 1839–1914. I. Title. II. Series.

B840.M46 1997 121'.68 C96-932017-5

University of Toronto Press acknowledges the financial assistance to its publishing program of the Canada Council and the Ontario Arts Council.

Contents

Introduction

Exordium

So I guess I had to embark on another book, which you now have in your hands. It all began almost a decade ago when I sifted through a pile of notes and wrote *Signs Becoming Signs: Our Perfusive, Pervasive Universe* (1991), which celebrated Charles S. Peirce's *processual semiotics*. Then, focus on *signs amongst signs*, that is, signs now actualized and offering themselves up to their interpreters – who are, themselves, so many signs – culminated in another book, *Semiosis in the Postmodern Age* (1995a). Finally, the general concept of signs growing, developing, evolving motivated the third volume of a rather self-indulgent trilogy: *Signs Grow: Semiosis and Life Processes* (1996). Following this meagre contribution to academic vainglory, why should I attempt – or even want, for that matter – to proceed?

Well, there remained this matter of the uncertain, vacillating *scandal of meaning*. I write 'scandal,' for throughout the ages meditation, speculation, deliberation, and debate on the nature of meaning has left the door open to opprobrium, ignominy, and unending frustration (the phrase 'scandal of meaning' also comes from a special session at the Charles Sanders Peirce Sesquicentennial Congress, Harvard University, 1989, where it was repeated on several occasions). The concept of meaning has been almost exclusively limited to the use of human language by human beings. This has more often than not culminated in unabashed 'linguicentrism' (which includes 'logocentricm'), with little regard for nonlinguistic semiotic modes. The fact of the matter is that meaning cannot live by language alone. Language, of course, is most comfortable in its familiar playpen and surrounded by an abundance of speakers with which to entertain itself. Yet it provides no guarantees regarding meaning: the reports of mystics, poets, rhetoricians, scientists, and our everyday stuttering and stammering bear witness to its notorious limitations. Neither is meaning available exclusively by way of the concepts of extension, denotation, reference, correspondence, and representation. That hopeful dream was put to rest some time ago, though many scholars are still hanging around to witness the last gasps of the senile world picture. It seemed to me that if any form or fashion of meaning is accessible to our finite, fallible intellectual faculties at all, surely it must incorporate the whole of Peirce's concept of the sign, which attempted to take on the indefinitely vast nonlinguistic sphere of *semiosis*. The idea began to captivate me. So eventually I had to go on, knowing full well that once again there would be no royal epistemological road to that venerable endgame, 'truth,' but hardly more than some vague, infinitely diverging, converging, set of cerebral goat trails lining precarious canyon walls enshrouded in an obstinate mist.

There were, to be sure, lingering doubts, sneaky feelings of inadequacy for the task ahead – after all, given my academic preparation I wasn't supposed to be meddling in this sort of thing – a sense of being tossed about in a sea of ambiguity, the lingering premonition that it would all come to naught. Of course, the very idea of meaning is presumptuous in the first place. Any and all attempts to wrap it up in a tidy package are in all likelihood predestined to end in 'scandal' of one form or another. For one's belief that one will be capable of coming to grips with meaning must surely be the greatest pretension of them all. But much the same could be said of the West's age-old quest for such imponderables as knowledge, 'truth,' and, above all, foundations regarding our most cherished foci of interest. To discover the ultimate building blocks of nature, to know the outer reaches of the universe, to give counsel regarding moral standards, to determine and define cultural values, to provide the ultimate criteria for excellence in art, to talk with God or with children or with the animals with the claim of understanding them: how supercilious all! Yet the rebuttal has it that to cease these predilections, queries, and impositions would be virtually to cease being human.

So yes, meaning. I suppose. Well anyway, why not?

Preliminaries

As things turned out, I expect the pages that follow will not strike you as just another volume on meaning. They begin on a tangential, yet nonlinear note. This is, I would submit, a reasonably poetic step, for Charles S. Peirce, whose thought influences this book, leaves few well-hewn paths with clear, distinct, and unambiguous slashes on nearby trees to mark the way. Quite the contrary. He intimates, suggests, implies, teases, and cajoles, but he also surprises, pushes, jolts, and at times insults. Consequently, how is it possible to present a neo-Peircean semiotic view of meaning in anything but a roundabout way? What can be said without vacillating allusions? Where can any solid anchor point be found, if one knows not from whence one came or whereto one should proceed?

Indeed, nowhere is semiotic indeterminacy more evident than on the question of meaning. In fact, the overriding theme of this inquiry will be that *indeterminacy*, at the heart of the *vagueness* and *generality*, the *inconsistency* and *incompleteness*, and the *overdetermination* and *underdetermination* of any and all signs, is no less than the fulcrum point of the life of signs and hence of their meaning (I cannot overemphasize the importance of the italicized terms to the thesis to be presented in this inquiry, as should become quite evident). But it is by nature a sliding fulcrum point. Consequently, the concept of meaning eludes one at the very moment it seems to be within one's grasp. Yet, signs and their meanings are inseparable, for signs would not be signs in the full-blown sense if devoid of meaning. So to the question 'Where is meaning?' the answer is 'Not in the confines of the skull, in the sign itself, in the thing to which it presumably refers, or somewhere in the imaginary – though illusory – conduit, that invisible conduit tube between sign emitter and sign receiver.' Meaning is nowhere and at the same time it is everywhere; it is in the interrelations of the sign interaction incessantly being played out on the stage of *semiosis*. Meaning is largely an informal, virtually unspecifiable and untheorizable, commodity.

Nonetheless, theories of meaning have abounded during the present century, with obsessive focus on language that has given rise to the likes of logical positivism, analytical philosophy, speech-act theory, hermeneutics, phenomenology, semiology, structuralism and poststructuralism, generative semantics, pragmatics, narratology, discourse analysis, and other 'linguicentric' practices, including even deconstruction. Many problems and questionable practices remain, however. Some scholars have a propensity to conflate words and their meanings, subjects and language, texts and authors and readers, and texts and the world. Others divorce language from their users and the world, as if contexts and thinking and feeling speakers did not exist. Still others pluck sentences out of common usage, or they invent perversely simple to highly improbable statements in order to test them in the mental laboratory of abstract theories. In the final analysis all these theorists are more often than not puppeteers holding on their strings not even so much as wooden speakers and hearers, or writers and readers, but nothing more than imaginary words, sentences, texts, narrative, discourse, and quite a lot of hot air. (The problem in this regard has been in large part due to the fact that much contemporary linguistic theory and philosophy has emerged from mathematical logic and metamathematics. This influence of formal logic on linguistic theory has been paralleled by the adoption of a linguistic account in metamathematical practices [see Stenlund 1990, for a critique of these practices]. It has frequently resulted in the concept of language as a calculus or formal system comparable to the systems of formal logic. Consequently, the rules, derived for mathematical logic and determining the technical use of words such as 'language,' 'proposition,' 'reference,' 'correspondence,' 'representation,' and 'interpretation,' and originally adapted to the description of formal systems, have been mistakenly appropriated for the study of ordinary language use. In the final chapters of this inquiry, it may appear that I too am guilty of this sin. My exoneration may be found, however, in my taking the entire range of signs into account, not strictly language.)

In spite of the many incursions into the depths of signs, their meanings have remained elusive. Meaning flows along within the *semiosic* process, resisting any and all artificial pigeon-holes. It is, as a result of this flow, plurality rather than singularity; it is many not one, continuous not discrete. Meaning does not emerge through some specifiable contact between people and people and between people and language and language and the world, but rather, it is the very process of emergence, the emergence of everything that *is* in the world, *our* 'semiotic world.' If we try to specify meaning in precise terms we are playing a tail-chasing-dog game inevitably ending in frustration. If we try to focus on it for the sake of analysis, the very focal point becomes that which we are in the process of producing. If we play a sort of quietist role of waiting for it to come to us, what we thought was its appearance in pristine form turns out to be our own reflection. The problem is that we would like to look for meaning as if it were an object coexisting with the sign, or as if it were in the sign itself, but once we become aware of it within the *semiosic* process, it has already passed on along the stream to become another sign. Signs, ultimately, speak for themselves. In a certain sense, they are their own meanings. Signs and the meanings that emerge from their interrelated, interactive dance are a shimmering mirage that refracts and takes on a new countenance at the mere suggestion of our futile, furtive glance. We cannot help but play hide-and-seek with ourselves in our relentless pursuit of the elusive meaning of our signs. (I should reveal at this juncture that I do not buy into the idea, common to many students of 'postmodernism,' that in our times we are experiencing a devastating loss of meaning, a notion especially prevalent in the writings of Jean Baudrillard [1981, 1983a, 1983b; also Kellner 1989:118, Pefanis 1991:11; for further in this regard, Merrell 1991a].)

Consequently, as is by now quite obvious, I remain critical of most formal and programmatic theories of meaning. I would say of meaning what Hilary

Putnam (1983b:xvii) says of 'truth.' It is 'as vague, interest relative, and context sensitive as *we* are.' And, as I shall argue throughout the pages that follow, we cannot help but fall victim to *vagueness* in our tireless quest for *generality*, and our *vagueness* will manifest an inevitable tinge of *inconsistency*, just as our *generalities* will always remain *incomplete*. In this regard, Peirce's semiotics can be alternatively regarded 'as a theory of meaning or signification, as a theory of communication, as a theory of inference and implication, as a theory of mind, or as a theory of knowledge and truth. (The list is not exhaustive.) It can be regarded in all these ways not because it is ambiguous, or because Peirce confusedly failed to distinguish these concerns, but because he adopted a point of view and forged out a system of concepts within which all of these concerns find a common basis of expression and articulation' (Ransdell 1979:51). In the most general sense, Peirce's semiotics by its very nature *includes* a theory of meaning. But semiotics is not about meaning in the ordinary way of taking it. It is about meaning engendered when signs are in their act of becoming signs, a becoming that includes sign interpreters as participating agents in the very *semiosic* process of becoming. I cannot overemphasize my contention that meaning is not in the signs, the things, or the head; it is in the processual rush of *semiosis*; it is always already on the go toward somewhere and somewhen. At least that is what I shall attempt to illustrate as the pages of this book pass from right to left.

But enough. There's really nothing more I can say before I get down to the task of trying to say what I hope I have to say. Before I do that, however, I should write a few words on the Preamble and the fifteen chapters that make up this volume.

The Layout

In the Preamble, I wish to set the tone for what is to follow with allusions to each of the diversity of topics herein discussed. I do this in the form of a dialogue between three characters, Alpha, Omega, and the Master. It is my expectation that this brief preview may whet the appetite for the main course, and at the same time afford a broad overview of the general theme to be discussed within the covers of this book. The focus of that general theme is above all, to put it bluntly, Peirce. Over the years I have come to an awareness of the importance of Peirce's philosophy and of his concept of the sign. I believe his thought quite effectively addresses itself to many contemporary issues – this I also attempted to present in *Semiosis in the Postmodern Age*. Consequently, though during a reading of this book at times pages may come and go without specific references to Peirce, he is always lurking in the background, awaiting his moment to reenter the scene and join in the dialogic ensemble voicing overtures bordering on and often entering the hazy arena of meaning.

In chapters 1 and 2 I attempt to paint the essential background for a Peircean discussion of meaning, which includes his concept of triadicity, self-other relationships, our rampant Faustian notion of individualism, and above all, the necessary distinction between 'real objects' and merely 'semiotically real objects' and the relations between signs and their/our 'semiotically real worlds.' This move calls for an initial presentation of the concepts, destined to become *leitmotifs*, of *vagueness* and *generality*, *inconsistency* and *incompleteness*, and *overdetermination* and *underdetermination*, all of which, I believe, are necessary to the very idea of 'semiotic meaning.' Chapter 3 argues that meaning cannot be divorced from notions of storytelling and fictionality. The engenderment of meaning in this sense demands presentation of *what is not as if it were* – the essence of fictions – which is impossible without the concept of *otherness*. In this sense meaning in distinctively human semiotics is primarily, though not exclusively, the *other* of the sign as it now *is*, that which the sign under other circumstances *would not be* – more specific to symbolicity than iconicity or indexicality. And the 'semiotically real' – as distinguished from the 'real' *an sich* – is the product of meaning, that which the 'semiotically real' *is not*. That is to say, the 'semiotically real' is the product of meaning, with which it is endowed by the *other* of signs, and the signs' meaning is *other* than the signs, that is, it is incorporated in the relationship between the 'semiotically real,' the signs, and their respective *other*. Meaning is in the interrelations, in the interaction, the interconnectedness. Meaning is thus in a sense parasitic on the 'real.' It severs it, carves it up, and at times mutilates it, in order to make way for the construction of signs and 'semiotically real' worlds of various and sundry stripes.

Chapter 4 engages in a discussion of Peirce's 'pragmatic maxim.' In order to develop this theme, the above-mentioned fiction/'real' distinction is provisionally introduced by way of Pierre Duhem's exposition on two alternative scientific views and methods: English empiricism and French rationalism. Attention is then turned to what might be considered an inevitable topic, in light of the sets of distinctions put forth in previous chapters: Peirce's concept of 'thought-signs,' and Alexis von Meinong's mental 'objects.' In spite of my rhetorical practices to that point, the argument will be presented that there are no absolute distinctions, classes, or taxonomies of which we as human semiotic agents are capable. During this argument, the fallacy of traditional notions of 'reference,' 'correspondence,' 'representation,' and 'objectivity' come to the fore. This issue brings with it implications of Peirce's somewhat unhappy concoction of 'idealism' and 'objectivism' – or perhaps one might say, 'realism' and 'subjectivism,' depending upon the vantage – which Peirce dubbed 'objective idealism,' a brief discussion of which will conclude this chapter. The next move, in chapter 5, inspired by philosophy of science and mathematics, brings *inconsistency* and *incompleteness* and their sister terms, *vagueness* and *generality* and *overdetermination* and *underdetermination*, to a shrill pitch. The accompanying suggestion is that *inconsistency* at local – and radically *incomplete* – levels can and in many cases should be tolerated, since sooner or later during our semiotic practices an anomaly or two will pop up anyway. But, the suggestion will be that we should try for *consistency* at larger levels, though there is no way we can really know without a shadow of a doubt if the whole is *consistent*, for there is no view, *sub specie aeternitatis*, accessible to us. In other words, the venerable concept of foundations is placed in question. In this regard at least, Peirce, it will become evident, is quite contemporary, and in line with much postanalytic, postpositivist, poststructuralist thought.

A brief Interlude follows, consisting of chapter 6. There, finally, I get to the meat of the matter. I present for further consideration what I hold to be the genuine Peircean concept of triadicity, in contrast to the customary semiotic 'triangle' and to semiological binary notions of the sign. I offer a preliminary discussion of Peirce's basic sign types and their interrelations, which will be used as a wedge to pry open the faults and fissures of 'standard reference theory,' particularly from Gottlob Frege onward. During this discussion, the concepts of *learnability*, *accountability*, and *knowability* are introduced by way of a brief return to *vagueness* and *generality* and *overdetermination* and *underdetermination*, with special focus on *acts of relating*, rather than *things related to*.

Chapter 7 continues the critique of Frege's concept of meaning, illustrating in the process that his program of 'linguicentrism,' of 'objectivism,' of a static view of signs and the determinacy of their meaning, is by and large inadequate. The work of Georg Cantor and Richard Dedekind with respect to sets and the problem of infinity emerges, which will have a bearing on future chapters, especially during considerations of Nelson Goodman, Putnam, W.V.O. Quine, and, of course, Peirce. In the following chapter I present various guises of what I dub 'linguicentric holism,' quite the vogue in some circles these days, and its limitations *vis-à-vis* '*semiosic* holism.' On so doing, I introduce Putnam's controversial yet intriguing rendition of the Löwenheim-Skolem theorem in his account of natural language use and the problematics of meaning. I attempt to illustrate how the theorem has a lesson for us regarding the now familiar terms *vagueness-generality*, *inconsistency-incompleteness*, and *overdetermination-underdetermination*. Chapter 9 then focuses on Putnam's 'There is no God's Eye view' in light of his 'brains-in-a-vat' thought experiment, which argues that meanings are not in the head, the object, or the sign, which also supports the idea, presented in chapters 2 and 3, that there is no determinable ahistorical boundary between fiction and the 'real' and the 'semiotically real' and the 'real.' This discussion then introduces, by way of a few Jorge Luis Borges–inspired examples, various paradoxes of infinity: how Peirce's concept of the sign bears on them, and why we cannot escape them once and for all. I suggest that, given human imaginative capacities, there is less closure to thought and to signs than even Putnam might be willing to admit. To make matters apparently worse, an intractable element of uncertainty, revealing our ultimate limitations, remains. Yet there is, in the final analysis, a vague sort of closure, if only because, after exhaustion ensues, or upon reaching a hitherto unforeseen point, we can go no further.

Chapter 10 extends the reasons why 'standard reference theory' is inadequate in view of Putnam's 'twin-earth' thought experiment. Peirce's concept of sign *translation*, I then argue, entails the process of meaning engenderment: signs becoming *other* than what they are, becoming a 'difference that makes a difference,' which is the very essence of semiotic meaning. Putnam's Löwenheim-Skolem model is re-evoked and briefly placed alongside Quine's celebrated but occasionally maligned example of a field linguist attempting to learn the language of another culture in his display of the 'indeterminacy of translation' and the 'inscrutability of reference' theses. This juxtaposition of Putnam and Quine brings on a reintroduction of *vagueness* – by way of the 'sorites paradox' – as well as *generality* and *overdetermination-underdetermination*, which constantly threaten to abrogate the classical principles of noncontradiction and the excluded middle. All these moves, I observe, are tangentially related to Peirce, who never ceased in his effort to bring abstractions in line with the 'concrete reasonableness' of everyday living. From the Peircean perspective I then argue that since I present a concept of meaning as indefinitely variable, alternative meanings can always pop up when least expected. Notice: the meandering, self-reflexive, at times convoluting and involuting path this book takes gently nudges us along, and the nebulous horizon becomes somewhat more distinct, though it cannot but remain vague, out there, somewhere, in the horizon; we and the meanings of our signs are one, and precisely for that reason our game of lassoing them in for an objective look is so aggravatingly elusive. Yet, we can't simply let meanings be, for they are us and we them.

Chapter 11 addresses what appears at the outset to be a hopelessly bizarre Putnam thought experiment: the apparently simple 'Cat on a mat' sentence mistaken for 'Cherries on a tree.' I use Putnam's story in an attempt to illustrate, via Borges's Pierre Menard, that the very idea of reference is even more radically indeterminate than Quine would have it, for all signs are indelibly caught up in the process of their becoming. Chapter 12 then addresses Goodman's 'new riddle of induction,' in conjunction with a brief discussion of the Duhem-Quine thesis, Ludwig Wittgenstein on rule following, and Carl Hempel's 'raven paradox.' I contend that a 'time-dependent logic,' a nonformal 'logic of vagueness,' predicated on Firstness in addition to Secondness and Thirdness – a 'logic' Peirce often promised but did not deliver – is necessary. In order to substantiate this argument, a synthesis of Frege, Putnam, Goodman, and Quine is brought into further relation with *vagueness-generality* and *overdetermination-underdetermination* in order to provide a new context for their interpretation. This brings me back, once again, to the idea of meaning. I suggest that even regarding natural and formal languages, meaning cannot live either by symbolicity and Thirdness or by indexicality and Secondness alone: a dose of iconicity is always present, whether we know it or not and whether we like it or not. Given this view, in my subsequent discussion, the body is at long last returned to the sign, and the icon to the symbol (via the index), which has also been a topic of much concern in our postanalytic, poststructuralist, postmodern times.

Chapter 13 offers a synoptic grasp of the thought experiments, perspectives, and conjectures discussed thus far. In their composite they are guilty of 'linguicentrism' (a product of the 'linguistic turn'). Peirce's *abduction*, the third leg of his tripod including *induction* and *deduction*, is introduced, with the contention that all three components of this triad are necessary for a 'logic' of creativity, invention, and construction, and for their incorporation into a given community's body of narrative of all sorts. Chapter 14 offers a crash course on Peirce's concept of the sign. One would expect that the first chapter of a book of this nature should introduce Peirce on the sign. But no. I have organized things in a roundabout way. The method of my madness is this: if the ephemerality, the elusiveness, of the very idea of meaning is first sensed, felt, intuited, from many angles, then the impact of Peirce's sign theory should be all the more intriguing. At least that is what I would like to think. With this in mind, I present the specifics of Peirce's three basic trichotomies, *qualisigns-sinsigns-legisigns*, *icons-indices-symbols*, and *terms(words)-propositions(sentences)-arguments(texts)* and place them in the context of the previous chapters. Then, I attempt to evoke the general notion that, if our signs and their meanings are at one with us and we with them, then there can be no body-mind distinction, but both, as signs among signs, are fused into the effervescent stream of *semiosis*. And finally, chapter 15 foregrounds the role of the body, of the contribution of kinesthetic, corporeal, visceral sensing and feeling in meaning engenderment. The recent work of George Lakoff and Mark Johnson is evoked, as is briefly that of Maurice Merleau-Ponty and others. Ultimately, I suggest, meaning is actually nowhere and nowhen, but always already in the process of emerging within particular *semiosic* contexts. It is, simply put, in the beginning 'felt,' and only then can it be articulated – albeit vaguely, incompletely, and indeterminately, as it were.

Now the body is squarely within the sign. But actually, it was there all along. We just didn't know it, or didn't want to acknowledge it, soporifically caught up as we generally are in what we would like to think is our venerable hard-nosed discourse, which remains divorced from corporeal and even visceral feelings, sentiments, wishes, desires, and needs – all of which is OK for common folk, but not for us. The message is that our signs are indelibly corporeal as well as intellectual, during the course of all our comings and goings. Yes. The sign is put back in the bodymind, after centuries of exclusive residence in the imaginary limbo of the Western mind that presumably remained autonomous of, and when at its best the imperious master of, the body.

The Design

A brief word on the strategies involved in this inquiry is also in order. After the *Preamble* was set on paper, I decided to eschew footnotes altogether in the remainder of this volume: footnotes tend to be cumbersome, a nuisance, often superfluous, and at times hardly more than the author's ostentatious show of pseudo-erudition and an insult to the reader. Some of what might otherwise go into footnote fodder is found in the text in the form of parenthetical material – as you already witnessed in the second section of this introduction. These asides can be taken or they can be simply ignored, according to the curiosity, patience, and whims of the reader.

Throughout the pages that follow, I allude often to semiology (in contrast to Peircean semiotics), poststructuralism, and deconstruction, without qualifying the terms. These allusions are for the most part to trends in continental thought, about which this inquiry is not. In the first place, I assume the terms are sufficiently familiar to the reader not to warrant detailed treatment here. In the second place, since I have offered commentary and critique on semiology, poststructuralism, and deconstruction elsewhere (Merrell 1985, 1991, 1992, 1995a, 1995b, 1996), I see no need to reiterate those arguments here.

In presenting my arguments, I avail myself of a host of examples, many of them in the way of paradoxes, to illustrate the various facets of my thesis on meaning as they emerge in the text. These examples should perhaps be taken as extended metaphors, conceits, or even parables: they are icons that indexically point out, however vaguely, the message of the story being told – or perhaps they may indicate the 'punch lines,' if you will, of cynical games and satirical twists. All in all, the text is a display to be gazed upon, contemplated.

It is not a linear argument against linear arguments; it is an intricate web, not a set of bifurcating pathways; it is a nonlinear rhizome, not roots and branches.

Acknowledgments

I suppose that by some stretch of the imagination it could be said that the words in this book are mine. But not really. The ideas implied by the marks on the pages that follow, to be sure, come from elsewhere. From reading, listening, looking, pondering, contemplating, or whatever. I doubt that there is a single novel idea in these pages, or in the other pages I have had the good fortune to see in print. If the ideas are not mine, then neither are the words, since all ideas are signs anyway. Consequently, whatever I have been able to put into traces on the monitor are by no means the result of closet thinking. I have been aided by many friends and associates, more often than not unbeknownst to them.

Though the many scholars who have influenced me during my mental wanderings are too numerous to list here, I cannot fail to make mention of certain individuals who are most prominent in my mind as I conclude this preface. First and foremost are Tom Sebeok, Marcel Danesi, and Ron Schoeffel, whose support was instrumental toward realization of this book in its present form. I also owe a special debt to those who attended a seminar I had the good fortune to conduct during the fall of 1993, during which time I was able to air out many of the ideas that follow. Anthropologist Professor Myrdene Anderson's moderative voice as an auditor was ubiquitous, as was the critical voice of literary theorist Professor Silvia Dapía. I thank them for their collegiality, patience, and input. Graduate student auditors from Spanish (Pithamber Polsani) and French (Anjali Prabhu) provided contributions far exceeding my expectations, especially in view of the fact that they were under the added pressure of forthcoming preliminary exams. And my students, hailing from Anthropology (Bret Bogart), Communication (Sibley Law), Comparative Literature (Denise Galarza, Yolanda Gamboa, Ozlem Ogut), and Spanish (Patricia Santos, Lucero Tenorio-Gavin), provided an ear, an inquisitive mind, a proper dose of doubt and scepticism to buffer my vanities, and plenty of creative input to prevent my expositions from lapsing into totally incoherent mumbling.

Finally, to Araceli, thank you, many times over. More often than not, wrapped within my own frail thoughts, and in single-minded pursuit of something – I never know what – I am not the easiest person to get along with. To you I owe whatever might be of some worth in these modest pages.

PEIRCE, SIGNS, AND MEANING

Preamble

Is Meaning Possible within Indefinite *Semiosis*?

The content, soul and spirit of science is lodged naturally in what in the last analysis its statements actually mean; the philosophical activity of giving meaning is therefore the Alpha and Omega of all scientific thinking.
Moritz Schlick

True sentences, observational and theoretical, are the alpha and omega of the scientific enterprise.
W.V.O. Quine

A philosopher is compelled to follow the maxim of epic poets and to plunge *in medias res*.
George Santayana

1. In It, Whatever That Is, Wherever We Are

Alpha: ... but ... any reliable account of meaning, it seems to me ... must use words that express what they have hitherto obscured. This makes unbearable demands on us, no? We are expected to say *what* our saying *is*, but we cannot say *it*, for it *is what* we are saying.

Omega: Good Lord! Like Nietzsche, Heidegger, Derrida, and other assorted poets, mystics, and nihilists, you gleefully embrace paradox. Forget paradoxes, along with Foucault, Baudrillard, Lyotard, and all other prophets of conundrums. The fact is that language must *refer to something*, for if not, it couldn't mean anything. Such intellectual giants as Frege and Russell have said so much.[1]

1 See Russell (1905) and more recently, Quine (1953, 1969) on the demand that that to which a sentence refers must exist, and for a general overview of this conception of things, Dummett

A: I rather doubt that meanings are available through reference, nor are they to be found in wave patterns in the air, in black marks on white, in the object of a sign, or in your skull for that matter. Granted, they must be made the object *of* our talk if we are to talk *about* them. But this is an impossible task, for our talk is caught within them. It's, well ... it's something like my saying 'I am lying.' Now if ...

O: Yes, I know. Cute linguistic tricks. The problem is that a contradictory sentence of the liar type is actually no sentence at all: it has a certain resemblance to a full-blown sign, but it falls short of the mark.

A: I merely brought up the liar in hopes of illustrating a flaw in your reference theory of meaning.

O: It's quite elementary, if you'll just listen to reason. Meaning exists in the *act of referring to* something. Your self-contradictory utterance refers to nothing other than itself, so it can have no genuine meaning.

Master: I fear we're getting nowhere. We were supposed to be engaged in amiable kibitzing without pretending we really know *anything*.[2]

O: Kibitzing Schlibitzing. All I want to know is *what* Alpha thinks he's talking *about*.

M: You must concede that his approach is intriguing. A sentence the likes of 'This sentence is not meaningful' appears to deny itself any condition of meaningfulness. Yet, if meaningless, it is nevertheless true, meaningfully true. And if true, it is false. We are capable somehow of imputing meaningfulness to the sentence before its *negation*, which renders it meaningless, has had a chance to become activated.

O: With due respect, your sentence, like Alpha's, lacks an object. It presumes membership to the set of all assertoric sentences, but it is deluded, for sentences that legitimately assert, assert *something about* an object. Your sentence merely 'talks of itself and only of itself and has no external relation whatsoever' (Peirce MS 340).

M: Agreed. Conditions of classical logic call for a sentence's having an *object*. But we must remember that for Charles Sanders Peirce, a sentence is subject to the medieval trivium: *grammar*, *logic* – which Peirce did not limit to its classical form – and *rhetoric*. The first is purely linguistic, while the second has been over the centuries construed as the *alpha* and *omega* of truth

---

(1978). Omega's view, which will surface as this Preamble unfolds, is generally in accord with a neo-Fregean concept of the sign, which will be subject to serious scrutiny in chapter 7.

2 'Kibitzing' refers to Rorty's (1979) 'conversation of mankind' – a phrase picked up from Michael Oakshott (for a critique of this facet of Rorty, see Malachowski 1990, Margolis 1991, Munz 1987, Sacks 1989).

conditions. The third, on the other hand, endows our liar sentence with respectability. Granted, the sentence is contradictory, but within the context of human communication (that is, rhetoric, pragmatics), we often manage to render such meaningless utterances meaningful. For example, Russell's Theory of Logical Types bars sort crossing, yet in the give-and-take of everyday communication we quite often violate his interdiction and get on with the practical task of communicating.[3]

O: I look for order, while you two apparently wish to propagate self-defeating paradoxes!

M: To paraphrase Kierkegaard, a thinker without paradox is like a lover without feeling: mediocre at best. By all means let us entertain paradox.

O: I still insist that a meaningful and properly constructed sentence must bear sober tidings of *reference*. Your self-defeating sentence cannot be other than fatuous. Since through its predicate the sentence only refers to the reference of itself as an *object*, that *object* being in turn a reference to its own *object*, and so on, ad infinitum, has no legitimate semiotic *object*. So 'it is absurd, which is the same as illogical' (MS 726; also Peirce *CP*:2.311).[4]

M: Not really. Granted, my sentence refuses to comply with what we ordinarily consider the minimal conditions for meaningfulness. However, its meaningfulness can be at least *tacitly* acknowledged, if it is so acknowledged against a background entailing its own *negation* – that is, a possibly meaningful string of (as yet unactualized) words.

O: Negation again! Now you make a hasty retreat in the face of insurmountable odds.

M: Yet you must admit that though the Liar Paradox *explicitly* asserts its own falsity, at the same time it *tacitly* asserts its truth. In other words, the sentence means two irreconcilable things (*CP*:3.447). Consequently, 'This sentence is meaningless' is not meaningless; it in a sense means too much; it is both true and false; it is *overdetermined* (*CP*:2.352, 2.383).[5]

O: You have now unfortunately embraced a *Principle of Included Contradictions*, deluding yourself into believing the most absurd of sentences can be true,

3 On Russell's Theory of Logical Types and the vicious-circle principle in this regard, see Rouilhan (1992), Hylton (1992).

4 The *object* to which I allude is from Peirce's concept of the sign. Briefly, an *interpretant* (roughly, meaning, but not to be confused with meaning in the ordinary 'correspondence theory' sense) and an *object* combine with a *representamen* (loosely, the sign, though a sign is actually much more [see Savan 1987–8]) to form the Peircean semiotic triad, in contrast to the Saussurean *signifier/signified* dichotomy – about which more *en passant*.

5 See Michael (1975) for further regarding this 'paradoxical solution to the Liar's Paradox' by way of Peirce (also the penetrating study by Pazukhin 1992).

or both true and false, as it were. Now *that* is *overdetermination* gone wild.[6] I'll stick to my guns. A self-referential, contradictory sentence without any subject other than itself and devoid of a semiotic *object* is meaningless, clearly and distinctly.

2. Of the Paradoxicon

M: Let me try to be more explicit. My paradoxical sentence implicitly alludes to what it *is not*, that is, it incorporates *negation*. A specific act of *negation* must bear indirect *relation to* something or other (itself in this case), the meaning of which is at least potentially specifiable – I prefer to avoid the term 'reference' here, for there is none, in the traditional sense at least. 'This sentence is meaningless' *relates to* itself, tacitly implying its own truth. In so doing it *negates* what it implies. But this very *negation* renders it meaningful, that is, meaningfully false, for what it implies – the truth of its expressed falsity – can be implied solely by way of its saying what it *is not*. It *is not* true, though its untruth is made possible solely by its implied truth. Without prior acknowledgment – at least tacit – of such a corpus of true sentences, *negation* loses its sting and falls from sight. In other words, *negation* requires a base to support it before it can act *negatively* on any-*thing*.

O: Can you prove *that*?

M: The next sentence I am going to utter will be true.

O: I don't follow you. Why should you *not intend* to speak the truth?

M: The last sentence I uttered was false.

O: It was? So simply withdraw it ... Oh, yes, I get it. Old Epimenides' paradox again, but this time by a devious – and perverted, I must say – route.

M: Devious, perhaps; perverted, no. My variation on the liar's self-destructive assertion should serve as a reminder that 'reference,' as you use the term, is often indirect, implicit.

O: You've lost me again.

M: To become aware *of* and explain meaning involves a certain degree of explicitness, and explicitness alone is capable of laying bare the device of contradiction. For example, the simple combination of a pair of terms composing the compound term 'square circle' implicitly contains no

6 *Overdetermination*, and its complement, *underdetermination*, as we shall note in the chapters that follow, are in part derived from Quine (1969), but more specifically I use the terms as a replacement for that mechanist-reductionist pair of terms, *overcoding* and *undercoding*, unfortunately often used in semiotic theory (for example, Eco 1976) (a preliminary definition of *overdetermination* is given in chapter 1).

contradiction; only when the terms in question are combined and construed with respect to their explicit definitions does contradiction surface. In other words, as long as a *superposition* of terms remains implicit, no contradiction has been highlighted: the terms remain *overdetermined*.[7] If the contradiction is rendered evident, it is so rendered by making part of what was implied by the *superposition* explicit (*CP*:2.603). But the implicit quandary in my sentence ordinarily presents no unbearable problem. In everyday language use it is often slipped in through the servant's entrance, and communication usually goes on quite well, thank you.

O: I continue to insist that we must banish paradoxes.

M: Actually, in many cases we can quite simply ignore them, since most of them are not really pernicious anyway. But if we wish to entertain them, we can more often than not do so pragmatically, and without getting in harm's way. In other words, from a more encompassing standpoint, my exemplary sentence 'This sentence is meaningless' is quite harmless (*CP*:2.315).

O: Aha! Tarski. I sense a distinction between an *object language* and its *metalanguage*. Your sentence, properly Tarskyianized, would be 'The sentence "This sentence is not meaningful" is true if and only if "This sentence is meaningful" is not meaningful.' The problem is that the sentence nonsensically refers to nothing but itself.

A: I thought that if we follow Tarski we are compelled ultimately to string out an infinite regress of metalanguages, so the problem is not really solved.

O: *Au contraire*, my dear Alpha. Tarski postulated a metalanguage, richer than the object-language, which refers to the object-language in such a way that it is capable of determining truth. If one wishes to know whether a particular sentence about the world is true, one must construct a metalanguage capable of asserting its truth or falsity. Putting Tarski's elaborate scheme crudely, to know whether 'Snow is white' is true, we address ourselves to the sentence by means of a metalanguage in the form of '"Snow is white" if and only if snow is white.' Then we *verify* the sentence and its accompanying metalanguage with the *evidence* at hand.

A: Yes ... I guess. But what about '"Nixon was not a crook" if and only if Nixon was not a crook'? Can anybody verify that to the satisfaction of the entire North American public? With what irrefutable evidence? And with what impeccable authority? Applying your method to the 'real' world, *our* world, things quickly become muddled, no?

7 What I wish to imply by *superposition* is a sort of quantum *eigenstate*, a scintillating, trembling, oscillating coexistence of possibilities without any of them having (yet) been actualized (see Merrell 1991, 1995a, 1996, for further).

M: The question is, whether Tarski's proof applies to natural language use or whether it must be limited to formal language. Tarski's theorem as a purely formal construct is closely related to Gödel's first theorem in this respect. The heart of Gödel's proof says that if a self-referential formal system is complete and sufficiently powerful, somewhere it falls into a contradiction the solution to which cannot be forthcoming from within it. So, *pace* Tarski, we jump to another level, and by so doing we think we can solve the contradiction. But eventually another one pops up, and so on, ad infinitum. The upshot is that although in formal languages paradoxes may presumably be avoided via Russell-Tarski and evaded via Gödel, my example of meaningfulness-meaninglessness never ceases to intervene in our ordinary language affairs. If meaning were conceived to be absolutely univocal in the sense of formal languages, then Gödel's proof would enter full force. But in actual everyday practices we are quite capable of rendering a surprisingly large number of our self-referentially contradictory sentences for practical purposes adequately meaningful.[8]

O: Your loose lumpenproletariat logic can only end in a blind alley of confusion. And we will be reduced to incoherent mumbling tantamount to Heidegger's 'Human beings remain committed to and within the being of language, and can never step out of it and look at it from somewhere else' (1971:134), of Derrida's '*There is nothing outside of the text*' (1974a:158), and of Nietzsche's '*We cease to think when we refuse to do so under the constraint of language*; we barely reach the doubt that sees this limitation as a limitation' (1968:522).

M: Look at it this way, Omega. Actual utterances as sounds in the air or writing as marks on paper are part of our physical world. But language itself is a *set of possibilities*. When a sentence hitherto unknown is engendered, meanings can be conjured up as a result of the interaction between addresser and addressee. Meanings are not simply there, in some Platonic sense. They appear only when signs are in the process of emerging within specific contexts. And when so emerging, they are invariably something slightly to radically other than what all previous meanings of the same words had been. Consequently, meanings are never co-present, absolutely self-identical, and univocal: they are fluid and indefinitely variable. They are derived from within the *semiosic* flow of signs. Language cannot give complete account of this flow, for it is 'inside' that very flow, and so are we (*CP*:5.310–17).

O: Once again, Russell would ride roughshod over such mental muddles.

M: And once again, Russell's prohibition is by and large innocuous regarding streetwise talk from within the *semiosic* woofs and warps. In this light,

8 This concept, which lies behind much of the disquisition that follows, is quite in line with the later Wittgenstein (1953, 1956).

commentators on Gödel's proof have suggested that not only formal systems, but also human thought in general, cannot be completely free of *incompleteness* and/or *inconsistency*. Yet the flow – and the thought it entails – may be capable somehow of saying much, though never the entirety, of what is known, and in so doing it says what it is for it to say something. Thus it says what it is without anything being said from a vantage point outside it. We hardly have any alternative but to pay lip service to the frailties of our language and thought while making fallible efforts to speak about our speaking, write about our writing, understand our understanding, and push along as best we can.

O: Do you really think you can salvage your metaphysical mush with such illogical tactics?

3. We Are Participants, Not Merely Actants

M: What body of thought as a totality is not illogical? Take quantum theory. It demolishes the split between observer and observed, yet the physicist is made of the very particles she describes. So how can she describe what she, herself, is? To paraphrase Max Planck, science cannot solve the ultimate mystery of nature, for in the final analysis we ourselves are part of the mystery we are trying to solve.

A: Yes ... I mean, that's what I was trying to say in the beginning. When the subject describes a minuscule portion of that which *is*, what her description asserts cannot be separated from the saying. Yet *what* she says is presumably independent of whatever meaning she might attach to her saying. In other words, the saying *is* what its object supposedly *is not*. So in the final analysis her description can say what *is* by saying what *is not*, which it, itself, in a roundabout way, *is*.

M: What you are vaguely suggesting might lead us to speculate on Peirce's notion that full-blown meanings can in the 'theoretical long run' be grasped by successive approximations, albeit with fits and jerks, and with many uncertain advances and retreats (*CP*:5.311).

O: Ah, yes. And now, that abominable Zenoesque asymptote.

M: Asymptote? In a certain way of putting it, I suppose. But for Peirce, any give-and-take approximation toward meaning is not continuous but punctuated by discontinuous breaks, and with no guarantee of success.[9] And you say

9 Mention of asymptotic convergence is in relation to Peirce's often maligned idea that science – and knowledge in general – is in a process of ever more closely approximating the truth (for a critique of Peirce's convergence theory, see Rorty 1991; for a discussion of the pros and cons, see Skagestad 1981; for a defence, Hausman 1993; and for expatiation on the discontinuity rather than continuity of Peirce's asymptotic approximation, Rescher 1978).

logic and reason reject Zeno? Not if we consider meaning to be radically *underdetermined* in the sense that there is no end to the future possibilities of meaning. For example, between two ambiguous meanings, A and B, at some point in time another meaning, A_1, a slight variation on A, may pop up, then another, B_{-1}, and another, A_2, and then B_{-2}, and so on. Gaps between A and B tend to be filled, but all the gaps can never be filled, so the game goes on.

O: And we now have a *Principle of Proliferating Middles* to accompany the *Principle of Included Contradictions*. To what extreme, this illogic? This radical *underdetermination*?[10]

M: *Underdetermination*, yes. And abrogation of the excluded-middle principle, quite possibly. It stems from the temporality, the transitivity, the incessant variability, of any and all signs and their meanings. If, as Peirce would have it, all signs refer to other signs, then we must be speaking of an unordered, nonlinear series. And if a sign is always in the process of becoming something other than what it was, then the series is not only indefinitely expanding, it also moves toward a state of *density*, or *continuity* – that is, the excluded-middle principle does not necessarily apply.

O: And our brains are ultimately reduced to a cognitive cabbage patch.

M: The notion of a *potentially infinite* – and *dense* – series is necessary, however, if it is the case that meaning can only be found in relations between signs, and relations between those relations. But actually, there is no real problem here, for the series is *potentially*, not *actually*, infinite, without any retrievable first or last sign.[11]

O: I still doubt that your ethereal scheme can be reconciled with the nuts and bolts of our concrete physical existence.

4. But Where Is the Mainstream of *Semiosis*?

M: Hm. Let me put it this way. Consider what Peirce (*CP*:5.441) called a 'cut,' that which precedes his categories of quasi-immediate *Firsts*, dyadic *Seconds*,

10 I will argue that just as *overdetermination* often shows little respect for the principle of contradiction, so also *underdetermination* does not necessarily embrace the excluded-middle principle. This, we shall note, is a radical departure from the notion of meaning in terms of *intentionality*, which by and large pays homage to both principles.

11 The concept of infinity comes in two flavours: *potential* and *actual*. According to the first, the furthest reach of human or computer computations at a given point in time is the whole of *our* conception of numbers, and although the addition of 1 or any other integer to this whole brings about its expansion, we will never reach the end. According to the latter, Platonist, view, the whole is always already there, and it is our charge to discover bits and pieces of it as best we can.

and mediate *Thirds.*[12] A 'cut' mars the 'nothingness' of pure *semiosic possibilia* (that is, that sphere preceding any and all divisions into *this* and *that*, *subject* and *object*, *semiotic agent* and *signs*). A *sign* is separated by a 'cut' from its *object* in some irretrievable present. But its *interpretant* emerges only mediately, since there can be no immediate consciousness *of* a sign *as* such. In this manner, an *interpretant* is an *interpetant* not of a sign in any raw, unmediated present, but of a sign of the next moment, which, by the time it has become a sign *for* some interpreter, has been mediated.

A: Must not the addresser and addressee also enter the equation?

M: Yes. The sign addresses itself to something or someone. In so doing it creates in the mind of the addressee a more developed sign, the interpretant, which is a sign in/of the mind. In this manner the mind's role as yet another sign suggests, nay demands, that the sign emissary and the interpreter must themselves be interpreting interpretants, and we have once again Peirce's triad, *Sign(Representamen)-Object-Interpretant.* While the components of the sign tripod are democratically situated, I would suggest that it is the location of the mediating interpretant that ultimately provides for meaning. As Alpha put it, meaning is not in the sign, the skull of the addresser or addressee, the air ripples between them, the object to which it relates, or black marks on white. Rather, relations between the components of the sign make way for, and engender, meaning. Although the object of the sign in a certain sense determines the sign, it is by way of further determination of the sign – its relation to the interpretant – that it means something *for* someone. Peirce qualifies this further determination as an interpretant, or translatant, of the sign, which in turn engenders another sign. There are no 'facts' of the matter – or pure, unmediated signs. Rather, the destiny of a sign demands that it be interpreted in (translated into) another sign.[13]

12 Peirce's three categories, Firstness, Secondness, and Thirdness, form the basis of his theory of signs. Though he arrived at the categories as a result of his criticism of Kant, he soon discovered that they serve a double function: (1) they are essential to the workings of the physical world and, more significantly, of life processes, and (2) they form the basis of all thought processes. In fact, it has been observed that there is a close correlation between each mode of biological evolution developed in the nineteenth century (Darwinian, Cuvierian, Lamarckian) and each of the categories: chance, brute existence, continuity. And the categories correspond to the three modes of thought by which scientific discovery, problem solving, and inferential reasoning in general proceeds: hypothesis (or abduction), induction, deduction (Wiener 1952). I will often allude to Peirce's categories during the course of this inquiry, though I will not expound on them in detail (for more, see Hookway 1985).

13 For a discussion of the interpretant as translatant, see Savan (1987–8; also Wennerberg 1962:124–30).

O: No! Signs do not constitute a referenceless hodgepodge of signifiers. There is a world out there crying out to be represented.

M: Granted, the external world *is*, and *remains as it is*, regardless of what you or I or anyone else may think of it (*CP*:6.327). Of that I have no doubt. But I am speaking of sign processes that know no fixity. *Interpretants* function as *translatants* of signs into signs. Each sign calls up an *interpretant*, that is, another sign, and consequently another *translation* has already taken place. For a sign is not a genuine sign unless it *translates* itself into another sign. In this sense signs relate to themselves, and the 'world' to which they also 'relate' – I avoid 'reference' here – is a 'semiotic world' of 'semiotic objects,' never absolutely 'real objects' of the 'real world' *as it is in and of itself.*

O: You're complicating the issue beyond repair. Our signs should set the ground rules for representing or picturing the 'real' world.

M: Yes. That was the early Wittgenstein's dream. But according to his later self, there are no fixed rules, methods, or meanings. We think we grasp a rule and with confidence go on. Then at some point one of us, wittingly or no, proceeds along some hitherto unimaginable tangential line. Or some stranger from a strange land thinks she grasps our rule and then makes mishmash of it.[14] Rule following in actual practice presupposes some unarticulated background, a web of de facto connections. Since the background is always changing, what makes up one community's set of rules – and therefore its 'semiotic reality' – can be another community's nonsense. Where, then, are the ultimate ground rules for picturing a state of affairs in the 'real' world?

O: Yeah, with your feet planted in thin air you think you can deny any and all foundations.

M: It is not a matter of affirmation or denial of foundations. The whole idea of foundations is simply ignored. Sign *translation* implies *triadicity*, which includes the sign's object 'out there,' to be sure. But in the first place, this 'object' is not the unmediated 'real world object.' It is a 'semiotic object,' that is, after it has become a sign available *to* some semiotic agent. In the second place, the sign in relation to its 'object,' if a genuine sign, is *translated* into its respective *interpretant*, that is, into another sign in relation to that 'object.' In this sense, every sign is related to the sign from which it engendered itself and to the sign that is in the process of emerging from it; the sign is not directly related to its 'object.' Triadicity pushes the sign along the rail of signification, which is not uni-, bi-, or tri-directional, but *n*-directional. Viewed as a whole, the process is radically nonlinear ...

14 The allusion here is to 'Wittgenstein's paradox' regarding rules, a problem I shall briefly take up in chapter 12.

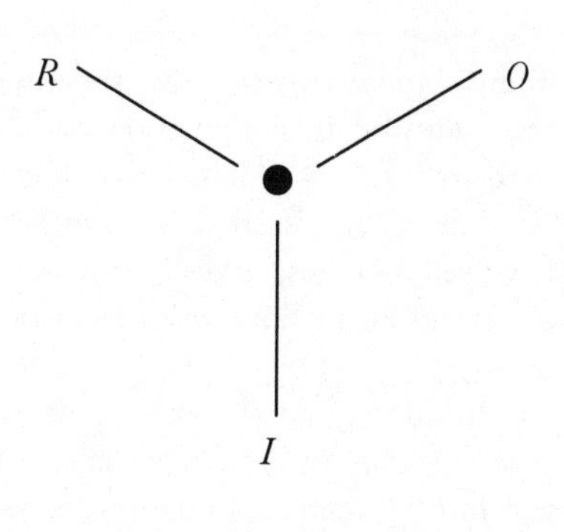

Figure 1

5. Meaning within the Flow, Then?

M: … Hm, by the look on your faces I fear I'm waxing excessively abstruse. Let me put things more concretely on the chalkboard. Let us call a sign – or *representamen* as Peirce often dubbed it – *R*, its *interpretant*, *I*, and the 'semiotic object,' *O*. We can diagram them thusly (Figure 1).

A: Why a node in the centre? Why not the customary triangle as per Ogden and Richards (1923)?

O: I suppose the node is the 'cut' before *R*, *O*, and *I* have come into existence.

M: You're quite right, Omega. The Ogden-Richards triangle (purportedly inspired by Peirce) links *R* to *O* and *I*, but as a triangle the relation between any pair of terms of the triad remains beyond the sphere of influence of the third element. In other words, what we have is a mere set of three dyads, $R - O$, $R - I$, and $O - I$. In contrast, our genuine triad, a tripod that includes the node, ties all elements together by means of a focal point such that the relation between any pair of elements depends upon the relation of each of these elements to the third one (*CP*:1.345–9).

O: But the *O* is that to which the *R refers* – I still insist on *reference*. The $R - O$ relation is quite clearly extensional, while the $I - R$ and $I - O$ relations are debatably intensional. So there is actually a difference between the *types* of relations.

M: Yes and no. The semiotic tripod is an interrelated whole. Its *interpretant* is like an interpreter revealing in a known semiotic sphere what was signified in a hitherto unknown, or at least unqualified, sphere. Relating this process to our *translation* model of *semiosis*, suppose you don't know the meaning of 'mundo,' and, looking it up in a Spanish-English dictionary, you find 'world,' corresponding to 'mundo.' You now know that whatever 'world' means for you, 'mundo' means *approximately* the same. So you know more or less how to use 'mundo' in conjunction with other Spanish words you have committed to memory. That is, you know that (1) 'world' is a mediating sign that relates to 'mundo' as a sign of the same object that this mediating sign itself signifies, and (2) if to say 'world' in English is more or less to say 'mundo' in Spanish, then 'world' is an *interpretant* of 'mundo.'

O: And we are again reduced to gutless, referenceless Saussurean signifiers.

M: Actually I'm not slighting what you call 'reference' at all. Granted, *translation* (or interpretation) is more a matter of relations between signs (specifically, *interpretants*) than between signs and things in the brute physical world. In this sense, we could say that (1) '"Mundo," "monde," "Welt," and so on have most of, but not all, the attributes common to "world," and vice versa, those attributes being approximately, but not absolutely, identical.' Or from a complementary vantage, we could say that (2) '"The world is spherical," and "El mundo is spherical," and "Le monde is spherical," and "Der Welt is spherical," etc.' In other words, (1) evokes the attributes of a sign, and in so doing, it partially express its *depth* (or if you prefer the standard labels, its connotation, intension). To say 'The "world" is a slightly imperfect sphere and it revolves around the sun in elliptical fashion and it is between Mars and Venus and it is habitable and its ozone layer is becoming depleted, etc.' gives the sign in question increased *depth*, though, regarding *translation*, which chiefly entails predication (2), it enjoys little substantial *breadth* (or denotation, extension, reference).[15] On the other hand, (2) lists a portion of the range of application of comparable signs regarding a particular attribute of the 'semiotic object' in question, but it hardly affords a glimpse of the *depth* of the signs, of their rich repertoire of attributes. *Breadth*, then, is a matter of relations between signs and their 'semiotic objects,' that is, of what you have preferred to call 'reference.' It entails *translation* between *interpretants* of different languages (but it could just as well involve *translation* between *interpretants* of the same language). 'World' could be *translated* into 'earth' – a change of the sign – or 'world$_1$ (as centre of the universe)' could be *translated* into 'world$_2$ (as revolving about the sun)' – a change of the interpretant. In either case, actual physical 'reality' remains *as it is*,

15 On *breadth* and *depth*, see Peirce (*CP*:2.253, 2.316, 2.364, 2.419, 5.471, 6.465), and for their discussion, Goudge (1952) and Liszka (1989). This pair of terms is generally placed in the context of *connotation-denotation* and *intension-extension*, but, as will become evident in the chapters that follow, I depart from their common usage.

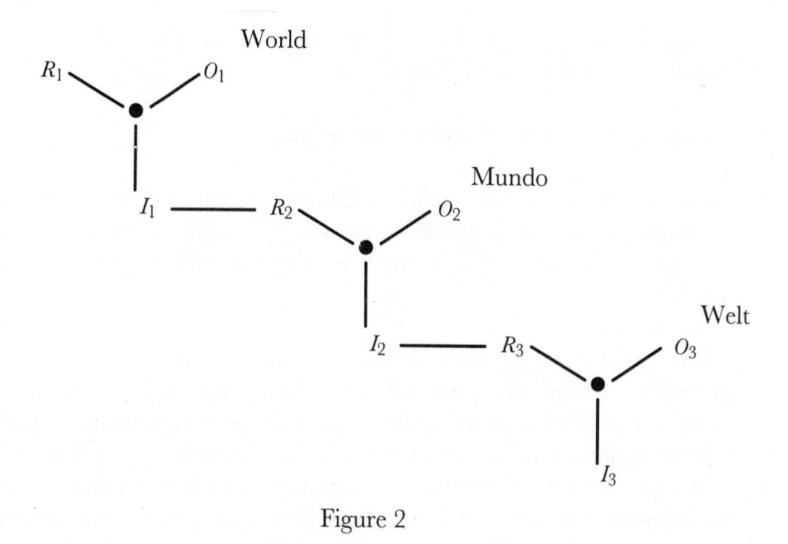

Figure 2

while different 'reality versions,' that is, 'semiotic realities,' take on different *translations*.[16]

O: That's not simply *translation*. It involves meaning change.

M: If meaning change is a matter of altered *I*s, and if an *I*'s alteration entails its *translation* into another *I*, then *translation*-as-meaning is indeed what we are talking about. Through *translation*, signs can take on additional *breadth* by expansion of their meanings when they are used from within different signifying networks (that is, 'Mundo' for a Latin American peasant does not entail 'a global concoction of nations, cultures, and peoples,' whereas 'world' for a middle-class citizen of New York does not entail 'concrete, intimate ties between human beings and the soil'). In this sense, proper awareness of *breadth* should accompany complementary awareness of *depth*: *breadth* without *depth* cannot enrich meaning, *depth* without *breadth* is incapable of extending meaning. To extrapolate our diagram with respect to *translation*, then, we have something like this (figure 2). Theoretically there is no end to the process.

O: And you have just articulated the radically equivocal notion of an *I* that engenders meaning for all those signs that do not engender meaning

16. 'Reality versions,' or what I will term 'semiotically real worlds' in this inquiry, are somewhat in the spirit of Nelson Goodman's (1978) 'world versions,' as will be implied in chapter 12 and beyond.

for themselves. The question is: Does the *I* engender meaning for itself? Russell's ominous gaze is still upon you.

6. Resorting to Not-So-Random Digressions

M: Look at it this way. Rather than a violation of logical types, it's like Quine's (1962) natural-language rendition of Gödel's proof: '"Is not an *I* when appended to this sign (i.e. this sentence)" is not an *I* when appended to this sign.'

O: Come again?

M: '"Is not an *I* when appended to this sign (i.e. this sentence)" is not an *I* when appended to this sign.' The subject and predicate are identical, and they make up a self-referential whole, but they are not coterminous. Unlike 'This sentence is false' the subject of which refers to the whole sentence of which it is a part, my – er, Quine's – variation of the Epimenidean paradox attributes falsity equivocally to itself, for it specifies a string of nine words and declares that if the string is put down twice with quotation marks around the first of the two occurrences, the result is self-contradictory. The subject is reduplicated in the predicate, and since the result of what the sentence says is the very sentence doing the saying, it is true if and only if it is false. And we have a legitimate antinomy. Yet, when contextualized, the sentence may be no more pernicious than my stating 'I am lying.' For example, attaching subscripts to the two occurrences of the term *I* in ascending order so as to differentiate between them, we have '"Is not I_0 when appended to this sign" is not I_1 when appended to this sign.' In other words I_0 is translated into I_1; they become two different signs; contextualized, they bear two different meanings. Thereupon the paradox, at least for the practical purposes of everyday communication, vanishes. This is the pragmatic counterpart to a contextualization of 'I am lying' in reference to one of my previous utterances, to my general inclination to state falsehoods, to an opening statement in a discussion of paradox, to a mere act of jesting, or whatever. It's all a matter of context, and incessantly varying sign use.

A: I get it, I think. If the predicate and subject are identical, then there appears to be no necessary *translation* (*interpretation*) of one sign into another, and the very signness of the two signs is placed in doubt. Yet, re-iteration of the 'same' sign within a 'different' setting renders it a 'different,' that is, a *translated*, sign. No?

O: On the other hand, your *recherché* scheme still fails to account for extension. You are reduced to that Quinean quagmire, the untranslatability of 'Gavagai.' Is it 'Rabbit'? 'Undetached rabbit parts'? Or 'A particular space-time rabbit stage'?[17]

A: Actually there is even less certainty than you may think. After all, bachelors can possibly be 'gavagais' if we overhear an attractive maiden from a strange land utter the sound string while gazing lustfully upon some young unattached lad. In such case she might mean 'An eligible male member of the tribe,' 'A desirable space-time entity whose sexual goals are indeterminate,' or 'A combination of certain sex-parts' – and all of them *translations* from one *I* to another one. She might even have a predicate, 'grue,' referring to 'green' bachelors before New Year's eve, 1996, and 'blue' bachelors after New Year's eve, 1996.[18]

M: Or she might have 'statile' and 'mobionary,' terms that refer to a 'stationary earth' and 'mobile sun' before Copernicus and a 'mobile earth' and 'stationary sun' after Copernicus. It all depends on the manner of the having and on who happens to be in charge. At the final stretch, the *depth* of signs is a bottomless pit.

O: This is inordinately pollyannaish, philosophical kibitzing rather than pretending actually to know something.

A: Isn't that what we were supposed to have been doing all along?

M: Let's not take these linguistic twists and turns lightly. The *object* of a sign to an extent *does* relate to that very sign and its *interpretant*. However, the *object* is a 'semiotic object,' properly speaking. Rather than refer to the 'real,' per se, a sign refers to the 'semiotically real objects' of other *interpretants*, whether within one language or across languages, and those 'objects' are erstwhile 'objects' of yet other *interpretants*, and so on. So if it is the case that an 'object' relates to its sign and respective *interpretant*, it is equally the case that the sign's *interpretant* relates to its 'semiotic object.' In this sense, to repeat myself somewhat, *semiosis* is not linear but radically nonlinear. Signs always stand a chance of meandering off to diverge, converge, involute, and convolute, becoming in the process something other than what they were. If the *depth* of signs is a bottomless pit, then their *breadth* knows no bounds. So if we take the broadest possible historical context into consideration, which includes the likes of 'Rabbit,' 'Space-time rabbit

17 I refer to W.V.O. Quine's (1960, 1969) elaborate argument – to be discussed in chapter 10 – regarding the *indeterminacy of translation* and *inscrutability of reference* for which he puts the coined term, 'Gavagai,' into service.

18 The 'grue/green' pair hails from Nelson Goodman's (1965) 'New Riddle of Induction,' about which more in chapter 12.

slice,' 'Green emeralds,' 'Grue emeralds,' 'Stationary sun,' and 'Mobionary sun,' almost everything conceivable becomes virtually possible from some viewpoint or other.

O: A gutter of undifferentiated sludge. Your *depth* coupled with *breadth* becomes even more labyrinthine than Derrida's 'bottomless chessboard.' Is there no *charity principle* by means of which we can find common grounds and talk like civilized women and men?[19]

M: Yes, but then, not really. Given Peirce's *indeterminacy – and hence fallacy – of reference* (not to be confused with Quine's *reference inscrutability*, mind you), we cannot hope once and for all to pin down a given sign and its meaning within the *semiosic* flow. Determination of the *interpretant* is never final insofar as a finite semiotic agent is concerned. However, regarding the *charity principle* according to which there must be common grounds in order that we may begin dialoguing, well, it is obvious, isn't it? Human beings *can* communicate with varying degrees of success. We *are* communicating, aren't we?

A: Then the 'semiotic object' never stands a chance of actually becoming a full-fledged item of the 'real'?

7. Syncopated Series in All Directions

M: No, ... not really, that is. Let me be more specific. Returning to my diagram, since I_1, the original interpretant of R_1, becomes itself a sign, it must in turn engender its own I. Let us call this interpretant I_1^1. I_1^1, during the process, becomes another sign, R_2, and its interpretant, I_2, in turn becomes the interpretant of I_1^1, which is to a slight degree different from the original interpretant – it has passed on and into I_2 and then into still another sign, R_3. And so on. We can construct a scheme thusly (figure 3). And *voilà*, we have a diagram of the potentially infinite regress of meaning. Well, actually, I'm extending Peirce's sign concept somewhat.

A: This web-like pattern leaves me uneasy. It is not exactly pleasing to the eye; it is unsymmetrical, like Bach's eternally rising canon, Escher's monks simultaneously climbing and descending a staircase, or Gödel's sentence that can't decide if it is true or false.

M: Something like that, it would appear. But rather than a tune in the order of four consonant notes per measure, it's a dissonance of three. It's *syncopation*, if you will. Each weak term of a triad becomes the strong term, and

19 The 'principle of charity,' which will have a bearing on the final chapters, was developed earlier by Wilson (1959, 1970), and has more recently been appropriated by, among others, Donald Davidson (1984).

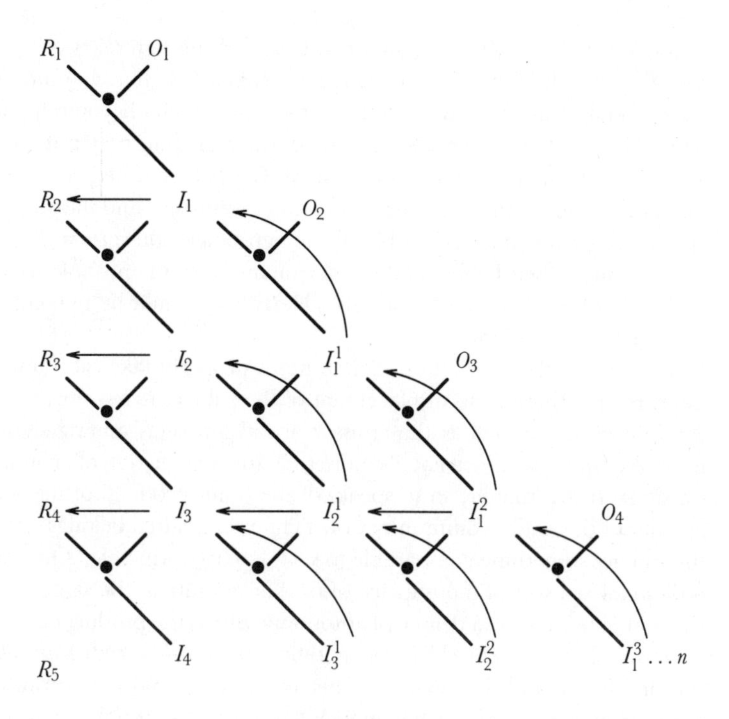

Figure 3

the ongoing waltz enters into a new cycle. It's almost as if things were perpetually out of synch.

O: I'd say it's an unruly jungle of shoestring signification.

M: Admittedly, it is an extreme form of abstraction, but at least a graphic illustration of a charmingly complex process – a sort of Peircean harbinger evoking 'strange attractors.'

A: I seem to sense a faint echo of Derrida's *différance* here: the sign is *different* and *deferred*, ad infinitum.

O: My aching back. It finally had to come to this.

M: Some commentators have speculated on the similarity between *différance* and Peirce's interpretant.[20] However, to put forth such comparisons is to overlook Peirce's enthusiastic inclusion of the interpreter as an integral part of the *semiosic* proceedings: the subject or dialogic self is definitely constituted

20 See Merrell (1985), on certain affinities between Derrida and Peirce, especially with respect to *différance*, trace, and the mediacy of sign processing.

as the focus about which the sign revolves, and the sign takes on meaning solely as a result of the emissor-interpreter-sign interaction. In other words, the sign-object-interpretant plus emissor and interpreter become apparently pentadic. But there is actually no pentad, since the interpreter and emissor are, themselves, signs among other signs. Sign-object-interpretant cannot function as such without an interpreter and an emissor, and the interpreter-emissor as such cannot exist without the sign-object-interpretant.

A: So meaning, albeit fallible and indeterminate, is made possible by way of *différance*? Most likely any respectable Derridean would be uncomfortable with such a proposition.

M: In contrast to deconstruction, Peirce more properly takes account of the interpreter – there is no displacement of the subject here – for, to repeat, the interpreter as well as the emissor are also a signs among signs. The process of human *semiosis* entails more than the mere action of an individual on signs. It is a matter, so to speak, of the 'joint product' of the semiotic activity of the entire community to which an individual belongs – perhaps therein lies something comparable to your 'charity principle,' Omega. The individual is a sort of mouthpiece of the community at the same time that she is able to exercise a degree of autonomy. She is the product of a dialogic exchange between herself and her (different and deferred) *inner other*, on the one hand, and the *otherness* of her community and her world, on the other. Hence meanings, engendered as a product of sign-object-interpretant and emissor-interpreter interaction, are therefore possible. Yet since they are endlessly possible, there is endless possibility of closure, therefore no possible closure, for meanings are always something other than what they were. Yet there definitely *are* meanings, however indeterminate, and texts *say* something potentially determinate *to* their interpreters within a situated time and place. In contrast, the Derridean text is a set of marks generated from within a machine-like sort of Cayley matrix allowing for infinite permutability, a happy-go-lucky *ars combinatoria*, and the reader engages in navel-gazing play to demonstrate that the text never actually means what it says or says what it means.

O: But *semiosis*, insofar as it is embodied in your scheme, is as closed to closure as is the Derridean text.

M: I see you remain fixated on the infinite series. Actually, if Firstness, we might say, *is* at least quasi-immediacy – unavailable *to* the mind *in* that immediate 'present' – and if Secondness entails a distinction between something and something else, then Thirdness involves the mediated relatedness between the two. And the *I* actualizes this relatedness in the interpreter's mind – such actualization being a mediate rather than immediate 'presence.' *Semiosis*, however, is an ongoing process: with each alteration the *I* is hopefully a step further along its tired road to completion. To be more specific, relatedness, the property of Thirdness, requires two terms, a First and a Second. But in order for a relation to hold between these terms, another relation must be related to them. That is, for the terms to exist in the first place, there must also have been a relation between the 'terms' and their relation.

A: Hm. Perhaps you could call this relation of the term and its relation a subsidiary relation. In this sense, each subsidiary relation inheres between a term and a relation, but the latter, now being related to by another relation, necessarily becomes itself a term.

O: Oh, yes, and we are off to the infinite regress race again.

M: The question is, How do the terms and relations I have spoken of relate to our schema on the chalkboard?

A: It seems that if each *I* can become an *R* for another *O* and another *I*, then the problem of meaning arises from and ultimately finds its possible determination in the *I*.[21]

M: Notice that the arrows in my diagram proceed backward from the *I*s. This is because *I*s are the primary authors of semiotic relations. True, the arrows represent relations, but there are no genuine relations until they are retrospectively called up, so to speak, by successive signs. Thus the *I*s' project is paradoxical, which is graphically illustrated in our diagram by its sort of syncopated swim against the current.

A: I believe I see. I_1 engenders relations between R_1 and O_1, and it is in turn transformed (*translated*) into R_2 by means of the action of I_1^1 having engendered a relation between I_1 and O_2, and, at the same time, I_1^1 is in the process transformed into I_2, which in turn becomes R_3 after engendering relations between R_2 and I_1, and so on.

O: The danger is that this infinite fission – or *semiosis* as you put it – could threaten to become infinitely strained soup. Take your set of willy-nilly orthogonals between sign components – assuming as you appear to do, that they are real numbers, or even complex numbers, given your obsession for

21 I should mention at this juncture that Peirce singled out three fundamental types of interpretants. Briefly, the *emotional interpretant* is that of feeling, or Firstness, symbolized by the initial sign. The *energetic interpretant* involves discreteness, action, change, bringing in something other: Secondness. The *final interpretant* entails *relata*, or better, it is the product of the relation between an emotional interpretant and an energetic interpretant. Since this relation is never static but always in movement, the interpretant is invariably destined to pass on – be *translated* – into another sign, which engenders its own interpretant, and so on. Just as there is no end in sight, so also there is no *final interpretant*, that is, *for* a finite semiotic agent or community of such agents. In other words, the *final interpretant* is always *incomplete*.

undecidable tactics of the $\sqrt{-1}$ sort. Cut them in half, then half them again, and again, and you will never reach the beginning, or the end.[22]

M: Good! Your mathematics background sheds additional light on the issue. But I must say once again that your allusion to Zeno is of no real concern. The fact is that we are, ourselves, signs. And as signs, we give hardly any thought to much or even most of what we do when we create and process other signs, notwithstanding the logical quandaries our actions imply. So not to worry, not really, that is.

A: I believe I perceive a further ramification for your set-up. R_1 is the sign of the object, I_1 is the interpretant of the sign of the object, and I_1^1 is the interpretant of the interpretant of the sign of the object, while R_2 is the sign of the interpretant of the interpretant of the sign of the object, and so on.

M: And the progression toward completion, toward futurity, is, and will remain, a potential. That is the essence of Peirce's conditional Thirdness.

O: A vicious *progressus* as well as a *regressus*.

M: But not perniciously vicious. Since each sign can become its own meaning, even though mediately so, in a manner of speaking meaning itself is virtuously vicious. A sign can become a sign in the full sense only through an *I*, but that *I* cannot exist as such unless it is – or has been – a sign for another *I*, and that for yet another one.

O: I arrived here with a few doubts; now I have nothing but doubts.

M: (*roaring with laughter*): Beware of paradoxes, Omega, lest they make a true believer of you yet.[23]

22 The mention of orthogonals and complex numbers entails what in geometry is called the 'Argand plane,' whose applications include quantum theory, and a variation of which I have elsewhere placed within the context of semiotic theory (Merrell 1991, 1995a, 1996).

23 The master's laughter is à propos, for the whole of this Preamble can be encapsulated in the following Buddhist-like mini-dialog:

> *Omega*: What is the meaning of *her* (the Master's) name?
> *Alpha*: Omega.
> *Omega*: No, that's no meaning at all; that's *my* name.
> *Alpha*: If you wish. In such case, then, it's Alpha.
> *Master*: (*roars with laughter*).

The Master is in essence the sign of the other two interlocutors; she is the mediating union of them. She would be nothing without them, and neither would they be anything without her. Our three dialogeurs thus embody genuine *semiosis*: signs becoming signs intermingled with signs incessantly growing into something other than what they were.

PART I

All Too Human?

1

Our Blissful Unknowing Knowing

This chapter and the next consist of reflections on: (1) Peirce's triadic concept of the sign; (2) relations between sign and mind and the 'semiotically real' and the 'real' in regards to a key set of terms that will pop up repeatedly during the course of this inquiry, *vagueness* and *generality* and *inconsistency* and *incompleteness*; (3) the dialogical self as a sign among signs; and (4) our vain individualism stemming from the imperious belief that we can make and break our signs by the sheer force of our will. This preliminary stage is essential, I believe, insofar as it provides a context from within which an adequate semiotic concept of meaning can unfold. (I might also emphasize my contention that, semiotically speaking, and as implied in the Preamble, there is no determinable 'representational' meaning in terms of 'correspondence,' 'denotation,' 'designation,' 'extension,' and/or 'reference,' as they are ordinarily conceived – my reasons for such should emerge as this disquisition proceeds.)

1. Triadology

Our Preamble consisted of an initial *sign*, a *First* (Alpha), and an *other* or *Second* (Omega), which involved the sign's 'semiotically real' *object*, both of which were conjointly mediated and moderated by a *Third* (Master), or, in another way of putting it, by an *interpretant*. These *First-Second-Third* and *representamen(sign)-object-interpretant* triads remain less than genuine without mind – that is, without semiotic agents, whether of human or nonhuman variety, in perpetual interaction with the signs surrounding them. Mind struggles to interpret its 'semiotic world,' and at the same time that 'semiotic world' is what mind (sign) put there in the first place. (What appears in these words to be a rather unsavoury collusion of 'sign' and 'mind,' 'realism' and 'idealism,' and 'objectivism' and 'subjectivism,' is actually of the nature of what Peirce calls 'objective idealism' – to be discussed at various stages below.)

In other words, mind finds in its *semiosic* surroundings that which it is capable of *constructing*, partly in accord with a given set of *conventions* (that is, 'constructivism' coupled with 'conventionalism,' especially as outlined by Skolimowski 1986, 1987). There is no 'reality out there' passively submitting itself to mind. Mind brings signs into existence at the same time that they serve to perpetuate the existence of mind. Each mind's 'semiotic world' is a staccato of signs intermittently presented to, and brought together by, that very semiotic agent who, to rephrase Niels Bohr (1958:119), is at once a spectator and an actor in the great drama of *semiosis* (compare to *CP*:7.347–50). For mind never ceases to intervene in and interact with its 'world' in a virtuously circular process that revolves about a central 'node' – cf. figure 1 – the fountainhead of all sign *relata* and the locus of meaning in flux. (This assertion will be qualified in the chapters that follow. For the moment, it bears pointing out that, as the Master stated, the 'real world' exists, for sure, but whatever 'semiotic world' we happen to inhabit is in large part a world of our own making. While I do not deny that there are stars and rocks and trees and things independent of our made world, I would also submit that the assumption of a finite community of humans capable of establishing an absolutely determinate line of demarcation between the mind-independent world and what has been selected and moulded into that community's world is by and large the product of deluded hopes and hollow dreams.)

Regarding the idea of an ongoing flux of signs in any and all 'semiotic worlds,' then, *semiosis* can be nothing other than a forever open and unfinished symphony within which the mind incessantly shifts and turns, presenting *to* and *for* itself a slightly to vastly different countenance at every bend in the stream. This time-bound nature of *semiosis*, I would submit, endows it with a form of 'logic.' It is a 'logic,' so to speak, of Peirce's categories of Firstness coupled with Thirdness, that is, a 'logic' of 'continuity' or 'vagueness' – which, we shall note, is quite alien to classical logic. Within the sphere of this 'logic,' both/and is not simply a wimpish embrace of two mutually exclusive poles, either/or does not necessarily entail a forced choice between incompatibles, and neither/nor constantly threatens to burst out of the logic of pure negation and into the hazy light of a distant, dreamy day. The transient nature of this *semiosic* 'logic' evinces ceaseless creation rendering epistemological postures ephemeral, conceptual schemes incomplete, and the very idea of foundations irrelevant (*CP*:5.438–63; this general theme is discussed throughout my rather presumptuously entitled 'trilogy' in celebration of *semiosis* [Merrell 1991, 1995a, 1996], and it will be extended here).

Specifically regarding language, primacy must be placed on the process of mediation between the actuality of what is said-written and what remains unsaid-unwritten but might otherwise have been said-written – I use the hyphenated terms to deprivilege both speech and writing. In another manner of putting it, what *is*, *was* a possibility that became actual *for* someone *in* some ephemeral 'here-now.' What *is not*, nonetheless, is that without which what *is*, *could not have become*; yet it remains as a motivating force for what otherwise *would have become* – that is, Alpha's enigmatic remarks on the role of negation. The *possible*, the *is*, and the *would be* constitute the essence of Peirce's Firstness, Secondness, and Thirdness. All three categories converge and diverge to engender sign sequences made meaningful at both tacit and conscious levels. What makes itself manifest, in the final analysis, is not the familiar presence/absence binary but a triadic *presence-absence: process* play, with the hyphen linking what have traditionally been conceived as intransigent terms and the colon signifying a mediating term. But this is not mere dialectics. Presence-absence does not constitute a thesis/antithesis dichotomy. It is, more adequately put, a *complementarity* between terms now emerging, now submerging, and in the process given equal time and equal weight when the entire picture is brought into focus. *Process*, in contrast to the more familiar term, synthesis, is the virtually limitless, liquid stage within which the free-form *semiosic* dance is enacted.

A root example of this *presence-absence: process* triad is found in Cervantes's invisible pen bringing the apparently incommensurable 'semiotic worlds' of Don Quixote and Sancho Panza into an oscillating *contrapuntus* ultimately providing a broad mural that could not have been depicted by the two 'worlds' standing alone and unrelated to one another. As narrative presence, Cervantes's pair of characters are the embodiment of what in Western discourse were to become obsessive dichotomies – 'truth'/fiction, appearance/'reality,' madness/sanity, subjectivity/objectivity, mind/'world.' The absent pen, guided by its master, is the force bringing about the *semiosic* textual process drawing the Don and his companion together into a larger whole. In this manner, both what is said and what remains unsaid compose a fugue-like process of foregrounding/backgrounding. But when speaking of one's awareness or consciousness *of* what is said and what remains unsaid, the shoe is on the other foot. If one attends to the said, the unsaid must remain largely implicit, though tacit assent to it may be in effect. Then, upon switching from what was said to some item of the hitherto unsaid, what was foregrounded becomes backgrounded, and what is now foregrounded becomes available – albeit mediately, not immediately – *to* the mind.

2. More Than Mere Talk

Much of Mikhail Bakhtin's thought is significant with regard to the Peircean triads that have hitherto emerged. Bakhtin includes discourse and all forms of verbal interaction in his author-text and context-reader equations. In the sense of Peirce's *dialogic*, this is in harmony with *emissor-sign-object: interpretant-interpreter* (that is, the pentad from the Preamble, where emissor and interpreter are, themselves, simultaneously that which interprets and the product of the interpretive act). In this involved and self-involving interaction, context is all-important, whether considering situated utterances or written sentences within their rhetorical contexts and their contexts of reading. The purest form of such contextualized meaning exists at the level of what Bakhtin terms *style-intonation*, which in its own turn lies at the frontier between said-unsaid and self-other – hence it demands contextualization in order to ensure proper understanding (Bakhtin 1981, Bakhtin-Volishinov 1973).

Style-intonation is predicated on the notion that verbal discourse is not self-sufficient, that language in use involves subtle nuances unavailable to formal notions of language and signs in general. Bakhtin-Voloshinov (1973:99) offers as an example of his concept of style-intonation a single word or 'holophrastic' sentence: 'Well!' Two people are in a room. One utters the expression and the other does not respond. To an outside observer unaware of the context, this abstracted 'conversation' would be utterly incomprehensible. Does the apparently simple evocation 'Well!' imply reproach? Indignation? Disgust? However subtly we analyse the phonetic, morphological, and semantic aspects of this solitary word, understanding remains elusive. Knowledge of the word's intonation helps fill the semantic void, yet it does not reveal meaning as a whole. Bakhtin-Volishinov writes that what is lacking is the utterance's *extraverbal context*, which depends upon three factors: (1) the interlocutors' *common spatial purview* (the empirically available physical surroundings), (2) their *shared storehouse of background knowledge*, and (3) their *common evaluation and understanding* of the situation. This *shared storehouse of knowledge* and *common evaluation and understanding* is related to what I alluded to in the Preamble as the '*joint product*' of the community of knowers – a term coined by Føllesdal (1975) and employed by Wheeler (1984) in what he dubs 'meaning physics' – about which more in chapter 14.

Bakhtin goes on to reveal that when the one-word utterance was made,

> both interlocutors *looked up* at the window and *saw* that it had begun to snow; *both knew* that it was already May and that it was high time for spring to come; finally, *both* were *sick and tired* of the protracted winter – *they were both looking forward* to spring and *both*

were bitterly disappointed by the late snowfall. On this 'jointly seen' (snowflakes outside the window), 'jointly known' (the time of the year – May), and 'unanimously evaluated' (winter wearied of, spring looked forward to) – on all this the utterance *directly depends*, all this is seized in its actual, living import – is its very sustenance. And yet all this remains without verbal specification or articulation. The snowflakes remain outside the window; the date, on the page of a calendar; the evaluation, in the psyche of the speaker; and nevertheless, all this is assumed in the word *well*. (Bakhtin-Volishinov 1973:99)

The moral to the story is that verbal discourse alone cannot any adequate form of meaning make. Of course one can run off a list of sentences of 'The cat is on the mat' sort whose simplicity borders on the absurd to illustrate one-to-one correspondence and no-nonsense semantics in terms of our familiar 'here-the-word, there-the-thing, thus-the-meaning' syndrome. Such Jack-and-Jill word strings hardly constitute the basis of living dialogue, however. Interlocutors most commonly encounter utterances that call for knowledge beyond grammar, beyond the *dictionary* and *encyclopedia*, beyond merely *what is said*. (I use the terms 'dictionary' and 'encyclopedia' in reference to the aborted project of a 'generative semantics' initiated by Katz and Fodor [1963] and, rather unfortunately, taken up by Eco [1976, 1983, 1990], among other semioticians.)

Moreover, in light of our Preamble, utterances more often than not require some awareness of preceding utterances and *shared expectations* regarding the range of possible utterances that stand a chance of emerging at future stages of the conversation. Such was the case of the Epimenidean sentence, whose internal paradox can dissolve when memory of past utterances and expectations of future utterances coupled with those of the present – the ongoing dialogic process – are taken into account. Dialogic life in the Peirce-Bakhtin sense, then, creates meaning through contextualization (Ponzio 1985, 1990). Signs exist in the full-blown sense only when they take on interpretants, and in this process they become charged with meaning; if not, it is because they have not been properly embraced (*put to use*) by some semiotic agent *for* some purpose or other *within* some context. I reiterate: a sign, in order to be genuine, must be known, but in order to be known, the knower must have some inclination in terms of what it would be for the sign to remain unknown. In other words to know what a sign *is* entails knowing at least in part what it *is not* but *might otherwise have been*. Without some inkling of the unknown and unactualized, whatever is known at a given moment would be no more than a self-sufficient, unrelated whole. It would not be able to gain entry into the general *semiosic* process wherein the known is known only insofar as it is, or can be, somehow related to the infinite stretch of the unknown. Without the unknown, the known, in comparison a mere infinitesimal sphere, would not mean; it would not 'live.' This notion that the unknown is potentially infinite in extension while the known remains infinitesimal, as we shall note below, is quite Peircean in spirit.

The idea of style-intonation as that which is capable of allowing the gaps to be filled in strictly defined verbal discourse is the rhetorical counterpart to Peirce's interpretation and use of the *enthymeme* (that is, an argument one of the essential premises of which has been suppressed but remains implicit). An *enthymeme*, giving account of the presence of the absence of the unsaid-other, creates an image of the listener-reader to whom the addresser addresses herself. It can serve as a dead give-away of the speaker-author's identity, biases, values, and ideology; it is the product of Peirce-Bakhtin dialogic. In this sense, Peirce and Bakhtin are conjoined, especially regarding the notion that meaning may be defined in terms of *translation* of signs into other signs (see *CP*:2.302, 4.127, 5.402 n3, 5.594; also Ponzio 1990).

Translation, as I used the term in the Preamble, by no means implies that the interpreter and interpretant are Humpty-Dumpties confidently making their signs mean whatever they want them to mean (that is, whatever they wish to *translate* them into). Nor are they monastic Cartesian *cogitos* solemnly divining ultimate meaning, and therefore 'truth' (without the need of *translation* from predecessor signs into present signs). Rather, interpreters and interpretants are nothing unless engaging in dialogic interaction with other interpreters and other sign components. Interpreters and their interpretants, as would be expected, are the locus of living dialogue. And their respective *others* are not mute, static signifieds, as Saussurean semiological parlance would have it: they are actually or potentially *other* interpreters and interpretants engaged in the ongoing process. Dialogic entails perpetual interaction between interpreters-interpretants and their *inner others*, on the one hand, and, on the other, their *social and physical world others*. It is the ceaseless creation of ever-so-tenuous-and-tentative meanings: endless *semiosis*. In short, style-intonation by way of dialogue is an implicit (tacit) indication (index) of the speaker-author's participation in a community's 'form of life' (Bakhtin 1984, Todorov 1984). In other words, as will become apparent in the final chapters of this inquiry, my posture deviates somewhat from W.V.O. Quine's notorious 'untranslatability thesis,' yet it does not fall victim to Donald Davidson's confidence-building program of 'radical interpretation' (or 'translation') (for Davidson in regards to Quine's view, see Evnine 1991, Krausz 1989, Malpas 1992, Ramberg 1989, and Werhane 1992).

Perhaps, following Bakhtin, it is in literature that we find the least blemished forms of dialogic interaction. Literary reception implies familiarity with 'forms of life' – Bakhtin's shared experiences – that put the reader in tune with the big band being conducted by its creator, the collective community of semiotic agents. The very capacity for the becoming of such awareness is intricately dependent upon *otherness* (Secondness). And *otherness* implies dialogism (Thirdness), whether we are speaking of Bakhtin or of Peirce. However, dialogism is by no means an exclusively literary phenomenon; it is implicated most blatantly in the very notion of self-consciousness and in the history of thinking about thinking, as well as in all aspects of textuality, whether discursive or narrative (Holquist 1990:14–39). One particular problem with some of the current poststructuralist conceptions of narrative has been that they tend to divorce the written sign from any form or fashion of the 'semiotically real' – to say nothing of the 'real' – which includes the entire spectrum of sign forms. To assert that a text takes leave of the world is to go against the entire grain of Peircean semiotics. For Peirce 'a sign is not a sign unless it translates itself into another sign in which it is more fully developed,' and thought (as well as the self), being 'in itself essentially of the nature of a sign, … must grow in incessant new and higher translations, or it proves itself not to be genuine thought' (*CP*:5.594). Furthermore, sign engendering and reception within a given cultural context cannot occur without sign emissors/interpreters, who are also interpretants, that is, signs. Signs develop. They grow, just as do their emissors/interpreters. Signs and selves interact to bring about, via their respective *others*, alternative variations, the composite of which is capable of engendering 'semiotically real' worlds (*CP*:2.222, 302). Insofar as their makers are concerned, and whether they are conscious *of* the fact or not, these worlds might come to be taken as simply the way things are, no more, no less. In this manner, all signs relate to some 'semiotic reality' or other according to their makers, be they *sign-events* 'out there' or *thought-signs* 'in here,' and be they linguistic (symbolic) signs or signs of other sorts (icons, indices).

In contrast, according to much standard poststructuralist rhetoric, signs – strictly linguistic signs – and texts remain largely autonomous. Insulated from their semiotic agents, they proceed to create a mere 'reality effect.' And the text by and large succeeds in producing its author and readers rather than production being a collaborative effort on the part of all parties involved. The problem is that this 'reality effect' is a product of the text's asserting its separation from 'reality' – empirical or otherwise – and diverging, as a sign, from a meaning that depends for its existence on the constitutive activity of that selfsame sign. Granted, in the Peircean sense all signs are destined, in a finite community of fallible semiotic agents, to remain at least a step removed from the 'actually real,' which will perpetuate itself as a receding horizon. But a community's signs are indelibly 'semiotically real' inasmuch as they are 'real' *for* their respective agents. I shall argue in the following chapters that a sign's closest approximation to the 'real' is from the word go made possible – albeit indirectly, and by circuitous routes – through iconicity and indexicality (both linguistic and nonlinguistic) in addition to symbolicity (on the stage of which natural language enjoys the starring role). In this sense, contrary to structuralist and even some poststructuralist assumptions, there is no categorical distinction between everyday language and literary language – or between scientific language and literary language. And there should be no priority either of written or spoken signs, for, as symbols, they depend upon other sign types (icons and indices) for their very existence.

Hence the coming into consciousness of meaning via Bakhtin's style-intonation serves potentially to weld said-unsaid and I-*other* into an indivisible whole. If, on the other hand, the two poles of the presumed dichotomies were to remain divided, their mutilated fragments would be incapable effectively of conveying meaning. So in a manner of speaking, part of what *is not* nonetheless *is*. It *is* – though in a roundabout way – *enthymemetic*. It stands on the absent shoulders of implicit signs. Peirce observes, in this regard, that a premise cannot be suppressed without ceasing to be a (tacit or implicit) premise. Consequently, part of the articulation of a train of thought may remain unexpressed in confident anticipation that the listener-reader will properly 'fill in the gaps' – that is, bring the *enthymeme* to completion. In such a case the possibility exists that a sign's meaning may be arrived at by a conscious inferential process on the part of the listener-reader.

Now, all this talk about the *is*, the *is not*, and *enthymemes* breeds tenebrous feelings, no doubt. And with reason. What is implied bears on what Peirce termed a 'logic' of *possibilia* or *vagueness* (Firstness) and on the *potential continuity of signs* (Thirdness) according to which everything that *is*, *is as it is* in regards to that which it *is not* – once again reminiscent of Alpha's strained mumblings. And everything that potentially *is* or *can become*, when a part of it actually becomes, *for* us finite semiotic agents, *will be* what it *is* only with respect to that which it *could have become* but *did not*. However, yet another dimension to this picture must be revealed: that which precedes everything that *is*, which Peirce dubbed 'absolute nothingness' (*CP*:6.217). All signs are *unfolded* from the *enfolded* sphere of 'nothingness,' that 'boundless freedom,' that 'nowhere' – that is, the 'node' in figure 1. The same is to be said of the *unfoldment* of meaning. Meaning emerges, during the *semiosic* process, and within the context of sign use, as if out of 'nowhere.' (For this somewhat Spinozistic *unfolding* of the *enfolded* [or the *explicate* being drawn from the *implicate*], as the terms are used here, see Bohm 1980, 1986; Deleuze and Guattari 1983, 1987; and Merrell 1995a, 1996; and, for Peirce's 'nothingness,' Baer 1988 and Merrell 1991.)

But please don't get me wrong: I do not intend to dish out a dose of bleary-eyed romantic drivel regarding meaning. Yet there is invariably a nebulous zone of unknowability and ineffability pervading our every effort to know the meaning of the very term 'meaning.' We would like to suppose we are the authors of our meanings; at the same time we would like to eschew all trappings of numinosity, of meanings available only to the anointed few. Nevertheless, quite often our role as authors of meanings cannot but remain minimal. In such events meanings emerge on their own accord, and whether we know it or not. It is precisely this enigmatic force of meaning that must somehow be addressed.

But for the present, it behooves us to do a quick jack-knife into Peirce's intractable sea of *semiosis* for a preliminary, and quite tentative, view of his 'logic of vagueness.' This is a necessary step, I would submit, since this 'logic' lies at the very heart of his concept of meaning engendering, and it entails two pairs of terms that will play an increasingly important role as my own story grows: *vagueness* and *generality*, and *inconsistency* and *incompleteness*. While I cannot hope to give full account of what Peirce wished to develop – but never brought to fruition – as a 'logic of vagueness,' I at least attempt to highlight an important aspect of it in the following section, and I elaborate on it as this volume unfolds. (See *CP*:6.185–213; for related work, see Black 1937, Brock 1975, and 1979, Dummett 1979, Eisele 1979:208–15, Engel-Tiercelin 1992, Nadin 1982 and 1983, Putnam 1983a, and Thibaud 1975; and, along comparable lines, Lakoff's 'hedges,' 1972, and his study of categories, 1987, Ross's 'squishiness,' 1972, and Goguen's 'logic of inexact concepts,' 1969).

3. Signs Gone Strange?

Peirce's envisioned 'logic of vagueness' (that is, of 'possibility' or 'continuity') is a 'logic' in 'the broadest possible sense,' a 'logic' fit for all seasons and all reasons. Although Peirce never made good on his promise of this general 'logic,' in 1908 he did envision and outline the makings of a 'triadic logic' of sorts based on 'real possibility,' 'actuality,' and 'real necessity,' which roughly correspond to his three fundamental categories (Fisch 1986).

Peirce points out that a proposition asserting actual existents (Seconds) lies at the half-way house between the poles of assertion of possibility (Firstness) and those of necessity (Thirdness). While assertions regarding actuals follow the tenets of classical logic, assertions of possibility and necessity do not, not necessarily, that is. In Peirce's words: 'that which characterizes and defines an assertion of Possibility is its emancipation from the Principle of Contradiction, while it remains subject to the Principle of Excluded Third; while that which characterizes and defines an assertion of Necessity is that it remains subject to the Principle of Contradiction, but throws off the yoke of the Principle of Excluded Third; and what characterizes and defines an assertion of Actuality, or simple Existence, is that it acknowledges allegiance to both formulae, and is thus just midway between the two rational "Modals," as the modified forms are called by all the old logicians' (MS 678:34–5).

What lies within the sphere of possibility (Firstness) by and large violates the principle of noncontradiction, which reigns supreme in the 'semiotically real' world of actuality (Secondness), following classical logical principles. Yet within the sphere of pure Firstness, neither does the excluded-middle principle remain intact. For, given the nature of unactualized Firstness as a superposed set of possibilities, in its complete form everything is always already there. It composes an unimaginably massive, continuous collage of compatible and incompatible, consistent and inconsistent, and complementary and contradictory, non-essences. In this sphere of pure chance, spontaneity, and infinitely diluted *vagueness*, nothing is (yet) specified and everything is at one with everything else: there are as yet no cuts, no borders, no taxonomies. There is no 'betweenness' as such, since what we have is not a static *plenum*, per se, but a Shiva's dance of effervescent, trembling, scintillating, fluctuating, flickering, superposed *possibilia* in mute expectancy of their actualization into some 'semiotically real' domain or other. Thus, the sphere of *vagueness*, as was implied in the Preamble, is thoroughly *overdetermined*.

The realm of necessity (Thirdness) includes mediary terms, with no end in sight. Since any and all corpora of signs remain invariably *incomplete*, something more, a *supplement*, can always be added – that is, the potentially infinite series of signs of which Alpha spoke. Hence, unlike the eithers and the ors of Secondness, within Thirdness the excluded-middle principle threatens to fall by the wayside. That is to say, between any two signs, given sufficient time and change of context and complexity, the potential always exists for other signs and their meanings, or the same signs and other meanings, to emerge. It is not a matter of the 'centre' of the universe *either* as the earth (Ptolemy) *or* the sun (Copernicus), but *neither* the one *nor* the other. In other words, the 'centre' for Ptolemy and the 'centre' for Copernicus is not simply a matter of *either-or* alternatives: with the demise of classical physics, the 'centre' is now conceived to be something else altogether (i.e. something entered the gap between the erstwhile *either/or* categories to render them *neither-nor*). Yet since at any given point in time the 'centre' cannot be construed as *both* the earth *and* not the earth, the principle of noncontradiction remains in force (recall, in this vein, Omega's charge that the Master and Alpha resorted to the *Principles of Included Contradiction* and *Proliferating Middles*). Consequently, at a given point in time, any and all conceptual schemes are destined to *incompleteness.* Owing to this persistence of *incompleteness*, *underdetermination* necessarily prevails.

Overdetermination, a concept with which I struggled throughout the writing of my 'trilogy' on the sign, includes the sphere within which a sign is not yet definitely or authoritatively decided, settled, or fixed – though according to the circumstances it presumably can be – and as such it is unbounded by definite limits or restrictions. I would suggest that *overdetermination* is related to the Peircean category of Firstness, as well as to the concepts of *vagueness* and *inconsistency*. However, *overdetermination* in the purest sense is actually tantamount to what we might label pre-Firstness, pure vagueness, before there is consciousness *of* a sign. Consciousness *of* a sign, once it has emerged into the light of day, remains vague, to be sure. During the process of this vagueness becoming more precise, a small number of the indeterminate range of possible specifications of the sign will become actualized as Seconds to take their place in what is perceived and conceived to be the 'semiotically real' world. But whatever specification might have been actualized, others remain as possibilities, some of them contradictory with respect to that which was actualized.

In other words, regarding the Secondness and Thirdness of signs *of* which there is consciousness and *regarding* which specification of meaning can be made more precise, *underdetermination* (related, I would suggest, to *generality* and *incompleteness*) inheres. In the sphere of *overdetermination*, mutually incompatible possibilities of meaning can cohabit quite comfortably (and the principle of noncontradiction loses its sting). In contrast, in the sphere of *underdetermination*, an actualized meaning within one time slice and context can become something slightly to radically different within another time slice and context (hence the excluded-middle principle is abrogated).

It becomes apparent, then, that the sphere of *vagueness*, of *possibilia* (Firstness), is timeless, while that of *generality* (Secondness developing toward the fullness of Thirdness) is time-bound. By the very nature of this interrelationship, signs of *generality* are destined ultimately to suffer a fate complementary with that of signs of *vagueness*. In this spirit, Peirce wrote that '[n]otwithstanding their contrariety, generality and vagueness are, from a formal point of view, seen to be on a par' (*CP*:5.447). *Vague* signs cannot be construed as *vague* unless endowed with at least a tinge of *generality*, and *general* signs, given their inevitable degree of *incompleteness*, are invariably somewhat *vague*. Peirce readily conceded that no sign can be *vague* and *general* from the same perspective and from within the same space-time slice, since insofar as the determination of a sign is extended to the interpreter – that is, the case of *generality* – it is by and large denied to the utterer, and insofar as it is extended to the utterer – that is, the case of *vagueness* – it lies largely beyond the grasp of the interpreter (*CP*:1.463–9, 5.447–57). By no means, however, do

I wish to imply that Firstness has a monopoly on *vagueness*, but rather, *vagueness* to a greater or lesser degree pervades any and all signs. This is in keeping with Peirce's abolition of clear and distinct, and precisely demarcated, boundaries (Rorty 1961). I must also add that the interrelationships herein implied between *vagueness* and *generality* – and *overdetermination* and *underdetermination* – is not usually forthcoming in twentieth-century philosophical discourse. Bertrand Russell (1923), for instance, relates the law of excluded middles exclusively to *vagueness*; in our times, 'fuzzy logic' tends to do likewise (Kosko 1993). On the other hand, Quine (1953, 1960) has focused almost obsessively on *underdetermination* with respect to scientific theories and, by extension, natural language (Føllesdal 1975, Gibson 1986), and more recently, Davidson (1984) has thrown *vagueness* into the same bag with *generality* and *incompleteness* without showing how they are agonistically set apart and at the same time intricately intertwined (Evnine 1991:105–14, Malpas 1992:105–26).

Every sign is in this sense at least partially determined, and its partial determination is contingent upon its varying degrees of *vagueness* and *generality*, depending on the vantage point:

> A sign (under which designation I place every kind of thought, and not alone external signs), that is in any respect objectively indeterminate (i.e. whose object is undetermined by the sign itself) is objectively *general* in so far as it extends to the interpreter the privilege of carrying its determination further. *Example*: 'Man is mortal'. To the question, What man? the reply is that the proposition explicitly leaves it to you to apply its assertion to what man or men you will. A sign that is objectively indeterminate in any respect is objectively *vague* in so far as it reserves further determination to be made in some other conceivable signs, or at least does not appoint the interpreter as its deputy in this office. *Example*: 'A man whom I could mention seems to be a little conceited.' The *suggestion* here is that the man in view is the person addressed, but the utterer does not authorize such an interpretation or *any* other application of what she says. She can still say if she likes, that she does *not* mean the person addressed. Every utterance naturally leaves the right of further exposition in the utterer, and therefore, in so far as a sign is indeterminate, it is vague, unless it is expressly or by a well understood convention rendered general. (*CP*:5.447; also 1.434)

Thus, 'a sign can only escape from being either vague or general by not being indeterminate.' Yet no sign 'can be absolutely and completely indeterminate' (*vague*) (*CP*:5.506). And a sign, 'however determinate, may be made more determinate still, but not ... absolutely determinate' (*general*) (*CP*:3.93). If a sign were totally determinate, it would always be as it is, its attributes remaining intact and changeless. In this respect, and regarding two terms introduced in the Preamble – that is, *breadth* (very roughly, 'extension,' 'denotation') and *depth* (very roughly, 'intension,' 'connotation') – an increase of a sign's *generality* marks an increase of its *breadth* and range of application, while an increase of its *depth* is marked by a decrease of its *vagueness.* It should become apparent, as these pages unfold, that meaning consists of interdependency and interaction between *breadth* and *depth*, *generality* and *vagueness.*

However, when the plethora of potentially variant space-time slices comes into the picture, the possibility of any absolutely determinate sign dissolves. There is a George Bush of 'Read my lips,' of 'No new taxes,' of 'Perhaps new taxes,' of 'New taxes,' and of 'New taxes, but the Democrats made me do it.' But there is no George Bush impervious to any and all change. Were a changeless sign to exist, it would be absolutely autonomous, individual, and indivisible. However, such absolutes 'can not only not be realized in sense or thought, but cannot exist, properly speaking. For whatever lasts for any time, however short, is capable of logical division, because in that time it will undergo some change in its relations' (*CP*:3.39 n1). So every sign must relate to some not-quite-absolutely-general 'semiotic object.' The 'object' cannot be the absolutely 'real object' as it is, for all 'objects' are related to all other 'objects' of a given field of signs. To be sure, all signs relate to some singular 'object,' at least potentially understood by all semiotic agents. But since the 'really real' lies perpetually beyond our grasp, there must exist some lesser sphere containing signs and their 'semiotic objects.' That sphere is partly shared by the semiotic agents involved in dialogic exchange, and those signs and 'semiotic objects' are to a greater or lesser degree *general*, though never absolutely so, and hence they are to a greater or lesser degree *vague.*

Vagueness and *generality* are in this sense *complementary* forms of *indeterminacy*. To reiterate, vague signs are those 'to which the principle of contradiction does not apply,' and general signs are those 'to which the principle of the excluded middle does not apply' (*CP*:5.448). A sentence can be determinately judged either 'true' or 'false' in the 'here-now,' though in the 'there-then' its value will have suffered a change, however small – Peirce's conception of 'logic' in the 'broadest possible sense' embraces temporality. And a sentence that has been determined either 'true' or 'false' in one respect may be neither 'true' nor 'false' in another. A sound can be neither blue nor red in the literal sense, though it may conceivably be both one and the other in the synaesthetic sense. Consequently, the predicates 'shrill' or 'mellow,' 'bitter' or 'sweet,' or 'blue' or 'red' attached to the sign can be both 'true' and 'false' from within the range of all possible conceptions.

Generality includes the Peircean terms potentiality, convention, necessity, conditionality, and regularity – all of the category of Thirdness – which implies process, growth, intellect, and mind (*CP*:1.340). *Generality* calls for ever greater account of particular signs and their attributes as types. Yet to expect absolute determinacy through *generality* is out of the question: there can be no more than an approximation toward a sign in its most general sense. *Vagueness*, given its nature as indefinite, ambiguous, and indeterminate, takes the terms possibility, chance, spontaneity, and novelty into its embrace. While *generality* entails relations to 'semiotic objects,' *vagueness* bears no form or fashion of relatedness of signs *to* other signs established *by* some semiotic agent. Pure *vagueness* (Firstness) is the superposition of all possibilities without any of them being actualized. On the other hand, *vagueness* of actual signs (Secondness) requires their concrete contextualization and their being related to other signs. Such actualized signs, according to their interpretation, can now take on *generality* (Thirdness). It is for this reason that while the onus of further determination of a general sign is left to the conceptual scheme, the criteria, and the style of reason, the 'logic,' and the wishes and whims, of its interpreter, determination of a vague, actualized sign depends upon further revelation and specification of its meaning by its author and the context of its engenderment.

General signs of the most general sort are found in the abstract disciplines: the physical sciences, logic, and mathematics. For example, signs of number theory hardly involve contexts, yet contexts are never entirely absent. The proposition 'Every even number is the sum of two primes' (Goldbach's conjecture) requires determination on the part of its interpreter, indeed, of an infinity of interpreters or a solitary immortal interpreter, if the plenitude of its determination is to be reached. Even with respect to this most general of propositions, consideration regarding the nature of the interpreter and the conditions of interpretation – that is, of context – cannot be entirely eschewed. In contrast, everyday utterances in a natural language, and especially the nonverbal cues within particular contexts accompanying them, are indelibly vague. As a consequence, living proof of their signness can only be adequately forthcoming through the contextualized pragmatics of human communication – that is, the above Bakhtin example. The sentence 'Give me a high five!' may remain relatively meaningless outside any and all contexts. Yet it is in certain situations quite effectively understood, and extended hands are slapped together without further ado. On the other hand, even though the sentence is contextualized as a sign of vagueness, it might demand the utterer's further elucidation in order that it be rendered adequately intelligible and determinate. In short, since there is neither absolute vagueness nor absolute generality in our world of actualized signs, neither is there an absolute absence either of vagueness or of generality.

Regarding the *complementarity* of vagueness and generality, Peirce writes that no general description can serve indubitably to identify the object of a sign or establish its meaning. A certain degree of identification of the object is always left to 'common sense' (Firstness, vagueness). For

> the common sense of the interpreter of the sign will assure him that the object must be one of a limited collection of objects. Suppose for example, two Englishmen to meet in a continental railway carriage. The total number of subjects of which there is any appreciable probability that one will speak to the other perhaps does not exceed a million, and each will have perhaps half that million not far below the surface of consciousness, so that each unit of it is ready to suggest itself. If one mentions Charles the Second, the other need not consider what possible Charles the Second is meant. It is no doubt the English Charles the Second. Charles the Second of England was quite a different man on different days; and it might be said that without further specification the subject is not identified. But the two Englishmen have no purpose of splitting hair in their talk; and the latitude of interpretation which constitutes the indeterminacy of a sign must be understood as a latitude which might affect the achievement of a purpose. (*CP*:5.448 n)

In addition to common sense, *purpose* is a watchword here. If two somewhat different conceptions of the same sign – one person's estimation of Charles the Second and that of another person – yielded meanings that were for all possible purposes equivalent, then the signs could well be considered equivalent. There would be no latitude of purpose, the sign would be general in the fullest possible sense. Nor would there be any room for vagueness, for the sign would always already have taken on the fullness of its generality, in the minds of its interpreters at least. However, in the context of human communication by way of natural language – and all other sorts of communication as far as that goes – there is no absolute identity of purpose, for the motivating force behind purpose itself involves common sense (intuition, inclination, belief, disposition, all of which have a foothold in Firstness and are inevitably tinged with some degree or other of vagueness).

Vagueness, then, is irreducible to the rank-and-file absolute determinacy of the 'semiotic object,' for there is always something indeterminable and left indeterminate. In Peirce's example: 'Suppose that the chat of our pair of Englishmen had fallen upon the colour of Charles II's hair. Now that colours are seen quite differently by different retinas is known. That the chromatic sense is much more varied than it is positively known to be is quite likely. It is very unlikely that either of the travelers is trained to observe colours or is a master of their nomenclature. But if one says that Charles II had dark auburn hair, the other will understand him quite precisely enough for all their possible purposes; and it will be a quite determinate predication' (*CP*:5.448 n1). The two interlocutors in question have no call for splitting hairs regarding their latitude of interpretation. Under ordinary conditions, fuzzy boundaries are established by a combination of tacit and explicit specifications, and talk usually goes on – that is, the Master's advice in the Preamble. In no case should it be assumed that, in good logical-positivist thinking, vagueness entails a deficiency of our knowledge or of our thought, William of Okham to the contrary (*CP*:4.344). Vagueness is every bit as essential to thought as is generality. For, in contrast to nominalist imperatives, a particular sign, its 'semiotic object,' or its interpretant, cannot be properly cognized in the total absence of the general nature of the semiotic entity in question. And unless there is some element of vagueness, there can hardly be any account of the entity's change over time: a changeless, timeless sign would be none other than a Parmenidean eternally invariant entity jam-packed with a host of other entities into a *plenum*.

To sum up, in a finite community of fallible semiotic agents, there can be no unadulterated sign of *generality* without at least a tinge of *vagueness*. And there can be no purely *vague* sign, for once actualized in order that it be made intelligible, a *vague* sign must take on at least some modicum of *generality* according to its interpreters' inevitable beliefs, habits, presuppositions, prejudices, and preconceptions. If any form or fashion of a 'logic in the broadest possible sense' there may be, it must include the spheres of both *vagueness* and *generality*, and hence the principles of noncontradiction and the excluded middle will not always be able to wield their terrible swift sword. The upshot is that if any and all statements regarding signs are possibly false (that is, *vague* and *overdetermined*, within the sphere of Firstness), then there can be no necessary *general* truths (determined from within Thirdness), that is, *for* us. Hence insofar as we finite, fallible semiotic agents are concerned, all *generals* are also possibly false (that is, the *incompleteness* of *underdetermination*), therefore they can be taken only conditionally as necessary, those conditions always remaining subject to their partial fulfilment, or in the event that they are false, to their unfulfilment.

Now for a further look at the *complementary* role of a sign's author and its interpreters – themselves also signs.

4. Signs Are Always Reaching Out

Taking into account the composite characteristics of possibility (Firstness), actuality (Secondness), and potentiality (Thirdness), a certain 'Principle of

Indeterminacy' is crucial to an understanding of the role of *absence* – from the *presence-absence: process* triad – in Peirce's semiotics (which is, he asserted repeatedly, tantamount to his ideal of a 'logic in the broadest possible sense').

Quite obviously, Peirce was keen on the idea that we dwell in a *vague* and *inconsistent*, and *general* but perpetually *incomplete*, world of signs. The ubiquity of *vagueness* and *inconsistency* breeds a tendency to embrace contradiction and paradox. And the inevitability of *incompleteness* in all signs of *general* nature allows for the entrance of unexpected thirds without conceivable end. Yet, according to Peirce, the collusion of possibility, actuality, and potentiality makes up our 'semiotically real world' as we perceive and conceive it, which, if we are fortunate, stands an outside chance of approximating some portion of the 'real.' Any and all 'semiotic worlds,' in this light, must remain radically uncertain, for

> [w]hen we busy ourselves to find the answer to a question, we are going upon the hope that there is an answer, which can be called the answer, that is, the final answer. It may be that there is none. If any profound and learned member of the German Shakespearian Society were to start the inquiry how long since Polonius had had his hair cut at the time of his death, perhaps the only reply that could be made would be that Polonius was nothing but a creature of Shakespeare's brain, and that Shakespeare never thought of the point raised. Now it is certainly conceivable that this world which we call the real world is not perfectly real but that there are things similarly indeterminate. We cannot be sure that it is not so. In reference, however, to the particular question which we at any time have in hand, we hope there is an answer, or something pretty close to an answer, which sufficient inquiry will compel us to accept. (*CP*:4.61)

To be more specific, Peirce does not use the pair of Gödelian terms, *inconsistency* and *incompleteness*, now commonplace in mathematics, logic, and physics, and 'buzz words' used and abused in the humanities and human sciences. However, his *vagueness-generality* dyad is brought in line with something reminiscent of a Gödelian framework by Rescher and Brandom (1979:124–6), though for a different purpose (see Merrell 1991, 1995a; Nadin 1982, 1983). The relationship between *vagueness-generality* and *inconsistency-incompleteness* and their relevance to *indeterminacy* becomes apparent if one sufficiently contemplates Peirce's suggestion that '[e]very utterance naturally leaves the right of further exposition in the utterer; and therefore, in so far as a sign is indeterminate, it is vague, unless it is expressly or by a well-understood convention rendered general' (*CP*:5.447). In other words, the indeterminately vague sign calls out to its maker for further clarification, since that which can render it less vague is more accessible to the possibilities that lie before her than before the sign interpreter.

An example of this principle is illustrated by an anecdote about Russell. In a social setting while discussing conditional statements, he remarked that a false statement can imply anything and everything. A sceptical colleague thereupon challenged him to prove that if 2 = 1, then he is the pope. 'Why,' Russell responded, 'the pope and I are two, but two equals one, therefore the pope and I are one' – the point being that it is useless to deal with inconsistent systems (in Bronowski 1978:79). During this exchange, confusion initially ensued upon Russell's uttering the vague signs, 'false statement,' 'anything,' and 'everything.' It was up to him, the signs' author, to provide their further determination, which he was most willing to do. One cannot deny that with Russell's engenderment of additional specifying signs, the original vague signs took on additional interpretative baggage. But the process was ongoing; for now, further determination of those signs as generalities rested on the shoulders of their interpreters. In this sense, the vague signs, 'false statement,' 'anything,' and 'everything,' remained alongside other specifying, yet to a degree general, signs, which combined to spell a potential for future semiotic engenderment on the part of both sign makers and sign takers.

If a sign of vagueness includes contradictions, then the sign's meaning for one community might be incompatible with its meaning for another community at another time. And if a sign of generality is never determined to the extent that it cannot be determined further, then an unordered set of potential interpretations exists with the characteristic that between any given pair of interpretations there can always be a third one. In other words, as we have noted, the excluded-middle principle loses part of its sting. A small group of mathematicians, the intuitionists, deny the excluded-middle principle altogether. They would discard statements the likes of 'Either there is a string of 18 consecutive 5s somewhere in the decimal expansion of π or there is not,' since they can most likely enjoy no proof in our finite world. That is to say, 'truth' is intimately linked to provability. For quite different reasons, a handful of quantum theorists also reject the excluded middle, in roughly the sense of Jan Lukasiewicz, the Polish logician of the 1920s, whose '3-valued logic' includes 'true,' 'false,' and 'undetermined' (indeterminate, intermediate). In fact, John von Neumann pioneered an alternative 'logic,' 'quantum logic,' especially tailored to the needs of quantum phenomena. Following the general implications of quantum theory and quantum logic, a sign's becoming a genuine sign depends upon the interpreter's interaction with it. Just as no 'wave packet' is an actualized 'particle-event' until it has come into contact with some aspect of its surroundings, so also no sign is a full-blown sign until it has been actualized (and *interpreted*) by some interpreter in some respect or capacity. (Of course there exists a veritable spate of alternative 'logics,' for example, three- and many-value logic, modal logic, dialectical logic, Buddhist logic, fuzzy logic, free logic, and, more in line with the premises underlying the present inquiry, Lupasco's 'logic of contradiction' [1947], Melhuish's 'complementary contradictory logic' [1967], Rescher and Brandom's 'logic of inconsistency' [1979], and the 'paraconsistent logic' developed in Brazil [da Costa 1974], none of which I intend to pre-empt here. I wish merely to open the door to a smattering of the many possibilities revealed by Peirce.)

An additional example may serve to illustrate the idea that (1) a sign is not a genuine sign until it has interacted with some semiotic agent, (2) within the (*vague*) realm of all possible signs, *inconsistency* and *contradiction* inevitably prevails, and (3) given the range of all actualized (*general*) signs, past, present, and future, there is no guarantee that the *excluded middle* applies, hence the meaning of any and all signs will be *incomplete*. Assuming I have little knowledge regarding a particular event reported in the newspaper, I may read each individual sentence with rather wide-eyed, innocent – and exceedingly vague – belief. Yet at a more general level I may also believe that this article, like all others, is in all probability the victim of at least some degree of biased reporting. I tend to believe each individual sentence as it stands, but at the same time I am willing to concede to the possibility that my belief in a given sentence can embrace contradiction, since I also believe that, lurking somewhere along the stream of black marks on white, there is undoubtedly some distortion of the 'truth.' So I take the article as a whole with a grain of disbelief, though I have not yet encountered (that is, actualized and interpreted) any expected sign of deceit: the sign remains a sign of possibility. Even though I might not have been able to catch the reporter at her devious game, I may still retain my faith that a closer reading will in all likelihood reveal some sort of inconsistency (that is, that the sign of possibility will be actualized). In other words, I believe the article is neither wholly 'true' nor wholly 'false,' but somewhere in between (following the teachings of the Master, we once again realize that banishing any and all contradictions and paradoxes is an interminable and hence futile enterprise.)

Extrapolating from Peirce's exclusion of the excluded-middle principle and his contradictory embrace of the principle of noncontradiction, it appears to follow that (1) an assertion of *possibility* (Firstness), having found newborn freedom from the principle of noncontradiction, rests chiefly within the domain of *vagueness*; (2) an assertion of *necessity* (Thirdness), liberated from the fetters of the excluded-middle principle, pertains primarily to *generality*; and (3) an assertion of *actuality* (Secondness) by and large, and for practical purposes, remains quite obedient to the demands of *classical logic*.

This collusion of vagueness and generality constitutes a fundamental principle, noted above, of what Peirce envisioned for his 'logic in the broadest possible sense.' According to the tenets of classical logic, once the identity of a proposition has been determined, it is either 'true' or 'false.' But for Peirce's more general 'logic,' as long as a proposition remains indeterminate – which must always be the case to a greater or lesser degree – it is not necessarily 'true' that it is either 'true' or 'false.' In fact, it may also be neither 'true' nor 'false,' for some newly born 'truth' may exist somewhere between the erstwhile horns of the presumed extremes of 'truth' and 'falsity' (a topic about which more below). And until the proposition is an absolutely determinate actuality – which will never be the case in a finite setting of fallible semiotic agents – it may be 'true,' given its vast range of all possible determinations at diverse space-time slices, that it is both 'true' and 'false.' Peirce's 'logic,' it tentatively appears, reflects a tension and potential mediation between *vagueness* and *generality*, the *individual* and the *universal*, and *discontinuity* and *continuity*, as well as between *self* and *other* and *self* and *sign*, in such a manner as to defy precise description. This accounts for the elusiveness of his hopeful 'logic,' and his obvious difficulty in bringing it to fruition. It also endows the terms in question with a flavour somewhat reminiscent, as suggested in the Preamble, of Bohr's complementarity regarding the wave/particle duality and Heisenberg's uncertainty, which, he argued repeatedly, is more a methodological and epistemological than an ontological necessity.

Since (1) complementarity and the uncertainty principle entail one's knowing now one character of an entity, now another character, without the possibility of knowing both characters in simultaneity, and since (2) Peirce's 'logic in the broadest possible sense' is time-bound, (3) a brief incursion – albeit tangentially by way of Kurt Gödel, if I may – into the nature of time behooves us.

5. It's About Time

Gödel's proof of 1931 has often been hailed by some as demonstration that machines cannot possess human intelligence nor are humans merely machines (see especially Lucas 1964). Actually, according to my modest understanding of the issue, he provided confirmation for nothing of the sort. According to Gödel's theorem, there are certain questions a machine simply cannot answer with a firm 'yes' or a firm 'no,' for a degree of *inconsistency* (*vagueness*) inexorably inheres. In our nitty-gritty world of human *praxis*, on the other hand, a number of questions exist that apparently cannot be *completely* (in the most *general* sense) answered at any particular point in time. But, given sufficient time and experience, and the numbing range of variable possible contexts, eventually a satisfactory answer can be forthcoming.

Moreover, if a question is posed we can – though with some vacillation – choose to answer neither with a definite 'yes' nor a definite 'no,' which is nonetheless also a decision. This *pro tempore* licence to vacillate between *this* and *that* and *yes* and *no* creates the possibility, at each new moment, of a slightly to radically different context. And context and time are all-important, for they hold some of the keys to the significance (meaning) of signs and of the semiotic agent's very existence. It is not that time heals all change but that through time, change ushers in new possibilities (Firsts), a minute portion of which are at particular space-time bifurcations and within particular contexts actualized (as Seconds) due to happy, and at times unexpected, collisions and collusions of memories, of present habits, dispositions, and conventions, and of anticipations of the future by the semiotic agent (via Thirdness). Most important, choices of one sort or another are exercised at each space-time juncture.

Now, if we replace *choice* by *decision* we are on the road toward approximating Gödel's turf. From within natural languages, *inconsistency* and *incompleteness* play havoc with the power of *decidability*, which depends upon manageable degrees of complexity. The problem is that, given a relatively rich and sophisticated field of natural language signs, the degree of complexity is such that it simply defies our finite, fallible human capacity for specifiability and decidability. The so-called Berry Paradox may give us a handle on the issue. This paradox comes in the form of an injunction: 'Find the smallest whole number that cannot be specified by a string of words with less than twenty-nine syllables.' The number of syllables in the Berry sentence itself, twenty-eight, can certainly describe some smallest number. And that smallest number is equal to the smallest number that cannot be specified by a string of words with less than twenty-nine syllables. We must conclude, then, that the least whole number not nameable by a string of words with fewer than twenty-nine syllables can in fact be named in twenty-eight syllables. The problem is that the sentence specifies a whole number that by its own definition it contains too few words to specify. Logically speaking, it should not be able to make a decision regarding such a number, for it cannot 'jump outside' itself to specify the number from some 'transcendental' vantage. If in this vein we take human finitude into due consideration, ultimately, the smallest number not nameable by the Berry sentence is for practical purposes virtually equivalent to the total number of our possible brain states: we cannot possibly hold each and every one of that mind-bogglingly monstrous collection of brain states in our purview for the purpose of deciding on and specifying its magnitude, for, logically speaking, we cannot do so without stepping outside our own brains, which we cannot do.

This impossibility of our grasping, surveying, deciding upon, and specifying the whole of a given corpus has a temporal-existential counterpart, which is revealed by another quandary known as the Prisoner Paradox. It is Sunday. The prisoners are told by their warden that the judge has decreed their execution on one day of that week, but they will not be informed which day it will be until the arrival of that very day, hence it will be a surprise (it seems that the warden, a humanitarian soul, wishes to spare them the anguish of a foreordained fate). The prisoners, however, happen to have found a quite astute lawyer. She reasons, after some deliberation, that assuming the warden has told them the truth, they cannot be executed, for if the fatal day is to be Saturday, then it cannot be a surprise, since the warden will have no remaining days when he can make a choice. By this mode of reasoning neither can it be Friday, for Saturday now having been eliminated, Friday is no longer a viable candidate. The same can be said of Thursday, and so on down to Monday. Therefore they cannot legitimately be executed.

Now, there seems to be a flaw somewhere, and there is, but it has nothing to do with timeless classical logic. The lawyer's reasoning is strictly by atemporal logical means; she can certainly afford to be logical, for her life is not at stake. Her field of signs, conveniently conforming to logical principles, is quite manageable, easily surveyable, and for her apparently decidable. In contrast, the prisoners' very existence is in jeopardy. They are rightly concerned over how much time remains of their lives, and time is precisely the issue here. The lawyer's logic is timeless, and within this framework, entailing a God's-eye grasp of things, the paradox springs forth in full force. In other words, as far as the lawyer is concerned, all events exist timelessly in the *before* or the *after* (that is, McTaggart's [1927] B-series). There can't be a 'day *after*,' regarding the prisoners' demise, for if there were, there could be no surprise, hence neither can there be a 'day *before*.' So the event of the prisoners' death at the hands of the firing squad can't occur, according to the lawyer's logic, that is. But the prisoners, their emotions having understandably taken precedence over their reasoning faculties, are condemned to time. They live in another world entirely, with a *past*, a *future*, and a knife-edged *present* racing from the former toward the latter (that is, McTaggart's [1927] temporal A-series). At any given *present* the warden can make his decision, the firing squad will be called up, and as far as the prisoners are concerned they will die. Hence, try as their lawyer may to convince them otherwise, she will not be able to reason away their expectations of an unexpected moment announcing their doom. Condemned to a time-bound set of *possibly*, *actually*, and *potentially* unexpected signs the complexity of which is beyond their grasp, they can conceive of no solution. There is for them no timeless God's-eye perspective of the sort apparently enjoyed by their lawyer.

The Berry Paradox traps the sentence 'within' itself and the interpreter within the sentence. The Prisoner Paradox traps the real flesh-and-blood objects of predication, the prisoners, 'within' the sentence, though a neutral interpreter can presumably remain 'outside,' maintaining a timeless logical slant on the whole. It is ultimately a matter of the capacity or incapacity to survey and give account of, and of the knowability or unknowability of, the whole of things. The lawyer thinks she can view the whole from a timeless perspective, as if she were gazing upon the undivided sphere of Firstness or of Thirdness completed once and for all. She sees an inconsistency, and, applying it to the prisoners' 'semiotically real' world of Secondness, declares that the judge's decreed event, the fulfilment of Thirdness, cannot logically come to pass. The prisoners, caught within their temporal existence and unable to survey the whole, believe that an event, so decreed by the judge, is surely inevitable, but they cannot know the point of its occurrence along the race of time. The judge claims he knows what the prisoners and their lawyer don't know; the lawyer claims she knows the judge cannot (logically) know what he thinks he knows; the prisoners know they cannot know what the judge knows, in spite of their lawyer's refutation of the judge's knowledge.

Is there no happy meeting ground uniting such apparently incommensurable mindsets?

6. The Time of Unknowing Knowing

Yes, there is a meeting ground of sorts, I would suggest. It plays on the limitations of *knowability*, that is, on the *incompleteness* and *inconsistency* of knowledge.

The judge, of the Prisoner Paradox, thinks he can justifiably set the day of the prisoners' execution, but the lawyer has discovered an *inconsistency* in his reasoning. The prisoners think they know not the day of the execution, and even though the lawyer points out the error of the judge's ways, they are not deterred from their learned sort of ignorance. They know their knowledge is destined to remain radically *incomplete*, for between a given future time-frame and a past time-frame, an instantiation of the present can always pop up within which their doom becomes manifest. In other words, at the very instant knowledge of the time of their execution is at hand, they are executed: their knowledge is now complete, but at the expense of their very existence. Whichever day the judge decides upon, an *inconsistency* will inhere. Whatever the prisoners think, their knowledge will be *incomplete*. The lawyer thinks she has dissolved the *inconsistency* by mentally strait-jacketing the judge and bringing the system to *completion* by discarding the possibility of a decision: things will remain as they are, timelessly. But the prisoners' 'semiotically real' world dictates otherwise, for the entire scheme is, from whichever vantage, either *inconsistent* or *incomplete* – or perhaps both – up to the instant their very existence is terminated. Each party, it would appear, is either right for the wrong reasons or wrong for the right reasons.

The point is this. The lawyer's timeless realm of logic, when placed in the living and breathing world of time-bound Seconds and Thirds, is not existentially valid, for it allows of no temporality, the very stuff life is made of. So from the subjective world of the prisoners, the lawyer's form of logic is relegated to the sphere of *overdetermination* (Firstness), where *inconsistent* signs are superposed as quite unruly bed partners. The lawyer, in contrast, wishes objectively to interject the timeless orb of her classical logic into the actualized sphere of Seconds, which allows for neither contradictory signs nor a proliferation of middles. But the lawyer's logic, from within the prisoners' own existential world, is a time bomb ticking out their destiny. It remains *for* them *incomplete*, within the sphere of *underdetermination* (Thirdness): they cannot know at what point in time the expected unexpected event of their death will occur, though they definitely think they know it will occur. When it does occur, their knowledge will have reached completion and the uncertainty of proliferating temporal middles between the judge's decree and their execution will no longer exist. But all will have been to no avail, for they will be no more.

Of course we would like to assume that such paradoxes are not pernicious and that we can always 'jump out' of the signs within which they are enshrouded to specify whatever we wish: we persist in our desire to think we are master of our signs. However, though we can occasionally exercise a move from one system to another of greater complexity, we are able to manhandle that 'lower' system from what we imperiously believe to be our 'metaperspective' only insofar as our own system – ultimately the brain-mind – is of greater complexity than that 'lower' system, and above all, only insofar as by some inconceivable stretch of the imagination it stands outside time. If not, like the Berry sentence or the lawyer of the Prisoner Paradox, we run the risk of attempting to – and presuming we can – survey the unsurveyable, decide the undecidable, specify the unspecifiable, know the unknowable.

That is to say, as I shall hammer out repeatedly through the remainder of this inquiry, given the sign fabricator and its interpreter – both hopeless meaningmongers in the event that they are high-handed humans – what is taken out of the sign is actually what was put there in the first place. What was put there is always subject, in time, to change of minor to radical sorts, and what is taken out, since invariably *incomplete*, is always subject, also in time, to further additions and deletions. In short, no *corpus* of knowledge in the time-bound world of our severely restricted capacities can be both entirely *consistent* and *complete*, though our thinking would like to make it so. As an afterthought, the assertions of the last few paragraphs will likely open me to the charge that I am mixing time and timelessness. This has been, of course, a perennial problem of Western metaphysics, and I harbour no illusions of being able to resolve it in one fell swoop. What I am very modestly attempting to illustrate by the prisoner and Berry parables is the impossibility of divorcing what is presumed to be timeless, objective thought from the concrete life-world, in other words, of divorcing mind from body, a topic the development of which I must leave for the final chapter.

And yet, our thinking can to a greater or lesser extent be made to give the appearance that what we think is the case is indeed the case. This making of our thought and of our thought's making what appears to be the case the case, at least *for* us at a given space-time juncture, is germane to the implications of what Peirce terms the 'pragmatic maxim' – given more detailed discussion in the appendix. The maxim is a method not for determining whether a set of signs, characteristically in the form of a sentence or set of sentences, is timelessly and undeniably 'true.' Rather, it is an indeterminately variable method for interacting with signs in such a way that the 'semiotic world' with which they relate appears to be the case, and in the process their meaning emerges: the maxim enables signs – including ourselves – to lift themselves up by their own bootstraps. To this end Peirce provided in 1878 his first incarnation of the maxim: 'Consider what effects, that might conceivably have practical bearings, we conceive the object of our conception to have. Then our conception of these effects is the whole of our conception of the object' (*CP*:5.402; also 5.2, 5.9, 5.18, 5.427, and MS 327).

The maxim in essence stipulates that the meaning of a sentence regarding what appears to be the case is the product of all conceivable consequences presented by other sentences – and their own consequences – engendered from the original sentence. This product of all conceivable consequences entails the *translation* of the initial sign or sentence into a series of conditional sentences the antecedents of each of which prescribe certain interactions between the interpreter and the signs in question. The consequences, ideally, consist of observable sign phenomena that should or would make themselves manifest in the event that the original signs or sentences are indeed 'true.' But 'truth' is not really the goal. Rather, the task at hand is to draw meaning from the signs being processed by way of interpreter-sign interaction. The interpreter takes the initial signs and creates a hypothetical situation by imagining what would most likely ensue. Then she puts her hypothetical signs to the test in terms of a thought experiment 'in here' or by interacting with the signs' objects 'out there' in order to see if she was right. If her hypothesis turns out to appear correct for the time being, the possibility nonetheless remains that other hypotheticals may at future moments present themselves, compelling her to repeat the operation. If her initial hypothesis is found deficient, then back to the drawing board for an alternative hypothetical, in which case she also repeats the operation. And so on.

By its very nature this process leads to an increasingly complex series of sentences. For example, the sentence 'This is salt' calls for the imaginative construction of all the conceivable consequences in all conceivable contexts. In the final analysis, I would suggest that the inclusion of all conceivable contexts knows no ultimate perspective, language game, or form of life. Nor does it prioritize any particular mode of knowing. It entails an entire range of possible sentences from the sphere of vagueness that predict what would most likely occur if the salt were dissolved in water, dumped in the water softener, sprinkled on a hamburger, used to treat a slab of pork, analytically subjected to spectroscopy, qualitatively tested in the high-school laboratory for chlorine and sodium, tossed on the city streets during a snowstorm, or whatever. Thoroughly to interpret the sentence in question – to arrive at its ultimate or final interpretant within the sphere of generality – demands knowledge of the behaviour of salt in all possible situations and all possible contexts. The ramifications are virtually limitless. Consequently, the plenitude of meaning regarding the initial sentence, 'This is salt,' given the plethora of subsidiary sentences derived from it, is in its fullness of numbing complexity. It exhausts our individual cognitive capacities and our capacity to know our world (Skagestad 1981). Our best possible hope is to catch snippets of the *semiosic* whole that lie within our finite grasp, interact with them in the world of our professional, practical, and leisure affairs, and get along somehow – that is, follow the Master's advice.

In formal systems (mathematical, geometry, logic, 'computer thought') the search is in essence not for new 'truths' either, but for reasons unlike those of the 'maxim.' The object of the quest, rather than meaning, is for axioms with which to enrich the system by erasing *inconsistencies* and moving toward *completeness*. Along complementary lines, the task of a human semiotic agent engaged in the everyday affairs of natural language use is that of interpreting signs – interacting with them in such a way that meaning emerges – in order to enrich her conception of the *semiosic* whole. It is not simply a matter of adding new 'facts' – new meanings – to an already bloated corpus of theories and their putative evidence, but of engendering new sentences capable of clarifying

– and at times of overthrowing – that corpus (Kline 1980). Quite justifiably, in this vein, it has been observed that Gödel's theorem can be viewed as 'a consequence of the limited complexity of any formal arithmetic system, a limitation affecting human minds as well as machine programs' (Paulos 1985:99).

'Fine and dandy,' one might retort, 'but this hardly separates the chaff of machines from the wheat of thinking and feeling humans; it merely illustrates that a machine endowed with time-binding human attributes is remotely like a human.' Fortunately, however, human *praxis* is not limited to the rigorous arguments of strictly formal languages – as the above observations on *vagueness* and *generality* suggest. In everyday human affairs we make decisions, the consequences of which at the time and within that particular context seemed plausible. But further experience often serves to determine that that particular decision was not prudent after all. For the set of implications presented by the whole system remained beyond our grasp, and we could therefore not be aware of the degree of *vagueness* and *generality*, and *inconsistency* and *incompleteness*, of our knowledge of that system in terms of its future consequences. In retrospect we might be able to become aware of the error of our ways, or we can congratulate ourselves on our sagacity, but at the time our decision was made, we exercised intuitive capacities the total ramifications of which we could not possibly have been aware. In other words, we are tenderly and rather helplessly fallible semiotic agents.

The conclusion seems to be that *actuality*, *vagueness*, and *generality*, coupled with *inconsistency-incompleteness* and the *principle of indeterminacy*, afford at least a premonition of the infinite series of conceivable consequences and their products arising out of the implications inherent in a given sentence engendered by the 'pragmatic maxim.' Vagueness marks the presence of an absent set of possible signs. Actuality is the presence of that which constitutes signs relating to the 'furniture' of our 'semiotically real' world. And generality, a mediator and moderator between the other two members of the triad, tones them, keeps them within reasonable bounds, and synthesizes them. In concert, *vagueness*, *actuality*, and *generality* not only pattern Peirce's categories, they are also the motivating force behind his unfinished 'logic' of *semiosic praxis*, which is quite compatible with much contemporary discourse, as we shall observe.

2

The Self as a Sign among Signs

1. Self-Referring, Self-Inferring Signs

Peirce's most basic trio of signs consists of *icons* (signs by resemblance – triangles for mountains), *indices* (signs whose very nature relates them to some *other* – lightning and thunder), and *symbols* (signs of convention – 'horse' related to a horse or to a/the class of horses). (I will briefly discuss Peirce's sign types in chapter 14, after a rather large expanse of terrain has been adequately prepared. For the time being, I would ask the patience of those readers who might be unfamiliar with Peirce's concept of the sign.)

Peirce's fundamental types of *symbols* include *terms*, *propositions*, and *arguments* (which, in the discourse of contemporary jargon, is tantamount to *word-sentence: text*, or when amplified, *words-sentences: [inter]textuality*). Consideration of *symbols* places us squarely within natural language signs. Yet, as we shall note, *symbols* are by no means free of *iconicity* and *indexicality*, for they are virtually worthless outside any and all consideration of those more fundamental signs. The tight *icons-indices-symbols* embrace is a far cry from most structuralist and poststructuralist circles according to which language (symbolicity) remains aloof and unaligned with the world as a set of free-floating arbitrary signifiers shorn of determinate hooks onto the 'semiotically real,' to say nothing of the 'real' (Merrell 1992, 1995a, 1995b). Peircean symbols inevitably carry iconic and indexical baggage along with them. This contextualizes them, for if totally divorced from all contexts and the situations of their use, they would be hardly meaningful. It behooves us, then, to consider the importance of *icons* and *indices* in terms of their life within *symbols*.

The remarks in chapter 1 on Bakhtin's style-intonation are quite in line with Peirce's notion of sentences as symbols the function of which includes a complex mixture of iconic (predicate) and indexical (subject) properties.

However, a sentence cannot be a mere 'verbal icon,' for if so, a genuine interpretant (Third) could not properly relate to any 'semiotically real' object (Second). In fact, if a sentence were a 'verbal icon,' there could be no genuine interpretant in the first place, for such an interpretant demands a mature form of symbolicity. Relations must exist between the sign and its object and between sign-object and interpretant, that interpretant in turn relating both the sign and its object to itself in the same manner in which they are related to each other. That is to say, a full-blown interpretant in terms of human semiotics must be a card-carrying member of symbolicity: it mediates between the iconic and the indexical character of the sign at the same time that each of those characters mediates between the other character and the sign's symbolicity.

A Norman Rockwell painting is an icon, to be sure, and certain of its elements give clues to indicate (index) the painting's creator. The painting's signature, 'Norman Rockwell,' a symbol, relates to and mediates between the icon and index in such a way that they relate to themselves both iconically (as resemblance) and indexically (as indication), and at the same time they relate to the symbol (in terms of a conventional link between a set of ciphers and the painter, his painting, that of which the painting is an icon, and those clues in the painting pointing to the painter and the painted). Iconicity and indexicality are there, whether or not there is any interpreter interpreting the signs. In contrast, a genuine symbolic interpretant requires a semiotic agent establishing links that stand on the shoulders of social norms and conventions, in addition to resemblance (iconicity) or natural or causal connection (indexicality). (Actually, during his early studies Peirce maintained that in the most fundamental sense propositions are of the classical subject-predicate form [*CP*:1.559, 2.472], though after beginning work on his 'logic of relations' he conceded that language resists such closure [*CP*;3.45–149]. This complexity and perpetual openness of language, which involves iconic and indexical processes embodied within symbolic processes, will be the focus of the final stages of this inquiry.)

A totally isolated icon, were that to be possible, would be nothing more than a 'possibility involving a possibility, and thus the possibility of its being represented as a possibility' (*CP*:2.311). Which is about as clear as mud until one becomes aware that iconicity in isolation is not yet anything *to which* there is any relation or *of which* there can be any consciousness *on the part of* some semiotic agent. The immediacy of Peirce's category of Firstness requires subsequent development of Secondness and Thirdness before there can be, properly speaking, consciousness *of* signness and self-consciousness *that* there *is* such consciousness. Yet, an intelligible sentence contains at least one icon (*CP*:2.251). In addition, a sentence also incorporates at least one index that manifests the sentence's nature, though it does not represent its whole nature

(*CP*:2.262). Indices are distinguished from other signs insofar as they have no significant resemblance to their semiotic objects; they direct attention to them through association by contiguity, or some natural or causal connection, that complements the resemblance character of the icon within the sentence (*CP*:2.306).

An index can function as the subject of a simple subject-predicate sentence and the icon as its predicate, which calls attention to the sentence's object of signification (*CP*:2.312). What surfaced in the Preamble was the problematics of such self-referring sentences. Icons unmediated and unrelated to anything else are by nature narcissistic in this manner; they are signs of themselves and themselves only. Indices, by nature binary in character, ordinarily relate to some *other*. But they can also be self-referring. Peirce offers the example of the collection of all even numbers, which is an index of the collection of all whole integers: the part (even numbers) indexes (indicates, relates to) the totality (whole numbers) and at the same time it indexes itself. In this regard the function of iconicity bears certain relationship to *depth*, and the function of indexicality to *breadth*, as they were tentatively outlined in the Preamble.

Self-referential statements of the sort presented by Alpha and the Master are also revealing. The indices (nouns, pronouns) in the sentences (symbols) 'This proposition is about itself' and 'Disregard this sentence' refer to themselves. The first statement is relatively harmless, while the second, requiring reader participation, contains an equally innocuous pragmatic paradox – as the Master pointed out, in everyday communication many paradoxes can be as a matter of course confronted, embraced, and tacitly surmounted (if not simply ignored), with hardly any attention to the matter. In each case the index points to the entire sentence (symbol), and to the part of the sentence that it *is not* – the predicate (or icon) – as well as pointing to itself. (Rather than a sentence of the simple subject-predicate sort, I use the terms icon and index, themselves of symbolic nature, since we are speaking of language. One must bear in mind, however, that icons and indices incorporated within symbols come in increasing degrees of complexity, since in sentences with various embedded clauses they can consist of compound sets of symbolic signs [see Murphey 1961]).

Although Peirce occasionally considered self-reflecting sentences to be 'unadulterated nonsense' – a characteristic that stands out in the sobriety given them by the spotlight of analytic philosophy – I would suggest that they offer much food for thought regarding the question of Bakhtin's style-intonation, which ultimately ushers in a question regarding what makes meaning possible in the first place. That is to say, the subject (index) of a simple sentence bears on intonation insofar as in its textual context it takes on the function of a 'shifter' or 'pointer.' Hence it remains to a degree *vague*, for the utterer is assigned the task of its further specification, which must remain an indeterminate affair, given the index's displacement with each and every instance of its use. And it must be to an extent *general* insofar as its interpreter shoulders the responsibility of carrying its determination a mite further, which is an equally interminable project. The subject, then, remains indeterminate: either the principle of excluded middle or the principle of noncontradiction does not always apply, whether we are gravitating toward *generality* or *vagueness*. Moreover, the subject is relevant to intonation in its social context as the nonverbal aspect of the sign-meaning, which, for obvious reasons, renders it even less determinate: the distinguishing features of the sign's intonation tend to be less discrete than their linguistic counterpart as sentential signs generated from within a particular universe of discourse. The subject also bears on style insofar as a sentence, once having become self-reflecting, begins to take on an opaque countenance. As an index it 'points to' itself, creating in the act a problem of self-determination. For the 'pointed to' is altered by the pointer, whose object is the 'pointed to,' which makes an about-face and turns back on itself to affect the pointer.

But to repeat, a sentence also incorporates an icon. This dual character of a sentence is dependent upon (1) a somewhat vague sense (quality, icon) relating the sentence to other sentences of comparable nature in order to render it intelligible, and (2) an act of volition on the part of both the utterer and the interpreter as an indicator (index) of that to which the sentence relates. It is impossible, Peirce argues, to construct a sentence of such pristine simplicity that it is entirely devoid of this duality. He offers the apparently unproblematic example, 'It rains' (*CP*:2.438). The icon ('rains') is 'the mental composite photograph of all the rainy days' the utterer and interpreter have experienced. The two 'photographs' are comparable, though never identical, for two given interlocutors. Yet they are incessantly in a process of variation. The index ('it') is everything whereby the utterer and interpreter from their slightly to radically distinct perspectival and conceptual scheme distinguish that particular day in their experience. And the sentence is the composite mental act whereby the icon, coupled with its respective index, marks that day as rainy (*CP*:2.360). If I may evoke the terms once again, the difference in experience Peirce observes regarding iconicity and indexicality and their role in the engenderment of symbolicity makes for an inextricable element of *vagueness* and *generality*, and hence *indeterminacy*, of meaning. However, lest the somewhat trite example, 'It rains,' evoke the common idea that icons are no more than simple images, I must emphasize that icons can come in increasingly complex forms (*CP*:2.440–1). A sentence, paragraph, or an entire text, can, in its compound form, evoke a general yet exceedingly vague, and simple on the surface though of myriad complexity, icon. Such is the case of works the likes of *Hamlet*, *Don Quixote*, *Anna Karenina*, and *Madame Bovary* (*CP*:2.344; for further, see Merrell 1995a, 1995b).

It is becoming increasingly evident that a crucially important feature of Peirce's triadic thinking being unfolded here is his notion of *interrelatedness*, which bears on the *dialogic nature of the sign*: for Peirce all signifying activity, in and of itself, is dialogic (in other words, *interrelational*) through and through (*CP*:6.338). Max Fisch (1986:442) observes that one of the most pervasive themes in Peirce's work is the idea that all thought is in signs, and it is dialogic in nature; even at its most private and silent it is nonetheless a dialogue between the self of one moment, which is, properly speaking, a sign, and the oncoming self of the next moment, a sign coming into existence. Peirce's dialogic, quite significantly, is germane to the current notion of intertextuality (that is, *interrelatedness*), especially in relation to the work of Bakhtin (see Ponzio 1985, 1990, and Baer 1988; and, for the semiotics of the self, Colapietro 1989, Fisch 1986, Sebeok 1979, and Wiley 1994). According to this *interrelatedness* idea, which includes the *dialogic self*, no term of any of the triads discussed in chapter 1 is separable from the other two. All triads are intimately linked and inextricably wedded to the self and, indeed, to the whole of *semiosis*.

It behooves us, then, very briefly to consider the role of the self as itself an interrelated and interrelating sign among signs. This may help provide a viable notion (1) of *semiosis* and the self's place within it as immanent, and (2) of meaning arising from within the signifying process as the result of a cooperation, collaboration, and at times collusion, of all parties involved.

2. The Self and Its Perpetually Shifting Other

One would perhaps like to assume that the self represents an 'object,' 'I-me.' Yet this 'object' is non-empirical: its 'presence' is marked by its 'absence,' and its 'absence' is dependent upon its 'presence.'

The problem is that the self is not unary, but *is* only with respect to what it *is not*, some *other* (as Alpha implied, negation is not a unary fact but a binary act). In addition, like signs in general, the self manifests a trinary character. Every self, in collaboration with its signs, addresses itself to some *other* (*CP*:5.253). For Descartes self-consciousness is immediately intuited and the self is autonomous: it is primary, existing independently of all external constraints. In contrast, Peirce's anti-Cartesian posture envisages a *mediate* or *inferred self* that, like all signs, must be related to *otherness*: it can never stand alone, for it is relational through and through. Consequently, like the eye that cannot see itself, the pure self as icon cannot maintain an immediate awareness *of* itself. As an inference, the self depends upon its own 'inner' other for its very existence. In fact, it can become aware of its inferred self only upon becoming aware of that other (*CP*:1.324). That is, the self, upon inferring itself into existence, sets itself apart from everything else in order that there may be a distinction between something and something else.

The self's becoming of awareness of itself entails a distinction enacted between it and its 'inner' other as well as between it and the physically 'real' – the other 'out there' – and the other selves of its community. There are, then, three dialogic others: (1) the 'inner' other, (2) the physical-world other, and (3) the collective social other. The 'inner' I-me relation is that of Peirce's self and its own other. The self and its 'outer' others entail I-you and I-it relations. The I is modelled as oneness (iconicity) and the you-it as action-reaction, or presence-absence (indexicality). The I as pure ego cannot dialogue with an 'outer' other except in the form of another person, the other self (you). Or it can dialogue with the 'outer' other of the physically 'real,' the 'it,' which is never completely accessible but only approximated by mediary Thirdness (symbolicity). This 'outer' other of Secondness, the physically 'real,' we shall observe in greater detail in chapter 3, is ultimately of the form of fiction – or perhaps better, fantasy. It is never a pure and unadulterated fact *for* the equivalent of some chimerical Cartesian hyperconscious supercogitator.

The self in this manner is of the nature of a sign, and more specifically, of the nature of Thirdness (Fisch 1986). In a manner of putting it, what Peirce calls the initiary 'cut' in the sphere of possible signs (that is, of 'nothingness,' as mentioned in the Preamble) enacts an I/you (this/that) split, which is dyadic. Symbolization, that is language, the premier form of triadicity, carries the rupture a giant step further to engender that familiar hierarchy of dichotomies about which much controversial ink has been disseminated in poststructuralist and deconstructionist circles – all of which bears on the existence of the self.

As (initially arbitrary) abstractions, the symbols of human language are endowed with the capacity to exercise dominion over their predecessors, icons and indices – whether of linguistic or nonlinguistic sort. But symbols can present another, even more ominous, threat: they evince a propensity to gravitate, at times apparently with the greatest of ease, toward dank nonconscious realms of the mind, thus eliciting sign use at times without their author's awareness that they are being so used – or better, symbols can use, and at times abuse, their authors' best of intentions. Once they have been submerged, have submerged themselves, into these nonconscious levels, they can become powerful authors of signification in their own right. They pre-empt their erstwhile authors – semiotic agents – who are now less implementors of symbols than instruments of their symbols' machinations. Putting it in the terms of poststructuralist discourse, signifiers, shorn of their signifieds, are now interpreted at tacit rather than conscious levels. During this process they can take over the whole show, authoring the very agents who originally engendered them. This submerging into consciousness of signs and their being put to use bears on Peirce's concept – derived from its mathematical use – of *de-generacy* [sign *embedment*, *entrenchment*, *automatization*] and *habit* (for further, see Merrell 1995a, 1995b, 1996).

In this manner, the 'inner' dialogic other, the 'outer' social other, and the 'real' physical-world other 'out there' alike, can threaten to cast an ominous shadow over the self. If they manage to do so, in their composite, these three others become construed as simply that which *is*. As such, they are tantamount to the 'I am that I am' (Firstness, the pure monad) of a vengeful Jehovah, the fascist state, the domineering father (or mother), suffocating group pressures, demands created by the media or by the exigencies of consumerist society, and so on. The self, as a consequence, collapses virtually to a point; it becomes devoid of almost all vestiges of its selfhood. This is the dark side of dialogic interaction to which Peirce occasionally addressed himself and which has been the focus of recent incursions in the name of postmodernism.

Fortunately, there is also a light side. Caught in the flow of things, the subject – author-interpreter-interpretant – can bear witness to the processual gush of living signs incessantly passing into other signs. This subject is in a sense partly autonomous – an icon, a First. At the same time, she is herself a sign in another ongoing *semiosic* loop – an index, Second, and a symbol, Third. If one facet of the whole is highlighted, she becomes, albeit artificially, identical with herself, a self-contained monad. Yet, if another complementary facet is highlighted, she becomes not exclusively autonomous but part of the ongoing interactive whole, for, as a sign, she merges into her environment and at the same time takes her environment into herself. The ongoing activity of the author-interpretant as *translation* of signs into other signs ultimately provides for the engenderment of meaning. That is to say, the author-interpreter interprets (draws an interpretant from) the sign at least in part according to how the others author-interpret it. The interpretation thus reflects back on the author-interpreter in the dialogic interaction such that she interprets herself interpreting the interpretant.

In the final analysis, the semiotic agent does not merely interpret signs, she interprets interpretation itself, she undoes the sign and the sign undoes her while she is in the act of undoing the sign. Her own meaningfulness is no more and no less than that which constitutes the meaning of any other sign. A sign-self is not a sign-self without its other, some other within a particular context. And meaning is other than the sign-self, yet, as something other than the others of the sign-self, it is never content with its status as other of the other, but is always in the process of becoming something else, of being *translated* into something else. This something else is neither spatial nor temporal, neither ever precisely *here* nor *now*, but a scintillating, trembling, quivering, vacillating drift betwixt the two poles.

Ultimately, as a consequence of this interactive process, engenderment of meaning is a community happening, and the individual self is by and large just along for the ride.

3. Our Vain Individualism

The centrality of the community bears on yet another Peircean triad, *feeling-volition: cognition*. Feeling is Firstness, quality – Alpha's vague sense of the paradox of meaning. Volition is dual: force and resistance, agent and patient, self and other. It is the result of interaction between the self and the 'real' (outer physical and social others) – Omega's reaction to Alpha, as well as indirectly to the Master – which gives rise to dyadic consciousness *of* ego and a non-ego (*CP*:1.334–5). Cognition, at the level of Thirdness, is the process of mediation between feelings and volitions. This is the Master's enacting a *conjunctionis oppositorum*, so to speak, uniting statements and counterstatements, intuitive assumptions and appearances, ideas and their negations.

Metaphorically put: 'Position is first, velocity or the relation of two successive positions is second, acceleration or the relation of three successive positions is third' (*CP*:1.337). Peirce's analogy is apropos. Position implies changelessness. Velocity is continuous change, but there is merely change of position. In contrast, acceleration is continuous change of change; both position and velocity undergo successive and continuous alteration. Feeling, volition, and cognition as First, Second, and Third correspond, I hardly need write, to Peirce's tripartite sign. The representamen is immediate. That for which it stands, the object, is other than the self and subject to volition. And the idea to which the representamen gives rise is its interpretant, which entails cognitive activity.

That is to say, since the object of the sign is not a 'really real' but a 'semiotically "real" object,' it can be none other than the object of another relation of which the first relation becomes the sign's interpretant, and that interpretant becomes another sign related to its object, which is now something other than what it was. In this manner, an endless train of relations can be conceived to have some 'absolutely real' object behind it as a limit, though it can at best be no more than approximated. In other words, the sign – as position, as First (feeling) – relates to the 'semiotically "real" object,' which is pushed along the rail of Secondness (volition) by the incessant transmutation of interpretants into other signs. And the interpretant as mover (Thirdness, cognition), accelerates, like the expanding universe bringing about the 'red shift' phenomenon, toward an ideal limit. This role of the interpretant is, once again, patterned by the Master, who mediates between Alpha and Omega in order to unite them, though the project is destined to perpetual incompleteness.

In still another way of putting it, feeling, possibility, a *might be*, is not adverse to *vagueness* and *inconsistency*. With regards to language (symbolic signs), the Firstness of possibility is most adequately exemplified by a predicate (icon) – a qualifying term or word as attribute, property, characteristic – whose self-sufficiency and self-containment leaves it wrapped up in its own 'egocentricity,' so to speak. Volition, the *is-ness* of things, is the action-reaction give-and-take of the self in incessant dialogue with its own other, its social other, and its physical-world other. Volition is incorporated in the subject (index) – a term or word as a sign that indicates (indexes) something or someone in the 'semiotically real.' Cognition, probability, a necessary *would be* or *should be*, is, as *generality*, invariably *incomplete*: it never ceases to exercise an obstinate push toward something in the order of the egocentric Cartesian ideal, though it has nary a ghost of a chance of getting there. At the same, time cognition is properly embodied in propositions, sentences, or utterances, whose task is that of offering themselves up as part of arguments, texts, narratives: intertextuality (that is, interrelatedness). In short, from position to velocity to acceleration, signs cannot help but reach out to other signs, interrelate with other signs, become *translated* into other signs, within the ongoing flow of *semiosis*. Within *semiosis*, the other is created by the passing of signs into interpretants, interpretants into signs, and the self of one moment into the self of another moment. The self cannot be itself, but only what it *was not* during the moment past, and what it not yet *is* – what it *will have been* – in the future moment. So how is it possible, if at all, to identify the self's 'internal' other?

Peirce observed that, regarding volition, there is a difference between intentionally willing, say, a muscle to contract, and the passive and unintentional volition that produces a shock of surprise as a result of an unsatisfied expectation, which results in a sense of externality, of the 'real' of Secondness, of the other (*CP*:1.334). This sense of exteriority, of the presence of a non-ego, is not merely a sense of the world 'out there.' It is the product of the dialogic 'I-me' (self and its 'inner' other), the 'me' resting tenuously between the 'I' and the 'it,' that is, the 'real.' When the relatively mature self is thinking, the 'I' uses signs by means of which to persuade the 'me' that something or other is the case. During this activity, 'a person is not absolutely an individual. His thoughts are what he is "saying to himself," that is, saying to that other self that is just coming into life in the flow of time. When one reasons, it is that critical self that one is trying to persuade, and all thought whatsoever is a sign, and is mostly of the nature of language. The second thing to remember is that the man's circle of society (however widely or narrowly this phrase may be understood), is a sort of loosely compacted person, in some respects of higher rank than the person of an individual organism' (*CP*:5.421).

The immediate 'I' as First (icon), relates to the object (index), or that which is the object of persuasion, in addressing itself to the interpretant (symbol), which is in the process of 'coming into life in the flow of time.' And the interpretant in turn becomes itself a sign with its own object (*CP*:2.274). In other words, the 'I' or more immediate self is itself split. There is the interpreting 'I' (First) as subject and the 'I' (Second) as object of interpretation. The first 'I' distinguishes itself and the sign from the process of interpretation; the second 'I' becomes one with the *semiosic* process. The first project, an impossible dream, is destined to remain incomplete, since there is no immediacy, only mediacy, of the 'I's' perception and conception of the other, hence the 'I' is not genuinely autonomous. The second project, a tail-chasing-dog game, is equally pathetic, for the 'I' cannot know itself as *it is*, but only mediately, as *it was*. Consequently, there is no independent, fixed, unitary self to be 'discovered,' which attests to Hume's often quoted passage: 'For my part, when I enter most intimately into what I call *myself*, I always stumble on some particular perception or other, of heat or cold, light or shade, love or hatred, pain or pleasure. I never can catch *myself* at any time without a perception, and never can observe anything but the perception' (1964:1,VI,iv).

The upshot is that there is no pure, absolutely autonomous 'I' or self. No sign – or self – is an island, an entity unto itself and absolutely autonomous. We, all signs, are thoroughly socialized. The 'I' addresses itself to its otherness, its social other as well as the other of physical 'reality,' both of which are 'out there' in contrast to the self's own 'inner' other. Part of that social otherness is that which is emerging and that into which the 'I' is merging: the 'I' is incessantly flowing into the otherness of which it is a *part of* and at the same time *apart from*. For, to repeat Peirce's words, 'a person is not absolutely an individual,' and at the same time, a person's 'circle of society' is a sort of 'loosely compacted person.' In spite of all this, our impoverished individualism is masqueraded about, bloated by our vanities, kept afloat by our modernist obsession for control, and in our postmodern milieu, it is frocked with high-tech glitter and glitz. All the while we continue in ignorant bliss, generally oblivious to our radical dependence on our social otherness, for 'the selfhood you like to attribute to yourself is, for the most part, the vulgarist delusion of vanity' (*CP*:7.571).

Thus, the presumed condition of a radical self/other duality compelling the self to become autonomous is false to itself. The self remains inextricably linked to its community, engaged in constant dialogue with its 'inner' other self, the 'outer' physical world, and its 'outer' social other within the parameters of that social other's host of prescriptions and proscriptions. This is not to imply that initially the individual self was not socialized and then at some point socialization became a fact. The self, since its inception, was always already embedded in a context – the community or 'semiotic world' as a system of signs. Consequently it is also embedded in itself, the self that speaks 'to that other self that is just coming into life in the flow of time.' In this sense the self, as a sign among signs, is itself a composite or conglomerate sign. From Peirce's belief that every thought requires a relation between the thought and something else *of* which one is conscious – since the content of consciousness as well as the self is not immediately intuitive but the result of inference – it follows that the self, consciousness, and the mind are all equally signs (*CP*:5.317). Or, in Peirce's rather enigmatic words, '[I]t is sufficient to say that there is no element whatever of man's consciousness which has not something corresponding to it in the word; and the reason is obvious. It is that the word or sign which man uses is the man himself. For, as the fact that every thought is a sign, taken in conjunction with the fact that life is a train of thought, proves that man is a sign; so, that every thought is an external sign, proves that man is an external sign ... Thus my language is the sum total of myself; for the man is the thought' (*CP*:5.314) (see also in this respect Burks 1980).

Now, what has all this to do with the central theme of the present inquiry? *Everything* and *nothing*. *Nothing*, because the self, as a bundle of signs, as a conglomerate symbol, loses itself within the universe of all signs: its ersatz individuality is at most a pale reflection of its signs, of all signs. Signs – the self included – are granular only during the ephemeral moment they have emerged from the *semiosic* soup *as* signs *for* some semiotic agent or other *in* some respect or capacity. Then they sink back into the continuum from which they arose. And *everything*, for signs, meanings, and minds mediating between them and some 'semiotically real' sphere or other are ultimately one and indivisible. (In the succeeding chapters I shall foreground the idea that the same is to be said of meaning: it is not a matter of signs there and meaning here to be trapped and held captive in its pristine purity from some God's-eye vantage, but of an ongoing, incessantly transient, affair – recall the Master's words in this regard.)

It becomes quite apparent that if author-interpreter, ego, and self are all signs, then they are their own interpretants, which calls for concession to the idea of ...

4. The Knowing Author-Interpreter (with)in the Interpretant

The individual may think she knows, to be sure, but this felicitous, Edenic condition self-destructs in Peirce's conception of things. Innocence becomes knowledge solely after one has been expelled, or better, when one has expelled oneself, from Paradise, and what was known becomes relegated to a cloud of unknowing. Learned ignorance ultimately rules.

The transformation from knowing (thinking) one knows to the knowledge that one knows not is the fruit of dialogic interaction. It is somewhat comparable to Hegel's law of inversion, the beginning of the master-slave dialectic: 'inner' and 'outer' arise when the self distinguishes itself from itself by pushing itself into, and then away from, otherness, that which had hitherto remained alien. Yet this image remains inadequate, for dialogic interaction is also circular, which can be either vicious or virtuous depending on the perspective. This aspect of dialogic interaction renders it much like Escher's hand drawing another hand which in turn draws the first hand, like Bach's 'endlessly rising canon,' or like a Gödelian sentence that bears witness to its own inadequacy. However, dialogic interaction is not only disjunctive and circular; it is, quite paradoxically, at the same time radically conjunctive. It is Nietzsche's or Walt Whitman's 'Every name in history is I.' It is the utmost of *generality* (everything) and at the same time the most primitive of primitives (nothing, utter *vagueness*).

However, such 'symbolic' interaction between *everything* and *nothing* is the product of an initial act of severance between *this* and *that*, the 'I' (icon) and the rest of the universe (*other*, which, in conjunction with the 'I,' make up an index). Symbols are in this sense derivative of their more fundamental predecessors, icons and indices. Consequently, symbols in the form of language should be for us the most alien and abstractive of sign forms. Yet we are obsessed with language. We lionize it as the alpha and omega of communication, that which makes us distinctively human. And we are inevitably to an extent deluded. Language's very nature is deceptive. As marks or sounds, linguistic symbols are apparently able to maintain their aloofness, their alterity, their 'itness.' But that primitive severance between 'I' and symbol was never absolute: at their extremities the conjointness of the two somehow manages to endure. Symbols and their meanings are not simply something other: *they are in us* and at the same time *we are in them*. As a result, although we obstinately persist in our attempts to exercise some sort of hegemony over our semiotic world, in the final analysis, of our presumed grounding signs we are made and to those baser signs we shall return.

An example of the interaction between sign and semiotic agent is in order. Suppose I spot a racist or sexist bit of graffiti written on the subway wall.

The object of the sign's content is something ordinarily prohibited by social convention from appearing in public places. There is, in addition, another semiotic object: the author of the sign. Someone has been here and left his 'signature.' Suppose the content of the sign clashes with my mindset such that my thought (= sign) gravitates from the graffiti to its absent author. The graffiti-monger via his 'signature' has now become the object of the sign. As such the sign is the sign of the present absence of its author, and my thought-signs regarding the fact that he was here is the interpretant. I almost instinctively reflect with ire on this unknown defacer of public property, my cognitive contact with his absence being mediated by the presence of the sign or representamen, the graffiti. As a result of my *habitual action*, my *disposition* to act and react in a certain fashion when confronted with a particular situation, I have revealed my attitude, my *belief* (= a set of embedded signs), concerning those who write on subway walls (the underscored terms are used in a specifically Peircean sense). The author's presence once determined the sign by putting marks on the wall, and perception of the sign and the inferential process leading to its interpretant is determined by my belief about him in his absence. Thus, indirectly, he determines what my belief about him would have been were he to have been present (see, in general, Boler 1964, Chisholm 1952, Gentry 1952, and Murphey 1961).

What I am implying is that symbolicity, given its capacity to convince us that it *is* what it *is not*, illustrates how meaning is forthcoming in spite of the absence of that to which the sign relates. And, given that absence, symbolicity draws us, as semiotic agents, into the equation: *we become signs among signs*. This bears on (1) our role as the embodiment of negation and error – what we don't know can't hurt us until we become aware that what we thought we knew *was not* what it now appears *to be*, (2) the abstract other of symbolicity and its role in compelling us to play an honest game, and (3) the game itself, which is unfolded in time, demanding, on our part as time-bound human semiotic agents, memory of the past and expectations regarding the future. In other words, we see once again that dialogue is not merely between the 'I,' the 'inner' other of the 'I,' and the others of the community, but also between the 'I' and the 'real' physical-world other, which is the most unrelenting opponent imaginable. All three others, it stands to reason, are necessary participants in the unfolding of meaning. Although the role of otherness might make sense of the *relata* between the three Peircean sign components, the business of meaning engenderment admittedly remains garbled. (I have substituted 'meaning engenderment' [or 'interpretation'] for Peirce's term 'meaning determination' for obvious reasons, not the least of which is the generally accepted notion – implicit also in Peirce's writings, to be sure – that meaning is 'indeterminately determinate.')

Meaning engenderment or interpretation, from the Peircean point of view, is by no means limited to signs autonomous of their authors-interpreters, nor does it exclusively involve either mentalist-subjectivist thought-signs 'in here' or positivist-behaviourist-physicalist-objectivist sign-events 'out there.' Neither is it strictly private or strictly public. Rather, it entails a confluence of all the above. It is production not product, process not being. It emerges while signs are in the making.

5. The Living Tempest of the Mind

It has become quite obvious that Peirce's account of sign *relata* and meaning engenderment, especially within the domain of symbolicity, goes much further than dyadism. For symbols are nothing if not shot through and through with the nature of Thirdness, of the *would be* of things.

The subjunctive conditional – at the heart of the 'pragmatic maxim' – depends upon certain future conditions that may or may not be actualized. And in the event that they are actualized, there is no absolute guarantee that what signs with greatest probability *would be* engendered *will have been* the case. Given Peirce's principle of fallibilism, a degree of indeterminacy will always inhere, which is the contingent character of the self-correcting universe of signs always subject to change. But Peirce's account is also in a sense participatory inasmuch as there is a perpetual collusion and collaboration between author-interpreter and interpretant. In fact, the term 'reader-interpreter' is also somewhat inadequate because there can be no author-interpreter without interpretants, and vice versa. Or better, in light of the above, the author-interpreter is herself an interpretant to/for her signs. In the act of her interpreting her signs, she is in turn interpreted by them, she becomes an act of signification by which she, as sign, undergoes a change at the same time that her signs are transmuted into other signs by her act of interpreting them.

Thus, what is construed to be the 'semiotically real' consists of the seeds sown by the sign emissary with the intention of their germination into interpretants of a certain character in conjunction with the interpretants actually engendered by the author-interpreter. The author-interpreter's interpretants do not fall from the clear blue; neither do they come to her *deus ex machina*. She finds in them only what she, her mind, the mind as sign, as itself an interpretant, put there in the first place. Thus, there is a three-way interdependence of signs, objects, and author-interpretant, which coincides with interpreter, 'semiotically real,' and interpretation, on the one hand, and mind, world, and knowledge on the other. Without the signs, there are no objects; without the author-interpreter, there is no 'semiotic reality'; and without mind, there is no 'world' (*CP*:5.213–37, 6:238–86). (This scheme of things is not a mere matter of mind, or even of language hopefully mirroring the 'world.' Heraclitus in his efforts to block Parmenides' architectonic dreams gave raw experience of the flux of becoming the upper hand, a view recently having emerged from within a spectrum of endeavours from chaos physics to deconstruction. In contrast, Kant's insight was blemished by his limiting the mind to the inflexible space-time categories of Newtonian physics. Consequently, the fall of classical mechanics spelled certain doom to his specialized categories of the mind. Peirce, a child of the nineteenth century, endowed the mind with free-wheeling evolutionary principles contingent upon his triadic dialogic spiral, beginning with 'chance' and ending in 'necessity.' But unlike Kant, he took a step toward liberating classical mechanics from its conceptual straitjacket, though he did not take the final step into the light of day subsequently made possible by relativity, quantum theory, the 'limitative theorems' of Gödel and others, and avant-garde movements in the arts.)

Peirce's triadic *relata*, it is becoming increasingly apparent, are exceedingly more subtle than their dyadic cousins inhabiting the continental Saussurean doctrine of semiology. The subtlety of triadicity intimately involves, among other characteristics, *negation* – as dyadic and triadic relations rather than a unary operations. Eco (1984:177–82) proposes that a chief, if not the chief, requisite for semiotics is the capacity to lie. Lying and other sundry forms of prevarication entail presenting an object, act, or event as that which it *is not*, and the sign must be in command of the same faculty: it must be construed as significantly substituting for something else. Like the lie, it must refer back to that which it *is not*, though in certain cases it conceivably may be in the future. And like the lie, it must possess the potential for producing an interpretant the nature of which is commensurate with what *is not as if it were.*

Though it is by no means certain that misrepresentation is limited to the human semiotic animal (Sebeok 1976), at any rate, the characteristic of the sign enabling it to lie transforms dyadic, transitive linearity into a back-peddling triadic carousel. In our graffiti on the subway wall example, someone engendered a sign (representamen) that evokes a response (interpretant) in me, my reaction being dependent upon that someone as mediator between the representamen and interpretant. In addition, my reaction was dependent upon some other graffitist in my memory bank, whether 'real' or imaginary, who scribbled something somewhere and at some time, evoking some reaction, that related back to a more remote graffitist, and so on (recall the regress of interpretants-as-translations, and its corresponding infinite regress scheme, in the Preamble). In this regard, the statement of fact, 'A graffitist graffitized this subway wall,' is not equivalent to 'The graffiti on this subway wall is a sign of the absent presence of a semiotic agent who, as both author and object of the sign, left something of his "self" in order that it become part of another semiotic agent-sign.' The former is dyadic, while the latter is genuinely triadic. It implies that the graffitist has some capacity as himself a sign to bring about some interpretant or other in my mind by way of a sign he has authored.

Thus, to repeat, an author-interpreter is at the same time a sign. When someone interprets (thinks) a sign (thought-sign), as an author-interpreter, she cannot help but construct another interpretant. In fact, the entire process is that of an interpretant constructing, being constructed by, itself, and mind, as it is at that moment, 'appears as sign' (*CP*:5.283). In its capacity as an interpretant, that selfsame mind becomes the sign of another interpretant along the stream of *semiosis*. So it is that Peirce solemnly and enigmatically declares: 'My language is the sum total of myself' (*CP*:5.314). Just as Thirdness is accelerated by the mind as sign within the *semiosic* flow of things, so also symbolicity (language), containing within itself vestiges of iconicity and indexicality, is a continuously changing displacement in space and time. And just as, Peirce observes, 'we say that a body is in motion, and not that motion is in a body,' so also we ought to say that we are *in* our thought-signs and not that our thoughts-signs are *in* us (*CP*:5.289 n1). In this sense, signs, like selves, are embodied, not gutless abstractions. They are concrete not merely conceptual. They are community not merely autonomy. And they never fail to bring along a good-sized load of Firstness (iconicity) and Secondness (indexicality): they are never exclusively Thirdness (symbolicity).

As an illustration of the concrete role of Firstness (iconicity), suppose, say, I had spied a piece of graffiti depicting genitalia rather than an instance of verbal graffiti. The sign as such does not directly evince the alienation of symbolicity. As an icon, the sign's temporality is unidimensional. It might appear that 'I' relate quite directly to its iconicity in virtually an instant and with hardly any mediation. Dutifully registering the appropriate reaction of repugnance, 'I' 'see' myself in 'it,' so to speak. It is not surprising that habit, by the force of years of Puritanical inculcation, produces this reaction in me, for 'I,' without giving the matter conscious or self-conscious thought, merge into the thisness of the sign. This is radically more direct than any mediated symbolic thatness, which would be at least twice removed from 'me.' But does not the graffiti embodied in written symbol-signs evoke the same or a similar response as if it were an icon? In a manner of speaking, yes. The word 'Commie' and the caricature of a hammer and sickle, 'Yalta' and a photo of Stalin, Churchill, and FDR seated together, the utterance 'I pledge allegiance to …' with a U.S. flag in the vicinity, the phrase 'Ol' Blue Eyes' and an image of Frank Sinatra on the screen, 'Air Jordan' and the real thing doing a gravity-defying slam-dunk, a caricature of George Bush with the caption, 'Read my lips.' In each case the symbol, if presented effectively and in the right context, stands a fighting chance of evoking some visceral, iconic response – as if the word were the thing, the map the territory (I have elsewhere termed this confusion of sign for object signified *embedment* or *automatization*, as mentioned above).

Just as symbols 'came into being by development out of other signs,' so also a symbol's interpretant – like my thought, my mind, my *self* – refers back to another sign. It refers back toward an original but now irretrievable sign such as in my graffiti example. Consequently, 'I' put myself in the symbol in spite of its character as a mere set of static – and arbitrary, as it were – spray-paint smudges on a wall. 'I' have been sucked into the trap, duped by the symbol's 'lie.' But its lure captivates me; 'I' cannot resist it; it has become 'my' master, 'my' own author – that is, as suggested in section 2. The sign's *depth* (a specific quality or attribute) exercises virtual authority over its *breadth* (range of contextualized uses). A particular instantiation of the sign becomes, for me at that particular moment, as if it were clearly and simply *the way things are.* The sign's necessary characteristic of negation or the capacity to lie, its very perfidy, brings about pathos as well as certain promise against which, for better or for worse, we have been properly warned from a diversity of vantages, from Plato and the early rhetoricians to Nietzsche and a plethora of contemporary thinkers, including poststructuralists and postmodernists.

And we have finally arrived at the meat of the issue regarding the strange dialogue between Alpha, Omega, and the Master, which leads us more directly to *negation and its bearing on what is known of meaning and what is meant by knowledge.* That is to say, we enter the domain of fictions and other fabrications of the mind – thought-signs – in order more closely to approximate the elusive problem of what it is to be a mind capable of engendering meaning (interpretants), and of what it is to be an interpretant (meaning) capable of becoming mind.

PART II

Or Merely What Comes Naturally?

3

Thought-Signs: Jungle or Wasteland?

In the preceding chapters I outlined what I perceive to be the essential background for a Peircean conception of meaning: triadic relations, self-other dialogic, self-mind as sign, the 'logic' of *semiosis*, the poverty of our pretentious individualism, and symbolicity's elusive, illusive capacity for 'deceit.' In chapters 3 and 4 I further address the fiction-'real,' and 'inner-outer' problems, which cannot but influence how we take our signs and how they mean. Then, in chapter 5, I begin entry into a discussion of the relevance of Charles Peirce to contemporary disquisitions and ruminations on the nature of meaning.

1. The Fictive Turn

We are incorrigible fabricators and repositories of fictions, whether in the arts, the sciences, the artificially pumped-up world of academia, or everyday living. Fiction – what *is not* presented as if *it were* – lies at the core of our distinctively human *semiosis*, and meaning can hardly be divorced from it.

After reiterating his contention that the product of our thought, the ultimate meaning of the signs around us, is to be found in actual 'reality,' and that 'our (semiotic) reality' hardly stands a chance of faithfully duplicating the 'really real,' Peirce asks: 'Now what is the difference between a reality and a fiction? A fiction is something whose character depends upon what we think about it; a reality is what it is whatever we may think about it' (Peirce *W*:II 45–6; MS 200). If we can maintain some control over our fictions – and our 'semiotic reality' – though not over the 'real' *an sich*, perhaps it is there that we should look for the source of meaning. For meaning emerges in the relations between ourselves and our signs within particular contexts, and fictions, remaining aloof from, but with a foot still lodged in, the 'real,' allow for greater awareness regarding both relatedness and context.

When Cervantes composed *Don Quixote*, he was, we would assume, at liberty to endow the land of *La Mancha* with whatever characteristics might suit his purposes and his fancies – even his vanity – in spite of many or most of the limitations presented by the geographical, cultural, and socio-economic conditions of Spain at the time. One might suppose that had Cervantes decided to fill the Don's mind with logic rather than lunacy, with no-nonsense realism instead of derangement, he would have been in comparison severely restricted. But as things stood, he was quite free to write as he saw fit, and he created the Don precisely as he created him. Consequently, Spain as Cervantes fictively reconstructed her had hardly any alternative but to correspond to the words he put down on paper. But Cervantes's motherland in terms of brute, physical 'reality' outside her existence as a cultural construct ('semiotically real' world) obstinately continued on basically as she was, Cervantes's wisdom, whims, and wishes to the contrary (*CP*:8.12). Even though *Don Quixote* might have turned out to be a 'realist' work, 'brute physical reality' would have persevered, remaining quite unruffled, thank you.

Now, though the character of a fiction depends fundamentally upon the will of its author and readers, and though 'brute reality' is what it is regardless of our willing otherwise, the fact remains that, *ab initio*, Cervantes had before him a potentially infinite range of possibilities, and the indefinite number of possible readers of his fiction over time have enjoyed, enjoy, and will enjoy, the freedom of a potential infinity of interpretations. In other words, *Don Quixote*, a fiction, leaves itself open to indeterminately variable interpretability, such interpretability being capable of altering the 'semiotic realities' of the range of all interpreters, past, present, and future. The fiction, its myriad interpretations, and the 'semiotic realities' within which it thrives, are to a greater or lesser extent dependent upon the 'real' for their sustenance, though the 'real' remains fundamentally unperturbed by their comings and goings.

However, I argue in the present chapter that, in the final analysis, we must concede that a given 'semiotically real' world, like the 'real' itself, is as unruly as the most complex fiction, for we can 'perceive,' 'meditate over,' 'think about,' 'conceptualize,' and 'theorize' it (that is, 'semiotize' it) in an indefinite number of ways without entirely exhausting it. And insofar as we cannot know the 'real' but only 'semiotically real' worlds engendered from it that hopefully approximate it, there is no absolutely determinate line of demarcation between the 'real,' 'semiotically real' worlds, and fictions. In this sense, fictions are *incomplete* and *incompletable* – that is *for* us – insofar as we are incapable of knowing everything that can be known of their characters, objects, acts, and events. The plethora of 'semiotically real' worlds engendered from the 'real' are also *incomplete* and *incompletable* – at least *for* us – insofar as, given their myriad complexity, we cannot hope to say everything possible about their characters, objects, acts, and events.

Yet, Cervantes's fiction, like whichever part of our world we may wish to consider 'real,' is taken in by us and, in fact, becomes part of us as we become part of it. With reason, Hilary Putnam observes that, regarding our experience of reading a novel such as *Don Quixote*, 'our conceptual and perceptual repertoire [become] enlarged; we become able to "see" Don Quixote, not only in the book but in ourselves and in other people. This enlargement of our stock of predicates and of metaphors is *cognitive*; we now possess descriptive resources we did not have before. And these are immensely valuable for their own sake' (1983b:166).

Putnam reveals what I suggested in the previous chapter: Thirdness cannot be divorced from Secondness and Firstness; symbols emerge from the terrain, oftentimes unsteady, of icons and indices. Putnam's 'seeing' begins with sensation and sentiment proper to Firstness, and his 'enlargement' of our 'conceptual and perceptual repertoire' upon our reading *Don Quixote* is an indexical projection of signs from within a fictive scheme into our 'real world' scheme. Both processes involve the feeling and acting body (that is, of Firstness and Secondness), as well as the thinking mind (of Thirdness). And they involve the mind's workings in relation to bodily activities, all within some particular social context. There is no autonomous, disembodied mind incessantly engaged in cogitating pure abstractions, but mind to a greater or lesser extent in tune with the *tones* and sentiments, and the particular sensations and their acknowledgment (as *tokens*), of what there is. Neither are there merely any quivering, palpitating, immediate bodily feels in complete isolation of the mind's penchant for mediating between the unique moments of present sensations, comparable past moments, and anticipations of future such moments (that is, the construction of *types*). So the comings and goings of body and mind is a process, never a finished product (*CP*:5.283–306).

Quite commensurate with this notion, Mark Johnson (1987) and George Lakoff (1987; also Lakoff and Johnson 1980) argue against the 'propositional,' 'objectivist view' of meaning, a rather unfortunate consequence of the analytical tradition and its reductionist tendencies that became paramount with the advent of the computer revolution and artificial-intelligence research. As an alternative, they propose that meaning emerges from within 'embodied schemata' (that is, it includes the Firstness of feeling and the Secondness of some *other* in addition to the Thirdness of cognition). In so doing, they question the assumption that only words and sentences have meaning, countering it with their own hypothesis that propositional meaning exists only by virtue of a complex web of nonpropositional schematic structures engendered from bodily experience (feeling, sensation, quality, iconicity, Firstness). Such 'embodied schemata' afford a continuous, analogue concept of meaning and understanding at once more concrete and more general than that allowed by the propositional model. Meaning, according to this body-in-the-mind account, is not simply a matter of mental images, however. In fact, pictures in the mind are not necessary at all; what is essential is a sense of 'feeling' (Firstness). The 'picture' as something other than what it depicts (indexicality, Secondness) comes along as a by-product of the initial 'feeling.'

In the Peirce view, these processes of Firstness and their entry into the stage of Secondness are public, not merely private; they are dialogical and communal, not merely autonomous; and they involve social, not merely psychological, construction. Don Quixote invented a 'language,' *his* language. Taken at face value, this language and the world construct issuing from it were not entirely incompatible with that of any other knight errant according to the myths, metaphors, and machinations, especially in the 'novels of chivalry,' of early-seventeenth-century Spain. The Don's behaviour within his world and by means of his perceptual and conceptual scheme hardly diverged from that to which any other well-intentioned *hidalgo* might aspire. The chief problem is that the 'language' by means of which he related to this world was his and his alone: it did not correspond to the perceived world and the conceptual scheme of the socially constructed 'semiotic reality' making up the Spain of his day for the average citizen. The Don went through all the motions of engendering meaning from the signs before him, but, with respect to his relations with the community to which he belonged, they were not charged with genuine meaning, for there was no legitimate dialogue between his self and its *other*, on the one hand, and Spain's social and physical-world *others*, on the other hand. (In other words, Quixote's method was that of 'tenacity,' which, along with 'authority' and 'introspection,' make up three of what Peirce proposed as the four basic methods for 'fixing belief.' Peirce discarded these three methods in favour of the fourth candidate, his own, which is properly 'dialogical' [*CP*:5.358–87].)

Quixote's signs were the yield of a self-contained, artificially autonomous semiotic agent out of synch with his surroundings. His world was a private, monological fiction – unlike the novel within which he dwells regarding our reading of it. In a word, he was at best a closet semiotician. The meanings of his signs were in a certain sense comparable to that of the Master's 'This sentence is false.' That is, his meanings were meaninglessly meaningful – or, if one wishes, meaningfully meaningless – when viewed from within his world. But when that world is placed within ours upon reading the book, his world, which ours *is not*, could nonetheless become pregnant with meaning, *our* meaning now applicable to *our* world.

Admittedly, regarding the Byzantine nature of the interplay between fiction, the 'real,' and the 'semiotically real,' Peirce is often quite diffuse. But rather than address myself to this issue I really should push on, for the very interface – or lack thereof – between fiction and 'reality' appears to have a more direct bearing on our capacity to engender meaning.

2. When a Fiction and When a 'Fact'?

Peirce occasionally made mention of our living in two worlds, a world of 'fact' and a world of 'fancy' (*CP*:1.321). The first is exterior, the second interior. We harbour an inclination to think we are the authors of our world of fancy. We would like to believe we have but merely to pronounce by fiat the existence of something in our 'inner' world of the imagination, and it emerges by the sheer force of our will.

In contrast, as far as our external world is concerned, 'we are masters, each of us, of his own voluntary muscles, and of nothing more' (*CP*:1.321). But we are also sly, Peirce continues, deluding ourselves with the mistaken belief that we have a grasp on our external physical world, the 'real.' Eventually, however, *expectations* generated by this *belief* collide with our experience, that is, with the brute force of the external world, which rudely disturbs our 'inner' world. The ways of our thought may then be subjected to modification. (My use of the term *expectations*, in conjunction with *belief* – also *habits* and *dispositions* from the previous chapter – generally follows the tenets of Peirce's thought, especially in regards to his essays, 'The Fixation of Belief' [*CP*:5.358–87] and 'How to Make Our Ideas Clear' [*CP*:5.388–410; also 5.411–37, 5.502–48, 7.388–596]. With regards to *expectations*, the present exposition is also quite in line with Popper [1963, 1972], whose affinities with Peirce are well known [Freeman 1983; Rescher 1978].)

Customarily, we patch up our belief system as best we can, in the future strive carefully to exclude such disturbances from our 'inner' world, and by and large life goes on. In this fashion, instead of waiting around for something interesting to happen and risking the onslaught of undesirable experiences, we tend to provoke our world 'out there,' to meddle with it, intervening in its affairs in order constantly to reconstruct it. And we consequently change our 'inner' world in such a way that those unwanted facts of experience that happen to pop up are generally either buried or conveniently buffered. This slippery – and, we must admit, artificial – distinction between 'inner' and 'outer' bears on Peirce's concept of an equally slippery demarcation between 'reality' and fiction, which, he disconcertingly tells us with hardly any justification, is 'plain enough.' In contrast to his *de dicto* pronouncement in this regard, he often puts forth a more elaborate defence of his notion that the 'real' existence of the internal depends on what we think of it, while external 'brute fact' remains independent of our vanities.

In another way of putting it, the internal is couched in *thought-signs* 'in here' that do not remain entirely independent of the 'real'; the external is independent of whatever character a given set of *thought-signs* 'in here' or *sign-events* 'out there' might happen to have. *Thought-signs* fall within the sphere of the internal; *sign-events*, in contrast, are what we take to be related to the 'real' (that is, our 'semiotic reality'), while the 'actually real' continues on as it is. Elsewhere, and in a comparable vein, Peirce writes that a figment or fiction

> is a product of somebody's imagination; it has such characters as his thought impresses upon it ... There are, however, phenomena within our own minds, dependent upon our thought, which are at the same time real in the sense that we really think them. But though their characters depend on how we think, they do not depend on what we think those characters to be. Thus, a dream has a real existence as a mental phenomenon, if somebody had really dreamt it; that he dreamt so and so, does not depend on what anybody thinks was dreamt, but is completely independent of all opinion on the subject. On the other hand, considering, not the fact of dreaming, but the thing dreamt, it retains its peculiarities by virtue of no other fact than that it was dreamt to possess them. Thus we may define the real as that whose characters are independent of what anybody may think them to be. (*CP*:5.405; also, in general, 2.141–2, 2.337, 6.328, and MS 333:19, 372:11, 609:7f, 683:33f)

Peirce hastens to concede that it would be a grave mistake to suppose that he has thusly clarified the idea of 'reality.' In the first place, he by no means asserts that dreams, as well as hallucinations and other figments of the mind, are in no sense 'real' (that is, in my terms 'semiotically real'). On the contrary, dreams and hallucinations, while occurring, are 'real,' though they are not substantive items of experience. Moreover, if we regard a fictive or hallucinated object, act, or event as indubitable, then it is just as one thinks it to be, and if one's judgment regarding it happens to change, then the object, act, or event is altered in corresponding fashion. We possess no comparable capacity willfully to alter the physically 'real,' hence an important distinction between 'unreal' domains and 'reality.' Peirce writes:

> Suppose that I experienced fifty years ago a visual hallucination. In that case it would be true concerning the hallucination that it consisted in my seeing something that was

not at the time in the place where I saw it; and this would be true though I had never mentioned it to anybody, or though it had never entered any person's head to suspect such a thing, and though I myself had totally forgotten it. The hallucination would have been real, provided we mean by the hallucination a certain psychical experience of mine. But the substance of the hallucination, that which I say, would be unreal, since everything that would be true of it would be true only in the sense that I, a determinate person, thought, or imagined (a species of thinking) that I saw what I say. (MS 852:11f; in Dozoretz 1979:78).

Yet, under highly improbable, though remotely possible, circumstances, the substance of a dream or hallucination could be construed as externally 'real.' As such it could stand a chance of becoming a 'real world' event apparently foreordained by a dream or hallucinated event. Or on a grand community level, perhaps it could become construed as 'real' by way of a scientific theory in the sense of Kuhn (1970), Feyerabend (1975), Hanson (1958, 1969), and Polanyi (1958), or a Wittgenstein (1953) 'form of life,' a Gadamer (1975) 'horizon of expectations,' a Goodman (1978) 'well made world.' So in the absence of any definable line of demarcation between fiction and 'reality,' and between mental worlds and what is 'out there,' perhaps we encounter the crux of the issue regarding the externally 'real' versus the internally 'real.'

As I shall argue in greater detail below, every sentence whatsoever in a certain manner 'relates to' a subject, whether or not it enjoys any sort of 'reference' in the 'physically real.' This subject is to a degree related to a singularity actually reacting upon the utterer of the sentence as well as on its interpreter, whether this action occurs within 'inner' worlds of thought-signs or 'outer' worlds of sign-events. And all subsequent sentences regarding this subject relate to the same singularity, that is, to a particular world of characters, objects, acts, and events, be they 'semiotically real' or 'real.' Thus, neither the 'real' nor the 'semiotically real' can be absolutely 'distinguished from a fictitious world by any description' (*CP*:2.337).

Was Hamlet mad or not? Are space and time infinitely or finitely divisible? Do quarks and black holes exist or not? Is the universe a four-dimensional space-time 'block' or is it a self-organizing, time-bound bootstrap operation? Did Sherlock Holmes have a mole on his left calf? Would Don Quixote have benefited from shock treatment? Such questions and the possible disputes arising out of them bear witness to the frequent need for indicating (relating to) something in some 'semiotic world' or other. Bohr's planetary model of the atom was not 'real' enough, so Bohr and other physicists, bowing to the demands of the strange new 'reality' that presented itself, developed the Copenhagen interpretation of quantum mechanics (a 'semiotically real' world) with hopes that it might be closer to the mark. On the other hand, Cervantes was not forced to give ground in the least, we might suppose; the Don was precisely as his author made him, no more, no less.

But such a conclusion is equally problematic. For, I would submit, what is perceived ultimately boils down to thought-signs, and thought-signs are, when giving their best performance, inventions – and often interventions – of the mind: they are pinned to the 'actually real' only at certain points, and on many occasions many of their pinnings are unintended. In other words, signs often emerge as 'inner' thought-signs with the hopes of attaining the status of 'semiotically real' sign-events, and, if fortunate, they may even capture a modicum of the 'real,' though there is no guarantee of such. Yet our obstinate push toward the 'physical real out there' and our frustration owing to our inevitable failure to grasp it bears on the interaction between fiction and the 'semiotically real.' Peirce observes, with respect to this interaction, that when the author of *1001 Arabian Nights* invented a lady named Scheherazade, he did not intend his readers to understand him as speaking directly of the 'externally real.' Scheherazade and her stories are a fiction whose attributes are what their author and readers give them. And the tale is strictly the product of imagination, 'the mere creation of the poet's thought.' Nevertheless, once the author 'has imagined Scherherazade and made her young, beautiful, and endowed with a gift of spinning stories, it becomes a real fact that so he has imagined her, which fact he cannot destroy by pretending or thinking that he imagined her to be otherwise. What he wishes us to understand is what he might have expressed in plain prose by saying, 'I have imagined a lady, Scherherazade by name, young, beautiful and a tireless teller of tales, and I am going on to imagine what tales she told.' This would have been a plain expression of professed fact relating to the sum total of realities' (*CP*:5.152). If dreams and hallucinations are conceived as autonomous entities, a certain form of 'reality' can be granted to Scheherazade, though not substance. At least not yet, for as long as she remains to a large extent autonomous (a First), and divorced from whatever may be taken for the 'real,' she is a sign without true otherness (Secondness), consequently she cannot be charged with genuine Thirdness.

It might appear, then, that signs of Secondness, of otherness, should be capable ultimately of distinguishing 'semiotically real' facts from fiction. However, it has become increasingly evident over the past century that even scientific concepts, most notoriously in Einstein's estimation, are 'free creations of the human mind and are not, however it may seem, uniquely determined by the external world' (Jammer 1962:4). Yet our culturally embedded and socially inculcated concepts (thought-signs), which have become useful in ordering things, can threaten to take on such authority over us that we forget their fallible human origin and embrace them as invariable (cf. the final pages of chapter 2). This authority comes chiefly in the way of the presuppositions, preconceptions, and prejudices of which certain hermeneuticists and their sympathizers, philosophers and historians of science, and social scientists speak. Even investigators of the most 'audacious spirit' and the finest instinct 'can be obstructed in the interpretation of facts by philosophical prejudices' (Einstein 1949a:49). (Regarding hermeneuticists, see Gadamer 1975, Bernstein 1983, Dreyfus and Rabinow 1982, and Heelan 1983; in philosophy and history of science, see Feyerabend 1975, Foucault 1970, Hanson 1958, Hesse 1980, Kuhn 1970, Margolis 1991, Polanyi 1958, and Toulmin 1982; in the social sciences, see Bloor 1983, Bourdieu 1987, 1990, de Certeau 1984, Geertz 1983, Gellner 1985, Phillips 1977, Rochberg-Halton 1986, and Tyler 1987.)

It bears pointing out, however, that what generally goes by the name of interpretation of 'facts' (Secondness) does not and cannot autonomously play the determining role in the interpretative drama. Firstness (the range of all possible constructs as free creations of the roving mind) has an important part, in conjunction with Thirdness (serving as mediator and moderator between Firstness and Secondness). For example, in the beginning, Bohr's planetary model as a hopeful indication (index) of the 'actually real' was at its deepermost roots an analogy, the result of a *Gedanken* experiment, an *abductive* (iconic, imaginary, creative, fictive) conjecture (of Firstness) from the realm of *possibilia*. Then it came to be considered a viable candidate (of Secondness) for modelling (indicating, indexing, relating to) the 'real.' Subsequently, dressed in its proper mathematical and linguistic attire, it became at least ephemerally a 'semiotically real' (symbolic) domain (of Thirdness). But at the outset that 'semiotically real' construct rested on hardly more than iconic piles driven into the dark, murky lagoon of *possibilia*: like all metaphors, models, and fictions, it could not have been so fortunate as to enjoy rock-solid foundations. Consequently, it was soon discarded and eventually replaced by another promising candidate on the scene. In light of chapter 1, just as the tone (intonation, iconicity) of a speaker gives an indication (via indexicality) as to whether or not he is sincere in what he says (via symbolicity), so also the subtleties of the world of appearances offer themselves up to the imagination of their observers, often with hardly more than a hint regarding the validity of some set or other of symbols relating to those appearances. And just as Scheherazade and Don Quixote, nonsubstances, indirectly enter our aesthetically and culturally 'semiotic worlds' possibly to alter them forever, so also Bohr's ill-fated planetary model radically altered our scientifically constructed 'semiotically real world' as hopefully another step in the long march toward a more adequate understanding of the 'real.' In all cases, symbolicity and Thirdness brought their other signs and categorical counterparts into the semiotic arena at the same time that those counterparts engendered that very symbolicity and Thirdness.

Quite obviously, our best of intentions when interpreting 'semiotically real' worlds or fictions are never quite good enough. For we are invariably deceived, we deceive ourselves, by putting into the world either by our own devices (constructivism) or as the result of our upbringing (conventionalism), some morsel of what we believed was subtly and vaguely suggested by the world or the fiction. Much in the spirit of Arthur Eddington's (1958) conclusion with respect to physics, and to reiterate my argument in chapter 1, what we find in the world (or the fiction) is in the final analysis what we put there in the first place. And what we put there is always an incomplete and radically impoverished diminution of the totality of what is 'real.' The same can be said of the multiply variegated, mutually interpenetrating, and at times contradictory interpretations of fictions.

At bottom line, neither the world nor fictions nor language can offer any Grand Infallible Index capable of telling us whether or not the 'world' as it is articulated is 'actually real' (*CP*:2.337). Consequently, Galileo's and Newton's 'Nature is a book to be read and quantified' and Descartes's 'Divide the world into smaller and smaller components and conquer it' ignore that necessary companion aiding and abetting indication (indexicality, Secondness) in its tenuous designation of the 'actually real' – via some 'semiotically real' construct (mediated by Thirdness) – and its distinction from the 'unreal.' That companion, consisting of the wellsprings of intuition, gut feeling, sentiment, and imagination, links any and all 'real world' constructs to fictional constructs. As such, our 'semiotically real' world we would like to call 'actually real' is quite often as much the product of our own 'intervention' as is any fiction (Hacking 1982). (Granted, scientific theories as 'free constructs of the mind' are, in comparison to fictions, figments, and fantasies, relatively restricted, since they must bear a certain degree of verisimilitude in order to convince their contemplator [Popper 1959]. In contrast, we ordinarily assume, creation of a novel is relatively unfettered by the restrictions of scientific theory–making. However, fiction demands its own form of verisimilitude [Todorov 1973]. Cervantes in all probability would not, we must suppose, have his hero charging fleeing hens instead of windmills, or gallantly coming to the aid of a jackass rather than a woman of ill repute. Under ordinary fictive situations the reader must sense she still has some sort of anchorage to 'reality,' no matter how fantastic the tale.)

It is not difficult to concede that once Don Quixote was made, he was as his maker made him, though after the fact of his making he was subject to innumerable interpretations by his readers according to the manner in which he affects them. But much the same can also be said of a given 'semiotically real' world scientifically and culturally fabricated and fashioned by its maker(s) rather than merely discovered in the 'real out there.' Ultimately, the Don and all other fictions as well as any and all 'semiotically real' worlds equally bear on the 'real,' in view of the labyrinthine plethora of interpretations it has suffered throughout history at the forever beguiling hands of humans in their attempt to model and portray it, whether in theories or in fictions. In this sense, what was fiction may stand a chance in some possible world of becoming 'semiotically real,' and today's 'semiotically real' may become tomorrow's fiction.

The problem with the 'inner' world for those of a conservative mindset grasping at fleeting remnants of the 'real' is that classical notions of reason and logic sooner or later suffer a knockout blow. For *inconsistency* (contradiction, ambiguity) and *vagueness* inevitably exercise their force, which is much as we would expect from purely imaginary constructs, but not, we would like to believe, from the world as we think we know it. Contradictions, ambiguities, and fuzzy meanings in a fiction ordinarily present few problems, as long as the fiction more or less conforms to our expectations regarding the genre to which it belongs. Contradictions, ambiguities, and fuzziness in sentences trying to pass themselves off as signs hooked to the world, however, are another issue entirely. For the sake of illustration, take an extreme case: 'square circles.' Peirce observes that a 'square circle' as a purely imaginary construct contains no implicit contradiction; only when the two conjoined signs are defined in 'real world' terms does the contradiction raise its ugly head (*CP*:2.603). He writes: 'Even if I think contradictory characters of an object, it possesses them both. Of course there is a sense in which I cannot conceive of an object with contradictory characters, but there is a sense in which I can do so, and for every thought of every kind the distinction of operation and object holds good. In one way, for example, I cannot conceive a foursided triangle, but I can so far conceive as to attach a meaning to the words more than to mere gibberish. This foursided triangle which is the object of a kind of thought is foursided, and is a triangle, and in consequence of the contradiction is an absurdity' (MS 333:34).

In another way of putting it, if the contradiction remains implicit, then it can be quite harmless in the arena of everyday talk, but when it becomes explicit, it more often than not becomes intolerable. Firstness, the sphere of *vagueness*, virtually knows no contradictions that must be barred at all cost. Contradiction barring becomes an obsession, however, when we enter the sphere of Secondness – which generally remains true to classical logical principles – and the unwanted guests are evicted by means of mental acts from within the sphere of Thirdness. But given an inevitable degree of *incompleteness* pervading Thirdness – in addition to the fact that it is never entirely devoid of *vagueness* – a few contradictions will always manage to hang on. Western mathematics, logic, and science can bear ample witness to this somewhat disconcerting, yet liberating, fact.

By this time knee-jerks must surely be forthcoming from many quarters, for I have entered that ethereal zone that includes the logically anomalous and the fictively tolerable, possible worlds and impossible worlds, and imaginary and unimaginable semiotic events. As a matter of fact, my venture into this forbidden territory will be repeated, as the pages of this inquiry continue to unfold, each time bearing further witness to the absence of legitimate demarcation lines between 'inner'/'outer,' semiotically 'real'/actually 'real,' and fictive/'semiotically real.' This being the case, a preliminary step toward dissolution of these traditionally venerable virgules should be taken, especially since they are intimately linked to the idea of *negation* as expressed above – and, we shall note, since they are a necessary companion to the effervescent comings and goings of meaning.

3. Either a Matter of Overkill or Underachievement

In the sphere of indeterminately fuzzy borders, *overdetermination* (pertaining chiefly, though not exclusively, to pure Firstness, *possibilia*) becomes the watchword.

The very idea of *overdetermination* strikes a blow at our discontinuous world of cuts, joints, and links making up the props, scaffolding, and pigeon-holes of what our tradition would like to call 'reality.' The 'real' has been the standard world mandated above all in this century by classical logic. It is that of an interrelated system of perceived 'facts.' This world of 'facts,' in objectivist, realist, physicalist, and in general positivist thinking, rigorously adheres to the laws of contradiction and excluded middle – pertaining largely to the realm of Secondness as articulated within Thirdness. Binary thinking rules this game. For in the world of 'facts,' we know, or at least think we know, in advance of experience, that certain things will be 'true' and others *not* 'true.' However, in postpositivist, postanalytic, postmodern thinking it is conceded that there is no innocent eye, that 'facts' are invariably laden with preconceptions and prejudices (habit and convention), and that the very classical notion of 'truth' is problematic.

In Peirce's conception of the *overdetermined* sphere (of Firstness), what is possible is *semantically possible* (that is, merely thinkable and/or describable, but not necessarily logical feasible or even picturable). The sphere of *overdetermination* consists of a *superposition* of all possibilities. It is an exceedingly *vague, indeterminate* sea of scintillating, tintillating, dancing, vibrating, quivering, undulating *possibilia.* It reminds one, once again, of David Bohm's (1980) non-Cartesian, non-Boolean, holistically intertwined *implicate order*, in contrast to the *explicate order* of actualized objects, acts, and events in the Cartesian cause-and-effect, linear physical world (of Seconds) in which we live and breathe. The *overdetermined* sphere of *possibilia* is not that of mere shadows, however. 'Qualitative immediacy' (sensations, or Firstness in the act of becoming experience, or Secondness), before its interaction with some semiotic agent, is still *overdetermined.* It can be interpreted in a limitless number of ways (astrology, varieties of magic, diverse scientific theories, myths and religions). In other words, no set of sensations and experience can be said univocally to call forth or prescribe a particular set of meanings. Nevertheless, sensations and experience are essential to the process of sign mediation (Thirdness): they are the very initiation of thought itself. Sensations and experience without thought can hardly be more than a senseless jumble; thought without sensation and experience is virtually empty. Or in another way of putting it, Firstness gives rise to Secondness, and both are necessary in order that Thirdness might carry out its mediary role. Since Firstness is germane to all thought and all interpretation, it inexorably pervades them with greater or lesser degrees of *vagueness.* Recalling Peirce's words: 'A sign is objectively vague, in so far as, leaving its interpretation more or less indeterminate, it reserves for some other possible sign or experience the function of completing the determination ... No communication of one person to another can be entirely definite, i.e., nonvague ... Much else must be vague, because no man's interpretation of words is based on exactly the same experience as any other man's. Even in our most intellectual conceptions the more we strive to be precise, the more unattainable precision seems. It should never be forgotten that our own thinking is carried on as a dialogue, and though mostly in a lesser degree, is subject to almost every imperfection of language' (*CP*:5.505–6).

The 'realist' in Peirce would like to insist that *generals* are by and large 'real.' A sign is '*general*, in so far as, leaving its effective interpretation indeterminate, it surrenders to the interpreter the right of completing the determination for himself' (*CP*:5.505). A *general* sign is of the mode of *necessity*, a *would be* (of Thirdness), in contrast to signs of the mode of *actuality* (experience, Secondness), and of the mode of *possibility* (sensations, Firstness). In addition, 'real' signs as *generals* 'can hardly escape being accompanied by the acknowledgment that there are, besides, real *vagues*, and especially, real possibilities. For possibility being the denial of a necessity, which is a kind of generality, is vague like any other contradiction of a general' (*CP*:5.453). *Vagueness* and the inevitable *inconsistency* accompanying it consequently pervade the sphere of *overdetermination*, and, as we have noted, the classical principle of noncontradiction does not necessarily hold – in complementarity with the excluded-middle principle's occasional impotency within the sphere of *generality*. A 'square triangle' or a 'gold mountain' can be articulated as assiduously as any geometrical form or Pikes Peak, Hamlet can be both sane and mad, Napoleon can be great and a scoundrel, $\sqrt{-1}$ can be both +1 and −1 (or it can be purely imaginary and part of 'semiotically real' world constructs), the Tooth Fairy can be 'real' and non-existent, or the sun can revolve about the earth and vice versa. Nothing is either one or the other, but thinking, believing, and saying can often manage to make it so. This is the 'idealist' side of Peirce. In conjunction with his 'realist' and 'objectivist' side, it makes up the essence of his 'objective idealism' that has stuck to the craw of philosophers of modernist bent striving to make heads or tails of his work while refusing to let go of their most cherished beliefs.

Although limitations of time and space do not allow for elaboration on Peirce's 'objective idealism' here, at least a few words would not be amiss – more will be forthcoming below. 'Objective idealism' might appear at the outset a rough combination of objectivism and relativism injected with immunization of what Bernstein (1983) dubs 'Cartesian anguish.' But 'objective idealism' is more, much more. It goes, to use Bernstein's qualifier, 'beyond objectivism and relativism.' One might surmise, then, that Peirce's intriguingly concocted philosophy must evince symptoms resulting from a rather unhealthy mix of subjectivism and some faint-hearted sort of realism. But not really. As we shall note below, 'objective idealism' dovetails quite handily with Putnam's 'internal realism' insofar as Peirce's philosophy yields no more than 'semiotically real' worlds as a consequence of mind acts, yet when the mind is in tune with the 'real,' to some degree it is assimilated into the 'semiotically real.' In another way of putting it, and as a discussion of Pierre Duhem in section 5 will reveal, 'objective idealism' is a happy collusion of *abduction-induction* (which can when on their best behaviour wed thought-signs 'in here' to sign-events 'out there') and *deduction* (especially in terms of the element of hypothetico-deductivism embodied in the 'pragmatic maxim' [see the appendix]). For Peirce, deduction cannot survive without the life-giving juices of abduction, which is to say that the process tends to collapse into a closed, tautological loop, though ongoing intervention on the part of the mind's vigilance can keep it 'open' and in give-and-take interaction with the 'real.' (For further on 'objective idealism,' see Murphey [1961]; for its relation to analytic philosophy, Hookway [1985:137–44]; for its implied 'antifoundationalism,' Harris [1992:150–4]; and for a discussion of 'realism' and 'idealism' with regards to links between Peirce and Wittgenstein, Rorty [1961].)

In view of these somewhat cryptic remarks on 'objective idealism,' let us focus our attention on 'semiotically real' worlds and their relation to the 'real,' while leaving fictions and other apparently unruly signs out of the picture for a moment. To be sure, the road culminating in a set of theoretical statements accounting for a 'semiotically real' domain is arduous, with dangerous curves and punctuated by potholes. It begins, according to the preceding paragraph, with Firstness, which, as the *superposition* of all possiblities – pure *vagueness* – is not (yet) anything. In regards to human semiotics, it can be no more than mere feeling, sensation, without there (yet) having emerged any form or fashion of consciousness *of* any particular object, act, or event (that is, any 'fact') from a 'semiotically real' world as 'such-and-such.' Since elsewhere (Merrell 1991, 1995a, 1996) I have expatiated at length on this sphere of *superposed possibilities*, I will here offer only a citing from William James, who was often an admirer of Peirce:

> Out of what is in itself an undistinguishable, swarming *continuum*, devoid of distinction or emphasis, our senses make for us, by attending to this motion and ignoring that, a world full of contrasts, of sharp accents, of abrupt changes, of picturesque light and shade ... [R]easoning is but another form of the selective activity of the mind ... [T]he mind is at every stage a theatre of simultaneous possibilities. Consciousness consists in the comparison of these with each other, the selection of some, and the suppression of the rest by the reinforcing and inhibiting agency of attention ... The mind, in short, works on the data it receives very much as a sculptor works on his block of stone. In a sense the statue stood there from eternity. But there were a thousand different ones beside it, and the sculptor alone is to thank for having extricated this one from the rest. Just so, the world of each of us, however different our several views of it may be, all lay embedded in the primordial chaos of sensations, which give the mere *matter* to the thought of all of us indifferently. (James 1950 I:284–8)

In Peircean terms, from the *superposition* of James's 'simultaneous possibilities,' myriad items of concrete experience can be actualized into Seconds, whose ephemerality – they are at this stage mere *haecceities* – becomes manifest as they quickly pass on along the stream of *semiosis*. By abductive-inductive-deductive acts, a crowd of them can be collected into classes, generalities, and universals (as Thirds), but any sort of order they countenance is the result of partly arbitrary or whimsical selections. As we shall note in section 5, the inclination to focus on selected Seconds as Seconds is most typical of the Anglo-American nominalist tradition. On the other hand, in good hypothetico-deductive style, items from the superposed realm can be carefully selected and actualized – as Seconds – then put in their proper place – by the mediating act of Thirds.

During this process an elegant formal system can be forthcoming whose nature as generality is highlighted, thus putting the erstwhile items of *possibilia* a few steps removed from the concrete – and consequently less mediated – 'real world.' If these items of *possibilia* resist being desiccated and squeezed into this cold, dry system of suspiciously harmonious balance, symmetry, and order, it is not ordinarily viewed as any cause for alarm. Things will surely average out in the long run. And business can go on. Or at least that is the elegant hope, while the hustle and bustle of concrete, everyday human living threatens to become increasingly alienated from the progressive abstractions legislated by the dinosaurs of modernity.

Now these summary observations are neither a revolt against rampant abstraction in our contemporary milieu nor a celebration of the virtues of listening to the birds, smelling violets, and writing poems. For better or for worse, we have grown to need our cars, quiche, computers, and the Internet as much as we do occasional moments of contemplation and the little things in life that give pleasure. The point I wish to make is that a certain, rather uneasy balance, with periods of dissonance, between objectivism and idealism and subjectivism and realism ('in here' and 'out there'), and above all, between Peirce's three categories, is essential. Firstness is the possibility of a sign's becoming in the realm of Secondness, such becoming governed by the mediating force of the mind by way of convention, habit, and all other propensities lying in wait in the realm of Thirdness. Regarding this role of mind, acts of Firstness are pervaded with 'subjectivism' and 'idealism,' Secondness with 'realism,' and Thirdness with 'objectivism' and 'realism.' But these categories do not correspond to disjunctive 'realms' at all. They are mutually penetrating, a constantly folding in and over one another. Their interdependence is essential to their very nature as categories.

Thus, Firstness without Secondness and Thirdness is nothing. Secondness without Firstness and Thirdness is surely dead. And Thirdness without Firstness and Secondness is well-nigh unthinkable. They all stand together; divided, they fall. (Some readers might at this point complain that I have not addressed myself sufficiently to literary texts. It is not so much that they are inapplicable. On the contrary, in light of the above, fictions are germane to any and all conceptions of the 'real.' The notion of signs of *overdetermination* as I use the term here, when subjected to the engenderment of interpretants, is generally in line with the concept in literary studies of 'overinterpretation.' The early Stanley Fish [1970, 1976] would be classified as a radical 'overinterpretationist' since, as he argues, every text can be made to yield virtually whatever meanings its interpreter might desire [Seung 1982]. In contrast, E.D. Hirsch's [1967] hermeneutics, with somewhat of a Popperian flavour, gives a nod to 'underinterpretation' regarding textual readings according to the various perspectives of a diversity of readers – the meanings they engender would be *underdetermined* – but Hirsch advocates radical textual determinism regarding the author's intended meaning. In more recent strains, while Jonathan Culler [1992] defends 'overinterpretation,' Eco [1990, 1992], for whom the likes of Fish and Culler are excessively subjective, leans toward the 'limits of interpretation.')

4. There's Always Room in the Gaps for Something Else

In conjunction with any disquisition on Peirce's categories, the terms *vagueness* and *inconsistency*, and *generality* and *incompleteness*, should be more properly foregrounded before we move on. Specific focus on these terms, I might add, is rarely forthcoming in Peirce studies, and, admittedly, Peirce himself did not always see the need of emphasizing them in his scheme of things to the extent that I have done here and elsewhere. Nevertheless, I would submit that in light of the current intellectual milieu, they should not be ignored.

Signs of Firstness cannot but remain *vague*, and quite often *inconsistent*; thus, to repeat, the principle of noncontradiction does not necessarily apply. Signs of Secondness, after emerging into the light of day, can – albeit partly arbitrarily – be endowed with what at the outset appear to be crystal-clear lines of demarcation. But as *haecceities*, their moment of glory cannot but be ephemeral. For they are destined to pass on into something other than what they are, even though the differences between each of their momentary flashes of existence are well-nigh infinitesimal – hence the classical identity principle runs the risk of falling by the wayside. Signs of Thirdness, it is assumed, must possess some form of continuity of existence; they are hopefully identical with themselves from one moment to the next, and they can be distinguished from other signs in terms of their character as *generalities* – though they cannot help being tinged with some degree of *vagueness*, for they are never free of Firstness via Secondness. But as generalities they are destined to remain *incomplete*, since there will always exist the possibility of other signs filling in the gaps between what had hitherto been construed as a set of precise categories, and hence once more we see that the classical principle of excluded middles does not necessarily inhere.

The upshot is that by and large there is a definite move toward some sort of ideal in terms of sign *generalities*, but at the expense of *incompleteness*. *Underdetermination* is the order of the day in this domain of *generalities*, since whatever sign – its quality as representamen, its value as interpretant, and the nature of its object – happens to be *underdetermined* at a given time and place, it could always have been something other than what it is. As a rule of thumb, *overdetermination* ultimately entails a *superposition* of all possibilities without any of them having been actualized into Secondness; *underdetermination* is the *juxtaposition* of what at a give slice in space-time is considered 'real' and what is relegated to the status of 'unreality.'

The underdeterminationist assumption has it that intuitively we believe something but not everything is 'real.' Since we cannot by empirical means discover what is 'real' without a shadow of a doubt, the matter is left to our judgment, according to our persuasions and propensities and wishes and whims. *Underdetermination* implies *incompleteness*, for what is 'real' could always have been construed otherwise, and what is 'unreal' may yet stand some outside chance of becoming 'real' at another time and another place. *Underdetermination* regarding scientific theories stipulates that competing and equally legitimate theories – equally legitimate from within their particular conceptual schemes, that is – can be generated on the basis of the same set of observations. In this vein, at the turn of the century, Duhem (1954) and Henri Poincaré (1952), and more recently, Nancy Cartwright (1983) and Hilary Putnam (1983b) argue that there will always be equally satisfactory alternatives to a given theory or general theoretical framework (paradigm), therefore there is no single story that can account for all the furniture of the world in one fell-swoop. This is, in essence, the Duhem-Quine scenario – in which Peirce is a principle actor, though his role is often overlooked – predicated on the radical underdetermination of theories (that is, they are empirically equivalent but logically incompatible) (see also Gähde and Stegmüller 1986, Roth 1987, and Sacks 1989).

For Quine (1969), one of the most ardent propagators of the underdeterminationist thesis – by way of Duhem's holism and the essentials of Peirce's 'pragmatic maxim' – a theoretical sentence in physics can have the same underdetermined relation to experiments and observation sentences that a sentence of natural language has to the observed objects, acts, and events that it is about (Vuillemin 1986). Quine writes that experience is never an infallible adjudicator for rejecting or embracing individual theoretical sentences. He conceives of theoretical physics as an interconnected web of sentences, procedures, and formalisms in contact with the world only at its edges, if at all. Any impact observation sentences may have on the web becomes distributed throughout the web such that no part of it is immune to change and no part stands alone in bearing the brunt of that impact. Additions, deletions, and adjustments of diverse sorts can often be made in the whole to accommodate the experience, but there is no infallible or unique method for making these adjustments. Four naturally occurring elements of the ancients or many elements, phlogiston or oxygen, Euclidean geometry or Reimannian or Lobachevskyan geometry, all during certain periods have been aided and abetted by empirical evidence of one sort or another. According to the dictates of a community's desires, what now appear to us as the most bizarre of theories could be, and at times have been, granted 'truth value.' And when fads, fashions, and tastes have suffered from the introduction of alternatives, theories have either followed suit, or they have served as stimuli for the most likely candidates from among those alternatives.

According to *underdetermination*, then, it is more often than not possible to formulate and embrace logically incompatible but empirically equivalent theories. As a consequence, competing and mutually exclusive theories may always be available to account for the observational data at hand. Arguments for determining absolute 'Truth' are thus rejected: we can at best only know what we (think we) know, for we can't know whether what we know is infallibly 'true.' That is, by Peircean refutation or Popperian falsification, we can't know that what we know is *not* 'false.' So the dominoes are set up only to be knocked down again without the possibility of quick-freezing them into a static phalanx never to be altered. (As an aside, with a certain degree of reason L.E.J. Brouwer and the mathematical intuitionists outlawed the law of excluded middle. According to intuitionism, occasionally mathematicians are bound to misunderstand and contradict themselves. Although 'intuited' thoughts – not to be equated with Cartesian intuition – are self-evident, when they are expressed, conflicts arise, because language can never be used with absolute precision [see Heyting 1964:61–3, Lehmann 1979].)

Peirce suggests that in addition to its denial of the excluded-middle principle, the sphere of *overdetermination* is vague, indeterminate, and inconsistent, thus at times it pays little heed to the principle of noncontradiction. Yet the hope persists in us that to all questions an answer can eventually be found, otherwise there would hardly be any motivation for continuing to play the game of inquiry. In other words, thought can potentially cure all ills, though when put into signs for communication with other semiotic agents, it often threatens to become *undecidable*. Some of Jacques Derrida's terms, themselves rendered *overdetermined* by overzealous disciples, are somewhat apropos here – recall also the Preamble. For example, *supplement* implies something added on, in order to carry the meaning of a text toward completion. The 'logic of supplement' is in this sense a logic of incompleteness, of neither-nor (which subverts the excluded-middle principle). The concept of *pharmakon* (both a cure and a poison) holds a meaning and its opposite in a tight embrace. The 'logic of pharmakon,' then, is that of vagueness, inconsistency, both-and (which subverts the principle of noncontradiction) (Derrida 1981).

Thus, it would appear that, according to Peirce and intuitionism, thought-signs are less blemished than linguistic signs (symbols, sign-events), and that our ideals are perpetually out of line with our real capacities. Such is the general nature of Peirce's 'objective idealism,' his 'pragmatic maxim,' and his doctrine of fallibilism. We see, therefore, with greater force that *overdetermination* and *underdetermination* apply to the very idea of fictionality, and especially to the inexorable fuzziness between fictions and the 'semiotically real.' The exact quantity of gold in Pikes Peak, the cause of Hamlet's dementia, the reason for Napoleon's decision at the Battle of Waterloo, Don Quixote's height, the use of $\sqrt{-1}$ in quantum theoretical equations, the absolutely precise nature of the sun with respect to all other entities in the firmament, are all *underdetermined* in that they are never so complete as to be immune to further determination. In fact, all signs are to a greater or lesser degree *underdetermined*, their 'reality' status or their fictionality status notwithstanding. Consequently, a community's fabric of signs is read into experience, and in the process it becomes the *world that is*, the 'semiotically real.' 'Semiotically real' signs pregnant with meaning ('mass,' 'energy,' 'Eucharist,' 'Big Foot,' 'Zeus,' 'UFOs,' 'mana,' 'witches,' 'AIDS,' 'cholesterol,' and the 'Cross' and 'Swastika') have become so impregnated because of the role they play and the place they occupy in their respective interwoven *semiosic* fabric. They do not describe experience; they are 'intersubjective idealizations' of experience – recall my reaction to the grafitti in chapter 2. Whether dressed in relatively concise and complete abstract language or in everyday language and enshrouded in vagueness, much of their meaning remains implicit.

Yet experience and the signs tentatively painting it are often, and in spite of their agents' wishes to the contrary, caught up in a quandary comparable to that of the positivist's 'observation sentences' and 'theoretical sentences,' following their objectivist 'correspondence theory of truth.' It was assumed that one could link up theory with experience by specifying rules with which to bridge the gap between the two domains of sentences, as in the case of identifying a statement about observable water droplets with a statement about electrons – that is, the Millikan experiment. The problem was that such identification was always to a degree dependent upon an arbitrary operation. Lower-level theoretical statements regarding the capillary properties of water that are easily observable can perhaps be deduced and derived from higher-level theoretical statements regarding the attraction of particles of opposite charge and molecular polarity. But statements concerning direct experience cannot always be in the same fashion deduced and derived directly from higher-level theoretical statements. There will always remain a certain unbridgeable gap between everyday lived experience and abstract theory, which testifies to the latter's perpetual *incompleteness* (companion to *underdetermination* in the sphere of semiotic *generality*) and the former's inevitable dovetailing with *vagueness* (companion to

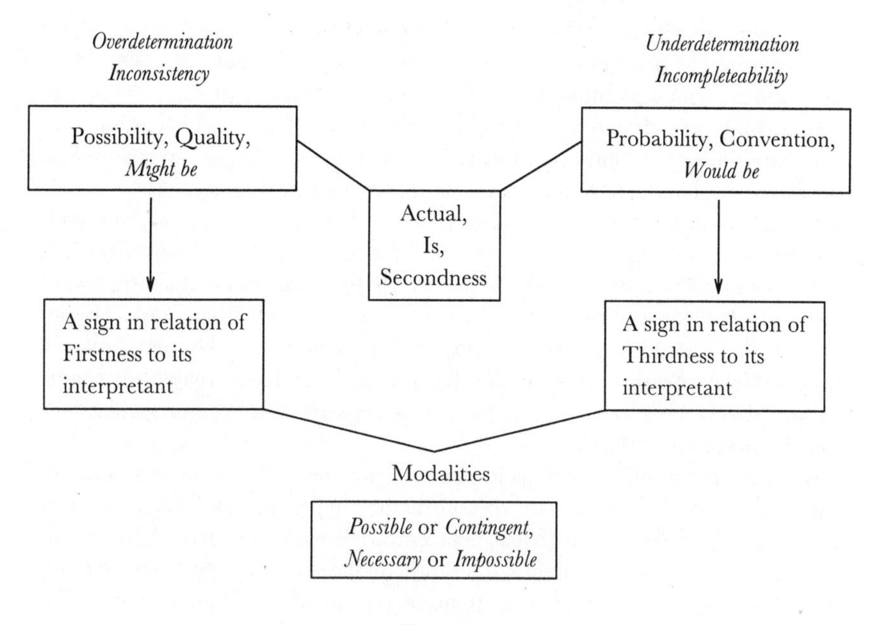

Figure 4

overdetermination in the sphere of semiotic *inconsistency*). In other words, experience (of presumed 'facts,' Seconds, entailing indexicality) is in a formal sense and at certain points incompatible with *overdetermination-underdetermination*, since it adheres to the tenets of classical logic.

5. Creative Bricoleur or Cerebral Engineer?

After all has been said and done, the *overdetermination(vagueness)-underdetermination(incompleteness)* pair itself is perhaps most economically viewed as two *complementary approaches toward knowing what is* (see figure 4; and see especially *CP*:2.322–3) (I must acknowledge a debt to Nancy Cartwright [1983] and Mary Hesse [1966] for much of this section).

The two approaches pattern the Heraclitus-Parmenides and Aristotle-Plato antagonisms. In their purest form, one is messy and unkempt; the other is of spit-polished brilliance. One is rich in the variety of its concrete particulars; the other is a parsimonious utopia of perfection. The one is a maze of tropical flora; the other is a barren desert converted into a grid of meticulously cultivated plots. Quite significantly, along these lines, Pierre Duhem (1954), himself a sort of hopeful Platonist, distinguished between these complementary approaches.

They evince characteristics essentially the equivalent of (1) *experienced sign-events* (empiricism, drawn from the *overdetermined* sphere of *vagueness*, collected as Secondness, and accommodated to the mind as Thirds) and (2) *thought-sign constructs or theories* (drawn from the sphere of mind as Thirds, but in conjunction with experienced Seconds, they invariably remain *underdetermined* and *incomplete*). (Recent trends in the hard sciences seem to corroborate this view. The Platonic approach to understanding the universe, founded on the dream of invariant, symmetrical, laws has led to the search for a 'grand unified theory' [GUT], a 'theory of everything' [TOE]. Since the 1970s an Aristotelian alternative of sorts has been on the rise in the form of 'chaos theory,' Prigogine's 'physics of complexity,' and Mandelbrot's 'fractals.' This alternative lays emphasis on observable happenings of everyday life rather than unobservable invariants behind them. Time and change have as a consequence become paramount [see Toulmin 1990:192].)

The first constantly threatens to produce myopia and shallowness of mind, while the second runs the risk of contracting hyperopia and narrowness of mind. The first, in line with classical empiricism Duhem would like us to believe, is generally the modus operandi of the English mind; the second, hypothetico-deductive in nature, is quite typical of the French mind. The English scientist loves details ('facts,' Seconds) and is relatively unconcerned with putting things into a tidy, compact, formalized package: she tends toward nominalism, though she occasionally avoids that trap. The French scientist strives for a unified, elegant, abstract grasp of the world (conceptualization, Thirdness): she tends toward, but does not necessarily fall victim to, realism (that is, of the rationalist-Platonic sort). The English investigator attempts to hold a perplexing concoction of particulars together, hopefully coordinating the gears, pulleys, nuts, and bolts of her world into a harmonious whole while imposing a minimum of abstract forms of organization on them and, by all means, resisting the temptation actively to intervene in their affairs. The Frenchwoman takes Newton's laws of motion and converts them into the elegant, abstract mathematics of Lagrange mechanics. The world of the first is a nonlinearly developing aperiodic fractal; that of the second ideally bears the image of a beautifully cut crystal. Or, in the terms of the present inquiry, in spite of her wishes to the contrary the first has a penchant for trying to jam-pack the world into the purest of generalities, which are the makings of her own mind; the second begins with vague assumptions – or models – with the idea that, subject to a few deletions here and some appendages there, her mental construct will become a map of the world.

In yet another way of putting it, the French garner the dream of a deep *holist* account of scientific theories, conceptual schemes, and even, we might surmise, modes of discourse and artistic styles – though Duhem does not go quite this far. As pointed out above, at its most extreme, holism stipulates that theories, thoughts, and beliefs face the tribunal of experience and judgment not on a sentence-by-sentence basis but as corporate bodies. All sentences, past, present, and potentially to come, are interlocked into an intricate web without ready-made structures, though they exact constraints on their speakers-writers. As a potential, these interconnections make up a fabric without fixed joints or junctures. The continuum's ruptures are partly conventional, normative, and perhaps necessary, but also at all times and all places there exists the possibility of partly arbitrary cuts. From a holist – and, I might add, antipositivist – point of view, theories, conceptual schemes, and languages are so laden with prejudices and presuppositions that it is virtually impossible to determine precisely which sentences divulge 'facts,' which fictions, and which merely fantasy or nonsense. Indeed, all sentences should perhaps be taken as provisionary 'fictions' eliminable, if at all, by some sort of move toward the 'truth.'

From the holistic glance, all theories, conceptual schemes, and languages are *underdetermined*: conflicting discourses generated from conflicting views can account, with equal cogency and validity from their respective views within their conceptual scheme, for the same items of experience. This is both the beauty and the bane of holism. There is no foreseeable limit to the number of explanations with which to give account of a particular corpus of data. Consequently, any ardent effort to eliminate inconsistencies insofar as possible – since they are a liability rather than an asset – is guided by the hope that an alternative theory, conceptual scheme, or language, can be found. For there must exist, following this hope, a viable alternative somewhere 'out there,' whether compatible, incommensurable, or contradictory with the present theory, conceptual scheme, or language, that could originally have been found but was not. Consequently, for the ideal Duhemian holist scientist of *cognitive depth*, nature is never so completely known that it cannot be subject to further inquiry. However, since, *pace* Peirce, nature cannot be so known by any finite community of knowers, knowledge is destined to remain *incomplete*, at best serving as a hopeful approximation to 'truth.'

Take, for instance, Boyle's laws of gases. They stipulate what ideally would be the case were certain conditions to be in effect. All actual gases come close to this ideal, some more than others. But as of this writing no gas has been discovered that is absolutely identical to the ideal. Moreover, no matter how internally consistent they are, Boyle's laws must evince, nevertheless, a degree of incompleteness. For there is no way we can know with absolute certainty that at some juncture or other new data will not pop up to demonstrate one or another of their inadequacies. The laws, to be sure, offer themselves up as a general account of a particular aspect of nature: they quite effectively describe, and in a manner of speaking even explain, the domain for which they were intended. But they offer little in the way of understanding. Following what was suggested in the previous chapters, it might be said that, for the holist, Boyle's laws are *general* insofar as 'the principle of excluded middle does not enjoy iron-clad application,' for the possibility always exists that some other theory might appear that is equally or more adept at describing and explaining the phenomena in question. In contrast, the English scientist's tentative assertions – as actualizations from the realm of *possibilia*, of *vagueness* – are valid only insofar as 'the principle of contradiction does not necessarily hold,' for, in the empirical world of particulars, one must be mindful that things do not have the talent for remaining absolutely identical to themselves for all time.

At bottom line, the French scientist, with ultimate visions of *cognitive depth*, can optimistically embrace ontological realism – coupled with a vague sort of epistemological idealism – but only if she realizes final knowledge will not be at hand, for any and all theories and conceptual frameworks are destined to remain *incomplete*. In other words, since absolute *depth* of knowledge is a receding horizon, indeterminacy cannot help but exercise its force. This must be the case, since there is no knowing whether a given sentence relates faithfully to the 'real' or whether it merely appears to do so, since it is conveniently coherent with all other sentences in the whole fabric. In contrast, the English scientist in search of *empirical breadth* can adopt methodological realism – coupled with a cloudy hint of ontological idealism – as long as she is aware that *inconsistencies* will always be lurking at some unsuspected bend in the road. That is, to repeat William James's (1950 1:287–8) words, since the mind 'is at every stage a theatre of simultaneous possibilities ... [i]t works on the data it receives very much as a sculptor works on his block of stone.' Since there are countless statues that could have been actualized in place of the one that now exists, 'the sculptor alone is to thank for having extricated this one from the rest.' In this manner, 'the world for each of us, however different our several views of it may be, all lay embedded in the primordial chaos [vagueness] of sensations, which give the mere *matter* to the thought of all of us differently [which at times bears on inconsistency].'

In this sense signs can be as indeterminate for Duhem's Englishman as they are for his Frenchwoman. On the one hand, at the level of Firstness, of pure possibility, there is no determining absolutely a sign's meaning owing to the elements of chance and spontaneity. And on the other hand, at the level of Thirdness, of necessity via habit and convention, the sign's meaning is also indeterminate, given the impossibility of knowing absolutely and without a shadow of a doubt whether a given meaning is 'true' and when that meaning will not be exchanged for some other 'truth.' Just as a potential infinity of statues can be sculpted from the stone, with no knowing precisely which one will have been sculpted at a further moment down the line, so also the gap between experience and preconceived theory cannot be absolutely bridged, for, as Duhem puts it, 'we can make an infinity of different formulas or distinct physical laws correspond to the same group of facts ... [A]ny other law representing the same experiments with the same approximations may lay as just a claim at the first to the title of a true law or, so to speak more precisely, of an acceptable law' (1954:168–72). Between theories (sentences) along an unordered series, another account can always be found. On the other side of the coin, given the infinite number of possible theories (sentences), contradictory accounts may stand a democratic chance of being selected at different times and places. The indefinite and unlimited range of possibilities cannot be crammed into the one and only 'true' finite theory (sentence), and over time, given the same infinite possibilities of experience, inconsistent and contradictory theories (sentences) can with little difficulty be used – albeit at times erroneously – as catch-alls for the whole of experience (more on this later, when the terrain has been properly tilled).

6. Re-enter Peirce

If we combine Duhem's two classes of scientists, we will have something akin to Peirce's indeterminacy of meaning and knowledge via his 'objective idealism.' This is a rarefied combination of a practical, hands-on sort of methodological 'realism' and ontological 'idealism' in conjunction with a vague, visionary nod toward methodological 'idealism' and ontological 'realism' – to say nothing of 'subjectivism' and 'objectivism.' It is a collusion of Peirce's evolutionary cosmology coupled with his no-nonsense 'realism' tinged with 'idealist' metaphysics (Rescher and Brandom 1979). It is not merely a matter of the *indeterminacy of underdetermination* according to Duhem's French hedgehog in contradistinction to the English fox. Rather, the very existence of *underdetermined* theories (sentences) depends upon the infinite possibilities of theories (sentences) that were there for the taking from the *overdetermined* sphere of pure vagueness – raw experience before it is mediated by the selecting mind.

The *superposition of possibilities* – the sphere of Firstness – contains the full range of all concrete items of the furniture of all possible worlds, past, present, and future, a minuscule portion of which can be actualized (into Secondness) at a particular time and place. This appears prima facie to be an unruly concoction held together only tentatively at best, and more often than not without stable rhyme or reason. Granted, the merging of contradictory *possibilia* into one monstrous package apparently flies in the face of the best of logic and of reason. But given the *underdetermination* of each and every theory, conceptual scheme, and language, if they are all piled one upon the other without limit, as a composite whole, even the most outlandish idea stands a chance of becoming 'real' at some other time and place, and the most logically cogent idea can become the most bizarre. This *indeterminacy* of *overdetermination*, complementary with that of *underdetermination*, affords the notion of *inconsistency* (*vagueness*) precariously coupled with *incompleteness* (*generality*).

Such, ideally, would be the way of Duhem's 'French mind' plus his 'English mind' striving respectively for *cognitive depth* and *empirical breadth* of thought. For Duhem, thought maintains the upper hand. The creator of his universe is a Great Cogitator, the ultimate French mathematician. This omniscient seer begins with what is hopefully the Absolute Posit, an unshakeable cornerstone emerging from the depths of her mind (Firstness, abduction), and she goes on to create a beautifully elegant hypothetical construct (Third, deduction), capable of accounting for everything that is (Secondness, induction). It is the scientist's task to create a simulacrum of that parsimonious construct our Grand Cogitator has left us, such simulacrum being the ultimate sign of *generality*. On the other hand, Duhem's Anglophile mind inclines toward concrete items of the world's furniture. She patterns her own creator's untidy construction of the universe by quite random hits and misses, finally accumulating a makeshift jumble (Seconds, particulars), which, after being subjected to literally countless perceptual grasps, can then somehow be collated and collected into certain tenuous *generalities* (Thirds) hopefully forthcoming by way of instinctive leaps of the imagination (Firsts). However, the sum total of all descriptions and explanations of scientists from both traditions cannot but be as *overdetermined* (from an ahistorical view, conflicting theories from different times and places can and have been embraced) as they are *underdetermined* (given a body of data, there will always be equally satisfactory but conflicting alternatives at other times and places). Consequently, neither the one nor the other has a monopoly on 'truth.' They are apparently in open competition with each other, yet they are not exactly an antagonistic, but rather, a *complementary*, duo.

Peirce would likely be sympathetic toward such a collusion of the Duhem holist-empiricist agonistics – a sort of Alpha-Omega fusion – in his obstinate effort to devise a method for determining 'truth,' if only in the 'theoretical long run' of things. As we have noted, for Peirce – and Popper after him – the semiotic agent cannot directly know the 'truth,' but only that which bears a degree of 'untruth.' So she swims along, now going along with the flow, now struggling against it, all the while finding fault with successive bits and pieces of conventional knowledge. With perhaps more luck than management, she may exercise a few moves closer to the ideal, though if she ever had it in its totality she would never know it, for, unable to see any 'untruth' in it, she would be incapable of distinguishing it from some unknown standard to set herself apart from it as a reactionary other in her dialogue with nature. In other words, the ideal could not be her object of knowledge, for she would be inside it. It would be as if nature were saying to itself that which is 'true' of itself and of its very saying what it is: its saying would be part of the object of its saying.

This paradox is implicit in Peirce's infinite *regressus* and infinite *progressus* regarding *semiosis*. Given such indeterminacy, how can we realize any advance instead of simply treading water? Peirce offers a tentative answer, which bears on the focus of the previous section: pragmatism, as a fallible and tentative separator of the sheep of the properly 'semiotically real' from the goats of the erroneous or merely fictive. To embrace Peirce's pragmatist, triadic concept of the sign is to embrace his 'pragmatic maxim,' and, as illustrated above, to embrace the maxim is by and large to forget about 'truth,' capital 'T' Truth, take signs and their meanings as they come, and get on with the game.

To this topic, which ultimately re-evokes the notion of fictionality, I now return.

4

Sign-Events Meet Thought-Signs

In light of the preceding chapter, there can no all-or-nothing line of demarcation between the 'semiotically real' and fictionality. What seems to hold is that the relation between the two involves meaning. For the meaning of something conceived as a 'real' entity (that is, the conception of it *as if* that conception were somehow coterminous with the entity itself) cannot be absolutely divorced from fictionality (the taking of some entity *as if* it were the 'real' article). In arguing this point, I briefly return to Peirce's notion of the 'real' in light of his enigmatic 'objective idealist' posture. Then I evoke Alexius von Meinong's strange world of 'mental objects' in order to round out the general nature of fictions as Peirce sees them.

1. Of the Subject and Its World?

Empiricism in this century has often held that the 'things' of our sensory world are about as close to 'reality' as we can get, while the 'things' of theory, though in the beginning they may have been fictions or 'thought experiments,' are nonetheless helpful in ordering the world of our senses – recall Duhem's English mind. In contrast, physicists the likes of Einstein, Planck, and Schrödinger have posited that the 'things' of theory are 'real,' while the 'things' of our everyday sensory world are mere appearances, which can coincide to a greater or lesser degree with the 'real' – somewhat comparable to Duhem's French mind.

One of the plethora of current lines, often held by those of poststructuralist, and postmodern or neopragmatist, bent, suggests that there are equally good reasons as well as equally poor ones for conceding and condemning the 'reality' of both sensory 'things' and theoretical or fictional 'things.' In this sense, neither the world of common sense nor the world of theory or fictions is purely 'real,' but both are merely 'semiotically real.' As a consequence, 'representation' and 'reference' are not necessarily any more or any less valid regarding theory and the 'real' than they are regarding fiction and the 'real.' If one continues to insist on 'representation' and 'reference,' one can have them only at the expense of conceding that they are relevant solely to the 'semiotically real,' which offers no fine-line discrimination between fictive and 'real.' 'Sherlock Holmes,' a 'partridge in a pear tree,' and the nearest 'cat on a mat' all equally 'represent' and 'refer to' 'things' in some 'semiotic' domain or other, and their 'representation' and 'reference' occur in basically the same way. In this vein, when taking all possible 'semiotic realities' into account, sceptical problems regarding (1) life as possibly nothing but a dream, (2) the unknowability of inductive inferences, or (3) the impossibility *absolutely of distinguishing* between scientific theories and poems tend to fall by the wayside. Whatever is 'semiotically real' *for* the citizens of a particular community is simply the world that *is*, and whatever is considered 'irreal' can nonetheless be as 'semiotic' as the 'real.'

Present-day objectivist-realist opponents of this idea of the 'semiotically real' – for example, Saul Kripke and Keith Donnelan – would charge that mere fictions cannot work like objectivist linguistic constructions. If they did, there would be no knowing whether or not life is just a dream. But it is not a dream, the objectivist-realist tells us; it is 'real.' And this 'reality' is accessible, if we would just get things right by correctly hooking words onto the 'world.' In this view, the terms 'representation' and 'reference' are quite legitimate: there *is* 'correspondence' between language and the furniture of the world. (See, in particular, the work on proper names and reference in Donnelan 1966, 1972, 1974, and Kripke 1972, 1977. For a critical view, see Rorty 1982, Davidson 1984, and the later Putnam 1981.)

Certain Peirce scholars would chime in. 'Granted,' they might begin, 'Peirce never claimed we can infallibly and objectively distinguish between "real" and fictitious by way of descriptions. Predicates, and even collections of predications as a result of successive observations, are incapable of accounting for the world. The only possible distinguisher rests in subjects, not predicates, indices and their respective icons properly embedded within symbols, not mere icons as islands unto themselves (*CP*:2.337, 3.363, 8.39–41). And granted, there is no Grand Transcendental Index pointing out the royal road to objective "reality" and "truth." But at the same time, there is, Peirce tells us, nothing that is absolutely uncognizable (unintelligible) in principle. We cannot objectively know anything beyond experience, but only what experience allows us to see. And what it allows us to see will be, in the "long run" of community opinion, "real." So ultimately "representation" and "reference" are legitimate concepts, and they entail viable methods and procedures.'

However, there is an undeniable tension in Peirce's thought on this issue. On the one hand, in view of the previous chapter, Peirce without apology embraced his own form of 'idealism,' which went something like this: if we cannot absolutely and infallibly know the world, then in part our knowledge will always be a mind-construct, so reality cannot be entirely external to the mind, but rather, the mind is embedded within the 'real,' which is, itself, mind. On the other hand, we have Peirce writing that 'the question of realism is a question of hard fact, if ever there was a hard fact' (*CP*:8.130), and that: '[a]ll reasoning goes upon the assumption that there is a true answer to whatever question may be under discussion, which answer cannot be rendered false by anything that the disputants may say or think about it; and further, that the denial of that true answer is false. This makes an apparent difficulty for idealism' (*CP*:8.126).

This tension finds a home in Peirce's 'objective idealism' according to which the properly tuned mind plays a somewhat faithful but always slightly discordant harmony with the melody of the universe of which the mind is a part and at the same time is its author in conjunction with all minds, with *Mind* (the notion that everything that is is mind lies at the heart of Peirce's 'objective idealism,' which views inorganic matter as 'effete mind' [*CP*:4.551, 6.102–8, 6.163, 6.24, 6.264–6]). Yet, as we have noted, according to Peirce the universe as a brute physical entity 'out there' remains unperturbed by whatever a given community of minds might happen to think about it.

So, in the final analysis, can Peirce's methodological 'objectivism' indeed dovetail with his ontological 'idealism'? – that is, according to Rescher and Brandom's (1979) interpretation of 'objective idealism.' How can what are to all appearances two perpetually antagonistic beasts be pacified? If, via 'objectivity,' a particular conception of 'reality' is 'true,' then surely it can't be refuted, and in such case we can't know whether or not it is 'true.' So if we can't verify the 'truth' of a particular conception of 'reality,' then obviously we can't know with absolute certainty where the line lies between 'real' and 'irreal' and between 'realism' and 'idealism.' On the other hand, if a conception of 'reality' is pure mind-stuff, then neither is there any possibility of distinguishing between what is 'real' and what is not, for most anything can be just as 'real' as many other things from one vantage point or another. But Peirce believed that the 'world,' our 'semiotically real world,' is not *merely* mind-stuff (subjective 'idealism') nor is it *pure* physical-stuff 'out there' to be had by the neutral observer (naive 'realism,' 'objectivism'). He wanted a happy meeting ground between the two horns of the dilemma: thus his 'pragmatic maxim,' a method for arriving at meaning rather than 'truth' in terms of tentative community opinion rather than a hard-nosed empirical look and a no-nonsense description of 'objective reality.' The 'maxim' is, as evidenced in the appendix, a way of concrete living more than a disembodied algorithm for generating theories and truths. It is a recipe by means of which signs enter into *relations* with other signs, semiotic agents with their signs, and those agents with each other.

In this light, regarding the 'maxim,' and according to the general tenets of this inquiry, I prefer to use the term 'relation' (and even 'interrelation') rather than 'representation' and 'reference.' Peirce engaged in a constant struggle with this terminology. He conceded late in life that 'representation' was 'injudicious.' He preferred 'mediation,' which is more in line with his category of Thirdness. Secondness, which he earlier dubbed 'relation,' was later changed to 'reaction' in his reformulation of the three categorical labels, *quality*, *reaction*, and *mediation* (*CP*:4.3). In the present essay I retain 'mediation,' and use 'relation' in a broad sense to include both dyadic and triadic *interaction*. I must emphasize *interaction* in order to avoid the 'stand for' epithet commonly evoked in many disquisitions on the sign as that which 'stands for' its object in the capacity of some sort of substitute or surrogate. Along the lines of Max Black's (1962) rejection of the *substitution* theory in favour of *interaction* in his account of metaphor, I would opt for the concepts of *relation*, *interrelatedness*, and *interaction* with respect to signs in general. In this manner, and to paraphrase Rorty (1982:130), the problem of demarcation between fiction (or 'irreality') and 'reality' simply does not raise its ugly head once allusions to traditional epistemological objectivism, ontological realism, and logical empiricism, at times unfortunately conjured up by Peirce's terminology, are laid to rest. Nor, for parallel reasons, does the fear of losing touch with 'reality' arise inasmuch as genuine Peircean 'objective idealist' language is used and 'correspondence,' 'reference,' and 'representation' are eschewed. In saying this I am, of course, swimming against the current of much conventional Peirce scholarship. The fact remains, however, that Peirce's texts are couched in terminology common to standard discourse up to and including empirical positivism. (Against this grain, Skagestad, for example, reveals Peirce's threefold modes of a sign's reference. A sign must be capable of [1] *referring to* and being interpreted by a subsequent thought or sign, [2] *standing for* some real object in the physical world, and [3] *representing* that object by some previous thought or sign [Skagestad 1981:121]. I put forth the present essay in an attempt to contextualize Peirce within our contemporary scene. In so doing, it becomes necessary to consider not always the letter but occasionally the spirit of Peirce's texts.)

This much considered, and with respect to the impossibility of an infallible distinction between the 'real' and the fictive ('irreal'), we might entertain the idea of a companion to Peirce's 'maxim,' let us call it the 'pragmatic mocksum':

'*In order to ascertain the meaning of a fiction (that is, something considered "irreal" but a possible candidate for the "real") one should consider what practical consequences might conceivably result from the consideration of that fictive conception as if it were "real" – and as a result, the sum of these consequences will engender the meaning of the fiction so conceived*' (a derivation from *CP*:5.9).

(I should hasten to add that in conjuring up the term 'mocksum' I mean no disrespect toward the 'maxim.' The problem, as I see it, is that in exegeses of Peirce's writings the 'maxim' is almost invariably placed within the context of indexical, linguistic [logico-symbolic – 'logocentric'], and inductive-deductive aspects of *semiosis*, while Firstness, iconicity, and abduction are slighted. In contrast, I wish to bring attention to that more basic aspect of sign interaction. 'Mock,' of 'mocksum,' pays homage to resemblance, proper to the iconic sign. Thus the term can be construed as a sign that 'mocks 'em' and at the same time as the 'sum' total of all possible 'mocking' signs interrelated with and overlapping one another by way of their conjoint Firstness.)

The 'maxim,' providing for the meaning of a set of presumably 'semiotically real' signs by way of their relation to another set of signs, makes tentative moves toward the conception of *generality* (the sphere of Thirdness, however *incomplete* it may be). The 'mocksum,' emerging from the sphere of Firstness (a juxtaposition of all possibilities the sum of which culminates in *vagueness*, however *inconsistent*), offers a clue to the nature and meaning of 'semiotically real' signs in terms of their relation to signs that *are not* what they would otherwise *be* as 'semiotically real' signs. The 'maxim' is often – and quite unfortunately – taken as a no-nonsense recipe akin to positivist verificationism; the 'mocksum,' product of imaginary flashes, conjectures, and tentative guesses, reveals the very idea of determinate verifiability as the repository of modernity's misplaced utopian dreams.

A fiction beginning with 'What if such-and-such were the case' calls for some conception or other, whether on the part of the fiction-maker or the interpreter, of the consequences of the original fictive conception. The initial posit, 'What if such-and-such were the case,' has the makings of a 'thought experiment' of sorts, which can give rise to various chains of possible constructs from each of which the meaning of a set of signs can be engendered. Subsequently, the *as if* of the fictive signs – what 'semiotically real' signs *would not* ordinarily *be* – can become a key opening the door to the meaning of a given set of signs. Upon taking on meaning, those signs are translated into other signs they *would not* ordinarily *have been* had they not been related to their respective fictive signs. The meaning of signs does not depend upon hard-nosed 'truth' and *generality* alone; it inevitable finds itself injected with a slight to a massive dose of *vagueness* and what might ordinarily go as downright 'untruth.'

In this sense, if we are to take Peirce's contrary-to-fact hypothetical at the heart of his 'maxim' seriously, then we are forced to admit what few would admit in his day, and what would most likely meet with widespread opposition even today: 'in the long run' knowledge, and consequently a given 'semiotic reality,' cannot but be gauged by some fictive standard or other. Moreover, in light of the previous chapters, we cannot know absolutely whether or not our bits and pieces of knowledge are 'true' ('real'). We can only (think we) know they are 'false' (fictive), and that the 'real' is something they *are not,* when we arrive at the wrenching discovery that we have been in error. This sobering realization should put a damper on our otherwise intractable vanities.

The bottom line seems to be that we may be to a greater or lesser extent ...

2. Lost in Meinong's Jungle?

Quite obviously, Peirce's concept of knowledge through a sort of 'learned ignorance' and its bearing on fictionality remains a far cry from the logical-empiricist conception of things. It is also divorced from Bertrand Russell's contention that whatever is referred to must exist, and that sentences about non-existents are about things that do not exist, therefore such sentences refer to nothing.

In 'On Denoting,' Russell (1905) criticizes Meinong's impossible 'mental objects' (that is, fictions and the like, as discussed in the previous section), suggesting that we should dispense with such unwanted guests. 'The gold mountain in Africa,' a Meinongian 'object,' presupposes that 'there is something which is both gold and a mountain.' But, Russell contended, there simply are no 'gold mountains,' and that's that. However, in view of the preceding, according to Peircean semiotics there can be no *absolutely absolute distinction* between existents ('real' objects, acts, and events) and non-existents (mere fictions). In Captain Nemo's time there were no nuclear-powered submarines; during the days of Rembrandt a Duchamp urinal as a work of art was, we must suppose, virtually inconceivable; during the heyday of classical physics, the idea of curved space would have been looked upon as a hoax; and so on. In this respect, Peirce seems to make tentative moves toward Meinong's jungle of imaginary, that is, of mental, 'objects.' This observation calls for a closer look.

Instead of Russell's 'Whatever is "referred" to must exist, for if not, it is not an object,' Meinong placed stock in 'Whatever is "referred" to must be an object by the very fact that it is that to which reference is made.' Russell, as would be expected, penned virulent protests. He assured us that if we take Meinong's idea that every thought has an object at face value, it inevitably ends in contradiction. If we construe a 'golden mountain' as 'an object which is such that it is golden and also such that it is not the case that it is golden,' according to Russell's 'theory of descriptions,' we have an intolerable condition: a 'golden mountain' can neither exist nor can it enjoy 'reference' of any form or fashion. However, according to some observers, 'reference' does not have to be 'true,' as Russell would have it, or even accurate, in the sense of Donnelan (1966) or Linsky (1971). A speaker can use 'reference' even if (1) it does not fit the 'referent' (it is false) or if (2) the presupposition of existence is not satisfied (see Lewis 1987; also Whiteside 1987, for the complementary idea of 'reference' in literary texts). My argument, on the other hand, is that in either case there is not really any need of the concept of 'reference' at all, for in the final analysis, there are only relations, and relations of relations, within the democratic *semiosic* gush.

Meinong, in his agonistic jousts with Russell, tirelessly argued against what he termed a 'prejudice in favour of the actual' – i.e., of Seconds – that is, Russell's 'robust sense of reality.' Cognition (Thirds), he believed, enjoy their own form of 'objects,' which, if not of the concrete existence of the physical world, are 'objects' nonetheless. A study of the 'objects' of cognition (thought-signs in Peirce's terms) is no more than the demand that what is already known as the 'object' of cognition is made the 'object' of study: it is part of the general study of signs, of semiotics. Russell, Frege, and the logical empiricists prioritized existents. In contrast, Meinong insisted that a proper study of 'objects' must consider the not (yet) existent (Firsts) that may or may not manifest a probability (Thirdness) of some future coming into existence (as Seconds), even if they are destined never to be actualized. In other words, it seems that Meinong would embrace the above-formulated 'mocksum' as well as Peirce's 'maxim.' The implications of this posture are, I would respectfully submit, far-reaching: they could aid in placing Peirce's pragmatism in the broad, virtually all-encompassing *semiosic* context it deserves.

Meinong, following Brentano (1973) who claimed that all mental states are directed toward something and thus they possess distinguishing features, proposed that what *is not* is as important as what *is*. According to this notion, knowledge not only pertains to existents, that is, to the empirical objects of science and metaphysics; it also pertains to the arts, imagination, and all inner experiences. How else, a Meinongian would ask, could theories of the 'real world' have come about except by virtue of imaginary (fictive and such) worlds couched in thought signs? – that is, Pythagoras's spheres, Dante's Inferno, phlogiston, the aether, Mallarmé's poetry, Einstein's space-time continuum, unorthodox logics, transfinite numbers, Dada art, recent developments in quantum theory, works by Joyce and Woolf and Beckett and García Márquez. We must conclude, the Meinongian would argue, that objects which do not, and perhaps cannot, exist, can nonetheless enjoy status as genuine mental 'objects,' thus they are part of the total experienced world (that is, subject to the 'mocksum' as well as the 'maxim') (see, in general, Castaneda 1979, Chisholm 1973 and 1982, Findlay 1963, Howell 1979, Parsons 1974, Routley 1979, and Schultz 1979).

This implies, first, that there are 'objects' that do not exist, and second, that non-existent 'objects' can nonetheless be spoken of in such a way that they can be made the subject of a predication conceived as if it were 'true,' hence they are constituted in some way or other. In this sense Meinong non-existent possibilities are rooted in our language-using capacity. This notion, given the above assumptions, must embrace possible as well as actual statements in natural and artificial languages, and once again the total range of non-existent sayable possibilities becomes limitless (Rescher 1975:212). (This characteristic of Meinong 'mental objects' will eventually come to bear on the 'anti-linguicentric' posture I take during the latter chapters of the present volume. Indeed, language is only one of the media through which Meinong 'mental objects' can be actualized. They can also gain entry into the physical world in the form of art, architecture, music, sculpture, and scientific models and metaphors, as well as all forms of nonverbal communication in everyday life.)

The Meinong strategy consists in selecting a subset of properties capable of serving as an identifying description of a particular 'object' and then giving it an articulation via a portion of those properties. This partial articulation brings the 'object' into mental 'existence' as a thought-sign, while the set of possible properties that remain unarticulated are relegated to the domain of the unmentioned (in other words, both the 'mocksum' and the 'maxim' are potentially brought into play). Though some of the unmentioned properties can subsequently be stated, a portion will always remain unmentioned and unmentionable at a given point in time and space, hence the 'object' must be to a greater or lesser degree *incomplete* in terms of its status as a *generality*. Meinongian 'objects,' insofar as they are mental, are 'objects' of articulation more than of sensation or perception.

Berkeley relegated material substrata to secondary status and argued that ideas (thought-signs) are sufficient. Kant stressed 'representations' ('semiotic objects,' sign-events), attention to which would help us forget about the inaccessible 'thing-in-itself.' Meinong, whose mental 'objects' are the object of identifying properties (predicates, adjectives, icons) that take precedence over particular things (subjects, indices) bearing those properties, carries the equation a giant step further. It is sufficient that an 'object' merely be said, whether it exists or not and whether it is logically possible or not. In this manner,

Meinong's strange hypothesis demonstrates how fictive but 'semiotically real' (that is, non-existent and possible or impossible) 'objects,' 'acts,' and 'events' (hereafter OAEs) can come into existence as 'semiotically real' world constructs. In other words, there are, *pace* Meinong, existent and non-existent, and ontological and nonontological OAEs, just as there are logically possible and impossible ones. What is considered at a given point in time to be the 'real' world consists of the range of existent OAEs, which excludes such oddities as 'gold mountains' and 'square circles.' 'Gold mountains' are counted among non-existent yet conceivably possible OAEs in possible worlds, while 'square circles' must take their place alongside non-existent and impossible OAEs. (I use the compound term OAEs in lieu of Meinong's 'objects' in order to account for the entire range of 'objects' [including living organisms] and their role in the semiotic 'acts' and 'events' making up a given 'semiotic world.')

Russell (1905) believed that Meinong's hypothesis, in addition to its unacceptable ontological premise, is groundless: his non-existent, impossible OAEs violate the principle of noncontradiction. But according to Meinong, if some OAEs are self-contradictory, there is no call for alarm. They cannot be existents precisely because they are self-contradictory, and if they were possible existents, in all probability they would be noncontradictory. The long tradition of Western notions of proper thinking demands a coherent 'reality' (limited exclusively to the 'maxim' in its narrow, verificationist interpretation). However, though such oddities as 'square circles' in a world of noncontradiction and 'curved space' in the Newtonian world are barred, the fact remains that at virtually any time and in any place they can sit rather comfortably in fictive worlds (potentially subjected to the 'mocksum'). And by use of a fudge factor of the sort common in everyday talk, their close kin – and occasionally even distant cousins as well – can earn citizenship to the sphere of our everyday life (through metaphors and other rhetorical devices, and at exceedingly more general levels, 'thought experiments' and scientific models). Moreover, 'circles' are generally considered 'round' and 'boxes' square or rectangular, yet there is nothing strange in calling a hat box a 'box.' So by a certain stretch of common talk what about a 'circular box,' or even a 'roundish square'? When considering the spectrum of possibilities between 'square' and 'round' and 'box' and 'circle,' and especially other terms potentially derived from them such as 'squond,' 'roux,' 'circre,' 'squale,' and so on (in the order of 'wavicles' in quantum theory or Goodman's 'grue' and 'bleen'), we enter into varying shades of *vagueness*. That is, a *superposition* of all the possible terms that could have been used but were not leaves us with areas of *inconsistency* as a result of those terms' *overdetermination*. Words of ordinary language tend to have a greater or lesser degree of 'squishiness' (Ross 1972) or 'hedges' (Lakoff 1972). In other words, they are 'fuzzy.'

Of course, science, according to the popular conception, calls for precision, while ordinary talk often breaks down logical exclusions and erases boundaries. Hitherto unknown scientific constructs may be quite clear, yet they often threaten to become muddied when dressed in ordinary talk tirelessly wedded to customary uses and more than a few threadbare images. For example, when relativity theory bounded onto the scene, it could hardly be understood in terms of familiar experiences and habitual natural-language practices. In fact, to this day it continues to endure as a theory of physical events that are, in a limited sense, for most people well-nigh inconceivable. The problem of the notion of conceivability is that our 'conceptions' regarding relativity-theory events hang onto temporal relations and worn out assumptions such as 'simultaneity,' 'time,' 'space,' 'mass,' 'light,' and so on (Gregory 1988). Habits, of course, are hard to break.

From another complementary perspective, just as commonsensical notions and ordinary talk are generally at odds with contemporary scientific theories, so also much of our perception cannot always be trusted. Richard L. Gregory (1966:107–8), to cite only one of many investigators, amply demonstrates our perceptual limitations through numerous examples of visual illusions. For instance, when the after-effects of a rotating spiral are examined, two curious features stand out: (1) movement may expand or shrink, yet (2) the object may appear to remain of the same size. It grows, but it doesn't grow. Along these same lines, from a biological perspective Francisco Varela (1984a, 1984b) draws from investigations by Beck (1972) and Land and McCann (1971), to demonstrate that there is no one-to-one relationship between light flux at various wave-lengths (primary qualities) and the colours (secondary qualities) we associate with 'real' objects. And regarding the aesthetics of worldmaking, we have Nelson Goodman's (1978) work, following investigations by psychologist Paul Kolers (1972), on the difference between what is seen and what actually happens when staccato flashes of light are erroneously perceived as continuous. The moral to the story: we should not put all our eggs in one basket of perception or conception, for our experience and thought will inevitably suffer from illusions at certain junctures, thus straying even further from 'reality' than we already find ourselves.

As a result of the aforementioned studies, and a host of others as well, it is becoming increasingly evident that the brain-mind does not and cannot faithfully mirror nature, but to a large degree – though not exclusively – it 'constructs' its own world with the neurophysical tools it has at hand. Perhaps we should do the best we can within our limitations, while conceding that there are many worlds, and that all of them in concert make up *the* world, that is, *some* world. If this posture appears unbearably concessionary – postmodern acquiescence – I would point out that in the aftermath of our loss of faith in objectivism, representationalism, referentiality, foundationalism, and the mirror model of 'reality,' any viable 'realist-objectivist' alternative hardly seems to be in the making.

It appears that we may be stuck with at least some diluted form of Meinongism.

3. Meinong, the World's Furniture, and Semiotics

Meinong's non-existent OAEs are, it hardly needs saying, quasi-infinitely more numerous than our repertoire of existents in the physical world. Admittedly, says the Meinongian, non-existents are in a sense inferior to existents, but this inferiority has nothing to do with their beingness or nonbeingness in a material sense. It involves their highlighted degree of *incompleteness*. Besides, the Meinongian continues, if we could just get rid of our pig-headed obsession for a rigorously consistent world and give in to a bit of *inconsistency* once in a while, we might at long last find peace of mind.

We have heard comparable notions above, especially in the Preamble. There is a plethora of *possible* 'truths' within the *overdetermined* sphere, some of which may be thought 'in here' or actualized 'out there,' and some not. Some of them can be *possibly* 'real' and some not, some are *inconsistent* with others and some not, and some can be relatively *completely* determined while others are destined to remain radically *incomplete*. A 'snow-capped peak' is possibly 'real' – though not feasible in the middle of Texas in July – a 'gold mountain' is a merely possible 'object' supposedly never to take its place among 'real objects,' and a 'square circle' is a contradictory impossible 'object' in some possible 'semiotically real' world, since at least two of its attributes are mutually exclusive. Regarding non-existents, there are no unicorns, but the term 'unicorn' can be used in relation to a *unicorn picture*, though it relates to nothing at all that can take its place among existents – Goodman (1978) has said so much. Peirce, incidentally, would maintain that there can be a 'unicorn phenomenon'; it is that to which the name 'unicorn' is given. Admittedly it is 'an illusory phenomenon, but a phenomenon nonetheless. It is not quite *purely* illusory, but only *mainly* so' (*CP*:8.82). In other words, what is *mainly* illusory goes with acknowledgment of the phenomenon as fiction, while the *purely* illusory would be tantamount to hallucinatory experience. On the other hand, lightning is a naturally occurring sign that relates to thunder *causally* (or, in everyday language use, 'cup' can relate to what it *contains*, the coffee, and 'wheels' can relate to that of which they are a *part*, the car). While the unicorn picture is an *icon*, the cause-effect – container-contained, and part-whole – sign relations are *indexical*. And sentences about fictions the likes of 'Quixote was deranged' relating to nothing 'real' are *symbols*: as linguistic signs, they are signs of *generality*, *regularity*, and *conventionality*.

The problem seems to be that if certain symbols of everyday language can be used with somewhat equal credibility to talk about fictions as wells as presumable 'facts' of the matter, about non-existents as well as existents, and about consistent as well as inconsistent existents, then we are caught in a bind. '2 + 2 = 4,' 'Square circles come in many colours,' 'O.J. Simpson is a wolf in sheep's clothing,' 'That is a unicorn picture,' 'C.S. Peirce was born in the U.S.A.,' 'I saw a lightning flash,' 'Holmes lived on Baker Street,' and '"Wavicles" are sometimes waves and sometimes particles' are all potentially placed on democratic footing: both the 'mocksum' and the 'maxim' apply. Icons, indices, and symbols can be talked about *as if* the words related to something. Even so-called natural signs can be subjected to what might appear to be incommensurable worlds. 'That is Jove's thunderbolt' for one culture can play the role of 'That is nothing more than an electrical discharge from the clouds' for another. In fact, 'mixed sentences' the likes of 'Jove's thunderbolts are electrical discharges from the clouds' mesh two apparently incommensurable worlds. What is for one person or community a goose may be a gander for another, and what for one is phlogiston is oxygen for another. Whatever 'truth' may be attached to the words used depends upon *tenable though always fallible assertibility*, that is, when we put sober-minded concern over 'truth,' 'rationality,' 'existence,' and other such untenables aside (see, in general, Woods 1974, Pavel 1986, Rorty 1976, and Merrell 1992: chap. 5).

With even greater force, then, we find ourselves compelled to embrace the admission that we should speak of '(inter)relations' rather than 'reference.' '(Inter)relations' are not hard-and-fast logical positivist 'correspondences' between theoretical sentences and observation sentences, between thought-signs and sign-events, or between words and things. They are implicit in the way we 'talk about' what happens to be the/a/our 'semiotically real' world. In Rorty's way of putting it (1979:127), all we need is a 'commonsensical notion of "talking about," where the criterion for what a statement is "about" is just whatever its utterer "has in mind" – that is, whatever he *thinks* he's talking about.' This entails a 'minimal gratification of Parmenidean needs' (Rorty 1982:135). It allows us to slap some sort of meaning onto the things of our 'semiotically real' world and render them 'true,' at least *for* us. In this sense, whatever we might like to think we 'refer' to is not-so-simply that about which we can talk. Rather, that about which we talk is by and large what we have to say about it, all notions of 'reference' aside.

In other words, we have, so to speak, signs of *First Order* (icons or monads, and indices or dyads, [inter]relations between properties and individuals), and of *Second Order* (symbols, [inter]relations between [inter]relations between properties and individuals). We can utter statements about 'unicorn-pictures,' 'lightning and thunder,' 'square circles,' and the fact that 'Chicago' is a 'big city' (use) and has 'seven letters' (mention). When in their most formal symbolic attire, the three orders of signs might appear to (inter)relate roughly with what might go as 'First'- and 'Second'-order logics. But this is not really the case. For, I shall hammer out in the pages that follow a conception of the Peircean sign that is shorn of ordinary notions of 'reference,' 'representation,' 'correspondence,' and 'truth,' and at the same time it embraces imponderables from everyday language that have alienated logical concerns and have thrown the whole enterprise into a veritable state of neurosis. In this vein, I hope to illustrate that it is not absolutely necessary for us to keep a stiff upper lip regarding Meinong OAEs that 'refer' in order to salvage a modicum of the 'maxim' by asserting that whatever we talk about must be the object of our 'reference.' We are free simply to engage in talk, and talk about talk – in addition to, of course, our interaction with signs of nonlinguistic nature. That is, we are free of the demands of *episteme*, and can become citizens of the relatively free society of *doxa*. In this sense, just as the 'real' things to which our signs (inter)relate are *incomplete* insofar as they are not determinately specifiable down to their most minute details, so also with respect to fictional worlds and their respective signs.

Now, if, as I have pointed out above, *noncontradiction* does not necessarily apply with respect to *vague* qualities, and if the same can be said for the *excluded middle* regarding the domain of *generalities*, then neither does the *identity principle* hold for OAEs. Quine (1953:4) makes this argument – though for reasons diametrically opposed to those of the present essay – in his allusion to

> the possible fat man in the doorway; and, again, the possible bald man in that doorway. Are they the same possible man, or two possible men? How do we decide? How many possible men are there in that doorway? Are there more possible thin ones than fat ones? How many of them are alike? Or would their being alike make them one? Are no *two* possible things alike? Is this the same as saying that it is impossible for two things to be alike? Or, finally, is the concept of identity simply inapplicable to unactualized possibles? But what sense can be found in talking of entities which cannot meaningfully be said to be identical with themselves and distinct from one another? These elements are well-nigh incorrigible.

One might respond that identity is valid at least regarding imaginary constructs that we can control in much the manner in which Cervantes dictated the conditions and happenings of Don Quixote's world. This being the case, we should be able to work toward such iron-handed control over 'real' OAEs, thus taking on knowledge of the 'real' world as it is. However, upon considering all possible alternative vantages and all possible spatio-temporal contextual slices applicable to imaginary and nonimaginary constructs alike, the conclusion forcing itself on us is that neither your image of a bed nor your reading this sentence nor the assassination of JFK can be absolutely apprehended in their myriad complexity. They can have one set of properties in the recent past, another set now, and still another set a step further down the road. Granted, a particular bed as pure Meinong mental 'object' might for practical purposes appear to be complete. However, its completeness can be forthcoming not only by virtue of its positive properties, but also its negative ones. The image of a bed you construct in your mind might be of one style, but it could have been of a hundred or so others: it might have been of one material but it could have been of others, of one colour but it could have been of others, and so on. So even though the Meinongian imaginary bed may presumably be complete as such, when considered in terms of what it *could have been* but *is not*, it must be considered incomplete. For the possibility exists that at any future moment it *will have been* something other than what it is. In the same vein, your reading the above sentence might have been and will have been something other than what it is in myriad different ways – and I choose to say nothing of the numbing complexity surrounding the event of JFK's assassination. The moral to the story is that there can be no self-identical and static OAE, whether mental or presumably 'out there.' Moreover, since the number of all possible sentences related to a given OAE is potentially infinite, that OAE enjoys virtually an infinite number of determinations.

So from a given finite perspective, whether fictive, 'semiotically real,' or 'real,' it is impossible to give total account of all the aspects of a given mental OAE. Moreover, since our conception of any and all OAEs is inexorably incomplete, then they may always and at every new moment be different from what they were, and at all future moments they may always be different from what they now are: potentially they are infinitely variable. The very idea of complete and self-identical Meinongian OAEs is a hope that can bear little fruit. Some of our most venerable metaphysicists have taught us that 'reality' packages eternal, unchanging entities: there simply is no place for many of the slithering Meinong OAEs lurking out there. This attitude has produced atoms, Platonic 'forms,' Cartesian 'minds,' and positivist 'data.' These and other concepts of comparable ilk have been both helpful and hazardous. In our own time at least, they have served to keep a host of academicians off the unemployment lines by their lending themselves to the writing of innumerable volumes. They have also influenced common talk with such concepts as self, soul, consciousness, ego, and mind, all generally conceived as self-identical and some of them even eternal. The problem is that these concepts (inter)relate not with some impossible dream of eternal essences but with fluctuating processes along the flow of *semiosis.* They are never complete, and somewhere along the line they are more often than not found to be in one form or another inconsistent.

4. The Nature of the Jungle

Relating the Meinong view to the initial sections of this chapter, 'semiotically real' knowledge of what is presumed to be the 'real world' enjoys no absolute priority over knowledge of incomplete, non-existent fictions. All fictions entail incomplete knowledge of incompleteable OAEs. Since the author of a given fiction could not possibly have provided knowledge concerning all the possibilities implied by the fiction, and since 'semiotically real' knowledge of their 'real world' counterparts is necessarily always incomplete, we cannot hope to know them except incompletely. In this respect the 'real' and the 'semiotically real' demand hardly any more respect than fictions. Only in this manner can it be said that a given 'real world' OAE emerges from the sphere of (fictional) possibilities containing all 'semiotically real worlds' (including Meinongian OAEs), and that all actualized 'semiotically real worlds' could always have been something other than what they are.

To restate the issue in the terminology of this inquiry, insofar as fictions and/or 'semiotically real' worlds are *incomplete* (*general* in Peirce's terms) they are *underdetermined*, and insofar as they contain a superposition of contradictories they are *overdetermined* (*inconsistent*, or *vague* in the Peircean sense). The fact that yesterday's fiction can stand a chance of becoming 'semiotically real' and vice versa – Peirce's pre-Quine critique of the analytic-synthetic distinction – cannot but point to the conclusion that whatever conception of the 'real' (or of any fiction) we may nurture, it is something other than what it could have been, and at some future moment it will have become something other than what it is. In this vein, *generality* demands allegiance *neither* to the one alternative *nor* the other, but in time, *either* one *or* the other, or even something else, may merit a leap of faith. This is positive generality. Things are never so tightly compacted that they cannot allow for a few additions. Positive generality has its negative counterpart in *vagueness.* In this sphere, given the somewhat peaceful coexistence of superposed, incompatible possibilities, it is not a matter of one thing and *not* its alternative, but of *both* as unactualized simultaneities. Virtually nothing is left out of the equation. By and large signs inevitably remain to a degree both *vague* and *incomplete*, and possibly or potentially either 'semiotically real' or fictive, or neither or both, depending on the whims and the compulsions of their beholder. (Recall that following Peirce, the maker of a fiction shoulders the responsibility of supplying sufficient determinability to her signs so as to render them adequately intelligible, while it is up to the receiver of that fiction to give it satisfactory determination as signs of generality.)

The snafu arises not only in cases of radically *overdetermined* OAEs, but also in radically *underdetermined* ones. The story, 'Puff was a magic dragon who lived down by the sea, the end,' and 'The sun revolves around the earth, period,' are radically underdetermined; in fact, they are to all appearances so incomplete as hardly to qualify as stories at all. At this far end of the spectrum knowledge becomes so schematic that the 'stories' tell us next to nothing; they contain hardly any ado about what could lend itself to much ado. On the other hand, the possible interpretations (meanings) of these radically schematic 'stories' are virtually limitless: they are capable of incorporating within their embrace an infinity of elaborations and variations. Were we mystics capable of seeing the universe in a grain of sand or in a solitary cipher, these 'stories' would be sufficient, for we would be in need of few details. But the element of intractable nominalism in us longs for a liberal scattering of particulars. We need Mickey Spillane as well as Jorge Luis Borges, Stephen King as well as Gertrude Stein. In other words, Spillane, King, and comparable yarn spinners provide a sufficient degree of sign determination so as to render their work relatively nonvague; hence they can usually be read rather passively and enjoyed, later to be recalled in the beer parlour, over gin rummy, or during amiable chitchat in passing the time of day. In contrast, Borges, Stein, and creators of 'high art' provide much vagueness, little interpretative security, and place stringent demands on their readers' capacity properly to generalize the signs they have left for posterity; hence their works, it might seem, are with more pain than gain brought to an acceptable level of meaning determinacy, which can make for presumptuous talk at cocktail parties, in lecture halls, and over a coffee cup at the nearest cafeteria.

Let us, then, gravitate to the other end of the spectrum and try constructing a complete OAE, following Rorty's (1982) proposal, by listing all the possible attributes possessed by Sherlock Holmes in the manner in which we would exhaustively list all of Bill Clinton's attributes. Upon so doing, any and all possible questions about Clinton can also be raised and answered about Holmes. Thus our fictive character must somehow be complete. The problem is that from a given perspective, just as by the very nature of nominalism some of Clinton's attributes are assigned either arbitrarily or they are coloured by prejudices and presuppositions, all the more so regarding Holmes. To make matters worse, given another set of space-time coordinates and another context, different answers will be forthcoming from the same questions and the same answers from different questions: consequently we see once more that OAEs cannot cease undergoing changes. The practical impossibility of listing all the attributes, asking all the questions, and providing determinate answers to OAEs is nevertheless no obstacle to saying that there are such entities, whether speaking of the 'real' world or of Meinong 'worlds.'

In other words, the traditional notions of 'truth-by-correspondence' or 'reference' are in jeopardy, which leaves us, Rorty concludes (1982:127), with two alternatives, either (1) a language-game approach allowing us to forget about 'reference' altogether, or (2) physicalism, according to which 'real world' causality determines 'reference.' Needless to say, Rorty opts for (1), which implies a more-or-less favourable nod to Meinong insofar as there is no absolute distinction between fiction and the 'real.' The distinction lies merely in our way of saying. So we are again forced to concede that there is no all-or-nothing distinction between possible or impossible fictional and 'semiotically real' worlds. Once again it becomes apparent that if the range of all contextualized 'worlds' is considered from a historical perspective, what for one generation is 'real' (that is, 'semiotically real'), for another might possibly be fictional, and what for one generation is possible and even existent, for another might be impossible.

The overwhelmingly broad character of Meinong OAEs is the source of their greatest weakness and their greatest strength. Unlike Frege and Husserl, Meinong assumes no distinctions between mental OAEs and levels of objectivity in advance, such as 'sense' and 'reference,' sign and thing. On the negative side, however, Meinong offers no easy way to distinguish 'truth' from 'falsity,' sense from nonsense, or 'real' from 'semiotically real.' It is this aspect of his hypothesis that has most aggravated logicians. For the infinitely expansive term OAE seems to tell us nothing: at bottom it is as epistemologically uninformative as Parmenides' everything that is is, as William James's blooming buzzing mess, as Hume's bundle of raw sensations, or as Derrida's *différance*. If everything consists of OAEs, what distinctions can possibly be made? What differences can there be that make meaningful differences? (Of course much the same could be said of Peirce's idea that everything is sign. However, one must bear in mind that a sign is not a full-blown sign without the participation of its respective semiotic agents, each with his/her particular role to play, which properly concretizes and contextualizes it.)

In short, the current neo-Meinongian does not flee from *indeterminacy*, *inconsistency* (*vagueness*), and *incompleteness* (*generality*), but meets them head-on. On so doing, she reaps the ire of those hard of nose desperately grasping at the last straws of certainty. So be it, she might conclude. Her reward is not forthcoming in the kingdom of that long-sought-for paradise punctuated with well-defined things and meanings. In fact, these days she finds more than a tinge of consolation, since her populous sphere of signs is suggestive of the wonders of a helter-skelter mishmash tantamount to the new physics of chaos, of myriad catastrophes, tangled fractals, prodigious fluctuations, and dissipative structures.

5. Then Can There Be No Legitimate Physicalist Language?

In fact, it can be argued that theoretical physics, apart from its reliance on mathematics, is loaded in every branch with talk about Meinong OAEs (Routley 1979).

Purely mental constructs such as the four-dimensional space-time manifold, quarks, charm, and black holes are worthy candidates. If we care for heightened drama, purely intensional idealizations in the form of predictions have become 'real' after enjoying appropriate verification from physical 'evidence' – the empty slots that once existed in the periodic table, Yukawa's mesons, Dirac's neutrinos, and so on. The euphoria of empirical positivism during the 1920s, 1930s, and 1940s was thus premature. The empiricist celebration of science actually ended in a brawl of competing theories and incursions into dark alleys in search of a Grand Unified Theory.

In this light, the sliding demarcation between existent and non-existent OAEs is reminiscent of Peirce's strange, and at times strained, combination of methodological 'realism' and 'ontological idealism' accompanied by an uncertain move toward 'ontological realism' at the same time that 'epistemology' and 'methodology' move tenuously toward 'idealism.' I reiterate my allusion, of course, to Peirce's cantankerous term, 'objective idealism.' From the broader Meinongian horizon, 'objective idealism' takes on an even more encompassing countenance. The first stage of the combination of 'methodological realism' and 'ontological idealism' making up 'objective idealism' is somewhat comparable to the Kantian notion that the methodologically real is ontologically ideal: the objects (Secondness) of knowledge (Thirdness) are the eventual intellectual products of the will to know, not of unspeakable transcendental causes (*CP*:8.15). Peirce's unlikely pair of terms I have repeatedly placed in the spotlight, *vagueness* and *generality* (≈ *inconsistency* and *incompleteness*) remains apropos. An idea or 'real object as engendered by the mind' is invariably *vague* (*inconsistent*), in its inception corresponding rather closely to Peirce's category of Firstness. *Vague* signs such as 'bald,' 'tall,' and 'heap,' and 'Napoleon,' 'Don Quixote,' and 'unicorn,' must remain at their roots the product of images, feelings, qualities (tones) that can be externally existent (tokens), or they may be merely imagined, in which case they can more or less conform to some conventional form (type). But as *general* signs, they hardly stand a chance of attaining identity status with that form: they will always fall victim to meaning indeterminacy and their interpretants will remain *incomplete* (*CP*:5.429).

In spite of these shortcomings, ontological 'idealism' is capable of endowing the range of all 'semiotically real' signs with the possibility of existence (phlogiston, quarks, black holes), whether or not they approximate the 'real.' And methodological 'realism' can account for the tendency of legitimate inquiry at least hopefully to approximate, albeit with fits and jerks, the 'real' (oxygen, atoms as largely vacuous, space-time manifold), though it can never exist as such in all its plenitude *for* us. Recall Peirce's example of a learned member of the German Shakespearean Society who embarks on futile speculation concerning how long it had been since Polonius had had his hair cut at the time of his death. Most likely the only possible response would be that Polonius 'was nothing but a creature of Shakespeare's brain, and that Shakespeare never thought of the point raised.' In this sense, it is what we call the 'real' (that is, the 'semiotically real') world that is most radically replete with indeterminable OAEs. As no more than 'semiotically real,' we cannot be sure that it is not the case that there are any indeterminable objects, though regarding the determination of any particular object we would 'hope there is an answer, or something pretty close to an answer, which sufficient inquiry will compel us to accept' (*CP*:4.61).

And so we are back to talk about 'things' and talk about talk itself. Some 'things' are the mere 'object' of talk – that is, OAEs – and therefore do not exist, at least for the time being, though they continue at least to enjoy mental 'objectification.' Polonius, like all such 'objects,' is inordinately *vague* and radically *indeterminate*, since Polonius's creator is no longer around to help carry the determination of the sign-object a mite further along its tired road toward completion. As a *vague* sign, it is not necessarily either 'true' or 'false' that Polonius had his hair cut, say, two weeks before his death, and there is no knowing whether it is or not both 'true' and 'false' – given the sign's radical *indeterminacy*, hence the open range of possible interpretations – that he had his hair cut at that particular time. So the Polonius-sign is virtually as *inconsistent* as it is *indeterminate*, and the principle of noncontradiction does not necessarily hold. Polonius is, moreover, radically *incomplete* as a *general* sign, since further determination of its interpretant is left to the whims and wishes of its interpreters during their pontificating in academic conferences and journals and dictating to numbed students in the classrooms. So the range of all possible interpretations is continuous, and the excluded-middle principle does not necessarily apply either.

In sum, classical logic demands an absolute conception of the 'real,' thus setting the standard for ontological talk of a rock-solid world. However, any and all 'semiotically real worlds' (that is, ontological 'idealities' coupled with methodological 'realities') thwart this enterprise, for they are inexorably feeble to not-quite-faithful accounts of the 'actually real.' We see with increasing force that Peirce's notion of what is and is not 'real' and what does and does not exist 'out there,' a notion ultimately embracing *vagueness* and *generality*, *inconsistency* and *incompleteness*, reveals the limitations of classical logic, which has for some time categorically barred the arts, narrative, major philosophical discourse, and a large portion of scientific discourse from the logician's playground. While classical logic (inter)relates with Secondness, its crystalline purity dissolves in Firstness's sea of *possiblia* and slips through the interstices of Thirdness's potential *continua* of signs and their interpretations (meanings).

Meinong's jungle, in the final analysis, trash-talks Russell-Quine's ontological desert and gives 'objectivity,' 'reference,' 'representation,' and 'correspondence' theories of meaning a swift uppercut. It would appear that any adequate semiotic inquiry into the idea of meaning must turn an eye toward Meinong's hypothesis. For, to reiterate the assumption stated at the outset of this chapter, the meaning of signs considered 'real' (*as if* the conception of those signs were coterminous with that to which the signs relate) cannot be absolutely distinguished from conceptions of that which is considered 'irreal' (insofar as, like fiction, it is taken *as if* it were 'real').

5

The Sign: Mirror or Lamp?

1. A Sign That Signed All Signs That Did Not Sign Themselves

After the foregoing, it might behoove us to turn our attention to what is traditionally considered the problem of *contradictions*, *inconsistencies*, and full-blown *paradoxes*, whether the result of a Meinong proliferation of signs or not, and whether in the arena of hard-nosed logic and formal systems, the carpeted surroundings of cultural concerns, or the give-and-take of the business world, politics, and everyday life in general.

I might as well lay my cards on the table by reiterating my contention that, outside the discourse of logicians, mathematicians, and philosophers, contradictions, inconsistencies, and paradoxes often lose their sting. Our recent tradition relegated whatever could not be whittled down and hammered into the cubby-holes of good logic and good reason to the trash bin of nonsense and meaninglessness. However, if the signs by means of which we give meaning to our world incorporate some form of disharmony and even contravention, in whatever style of reasoning we use, and if in spite of this we generally manage to make them meaningful in our day-by-day affairs, then contradictions, inconsistencies, and paradoxes are perhaps not as monstrous as their billing has had them. In this sense, meaning often allows for what has perennially been dubbed illegitimate and irrational thinking. Of course no serious scholar searching for rightness of fit in all things would wish openly to embrace contradictions, inconsistencies, and paradoxes. The drive for completeness belies an equal obsession for systematic adequacy, for a coherent, harmonious combine of concepts, content, and expression. Yet, awareness of one's fallibilism should most certainly breed tolerance for some degree of inconsistency in hopes that, though the terrain is rocky, a lush valley might be spread out beyond the next rise.

However, though all holistic self-contained, self-sufficient, self-referential cosmologies thus far developed by humankind have been at their roots anomalous in one form or another – and therefore we have no guarantee whatsoever that a consistent one will pop up in the future – the struggle for some sort of well-formed conceptual scheme offers some solace and evinces a modicum of promise. In order more often than not to map out the route in that direction, it may at times become expedient at least temporarily to embrace contradictions, inconsistencies, and paradoxes at local levels. But this presents us with an apparent quandary. If they are embraced, even at local levels, does not the entire *semiosic* fabric thereby become tattered? Our concoction of signs, we would like to assume, is either consistent or it is not. If not, the inconsistency must certainly be due to some flaw in the cornerstone of the edifice that will eventually bring about its downfall. To say our *semiosic* fabric is only a little bit ragged and incoherent is as futile as the anguished teenager's justification that she is only a little bit pregnant. On the other hand, some theorists of logic are steadily gravitating toward the idea that a contradiction does not automatically diffuse throughout the entire universe of signs. Rather, it is possible to 'distinguish between pervasive inconsistency (of the disastrous, "anything goes" form) and merely local anomalies, isolable incompatibilities whose logical perplexity is confined to a small, localized region of a wider system' (Rescher and Brandom 1979:53). In other words, consistency, like coherence, balance, and structure, admits of degrees in regards to the unfathomable whole of *semiosis*.

Nonetheless, the attitude toward apparent irreconcilables has traditionally been more bellicose than benign. At the turn of the century mathematician David Hilbert announced that the discovery of paradoxes in set theory rendered the situation in mathematics intolerable, and he subsequently founded a hopeful program to establish the consistency and completeness of any and all systems. In 1931 Kurt Gödel threw a monkey wrench in the works with his now notorious proof. At about the same time along came Wittgenstein, whose much maligned critique of mathematical foundations declared problems of irreconcilables by and large innocuous: the good therapeutic philosopher should do no more than bring them into the light of day, then they can properly be dissolved and forgotten. For Wittgenstein, if an inconsistency or paradox is hidden, then there is no cause for alarm, because in our everyday language use we are not ordinarily aware of its existence. And if we happen to find it, then there is still no call for hand wringing, since more often than not it will prove to be relatively harmless anyway – recall the Master's advice.

This notion – which should strike a responsive chord with many 'post-moderns' – is related to Wittgenstein's attitude toward *surveyability*, or the lack thereof, of mathematical proofs. The idea of surveyability is of import to the present disquisition, since to grasp meaning, traditionally conceived, entails the very graspability – with implications of surveyability – of that which is meant. It was conceived by formalist mathematicians, following Hilbert, that to assume a mathematical proof as intuitively grasped or self-evident entails that the 'truth' it expresses is surveyable in its entirety. Such surveyability presupposes that if there is a 'hidden inconsistency' somewhere in the *semiosic* fabric, it must have simply been 'overlooked.' The mathematician should reprimand himself for his myopia and exercise more caution the next time around. In other words, an inconsistency lies within the field of inquiry like a disease, and it is the task of the investigator to dig it out and restore the infirm body of discourse to good health.

All of which is absurd, Wittgenstein claims. Surveyability and scrutiny of the field rules out the possibility of merely overlooking an inconsistency. A distinction must therefore be made between mere carelessness and unsurveyability. Besides, one cannot speak of 'overlooking' an inconsistency without assuming that the possibility exists for excluding such 'overlooking,' which entails the capacity to survey the entire field. As the later Wittgenstein (1956) would most likely put it: I have found a contradiction – did I have from the very beginning a method for discovering it? If so, there's merely been an oversight; I failed to check all the possibilities. If not, then the possibility of a contradiction shouldn't arise in the first place, for a contradiction is yielded only by the application of some method for discovering it.

Thus, for Wittgenstein there simply is no transcendental subject capable of surveying the field of mathematics – or any other discipline for that matter – in one gulp: such a Laplacean Superobserver is pure chimera (in this light, recall the Berry paradox and our incapacity to resolve such problems owing to our incomplete grasp of the whole). My introduction of the term *surveyability* as it is used in the philosophy of mathematics does not follow from the Hilbertian assumption that mathematics is the grandfather of all lesser fields of inquiry. The capacity to *survey* the universe of discourse in any discipline from a God's-eye vantage is actually germane to the tenets of modernity and unnecessary to the assumptions of this inquiry, for, baldly put, we simply cannot *survey* the field, any field, in its totality. The bottom line is that we are in the *semiosic* field we are in; we are immanent.

This posture evokes various and sundry suggestions the likes of Derrida's (1974a) *we are always already in the text* or Quine's (1953) *web of knowledge and belief*, as well as the *radical textualism* of 'new pragmatism' (Margolis 1989, Rorty 1982) and recent ethnographers (Clifford and Marcus 1986, Marcus and Fischer 1986, Tyler 1987). A field, whether mathematical, linguistic, or consisting of the *intersemiosic* process in general, is simply unsurveyable in its entirety. In other words, there is no 'representation' by some surveyable language in the here and now to the eye or the ear and deposited in the venerable public archive as 'facts' (of an equally surveyable world) and their meanings, signed, sealed, and delivered. The idea now growing by leaps and bounds has it that what becomes permissible is inextricably conventional, and it will always hover – because it is suspended there – between pure chance (Firstness) and pure necessity (Thirdness). There is no absolutely frivolous free play nor is there absolutely blind compulsion as a result of nature's or nurture's iron-handed demands, but only the game within which we happen to have found ourselves. Consequently, what is permitted is unassailable in a manner comparable to our 'suspension in language,' as physicist Niels Bohr was wont to put it (in Petersen 1985:302). There is no Archimedes fulcrum point 'out there' with which to move our universe of *semiosis*.

In sum, perhaps we should practise tolerance toward local contradictions, inconsistencies, and paradoxes, and reserve the right to maintain a posture of intolerance toward those who are intolerant toward our tolerance. Then perhaps we might stand a chance of constructing at least a relatively consistent account of the world, a world accounted for somewhat consistently, an account of the world that is by and large consistently put forth, whether that world is ultimately consistent or not – currently there is actually no fool-proof evidence either one way or the other. This is not the same as the dream of accounting for a consistent, and hence meaningful, world. In fact, it is somewhat commensurate with Bohr's philosophy (see Folse 1985, Honner 1987, Murdoch 1987, Rosenthal-Schneider 1980). Bohr conceded, though reluctantly at the outset, that certain aspects of the world – at least insofar as we can know it – might just contain irreconcilables. To wit, at the most basic of 'realities,' quantum phenomena, matter is conceived as either particles or waves, or both, or neither, depending upon the perspective. Bohr continued in his belief that it would ultimately be possible to describe each of the pair of complementary pictures of quantum reality with classical mechanics and classical computations, but not both at the same time with the same formal language. This must be so, he reasoned, for the world will continue to appear strange, no matter what kind of cross-eyed look we give it.

Einstein disagreed, retorting that the world is perfectly consistent; it is our knowledge of it that is in need of a healthier diet. Bohr countered that we cannot know that what we know is not all we can know until by some quirk the illumination on the walls of our cave takes a dramatic shift, and then, if we are lucky, we can know a bit more, though there is still no guarantee that this new knowledge will mirror a consistent world. Einstein balked with the rejoinder that God does not play dice with the universe. Bohr cautioned that we have no right to dictate how God is to conduct his affairs. And the intellectual titans continued to lock horns.

Actually, Bohr was considerably more conservative and Einstein more radical than historical accounts have customarily granted them. Einstein was Kantian enough to concede that since theories are free constructs of the mind, try as the scientist may, she stands hardly a chance of stumbling onto the absolutely correct answer. And Bohr remained to the end reluctant to abolish his complementary classical pictures and languages with which to give at least two complementary accounts of a perplexing world. In contrast, some of today's deconstructors, postmodernists, neopragmatists, poststructuralists, and such are gravitating toward the radical irrationalist, relativist, extremes of the spectrum (while their antagonists are taking refuge in their hopeful search for ethical values in a cultural milieu they think has gone mad). However, what they are not always mindful of is that to embrace inconsistencies at local levels is not necessarily a slide into the mire of irrationality or a happy-go-lucky 'anything goes' carnival of relativism regarding the whole (see Margolis 1991). In contrast, at the other end of the spectrum the conservatives of various leanings view any and all inconsistencies as the cognitive equivalent of computer viruses instantly creating an epidemic of nihilism, anarchism, and other lethal diseases.

It is, of course, difficult to free oneself of the assumption that what one talks about must exist, for if not one is merely spouting nonsense. Consequently, one may give in to the tendency to practise little tolerance for inconsistent and incomplete entities. One might even find a modicum of consolation in the belief that existent entities are ultimately determinate in every respect. Such determinacy, however, is dubious. We have the notorious indeterminacy of quantum events, which causes a breakdown in natural language. But we need not go that far. Undecidables are found with respect to many phenomena we generally take to be quite natural. Where, precisely, does the mountain end and the prairie begin? How many bees are in a swarm? How many grains of millet seed make a heap? What is the absolute weight of a bowling ball? Where will the river bed of the Mississippi be fifty years from today? How can one write a complete autobiography? Such imponderables are due either to inconsistency or incompletability or both. According to the definition of 'prairie,' the mountain might end at one spot; according to the definition of 'mountain,' it might end at another spot. A bowling ball, in order to be assigned its absolute weight, will require a balance of infinite accuracy. The number of millet seeds in a heap evokes the 'sorites' paradox. The problem of a complete autobiography evokes the image of Tristram

Shandy's notorious paradox. Predictability of many natural events such as the future of the Mississippi's causeway is impossible. The 'new science' of chaos adequately bears witness to many of these quandaries. But this shouldn't shock us, for indeterminacy of natural phenomena is hardly news these days anyway.

Our signs presumably 'representing' natural phenomena are also indelibly indeterminate. We would like our signs to enjoy the fullness of their function as signs for all time. Unfortunately, this desire for well-formed signs is not possible, given the rift between our bloated ideals and the limitations of our real capacities. In light of the topics discussed thus far, the distinction between what we would like from our signs and what they can actually deliver applies also to the 'real' entities of science. So one would like to ask the question, In what manner is the class of things scientific necessarily superior to classes of things nonscientific? Peirce was somewhat ambiguous on this issue. To be sure, he constantly revealed, and without misgivings, his bias in favour of scientific inquiry: he ceded to the temptation of defining 'truth' in terms of scientific method. On this point at least he was a respectable nineteenth-century 'epistemologist.'

But in spite of Peirce's championing science, he was willing to concede that since the only way we can hope to approach the 'real' is through signs, and since all genuine signs are invariably to a degree either vague or general or both, so also is our knowledge of the 'real.' To put matters on even more tenuous grounds, if every thought is a sign, and if all signs are mind-dependent – per Peirce's ecumenical interpretation of mind – then we cannot hope to free ourselves entirely from the bonds of some degree of 'idealism.' Or better, our 'semiotically real' world is *ipso facto* destined to remain tinged with some degree of ontological 'ideality.' Since Peirce's methodological 'realism' yields a particular 'semiotic reality,' and if in the Peircean sense there is some form or fashion of convergence toward the 'real,' then a given 'semiotically real' limit-world cannot but remain plagued by *vagueness* and *generality*, *inconsistency* and *incompleteness*. In other words, any and all 'semiotically real' worlds will be laced with a weak to strong dose of 'unreality.' Thus, their standards cannot help but be at least partly fictive, dreamy, fanciful. Such is the nature of all signs, and of Peirce's 'objective idealism.'

To make matters apparently worse, there is yet another tale to be told that bears on Peirce's sliding 'real'-fiction interface: scientific theory-making and its relation to stories – the sole avenue by which thoroughly embodied meaning can emerge – which brings contradictions, inconsistencies, and paradoxes to the fore once again.

2. Fiction, Fact, and Fantasy

I take my cue from Rom Harré (instead of Harré, I could have evoked the names of Jacques Derrida, Paul Feyerabend, Jean-François Lyotard, Michel Serres, and a host of others, but I opted to cite a philosopher from within the mainstream who, perhaps quite surprisingly, has much the same message to offer).

Upon historicizing scientific theories, Harré (1972) plays loose and fast with the notion of scientific hypotheses as fictions. Most philosophers and scientists, he notes, are willing to concede that there are at least two fundamentally different types of scientific knowledge: (1) that of empirical and adequately describable phenomena, and (2) that of theories. The distinction, however, should not be construed as a dichotomy. Generally speaking, a fundamental difference is recognized between 'The precipitate weighed 2.304 grams' and 'Atoms with eight electrons in the outer shell are inert,' even though present theory and ghosts of past theory tend to infect the latter, while certain virtually indubitable 'facts' appear relevant to the former. This difference can be understood, Harré suggests, upon intrepidly considering theories as fictions and taking them accordingly. In its most skeletal form, his equation is: *theories are roughly to fictions as novels are to histories.*

We read novels like what are ordinarily construed as factual accounts that ostensibly function in a manner commensurate with the logic of ordinary description and reference, though it is tacitly assumed that they are works of the imagination. A novel depends for its element of verisimilitude on the use of the apparatus of historical reporting, which in real life is supposedly under the control of 'truth.' But it is not 'true,' although its episodes may be coherent and quite convincing. The craft of fiction consists in constructing characters and endowing them with attributes at least plausible enough so that the reader is willing to accept them *as if* they were 'real' people, or at least people who are credibly 'real' in some alternate 'reality.' This is necessary, for the characters of fiction must to an extent coincide with what are conventionally considered to be 'truths' about 'real' humans – recall the above on *Don Quixote.*

In comparable fashion, a plausible scientific theory uses presumably known laws of nature in describing the behaviour of the entities with which it deals. But these entities as yet have no more claim to 'reality' than the characters of fiction, and at this stage the terms used to describe them hardly need be any more 'real' than Sherlock Holmes and Baker Street: Baker Street is 'real' of course, but, when placed in a fictive context, it is part of a set of 'unreal' conditions. This characteristic of scientific theories is most common during periods of crisis when hypotheses, some of them mutually exclusive, proliferate, and there appears to be hardly any resolution of the issues between them. During such trying times, as we have noted, many philosophers and scientists have attempted to clarify the reigning confusion by labelling competing theories 'fictions,' or merely 'false,' 'nonsensical,' or 'meaningless,' while attempting to establish hardly more than pragmatic or heuristic distinctions between them. Ideal theoretical knowledge consequently becomes itself the most adequate sort of fiction, which is understood as being 'the neatest, the shortest, and the most elegant. The search for truth, for the confirmation of one theory at the expense of others, is abandoned. Truth is claimed to reside only in the relations of phenomena. There are thus held to be two radically different aims and ideals, and so radically different criteria of excellence' (Harré 1972:81). Among other episodes illustrating his point, Harré cites the formulation of Bohr's complementarity principle, a fiction that matured when all attempts to reconcile the wave nature and the particle nature of the electron had ended in failure. Under the complementarity view, consistency was in a roundabout way preserved, since the two incompatible pictures need not be applied in the same breath: when one is applied, the other necessarily remains dormant, and vice versa. To a degree this fictionalist attitude has by and large prevailed up to the present, though, Harré speculates (1972:82), most likely the view 'will seem as obtuse to scientists of the twenty-first century as do those of the rival astronomers of the sixteenth century to us now.'

Harré adds that scientists, philosophers, and scholars in general, if pressed as to the 'truth' or 'falsity' of a work of fiction, are increasingly prone to concede that it is in a certain sense 'false.' There are some sophisticated logical theorists just as there are possible-world semanticists who would create a limbo of 'neither true nor false' sentences (recall the above on generality and incompleteness with respect to the excluded middle). Yet the fact remains that fictions, conceived in terms of makeshift theories, do not exactly correspond to the 'real' world as it is conventionally conceived at that particular point in time. The theory may appear to offer a 'true' conclusion, even though its underlying assumptions or premises are considered 'false' (that is, fictive). In this sense the criterion for a theory becomes logical rather than empirical. The trick of the trade is to devise a theory meeting the logical criteria (1) of validity encompassing the known world, and (2) of accountability for the consequences that are demonstrably and presumably 'true' by observation of that world. If the theoretical formulation is simple, elegant, and parsimonious, so much the better. In this manner, if one asks which theory is 'true' and which 'false' one simply misses the point: the aim of theorizing is to create the most satisfying fiction possible – in spite of its unsurveyability.

In fact, the principal motive for treating hypotheses as fictions stems from the alleged impossibility of determining once and for all which hypotheses are 'true' and which 'false.' Much in line with Quine and the earlier Peirce, Harré observes that many, indeed infinitely many, slightly to radically distinct – at times even mutually contradictory – hypotheses can be generated from which statements describing the known facts can be deduced (that is, they are *underdetermined*). Hence, any criterion based on the absolutely rigorous logical validity of hypotheses cannot but be equivocal. However, the fictionalist would advocate that, whenever it is possible, choices among hypotheses can most adequately be exercised by reference to their logical power and coherence (that is, the 'coherence theory of truth'). Nevertheless, the hypothesis deemed most closely to correspond to these criteria might just happen to be 'true,' but then again, it might not. The question cannot be absolutely settled.

The upshot is that Harré's account of fictions in science stacks up quite well with Peirce's scepticism regarding any determinate cut between the internally 'real' and the externally 'real.' Over the long haul, it might appear that since, in view of Peirce's notion that dreams, hallucinations, and fictions enjoy 'reality' status at least until they come into interaction with their significant others – that which is perceived and conceived to be 'real' – everything is at the very outset just as 'real' as anything else. And we are back to square one. How can we entertain the idea of meaning without some concession to 'objectivity,' 'correspondence,' 'reference,' and 'representation'? Must we concede to our status as that of prisoners in the empire of 'floating signifiers' over which some poststructuralists and deconstructionists have recently made much intellectual hay?

A further look at our 'inner-outer' problem from Peirce's concept of intuition in the most abstract of disciplines, mathematics, and in light of mathematical 'realism' by way of Kurt Gödel, might shed light on this issue.

3. Can a Sign Be Pure Idea?

My initial allusion to Gödel might have appeared off the wall. By the time the present section draws to a close, however, I would hope it might be looked upon as timely. A mathematical 'realist' of the first order, at the outset Gödel strikes one as a far cry from Peirce. Yet, an understanding of where Gödel and other such 'realists' come from may help us better to understand where Peirce comes from, since Peirce occasionally leaned toward a sort of 'realist' posture at the same time that he denied chipped-in-marble distinctions between 'realism' and 'idealism' and the 'real' and the fictive.

Gödel claimed the 'truth' or 'falsehood' of the axioms of a mathematical theory or of set theory can be settled by actual 'perception' of the 'objects' of the theory (my use of the term 'object' in the context of Gödel's 'realism' is to be distinguished from the composite term 'OAE,' which is related to Peircean sign theory denying any crystalline distinction between a thing as generality and its becoming at every moment). Despite the 'remoteness from sense experience' of any and all axioms, Gödel's mathematician has something like 'a perception of the objects of set theory, as is seen from the fact that the axioms force themselves upon us as being true. I don't see any reason why we should have less confidence in this kind of perception, i.e., in mathematical intuition, than in sense perception, which induces us to build up physical theories and to expect that future sense perceptions will agree with them' (Gödel 1964:27). In other words, in Gödel's 'realist' view there is the 'inner' counterpart to what Peirce called the 'outward clash' that 'enters into all cognition and serves to make it mean something real' (*CP*:8.41). This entails, it would appear, essentially the world of Peirce's Secondness, the encounter with 'hard fact,' the inevitable and undeniable shock of contact with the 'outer world' and its forcing itself on our senses (*CP*:1.334 – 6, 6.95). It also entails perception of the thought-signs of 'inner worlds,' much like Gödel's use of the term with respect to mathematical 'objects.' In both cases, the 'objects' act on the observer. Thus, regarding thought-signs 'in here' or sign-events 'out there,' Peirce seems at times to move ever-so-gingerly toward a Gödelian sense of the impact of signs on the intellect. Jerry Dozoretz (1979) offers an intriguing study on Peirce's view in this respect, while highlighting the distinction between internally 'real' mathematical entities and the 'unreality' of fictions. The problem is that, as Peirce was well aware, percepts require perceptual judgments that are never entirely innocent, for seeing is always already interpreting (Hookway 1985: chap. 5). In this sense thought-signs and sign-events are not exactly 'apart from' the self but intimately entangled with it.

Peirce illustrates this self-sign entanglement with various case studies and optical illusions, the most familiar of which is the ambiguous 'Schroeder stairway' that goes either up or down (*CP*:7.643). Initially ,the observer has hardly any control over the matter. She looks at it and it is a stairway going up, she looks at it again and the image is inverted. According to Peirce, this is an illustration of the externally 'real' forcing itself upon her. Perceptual judgment and perception itself seem to shift 'from one general aspect to the other and back again,' a phenomenon that functions as an example of the 'true connecting links between abductions and perceptions' (*CP*:5.183). Yet after one becomes familiar with the Schroeder stairway, one can learn to exercise a degree of control over it, manipulating it according to one's whims and wishes. In this manner, the percept becomes at one with the self rather than remaining autonomous of it, which now seems to go against the grain of Gödel's mathematical 'realism.'

Furthermore, perceptual judgments can with surprising frequency be revised (within the sphere of *underdetermination*) when the percept of an ostensible physical object is rejected as a mistake, an illusion, or perhaps a hallucination. So Shakespeare's Macbeth conducted the experiment of trying to clutch the dagger apparently before him to find out if it was 'real.' The feeling (Firstness) of dagger photons striking his retinas, when converted into neuronal firings, caused a clash or shock of surprise (Secondness) as an indication of what to all appearances existed, though things should have been otherwise. This shock of Secondness was then subjected to verification (via Thirdness) by Macbeth's effort to come into contact with the apparition that, if actually 'real,' would have resisted the pressure of his hand. Since we have it on high authority that the appearance of Macbeth's dagger was just that, an appearance, we can suppose that after carrying out the proper verification procedures, a postulate regarding the 'reality' content of the apparition would have been 'falsified.' And Macbeth, now cognizant of what a particular aspect of his world of appearances was not, would be in a position to know a bit more about his surroundings.

The mental 'object' – or thought-sign if you will – was, as such, nonetheless 'real.' It acted on Macbeth through his sensory channels as if for all intents and purposes it were a sign-event 'out there,' and in turn Macbeth acted on it by subjecting it to other items of his world of physical appearances: he put forth his hand to clutch it. However, other possibilities existed within the *overdetermined* sphere. Perhaps he could have conjured it out of existence, implored to God that He might cause it to disappear, summoned a friend to ask him if he saw it, or we could even have him in some imaginary world try to take a snapshot of it or strike it with a baseball bat. Such also is the presumed impinging of Gödel's mathematical entities on the mind, yet in a non-Gödelian sense the mathematician determines their validity by her acting on them and forcing their interaction with certain other related entities. It all comes down to the same story: the supposed virgule between 'mind stuff' and 'thing stuff,' an 'inner clash' and an 'outer clash,' 'intensional' and 'extensional,' thought-signs and sign-events, or, in another manner of speaking, dreams, hallucinations, figments, and the 'real,' becomes fuzzy.

The telling tale regarding Peirce's departure from a straightforward 'realist' impingement of thought-signs and sign-events on the intellect revolves around his contention that the coming of awareness *of* the interaction between the self and its signs is the product of mediate rather than immediate perception. Peirce posed the problem in the first of his anti-Cartesian papers, 'Questions Concerning Certain Faculties Claimed for Man.' He asked whether, 'by the simple contemplation of a cognition independently of any previous knowledge and without reasoning from signs, we are enabled rightly to judge whether that cognition has been determined by a previous cognition or whether it refers immediately to its object' (*CP*:5.213). He concluded that, while cognition relating 'immediately to its object' is an intuition, the only cognition *of* which we can be aware is connected to previous cognitions, and available to mediate rather than direct knowledge. Thus, Peirce's denial of any infallible method for distinguishing between mediate knowledge and immediate intuitions. Rather than directly intuited, 'objects' of knowledge are mediate and relative to the mind (*CP*:5.311). Such 'objects' represent an ideal limit; they can be known with certainty only by an indefinite and ideal community of knowers. This is in essence a radical posture. If all knowledge is mediated, an infinite regress is implied, as Peirce readily admits, hence there can be no ultimate foundations upon which knowledge can be edified.

Peirce's philosophy not only slams the door on Cartesian introspection and Kant's ultimate forms of intuition, but in addition, as Murphey (1961:109) points out, '[t]he denial of intuitions is Peirce's boldest stroke against the British school, for Locke, Berkeley, and Hume all require the existence of intuition as an axiom.' For Peirce an 'intuition,' when finally grasped by the mind, should be taken as a premise, not a conclusion, hence in the throes of its very inception it is merely the possibility of a possibility (a First). It is not (yet) 'real,' though it is absolutely necessary to human thought processes. Yet, upon denying any secure foundations edified upon intuitions, as Peirce so denies them, every premise must at the same time be the conclusion of another premise, and so on, in the same fashion as interpretants that incessantly become other signs, whose interpretants in turn become yet other ones. From this view, mathematical knowledge must be subject to the same critique: Peirce's non-Cartesian 'intuitions' are neither immediate nor infallible, but depend on other 'intuitions,' and those on yet others. So in the final stretch, a bootstrapping sort of coherence theory of 'truth' edified on the notion of the impingement of signs on the intellect, if correct, is as foundationless as Peirce's mediated knowledge of the 'internally' and 'externally real.' If there were any causal or 'clash' effect of mathematical or any other intuitive 'objects' on the other hand, they would be placed in the same bag as empirically 'real objects.'

According to Peirce's mediary *semiosis*, then, both thought and perception are inferential, not intuitive or introspective in the Cartesian sense – this is quite evident in the injunction implicit in his 'pragmatic maxim.' All thought, consequently, 'is in signs' (*CP*:5.253), and, rather than there existing a dyadic relation between the cognizing subject and passive OAEs, mediated triadic interrelations between interpreters, signs, and OAEs are the order of the day (*CP*:5.283). In this sense, both worlds, the 'inner' and the 'outer,' are in part a result of the 'clash' of Secondness drawn from the multitudinous possibilities of Firstness, and in part the product of mind (Thirdness) as mediator and moderator of Firstness and Secondness and arbiter as well as construction engineer of what ultimately becomes the 'real.' For Peirce there is exclusively neither tunnel-minded imperialist 'realism' nor solipsistic 'idealism,' neither 'objectivism' nor 'subjectivism,' but 'objective idealism,' a rather strange yet happy meeting place for both 'thought-signs in here' and 'sign-events out there.'

It appears that Peirce, like postanalytic, postpositivist thought, offers us no hard-line criteria for distinguishing between 'inner' and 'outer,' and between 'really real' and 'semiotically real' or 'fictive' OAEs. What is taken to be 'real' or 'unreal' largely depends upon the way of the taking. This perhaps uncomfortable conclusion does a slam-dunk in the face of those primrose purveyors of meaning as the product of 'objectivity,' 'reference,' 'correspondence,' and 'representation.' It appears that if by any stretch of the imagination we can talk about meaning at all in these times, it must come through a meeting of minds and their signs, not by the grace of invariant 'correspondences' between signs and things; through mediation, not thanks to the existence of immediately present signs, things, and our knowing them; through a mergence of 'inner' and 'outer,' subject and object, knower and known, not by way of an imperious totalizing grasp of the whole of things as they are.

Now for a closer look at the concept of the sign, before embarking on early-twentieth-century theories of meaning.

An Interlude

6

Whither Meaning, Then?

1. Good and Bad Triadicity

A legitimate Peircean notion of triadicity to which I have summarily alluded in the preceding chapters sheds light on a serious flaw in what is customarily portrayed as a 'semiotic triangle.'

Nevertheless, semiotic triangularity has persisted. There is an ample chorus of models to choose from: Ogden and Richards's (1923) *symbol*, *thought*, and *referent*, Carnap's (1942) *lexis* (sign), *intension*, and *extension*, Charles Morris's (1938) *sign vehicle*, *designatum* or *significatum*, and *denotatum*, Frege's (1970) *Sinn*, *Zeichen*, and *Bedeutung*, and Peirce's *representamen*, *interpretant*, and *object*, to mention only a few. These sets of terms are in most instances dutifully and delightfully presented as a three sided, enclosed geometrical form, a triangle (for example, Whiteside 1987). The problem with semiotic triangularity is that it evinces no genuine triadicity, but merely three-way dyadicity. Genuine triadicity was properly depicted by the tripod in figure 1, where each sign component is related to the other two on a democratic basis by way of the 'node.'

Peirce's *representamen* is only very roughly comparable to what customarily goes by the name of 'sign' (Frege's *Zeichen*). The Peircean sign, in the full sense, encompasses much more. It is a label attachable also to the *interpretant* and the semiotic *object*, for all three sign components are, are becoming, or will become (will be translated into), signs themselves in their own turn. Peirce's 'semiotic object' – never absolutely coterminous with the 'real object' *an sich* – is roughly what is traditionally taken as 'reference,' 'denotation,' 'extension,' 'breadth' (Frege's *Bedeutung*). And the interpretant, the crowning feature of all thought-signs and sign-events in terms of the manner in which they affect the mind of their interpreter, consists of an *act of relating*, somewhat comparable to 'connotation,' 'intension,' 'depth' (Frege's *Sinn*).

Extending figure 1 to include Peirce's three basic trichotomies – each term of which is a sign in its own right – we can construct figure 5, with the 'nodes' of the three lower rectangles triadically interconnected to the basic sign components – the 'mother matrix,' so to speak – through the 'node' of the upper rectangle. Very briefly – since the fundamentals of Peirce's sign types will be presented in greater detail in chapter 13 – a *qualisign* is a sign of pure sensation before there is consciousness *of* the sensation as such. A phenomenon presented to the mind as a *sinsign* is that of an individual or singular *extensive* or *intensive* 'semiotic' object, act, or event (OAE) – a *token.* In traditional parlance it entails the 'referent' of the sign – 'reference' being replaced in this inquiry by the preferred term, 'relation.' A sinsign evokes awareness in the mind *of* a 'semiotically real' OAE, a 'semiotic' object, which is itself also a sign insofar as it is properly 'semiotic,' not what actually *is.* Active entry of the mind onto the scene involves the *legisignness* of the OAE as a general sign (*type*) by way of habit, convention, re-cognition of some generality. In other words, interaction of the mind in the *semiosic* process enhances the engenderment of yet another sign, the *legisign.* This interaction involves the mind's entering into relation with a *sinsign*, itself related to a *qualisign* – which had hitherto remained at implicit or tacit mental levels – to bring both the *sinsign* and the *qualisign* into interrelation with a *legisign* that is in the process of emerging into the light of day. And during this entire process, an interpretant is potentially engendered.

The *qualisign-sinsign-legisign* trio can be contained within, and can thus become, a single sign in the mind. It makes up an even larger, more encompassing triad, which includes its own (now somewhat altered, translated) representamen, 'semiotic' object, and interpretant – recall figures 1 through 3. In terms of signs 'out there' and apart from their existence in the mind, a representamen can be depicted as an actualized *iconic*, *indexical*, or *symbolic* sign – or some combination thereof. An *icon*, a sign of resemblance, stands as it is: it is self-contained and self-sufficient. An *index*, a sign relating to (indicating) its object by some natural means – smoke for fire, cause for effect, cup for coffee – can also sport some degree of *iconic* properties. A sign's *symbolic* exemplification is made possible by means of convention, and by habitual relations in terms of the sign's generality, its regularity. Language being the prime candidate for symbolicity, a symbol can appear in the form a *term* (word), a *proposition* (sentence, a combination of terms), or an *argument* (text, intertext, a combination of sentences). Each of these signs enjoys an interpretant and a 'semiotic' object – in addition to some degree of *qualisign-sinsign-legisign* and *icon-index-symbol* properties according to their particular sphere of *semiosic* influence. Just as, regarding consciousness, the *legisign* plays a mediating, synthesizing role, so also the interpretant, as well as the *symbol* and *argument.* And just as there are three

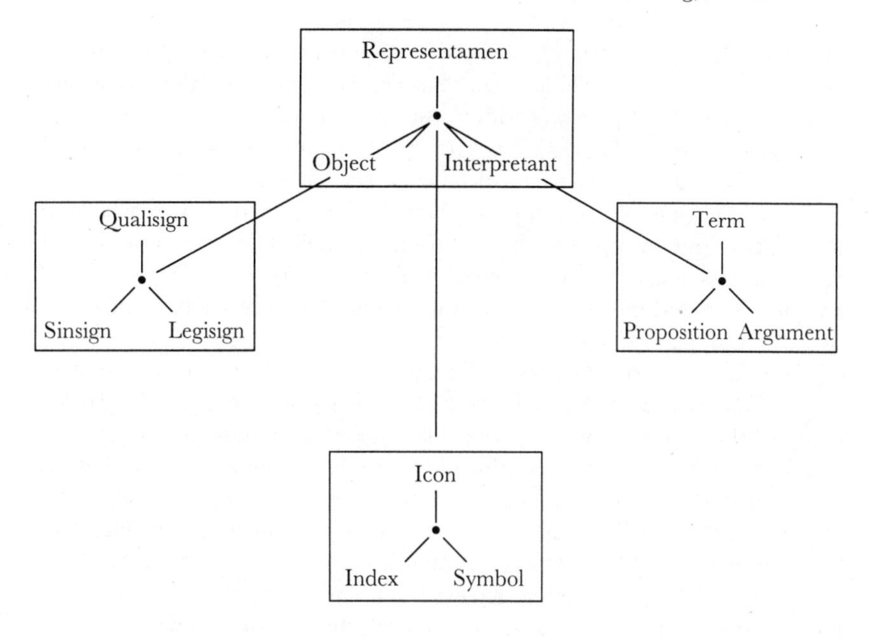

Figure 5

levels of *semiosis* with respect to the qualisign – *unary* immediacy, *dyadic* relations, and *triadic* or mediary relations – so also with the *sinsign* and *legisign* and with the other triads, *icons-indices-symbols* and *terms-propositions-arguments*. In short, the three lower triads of figure 5 are included within the full extension of the upper triad. They are sign components that in turn can make up the components of a more complex, conglomerate sign. This conglomerate sign is a sign whose character, as acknowledged by some interpreter, is a heterogeneous mix of the terms in all the triads. (I must add, regarding natural and formal languages, that icons and indices are symbols chiefly of qualisign and sinsign character respectively, but all genuine symbols are necessarily legisigns of one form or another).

The equation can also be reversed, as has been intimated above: an entire *text*, say *Hamlet*, can become generalized (*embedded*, *automatized*, *entrenched*) in the mind to the extent that the mere mention of the title of Shakespeare's work, as if it were a relatively uncomplex symbol, is capable potentially of conjuring up in the mind a plethora of images, words, sentences, and interrelated meanings. In other words, the conglomerate word-sign has become condensed in the mind in such a manner that it carries with it all the implication of its respective undiluted whole consisting of a collection of sentences making up the text in question. It is as if the solitary sign, '*Hamlet*,' were no more than a fleeting image, an *icon*, but possessing within itself the capability of spinning out, in nonlinear fashion – like a *semiosic* 'strange attractor' – a virtually unlimited array of signs the complexity of which defies ready articulation.

Some brief examples are in order. Jane's older sister, June, sees a balloon in the sky during the opening day at a shopping mall. The balloon, we would ordinarily assume, is simply a physical object 'out there.' It is also a sign customarily found in social situations involving play, recreation, commercial hype, and so on, thus signifying certain cultural, context-dependent activities. June remarks 'Balloons are pretty.' A simple sentence. Yet not quite so simple. The *semiosic* process leading to the engenderment of the sentence string is more complex than initially meets the eye. First, the raw sensation of a balloon as a physical object is a qualisign, which, after having become an acknowledged image in the mind of a balloon, draws forth an index as yet unrelated to anything else. Upon the image's being consciously and intentionally related to some experienced physical object 'out there,' it becomes a rudimentary sinsign. After the fact of the distinction having been made between a sensation of a balloon and the balloon as a semiotic object, the sensation and the balloon can then be placed into the general class of things (as types) of which they are members (as tokens). Then, the strings of syllables making up symbolic signs, 'balloon' and 'pretty' (words, or *terms* as Peirce labelled them), linked by a copula, can be forthcoming. But this further development does not stand alone; it involves a recapitulative return to iconicity and indexicality, and qualisignness and sinsignness. The mere sensation of 'prettiness' regarding the physical object labelled 'balloon' is a qualisign, which, as an icon encompassing a property or attribute of something – a particular sinsign related to something else in indexical fashion – qualifies that object. Finally, the predicate 'pretty,' when related to 'balloons' by the connective, makes up the sentence (or proposition in Peirce's terminology), 'Balloons are pretty.'

However, in the give-and-take of human interaction, the story cannot simply end here. The sign, 'balloon,' has thus far been presented as hardly more than a token. June actually used the word in the plural, as a type of things belonging to the general class of 'balloons.' As such, the sign enjoys genuine legisign properties. Now, dialogue can ensue regarding 'balloons' as a general sign the use of which is guided by social conventions and individual habits of thought. For example, after June's rather spontaneous evocation, 'Balloons are pretty,' Jane might ask: 'What's that?' June responds: 'It's a balloon,' while pointing it out with her index finger. Now the generality, 'balloons,' is itemized as a particular token, *that* 'balloon,' by yet another indexical sign, June's finger indicating the 'semiotic object' in question. Jane continues her inquiry: 'Why is it a balloon?' alluding to the sign in question as a generality once again, and is given the response: 'I think it's called a balloon because it's like a big soap bubble.'

Jane's ongoing curiosity has served to boot the token-sign to a type-sign calling for its qualification in terms of attributes possessed – according to convention – by any and all particular items of the class of things called 'balloons.' June, however, relates the token of the class of 'balloons' to still another token, a metaphor, that relates to another class of things. A 'balloon' (sinsign, index-symbol, word) is the member of the class of 'balloons' (legisign, index-symbol, word), which, when elevated to and interacted with the class of 'soap bubbles' (legisign, index-symbol, word), reveals some particular attributes ('roundness,' 'delicateness,' 'prettiness,' 'ephemerality,' and so on) that render 'soap bubbles' like (as qualisigns, icons, words) 'balloons.' 'Balloons' and 'soap bubbles' can be made the subject and predicate respectively of a sentence relating one class of signs to another class by way of various sign types. And all this having been developed out of the initial raw sensation of some coloured patch in the sky.

Another example. When Sancho Panza fixed his gaze on a windmill, his mind might have rested on 'windmill' as a generality, perhaps, let us assume, coupled with the thought: 'Ah, windmills, authors of the stuff of life.' Or more likely, our pragmatically minded squire might have made a remark about that particular windmill to the Don at his right, with a gesture of the hand, 'That pile of rubble is badly in need of repair.' Panza has actualized a sign type (legisign, symbol, word) and couched it in a sentence relating to a 'semiotic object' quite in common with shared practices of the Spanish community of the times. The Don, however, lives in another world altogether. His observation might be: 'Yonder, a menacing dragon against which I, having been duly commissioned by my Lord, and while invoking the name of my lovely Dulcinea of Toboso, must wage battle.' His utterance is the result of a metaphor, as if he had stated: 'That windmill is like a menacing dragon.' The Don iconically relates 'windmill' to another word (index-symbol, word), 'dragon,' whose immediate 'semiotic object' is not the physical entity 'out there' but another sign, 'windmill' in this case, that enjoys relations to something other than that to which it would ordinarily relate. The metaphorical (iconic) relation of resemblance has been suppressed such that the 'semiotic object' is taken not for what it is but *as if* it had been transformed into that which resembles it. This is, so to speak, *embedded, automatized, entrenched, tacit semiosic* activity (for further regarding the underscored terms, see Merrell 1991, 1995a, 1996). It is the result of an implicit iconic relation between the tenor and the vehicle of the metaphor transforming an erstwhile sign into a 'semiotic object,' and that 'semiotic object' into something other than what it would customarily have been. The resemblance has become the presumed thing itself. The map has, so to speak, been confused with the territory. (A worthy example of this confusion of map and territory occurring on a massive social scale is the 'machine metaphor' of the universe, which, over the generations, came to pervade the minds and habits of Westerners, much as if it were a form of 'collective hallucination' [see Capek 1961]).

In comparable fashion, the general statement 'Square circles are Meinongian "objects"' can be tokenized or indexicalized into 'I'm thinking of a square circle.' And that statement can become iconized into 'Constructing a square circle is like Escher's constructing his "Möbius strip" lithograph.' This sequence has been limited exclusively to thought-signs, and to make matters more trying, the thought-signs are unimaginable. However, even though an image cannot be conjured up of square circles, square circles can quite effectively be the 'semiotic objects' of thought and of talk. In the Meinong sense, imageless thought-signs, like all thought-signs, are quite capable of standing on their own. They are signs, though they do not enjoy relation to any exterior 'semiotic object,' as do sign-events. But this is no severe handicap. The chief difference between thought-signs and sign-events is that the 'semiotic objects' of the one can presumably exist, according to the conventions that be at a given juncture in time and space, and those of the other ordinarily do not.

However, in light of the above on Meinong, what has at some time and place or other been considered 'existent' (phlogiston, ether, Homer's gods, Maxwell's demon, Atlantis, the Seven Cities of Cibola, atoms as impenetrable spheres, Piltdown man, Russia as the 'evil empire,' humours) can often be relegated to the bin of 'non-existents,' and even the 'nonsensical.' Conversely, what was previously 'non-existent' or simply a hitherto unannounced possibility (the American continent, oxygen, a rotating earth, *Guernica*, the space-time continuum, Milton's *Paradise Lost*, the Virgin of Guadalupe, Joyce's *Ulysses*, sentient computers, coelacanths, Cro-Magnon man) might stand a chance of taking its place among the world of things. What is a genuine sign and what is not, in the final analysis, often depends on the eye and mind of the beholder, in addition to the space-time slice within which it happens to appear. I repeat: no sign is either genuine or nongenuine, but the thinking (Thirdness) of some semiotic agent or other can often manage to make it so.

This is not to imply, I must reiterate, that symbols are more essential than indices or icons. All three are absolutely necessary for the whole of the *semiosic* process, the reasons for which are quite obvious. Without the Firstness of iconicity there cannot be any *other* of the First. This *otherness* brings on a Secondness of the universe split into an indexical (indicating) relation distinguishing between and specifying what is *this* and what is *that* – which is no Cartesian bifurcation, mind you, but, rather, a precondition for the existence of sign and 'semiotic object,' and of semiotic agent and sign. And Secondness necessarily precedes any and all manifestations of Thirdness (symbolicity), for without a distinction, there can be no mediation bringing two otherwise antipodal elements into relation with one another.

The 'nodes' in figure 5, those infinitesimal 'points' of demarcation tying the sign components together, set the limits of one sign component in its relation to the others, and at the same time they offer the possibility of *limitless* or *indefinite semiosis*. It is this set of 'empty sets' from which the universe of signs gushes forth (Merrell 1995a). This set of sets is the author of all that *is*, which includes thought-signs and sign-events, and existents and non-existents alike. Furthermore, it does not discriminate: all signs are born equal, and if some become privileged over others, that is chiefly the fault of their interpreters, be they honest and innocent or conniving and beguiling.

Which brings up the question of the very *presentation* of signs *to* their authors-interpreters.

2. In the Sign, the Mind, or the Thing?

One of the Peircean triads evoked above, *feeling-volition-cognition*, was compared to position-velocity-acceleration. Position is Firstness. It is monadic, without relation to anything else and without change. Velocity, Secondness, involves two variables, position and speed; there is change, but no real change (*Plus ça change, plus c'est la même chose*). In contrast, acceleration, Thirdness, involves three variables, position, speed, and change of speed. It entails change of change.

Consider in this light another triad, commensurate with feeling-volition-cognition: *presentation* (of a sign as the Firstness of a representamen), *indication* (the indexing nature of Secondness of the sign), and *mentation* (the construction of Thirdness, the interpretant, of the sign). Presentation offers itself up in terms of the sign's *learnability*, indication puts forth its *accountability*, and mentation incorporates its *knowability* (these two sets of triads, I should add, are not originally Peirce's but of my own making, and I must accept full responsibility for their shortcomings). What from the realm of possibility can be learned can be to a greater or lesser degree accounted for, following proper rules of language use and classical logical principles, and an account of a set of signs opens the door to knowing. More specifically, learnability has to do with the initial presentation of the sign as representamen from which the object and interpretant emerge – also in and of themselves signs. Signs are where, when, and what they are, *for* their semiotic agents: where there is presentation of a

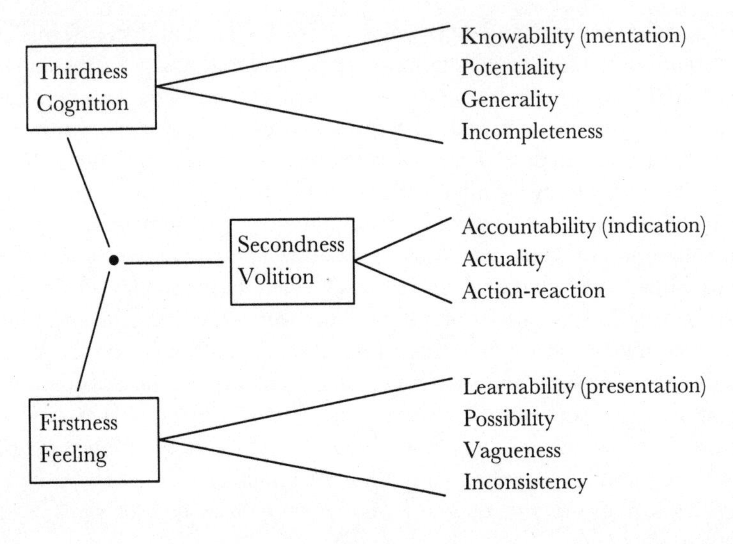

Figure 6

sign there is the possibility that learning of one sort or another can take place as a result of the sign's having presented itself *to* its respective audience (see figure 6).

This presentation I speak of is not limited exclusively to actuals, but, in addition, it can involve unactualized possibilities regarding both sign-events and thought-signs. Western metaphysics's 'prejudice in favour of the actual' gives up the ghost here, for existents as well as non-existents, 'objects' of the 'semiotically real' as well as of imagination, hallucination, dream, and fictions of all stripes, are equally up for consideration. What is more, presentation is not that of something actually presented to the mind and 'real.' It is the living *act of presentation* itself. In this sense, the initial stage of presentation is that of the Firstness of sensation, feeling, and imagination. Hearing an undifferentiated sound, sensing a coloured patch, feeling warmth or coldness, and all comparable states of imagination and sensation as well as the unmediated experience of joy, fear, hope, anger, love, desire, hate, despair, wonder, contempt, and so on, are examples of the Firstness of presentation. Such manifestation of Firstness can become Secondness once the presentation is *set apart from* something else – a physical phenomenon such as a particular sound, colour, temperature, feel, odour, taste, and so on, which is then sensed as something *other than* the raw monadic quality. Then, it can become Thirdness once it has been placed within a general class of things by the intervening mind. Every judgment, recollection, expectation, inference, opinion, induction, and deduction of this sort is at its roots an *act of mind.*

Such mind acts can be *intentional,* for sure, in contrast to raw presentations of Firstness and actuals of Secondness (whether in the mind or the 'semiotically real' world). Intentional acts involve judgments of one form or another. However, an initial presentation (Frege's *Vorstellung*) remains distinct from a judgment (*Urteil*) regarding it, insofar as presentation and judgment are two different modes of consciousness *of* an item of experience. They correspond quite closely to Peirce's Firstness and Thirdness, with Secondness involving the actual item to be experienced. But this is still not the whole story, for there are actually three levels of presentation: (1) a mere sensation (Firstness of the First), (2) consciousness *of* the sensation (Secondness of the First), and (3) a (as yet vague) thought *about* it without any judgment having yet been enacted (Thirdness of the First). These three levels involve 'inner' perception, presentations *to* the mind. There is also a corresponding three-tier presentation of the 'semiotic' object to be judged and its relation to the sign, and another trio of presentations regarding the mind's judgmental intervention into the two-way affairs of the sign and its respective object in order to draw out an interpretant. Moreover, it bears mentioning that the Firstness of the presentation offers itself up to *learnability,* Secondness to *accountability,* and Thirdness to *knowability.* There is a teeming jungle of sign activity preceding judgment, cognition, and intention, all most properly of *embedded, automatized* sign processing. (Some Peirce purists might baulk at these words with the rebuttal that there is a representamen, two objects, the immediate and the dynamical, and three interpretants, the immediate, the dynamical, and the final [other comparable terms have occasionally been used by Peirce in place of the last two]. However, here I am attempting to give brief account of the 'ordinals,' Firstness, Secondness, and Thirdness of each sign component as designated by the 'cardinals,' 1, 2, and 3 [that is, representamen, object, and interpretant, but not necessarily in that order].)

Thus, the Frege sign triad, sign-sense-reference (*Zeichen-Sinn-Bedeutung*), is up for reform on all counts. The sign, either as a material phenomenon (sign-event) 'out there' or a mental entity (thought-sign) 'in here,' is something affording some degree of *learnability* and *accountability,* but whose *knowability,* like all 'semiotic objects,' whether 'semiotically real' or mere figments of the mind's making in light of the foregoing chapters, is destined to remain *incomplete* (as a *generality*) and/or *inconsistent* (*vague*). For this reason neither sign nor 'real object' (which remains independent of *learnability, accountability,* and *knowability*) can enter the equation defining distinctively human semiotics. More properly speaking regarding human semiotics, the concept 'sign' should be construed as an 'act of presentation,' and 'reference' to 'real objects' should give way to the idea of 'semiotic interrelations.' A sign *presents* itself, but at this initial stage it is part of the 'independently real' world as a raw physical or a mental entity, a qualisign. What must be included in the equation is the sign's *presentation of* something possible *to* someone *as* something *in* some respect or capacity. That is, from the initial *presentation* (Firstness), all else follows: the *presentation of* something *other than* the self of the semiotic agent (Secondness) evoking some interpretative act (Thirdness). It is not merely a matter of a sign provoking a response in dyadic fashion, or of a three-way dyadic sign-object, sign-meaning, and object-meaning relation. Rather, the three components of the sign gyrate about the central axle, the 'node,' which allows each component to remain in tune with the whole.

This move gets rid of the tendency toward a behaviourist approach to the sign via Ogden and Richards, Morris, and Carnap and the logical positivists. It also serves to debunk any putative connection between Peirce, semiology-structuralism, and narrowly defined information theory via Roman Jakobson, Eco, and others. And it serves as a safeguard against interpretations of Peirce's 'pragmatic maxim' as a strictly defined verification theory of truth or meaning. This is not to imply that the sign becomes tantamount to the poststructuralist's 'floating signifier.' Unlike the homeless half of the Saussurean sign dyad, the Peircean event of sign presentation cannot be divorced from indication and mentation, the representamen cannot exist as such without linkage to its respective 'semiotic object' and its interpretant (themselves also signs), and the symbol either contains or depends upon iconic and indexical processes, as does the legisign on qualisign and sinsign properties. Neither do I wish to imply a mere dismissal of what traditionally goes as the 'referent,' nor am I guilty, I would submit, of the 'referential fallacy,' in the order of Eco (1976:162–3), which consists in 'assuming that the meaning of a sign-vehicle has something to do with its corresponding object.'

Eco's 'referential' or 'extensional fallacy' relegates reference (extension, denotation) to a theory of 'mentions' that determine a sign's truth-value in terms of its 'referent.' Such a theory presumably places the sign in contact with the 'actually real' furniture of the world by means of indexicality, which, according to Eco, is a travesty. For the legitimate semiotic function of the sign is that of 'referring back' to something that is *not* 'out there' in the *here* and *now* (*aliquid stat pro aliquo*). In this sense, the sign's 'semiotic object' can function equally well whether it is present or not. With a stroke of the pen, it appears, Eco tosses the traditional notion of 'referentiality' into the trash can. Whatever might remain of 'reference' in Eco's conception is that of what I have called the 'semiotically real' rather than the 'really real.' The 'semiotically real' takes into its embrace Meinongian 'objects' as well as fictions, imaginations, hallucinations, dreams, and the airy nothings of the realm of *possibilia* (Firstness) as well as the virtual entry on the stage of the world drama of that which is expected in terms of habits of response, propensities to act, and the realm of *probabilia* (Thirdness). From this vantage, a sign is neither 'referential' nor 'nonreferential,' strictly speaking. It 'refers' neither to an 'existent' or a 'non-existent' 'semiotic object.' Rather, a sign *interrelates* with other signs and with its 'semiotic object'; it does not 'refer,' that is, in the traditional sense of the term. In this respect at least, I wholeheartedly agree with Eco.

In sum, as semiotic agents we enjoy the potential for (1) *learnability* (of what *might possibly be*, whether thought-signs or sign-events – an *overdetermined* ensemble), (2) *accountability* (of the 'semiotically real' world of 'semiotic facts,' not the 'real,' which remains independent of any and all 'semiotically real' worlds), and (3) *knowability* (of the *underdetermined* realm of potentially *would bes* or *could bes*, whose display on the stage of *semiosis* follows temporal development, and the conglomerate of which can approximate the 'ideal,' though never actually reach it, for to do so would entail a leap outside history). What is *overdetermined* (the field of all possibilities), cannot but become, after account has been rendered regarding that which was actualized from the possible, *underdetermined*, and hence there will always be something left unknown. For to know is to know at least in part what could otherwise have been the case, and it is to expect what most likely will have been the case at some space-time slice on down the road. Yet, as a result of semiotic interactivity by way of Peirce's infinite community of semiotic agents, gaps between the either-or of Secondness will eventually be filled by the excluded-middle barring activity of Thirdness, and the *plenum*, the continuum, will finally be at hand. But that task is for some ideal realm of omniscient beings. It is not for us.

PART III

Or Perhaps Merely Signs among Signs?

7

Fabricated Rather than Found

The general thrust of Whitehead's *Process and Reality* (1946) is that our minds are finite, yet even in these circumstances of finitude we are open to possibilities that are infinite, and the purpose of life is to grasp as much as we can of that infinite sphere, however infinitesimal our yield may be. In this chapter and the next, I attempt to expound on this theme.

1. Some Questions

What is grasped from the indeterminable array of possibilities directly involves Secondness – the act of fishing *actuals* from the sea of Firstness and placing them in conventional categories of Thirdness. The experienced angler's plan of attack must accord with some tentative and tenuous determination at some particular time and place regarding which of those particular actuals will have ended up on her hook as part of a given 'semiotically real' world, what tackle and lures will have been used, and what the rules of the sport will have been. My use of the future conditional might be questioned on the grounds that the past – history, memory traces – exercises its inevitable force, as do conditions of the present. But what in many cases is even more important, expectations concerning what *will have happened* inexorably colour what is taken to be the case at each and every present. Fish stories, of course, are notorious in this regard.

But questions arise: If the number and variety of actual fish that can possibly be caught is infinite in number, and if the set of fish a given semiotic agent pulls in from the infinite sea of possibilities could have been any one of a potentially infinity of other sets, then could the rules of the sport have been fixed from the beginning? Or might there not have been an indefinite number of possible rules and methods for their execution? And if the number of possibilities that lie before one at every moment is infinite with respect to incessantly changing contexts, can generalities remain 'true' to themselves over time? Or do we not find ourselves in an unruly, well-nigh chaotic sea of change? In line with the tenets of this inquiry, is there not simply one method, theory, 'truth,' and world, but many? And if so, how can we maintain a modicum of order? How can we give meaning to the gush of signs within which we find ourselves? These questions must engage us, especially in light of Peirce's preoccupation, even obsession, with continuity versus discontinuity – the one and the many, infinity and finitude.

But first, a further word on Frege, if our central focus is ultimately to rest on meaning.

2. Signs, and the World

Frege is often regarded as the prime initiator of 'logicism' – the wedding of logic and mathematics, with the former hopefully becoming the patriarchal repository of all thought and the latter the queen of the sciences. This grand project called for a preliminary divorce of signs in general and most particularly arithmetical signs from psychologism. It would be unfortunate indeed, Frege believed (1953:38), if arithmetic, the most exact of the sciences, were forced to perpetuate its cohabitation with psychology.

The idea was to purify language, to rescue it from the swamp of semantic muck into which it had unfortunately wandered, and use it against itself in elevating it to the clarity and precision of the rugged heights of snow-capped mountain peaks. According to Frege and all kindred thinkers of succeeding generations (Russell, the early Wittgenstein, logical positivists, many analytic philosophers), if language could only be liberated once and for all time from vagueness, ambiguity, and sticky generalities, it could become an adequate instrument of unequivocal thought. Then, in the conception of Wittgenstein of the *Tractatus*, it could be used to paint a faithful 'picture' of any and all meaningful states of affairs. In other words, so the venerated story went, by 'logicizing' language, its weaknesses could be strengthened, its blemishes could be erased, and future mistakes could be avoided. From the Olympian reaches of the highest rooftops the world could eventually be seen from a detached God's-eye vantage. This vantage would govern the construction of a new crystal-clear language free of any and all contexts that might threaten to frizzle its words. However, the dilemma coiled within this project soon became obvious. No real flesh-and-blood feeling and thinking mortal could expect to survive in the Fregean desiccated world affording such purity of expression. If all fuzzy edges could somehow be smoothed for all time, then eventually even the artist's brush would run dry, the musical score would contain no notes, the dance troupe would be paralysed, the poet would be condemned to silence and the blank page, and even science would find itself suffering from interminable catatonia. So most likely any privileged guardian of a *sub specie aeternitatis* view would soon opt for a return to the rough ground in hopes of getting her hands dirty with the grimy, yet quite familiar, world of natural language.

Nevertheless, Frege and many of those who followed him continued their quest with optimistic sugarplums of foundationalism dancing in their heads. It is generally assumed that Frege's distinction between 'sense' (*Sinn*) and 'reference' (*Bedeutung*) announced the beginning of modern logic and brought about unprecedented repercussions in Algo-American philosophy. (Quine, in *Methods of Logic* [1950] points to 1879, when Frege's pathbreaking work, *Concept Writing* [followed by *The Foundations of Arithmetic* in 1884] was published, as the year logic became a substantial field of inquiry, and van Heijenoort, *From Frege to Gödel: A Source Book on Mathematical Thought* [1967], makes a similar claim. Putnam, by contrast, is not taken in by this 'bias.' He writes that 'Frege tried to "sell" a grand logical-metaphysical scheme with a dubious ontology, while Peirce [and, following him, Schröder] was busy "selling" a modest flexible, and extremely useful notation' [Putnam 1990:257].)

According to Frege, 'sense' is grasped when a sign is understood, the sign opens itself to its 'sense,' and its 'sense' determines its 'reference.' The task Frege set for himself by way of this 'sense/reference' distinction was monumental: to establish a method for determining linkages between the objective world and its representation in signs. Equality of meaning of different signs referring to the same object became the watchword. If such equality could be attained, a logically perfect language as a calculus with fixed rules embodying the logician's ideal of complete precision would soon be at hand. The dilemma was that Frege's grand game plan involved rendering two virtually incompatible domains virtually equivalent: language on the one hand and the furniture of the world on the other. Frege argued that while two signs with the same 'reference' – *Venus*, for example – could have two senses – the 'morning star' and the 'evening star' – two signs with the same sense could not enjoy the luxury of different 'reference.' The relation between signs and the world is not that of mirror imagery or symmetry, but asymmetry of sorts. However, this problem was in a manner of speaking pushed under the rug, for the sign's *intensionality* (*sense*) was highlighted somewhat at the expense of *extensionality* (*reference*), and language itself, that apparently ubiquitous partner to mind, held the trump card. Which is what we might have expected, since the deck was stacked from the beginning. (By way of definitions, in brief, the *intension* of a sign consists of the conception of the sign, irrespective of that to which it refers. *Extension* consists of the things to which that conception refers. *Intension* used in this context must be distinguished from *intention* [of *intentionality*], a phenomenological term entailing the property of consciousness whereby it refers to or *intends* an object. The intentional object is not necessarily existent, but can be merely what the mental act [thought-sign] is *about*, whereas *extension* presumably involves the 'real' furniture of the objective world.)

Nevertheless, with the appearance of Frege's work on the scene, things seemed to be moving along smoothly. A Fregean, relatively uncomplex sentence, patterning the equation '$A = B$,' was considered straightforward enough. It simply means one sign is the same as or synonymous with another sign. The thorn in the side of Frege's formal system is that both signs, A and B, are variables, and can represent most any set of objects. So when unproblematically jotting down the unspecified sentence '$A = B$,' one actually refers to an abstract relation between two signs, not between signs and things. For example, 'The morning star is Venus' might be written for the purpose of referring not to an astral body but to different uses of the signs in question; that is, the signs are mere *mentions* of the possible *use* of these and perhaps certain other signs. In this sense, '$A = B$' is hardly more than, and indeed it can be and was construed to be the same as, '$A = A$.' Like '$A = B$,' '$A = A$' is an identity equation. The difference is that '$A = A$' is purely tautological, the stark embodiment of an analytical statement that tells us nothing new. At least '$A = B$,' if not in error, can hopefully impart some sort of information to us that we might not have known beforehand. '$25 = 25$' is tautological, while '$10 + 15 = 25$' tells us that 10 and 15, when combined, will yield 25, or that 25 can be subdivided into 10 and 15.

Placing this in the Fregean framework, it all seems quite elementary. 'Venus is Venus' is tautological, while 'The morning star up there in the blue expanse is Venus' is not; it is synthetic (that is, it bears on Quine's [1953] devastation of the analytic/synthetic distinction). So as long as we provide extensionality for our signs, there need be no error once we clear up all subtleties and nuances that can lead to misinterpretation. Moreover, one can go on by stating that 'The evening star is Venus' and 'The morning star is Venus,' concluding that 'The evening star is the morning star.' In other words, the 'morning star' does not bear the same *Sinn* as the 'evening star,' though they enjoy the same *Bedeutung*. Apparently no problem exists, since, whether we use an abstract calculus or natural language, inasmuch as we specify 'reference' to objects in the physical world, it is smooth sailing toward clear and distinct thinking and meaning.

But more questions arise: Do these sentences impart any information regarding their presumed objects of 'reference' (*Venus*, *morning star*, *evening star*), or simply about the signs themselves ('Venus,' 'morning star,' 'evening star')? If the latter is the case, then how comes it that we would like to be comforted by the soothing idea that 'reference' is fixed, while meanings may suffer alterations? If meanings change, how can signs actually 'refer to' the same things in the world insofar as they are perceived and conceived by the semiotic agents of the meaning changes? If the signs do not necessarily 'refer to' the same things but to variable 'semiotic entities,' then do the 'real' things of the world actually make much difference regarding the engendering of meaning? Can meanings be something found in things 'referred to' exclusively in the head of the sign users, or are meanings embodied within their respective signs?

3. Frege Meets Peirce

Actually, the demarcating line between Frege's 'object' and 'reference' is quite tenuous. It seems safe to say that the idea of 'reference,' in light of above chapters, is not coterminous with the percept and the concept of a 'referent.' More adequately stated, it entails the *act of referring*, or better, the *act of relating*. Once the act has occurred, an 'object' then bounds onto the scene, which is now the incorporation of what is in the Fregean tradition called the sign's 'reference.'

But this is all quite confusing, for the 'referent' is neither the thing nor the 'object' (as a 'real' physical entity). It can be no more than the *intended* 'object' (for instance, a product of *intentionality*). It is what I have termed throughout this essay and elsewhere the 'semiotic object.' By way of community opinion, if we are fortunate, the 'semiotic object' can navigate along a successively more adequate route toward the 'real object,' but will never actually reach it short of an infinite stretch. Yet if 'reference' involves the intended 'object,' then it must be somehow related to the sign's meaning. And if so, then it cannot be divorced from 'sense.' 'Reference,' or the thing 'out there' (extension) to which the sign is attuned, also includes the 'referred' to (intensional) 'object,' a 'semiotic object,' which brings in its bag of tricks not the sign's 'sense,' per se, but rather, a modular communicating device relating it to the Peircean interpretant. In other words, the 'semiotic object' relates to both sign and interpretant through the 'node' of the semiotic tripod depicted in figure 1. (It should by now be apparent why I use the term 'semiotic object' for the purpose of differentiating it from the 'real object,' which, for Peirce, is as far as our severely limited capacities are concerned, inaccessible. Given the thrust of the present inquiry, I do not feel the need to evoke Peirce's distinction between the 'immediate object' and the 'dynamical object,' the first corresponding to the category of Firstness and the second to Secondness. Neither do I pretend to resolve the problem of relating Frege's 'object' – much less 'reference' – to what I call in this inquiry the 'semiotic object.' Rather, I more modestly wish to point out the inadequacies of Frege's logical calculus *vis-à-vis* Peirce's more general concept of the sign.)

The 'semiotic object's' relation to both sign and interpretant does not imply that meaning has been subdivided into 'sense' (*Sinn*) and 'reference' (*Bedeutung*). Rather, meaning emerges only through the lines relating the three sign components (that is, Frege's *Zeichen-Bedeutung-Sinn*). So the 'referent' (the 'semiotic object') is at once a 'thing' (though never the thing *an sich*), and a relation, which accounts for the customary difficulty in distinguishing adequately between 'object' and 'referent.' In such case, the Peircean 'semiotic object' is no synonym for Frege's 'referent.' On the contrary. The concept of a 'semiotic object' entails the *act of relating*. That is to say, the 'semiotic object's' style of 'reference,' if some sort of 'reference' there must be, is not simply Fregean 'reference,' since the latter involves a collusion of the *extension* (interaction with the 'semiotic object' and other sign-events 'out there') and *intension* (interaction with the conception of the 'semiotic object' and other thought-signs 'in here'), with relatively little regard for the interrelationships between the trio of sign components (see Dummet 1978).

Now admittedly, my summary comparison of certain aspects of Peirce and Frege on signs is far from definitive. But, I would suggest, it can give support to the issue regarding Meinong non-existents and their relation to Peirce as introduced in chapters 2 and 3. According to Frege (1970:58–63), 'truth' has no real truck with non-existents, at least when they know their place – in fact, as pointed out above, all scientific theories need imaginary 'objects.' But 'truth' does not allow non-existents immigrant status to its meandering streams and lush meadows, for the great fear is that they would soon turn it into a tangle of thistles. 'Odysseus' – Frege's example – obviously has some 'sense' to offer, though there is no 'reference.' And 'reference' is mandatory in the Fregean landscape – he does not tolerate a wilderness of signs here and things 'out there' with nothing in between. 'Sense' alone simply is not enough, for the Fregean view is chiefly concerned with 'truth' value that can be forthcoming solely through validation by 'reference' in terms of some circumstance that makes a sign either 'true' or 'false.' It is precisely 'the striving for truth that drives us always to advance from the sense to the reference' (Frege 1970:63).

Moreover, the 'object' of the sign, the goal of 'reference,' it must be noted, is in this sense coterminous with what is construed to be 'real.' Frege writes that the axis of the earth is objective and 'real' (1953:35). Though the equator is often spoken of as an imaginary line, that is not to indicate that it is a mere creature of the mind's making. It is 'real,' clearly and simply. I would, however, take issue here. The equator as an imaginary line traces the circumference of a sphere, even an ideal sphere, if you will. But actually, the earth is not exactly a sphere at all in the genuinely ideal sense. Where is the equator of a slightly pear-shaped object? But the earth is not exactly pear-shaped either, that is, in the ideal sense of the term. Its irregular coastlines, its mountains and valleys, its earthquakes and volcanoes, its periodically bearing the weight of ice build-up at its polar regions, its increasing rate of erosion owing to deforestation, and so on, render it quite unfit for the realm of ideal geometrical 'objects.' The earth is only somewhat vaguely pear-shaped, the result of aperiodic fractal geometry. If equator there be, it consists of an infinity of infinitesimal fits and jerks, zigs and zags, mountains and valleys. There is no Platonic perfection here, but an infinity of well-nigh infinitesimal wanderings from the straight and narrow path, whatever and wherever that may have been, is, and will have been.

In contrast, by smoothing his concept of 'sense' and spit-polishing it to a brilliant lustre, Frege believed he gave it the charge of remaining aloof from unreliable perception and unruly, idiosyncratic representations that might otherwise have blemished its pristine purity. If the 'real' object appears crude, 'sense' can be refined in order to present it as it deserves to be presented; if the object is short of the ideal, thought can refine it; and if for some reason 'sense' and thought cannot effectively be passed from one speaker to another, then perhaps at least we can depend upon signs themselves somehow to do the trick. Frege insisted that in spite of varying contexts of sign use, the same invariant 'sense,' or thought – consisting of a commonality between speakers – must persist, for if not, there could be no communication to speak of. Semantic anarchy would surely prevail, and we would revert to past ages of barbarism. There must be for Frege, then, a near identity, if not absolute identity, of the meaning of signs from one context of usage to another, or, by means of translation, from one language to another. Thus we withdraw into a fantasyland of virtually intransient 'sense,' signs, and 'reference' – as the function of 'referring to' the equally intransient 'object.' Nevertheless, in the Fregean view things must remain objective at all costs; otherwise we fall victim to psychologism, to subjectivity – the methods of equally barbarous pursuits – which jeopardizes language's usefulness as a reliable instrument with which to get a vice-grip on 'truth.' For the intellect must be vehemently defended against the threat of chaos. Equilibrium and linear order must prevail against the disequilibrium and nonlinearity or disorder.

The upshot is that, in light of chapter 3, Russell, like Frege, demands an extensional 'object' and no-nonsense 'reference to' it, for without 'reference,' a sign can bear no legitimate meaning and is therefore incapable of any form or fashion of 'truth' value. On the other hand, unlike both Frege and Russell, for

Meinong, 'Odysseus' as a matter of course bears 'sense,' and it also has a form of (mental) 'reference.' The difference is merely that Meinong's 'Odysseus' lacks an existent (extensive) 'semiotic object' – a notion barring any and all Meinong non-existents from Frege's and Russell's logical Garden of Eden. Frege's and Russell's foundationalist conception of 'truth' is contingent upon extensional 'reference,' not mere 'sense,' though 'reference' might presumably depend on community shared 'sense.' As a consequence, if we were to insist on eliminating 'reference,' then we would be forced to live without 'truth.' A neo-Meinong sort of 'truth,' on the other hand, is whatever and wherever it can be constructed, whether 'in here' or 'out there.' If the existent 'semiotic object' of a particular sign does not exist, that is not necessarily any call for biased opinion regarding the sign's value. After all, 'phlogiston' once boasted of meaning and 'truth' value, but, as it turned out, the elusive substance was found to be non-existent. 'Black holes' enjoy no absolutely undeniable 'truth,' but some committed parties tell us it is a pretty safe bet that they will in the future. And 'UFO's' continue to bask in the ardent belief of their persistent and hopeful followers, though their existence will most likely remain dubious for some time. It's all a matter of who's saying what, with what authority, and when and where they are saying it, the Meinongian would contend. (It would be interesting to relate this idea to current Foucauldian talk about 'power-struggles,' Lyotardian talk of 'master narratives,' and Derridean talk of the 'metaphysics of presence.' But that must be left to another time and another place.)

The problem here is that Frege – like Russell, the logical positivists, and Saussure and many of his followers, and unlike Meinong – eschews 'diachrony' and spends his time sharpening his tunnel-minded focus on 'synchrony': there is no legitimate appreciation for the *process* of sign development and evolution. And language, at a particular 'synchronic' slice, is conceived to be virtually immutable: it is for the purposes of analytic practices a bedrock of order and stability. According to this notion, 'sense' remains fundamentally the same independently of any and all individual sign users within specific contexts. It cannot be held slave to the caprice and frivolity of a loose grouping of individual, idiosyncratic subjects: it must ultimately be grounded in rock-solid objectivity. It must exist outside all individual consciousness in order that there be communication at all, yet at the same time it must be readily available to any and all speakers. If we take this foundationalist posture at face value, then it seems that we have no recourse but to toss time, process, change, and history in the trash heap (for further, see Merrell 1996).

Thus, Frege's project was no call for any sort of militant *Putsch* against received conceptions of signs and language, or against traditional theories of meaning, but a last-gasp effort to salvage knowledge, traditionally conceived. It was the beginning of the end of modernity as it had been known to that point. It was marked by that pistol shot when the 'linguistic turn' zoomed out of its starting blocks and made a mad dash for the infinitely receding tape somewhere out there without realizing it had left its baton behind and had nothing to pass on to its successor. It was an attempt to erect an impenetrable wall around classical science, which was at that time presumed to be nearing its plenitude after a few more decimal places had been computed in honour of the reigning theories. It was an attempt to boost the mathematicians' efforts to find ultimate axiomatic groundings and finally to realize the program of 'logicism,' which would bear the whole of knowledge on its robust shoulders. Then along came Einsteinian relativity and quantum mechanics; Gödel incompleteness and the end of certainty in mathematics; Heidegger, Wittgenstein, Derrida, Foucault, and Rorty following Nietzsche, James, and Dewey; Quine, Putnam, Goodman, and Davidson deviating from Frege and Russell; and a veritable smorgasbord of alternative logics that revealed classical logic as the stodgy, humourless old fellow he had always been.

And it appeared to many that life had become capricious. But there was no call for alarm, not really. This uncertain trumpet rested at the heart of the classical mode of perceiving and conceiving, though it had been muted to near inaudibility. Let us, then, turn to this aspect of Frege.

4. Meaning: Private, Shared, or Some Combination Thereof?

Frege's qualifying 'sense' in terms of some all-engrossing and mysterious yet objective common stock of thought banished a very essential actor from the stage of *semiosis*. I refer to his *supplemental* term, *Vorstellung*, that had no recourse but to occupy that infinitesimally thin and virtually non-existent demarcation line, that veritable semantic continental divide, separating *Sinn* ('sense') from *Bedeutung* ('reference'). (As one might expect, translation of the term *Vorstellung* into English presents difficulties. I have consulted various native speakers, but there seems to be no consensus on the matter [however, see Avni 1990: chap. 3]. The translators of Frege's *Posthumous Writings* [1979:vii] observe that '"Vorstellung' is a notorious crux for translators and we have by and large rendered it by "idea," preferring this *in general* to the quasi-technical "representation' with its Kantian overtones and the too narrow "image."' Frege himself remarks in his *Foundations of Arithmetic* [1953:x]: 'I have used the word "idea" [*Vorstellung*] always in the psychological sense, and have distinguished ideas from concepts and objects' (brackets added). In this inquiry *Vorstellung* will be used much like Peirce's 'idea' in the sense of Firstness, while 'object' will hereafter be the 'semiotic object' or Secondness, and 'concept' will be related to Thirdness. This use, I might add, is quite removed from the *Vorstellung* of Hegel and Lacan, perhaps most adequately translated as 'representation' [Wilden 1968:104], which remains closer to Peirce's Secondness than does my use of the term.)

In general terms, *Vorstellung* was considered what is individual, subjective, unspecifiable, and even idiosyncratic. Hence, the reasoning went, it must not be allowed entry into the kingdom of communal, objective, and determinable 'sense.' *Vorstellung*, as a subjective, individual, and even idiosyncratic idea – the most unreliable of things – was placed in opposition to meaning at the core of 'sense.' Meaning is enduring and public, while *Vorstellung* is private and fleeting. The meaning of the Pythagorean theorem, so the Fregean story goes, is possessed by nobody in particular and everybody in general. It is that precise, minimal, and unchangeable objective semiotic charge. *Vorstellung*, in contrast, is the private mental and largely pictorial (iconic) aspect of one's relation to the world that persists in eluding the grasp of a strictly logical formulation: it is the repository of creations, imaginations, feelings, moods, and sensations. Taking into account 'sense' and 'reference' to the exclusion of *Vorstellung*, Frege assumed he was hot on the trail of a hard and fast rule with which to hammer out stable meanings for terms referring to the furniture of the world. This project, I intend to argue, is diametrically opposed to Peirce's notion that meaning of a supple, yet resilient sort plays a major role in the flux and flow of *semiosis*. (I take *Vorstellung*, then, as 'ideas' regarding sensations, in contrast to *Bedeutung*, presumably 'clear and distinct reference' between signs and the furniture of the world, and in contrast to *Sinn*, which entails hopeful categories of thought, names and descriptions, and their *meanings*, all chipped in stone. The three Fregean terms, I would suggest, are most properly conceived as tightly interlinked. You simply can't have one without the others; and one simply can't be privileged over the others. If the three terms are democratically united, the very need for soothing distinctions between 'reality' and dream, 'true' stories and fictions, and representations and signs relating to other signs and to their 'semiotic objects' can be tossed. And *Vorstellung* takes its rightful place in the semiotic tripod with *Sinn* and *Bedeutung*.)

Frege's 'evening star' and 'morning star' are supposedly linked to the same 'real' object whose meaning is stable. In contrast, with respect to the 'semiotically real' object as I have used the term, 'evening star' is linked to its particular 'semiotic object,' while 'morning star' takes on a different 'semiotic object.' Consequently, the respective significations for 'evening star' and 'morning star' do not exactly coincide, for there is no absolute synonymity: two different signs will inevitable bear two different interpretants. Even if all other things could be equal, the contexts of their use would spell a difference, for they cannot be used within the same context at the same instant. Moreover, neither is the 'same' sign identical with itself from one moment to another. Signs never merely tread water: with each iteration, a *difference*, however slight, never ceases to make itself manifest. Frege's 'reference' is thus derived from what has been alluded to as the 'joint product' of the interpretants of 'evening star' and 'morning star.' Such a 'joint product' provides the semiotic space whereby translation from sign to sign can be approximately, but never exactly or wholly, realized (for further, see Merrell 1995a). In this manner, from the terms, 'evening star' and 'morning star,' sentences and arguments are capable of encompassing ever-broader contextualized semiotic spaces as they make their way along that interminable road toward the fullness of the interpretant – the final interpretant – of the term 'Venus.' So there are neither hard and fast rules nor methods chiselled in stone for ascertaining meaning, nor can there be any stable set of meanings either 'out there' for the taking or 'in' the 'here' and 'now' of the collective brains of the community. If 'meaning' in the Fregean sense there be at all, it is never stable but always already on the go, within the stream of *semiosis* (as the later Wittgenstein once put it in much the Peircean spirit: 'Only in the stream of thought and life do words have meaning' [1970:173]).

A Peircean concept of 'meaning' would be somewhat comparable to Frege at least in the sense that it leans on convention, on community opinion, and on ('semiotically real') 'reference' to something that in the theoretical 'long run' would turn out to be the 'real.' The fundamental difference is that Peirce's community, like its shifting, turning repertoire of signs and their meanings, cannot afford the luxury of sitting down for a breather: the rush of *semiosis* continues to drag it along at the same time that it perpetuates itself. Moreover, as suggested above, meaning can also be the product of a community's thought gone astray, as well as of collective anthropomorphisms, ethnocentrisms, and prejudices, and personal whims, fancies, and idiosyncrasies. In such cases there is always the possibility that the ways of individuals and communities can be mended and changes wrought: we learn from our errors, Peirce reiterated time and again, and from our learning, new ways of accountability and new knowledge can emerge. If Frege's presumably objective – and intensional – 'sense' (coupled with 'reference') promises stable 'meaning,' it ignores the other side of the coin: (inter)subjective, tenuous, and always fallible associations. These associations make up that necessary frosting giving an undefinable number of possible embellishments to the community's storehouse of signs, thus altering the appearance, and perhaps even transforming the constituency, of the cake of convention.

This '(inter)subjective' regard for 'meaning' does not necessarily comprise 'sense,' but rather, it takes 'sense' as well as something akin to Frege's *Vorstellung* into its embrace. *Vorstellung* is much like an associated idea, while 'sense' serves to bring the idea in relation with its respective 'semiotic object,' whether mental – thus composing a thought-sign – or 'out there' in the physical world – in which case a sign-event is engendered. In a manner of speaking, *Vorstellung* is what the mind, whether playful, constructive, or by the force of habit, makes the senses tell us (Frege 1970:58–9). It is that instrument we use in constructing our world. Yet, since it is subjective and individual (psychologistic), Frege insists that it must be distinguished and alienated from 'sense' and 'reference.' For if the idea or image in the mind of one person is not the same as the image in the mind of another, it cannot enjoy the level of objectivity necessary for legitimate meaning. Hence, for Frege *Vorstellung* differs radically from the 'sense' (intension, connotation) of a sign, which must be the common property of the linguistic community at large, as well as from 'reference' (extension, denotation), which presumably accounts for objective, determinate links between words and the world. In another way of putting it, 'reference' is established well enough by a word's extension and its 'sense' by intention, which draws from the community's storehouse of meaning transmitted from generation to generation. Thus *Vorstellung* supposedly need not enter the picture (ibid.:59–60). This picture consists of the linguistic commitments of speaker and hearer overlapping in varying degrees. You can think, mean, and believe some of what I think, mean, and believe, but not all. And you can understand part of my language and I part of yours, but not all. The partial overlap is accounted for by sense and reference, while that which renders individuals individuals is relegated to *Vorstellung*, that which remains unspecifiable, a sea of undesirably vague and ambiguous countenance.

And yet, this inevitable element of uncertainty, this *vagueness*, is a manifestation of the shifting, twisting current of *semiosis*. *Vagueness* is quite essential to the idea of an interpersonal dimension of language and of signs in general. The whole of our cultural fabric of signs, of which each of us enjoys a few snippets here and there, is that to which the Peircean counterpart to *Vorstellung* – *vagueness*, Firstness, qualisignness – may provide access to *learnability* of some sort, to which 'reference' or *accountability* stands a chance of giving at least a partial expression, and to which a certain degree of *knowledge* may hopefully be forthcoming. In a rather loose way of putting it, if I may be permitted, *Vorstellung* is to Firstness (icons, qualisigns), as 'reference' is to Secondness (indices, sinsigns), and as 'sense' is to Thirdness (symbols, legisigns).

Vorstellung, then, plays an essential role in the engenderment of meaning. This role entails the enactment of a necessary element of Firstness. Frege

(1970:60) once imagined two different people observing the moon through a telescope. Both use the same sign (*representamen*) – in English, 'moon' – they use the sign in 'reference' to the same *moon* (the *object*) as seen through the mediating instrument, and they are privy to the same 'sense' (roughly, the *interpretant*). But *Vorstellung* is not the same for them in the manner that the Pythagorean theorem would be the same, since 'moon' is pregnant with cultural-bound subjectivities. Consequently, the image or sensation (Firstness) of the *moon* that the two moon gazers experience can be slightly to radically at variance. This inextricable element of subjectivity found at the heart of *Vorstellung*, according to Frege, renders it an irresponsible playmaker on the hard-nosed logical stage of intellection and meaning. However, contrary to Frege, the *moon*, and consequently its meaning, cannot be directly available to the intellect exclusively in terms of 'sense' and 'reference.' Rather, in Peircean terms, meaning is the result of a particular perceptual and conceptual grasp – 'sense' (roughly, the *interpretant* of a thought-sign) – mediating between the 'semiotically real object' in the firmament and the 'mental image' – *Vorstellung* (sensation, image, quality) – constructed by the observer of the 'actually real object out there.' In other words, the *object* is never absolutely coterminous with the 'real' but inevitably tinged with some degree of semiotic input consisting of a mild to massive dose of *Vorstellung*. (Frege's example, evincing faith in objectivity, would be deemed part and parcel of the 'ocularcentric' [and/or 'logocentric'] bias of modernity. Modernity's 'ocularcentrism' was reinforced with the invention of printing [McLuhan 1964; Ong 1967], it was privileged in scientific discourse with such mediating instruments as the telescope and microscope [Eisenstein 1979], and it has held metaphysics captive by its having engendered the 'metaphysics of presence' [Derrida 1974a, 1974b; Wittgenstein 1953].)

The semiotic role of *Vorstellung* is that of creating the space of possibilities one or more of which at a particular space-time slice can be actualized in place of what would otherwise have been but is not. This role renders 'sense' incessantly transient: with each moment of a sign's use within a particular context, it is something other than what it was or would otherwise have been, even though to a virtually infinitesimal degree. In this sense, *Vorstellung* presents the possibility of separating some morsel of the wheat of 'meaning' from the chaff of all possibilities that might have been selected. 'Reference' is the turbulent flow revealing here and there bits and pieces of the observer's 'semiotic world,' though at times forcing her along unexpected channels – owing to *Vorstellung*'s role. And 'sense,' though apparently hanging in limbo between the 'real' and the merely 'semiotically real,' mediates between 'reference's' hard-core dyadism and *Vorstellung*'s soft-line suggestion of many possibilities.

In all fairness it must be said that, somewhat closer to Peirce, Frege does note that 'a painter, a horseman and a zoologist will probably connect different ideas [*Vorstellungen*] with the name "Bucephalus." This constitutes an essential distinction between the idea [*Vorstellung*] and the sign's sense' (1970:59–60). *Vorstellung* depends upon one's context and background knowledge (part of the whole fabric), whether one is a painter, horse enthusiast, zoologist, compulsive gambler, or dogfood manufacturer, and whether one is at the easel, out for a ride, doing fieldwork, at the hippodrome, or in the nearest cannery. Ideally, *Sinn* is that precise minimal and unchangeable semantic charge Frege terms 'objective.' In contrast, *Vorstellung* – the world of fleeting sense-impressions, images, feelings, and moods, a world of inclinations, desires, and decisions – is an unruly jumble of 'subjective' mental activities that for the Fregean is best ignored in order not to muddle the search for clear and distinct meanings. One person's *Vorstellung* is never-quite-exactly that of another, for the 'same sense is not always connected, even in the same man, with the same idea,' but rather, focus must rest on 'to whom it belongs and at what time' (ibid.:59–60). Peirce's 'pragmatic maxim' comes into focus once again. To know the meaning of the sign-utterance 'This is salt' thoroughly, all the conceived possibilities of human interaction with 'salt' must enter the scene. Thus, the merely imaginary or possible, which definitely has a bearing on the 'maxim' and on the engenderment of meaning, disallows any clear-cut line of demarcation between *Sinn* and *Vorstellung* and between *Bedeutung* and *Vorstellung*.

In other words, with respect to figure 6, *Vorstellung* includes Firstness and at the same time it acts as a sort of half-way house between Firstness and Secondness. The unmediated experience of Firstness is never immediately accessible *to* the semiotic agent, and when once it has entered the consciousness *of* the agent, it is never uninterpreted. It has now entered into the exclusive sphere of shared sign use – Frege's 'sense,' which exists in Netherland between Secondness and pure Thirdness, since it inevitably remains tinged with some vestige of Firstness. Never 'real' but merely 'semiotically real,' 'sense' is not as clear-cut as Frege believed and as hopeful epistemologists would like. Nor is there any neat 'objective' entity, the 'object' of the sign and 'reference' to it, lying in wait for all enlightened citizens of the community of knowers. For Frege's 'reference' does not belong exclusively to Secondness, but remains infiltrated by Firstness and in turn infiltrates Thirdness, since what is considered 'real' cannot but remain merely 'semiotically real.'

In sum, Frege, in his relentless efforts to rid himself of *Vorstellung*, of subjectivity and psychologism, departed from the spirit of Peircean triadism. In the first place, he posited that ideas are not 'objects' of perception in the mind; they cannot be touched, smelled, tasted, or heard. In contrast, Peirce believed, as we noted in the above on Meinong, that thought-signs can have a 'reality' every bit as legitimate as sign-events. In the second place, for Frege, ideas are the exclusive right of individuals, and their being shared by members of the community at large is unverifiable. Peirce, by contrast, argued that if there is no sharp line of demarcation between thought-signs and sign-events, and between mind and matter, then ideas *are* public, whether we know it or not and whether we like it or not, on conscious as well as tacit levels. Given the slippery nature of *Vorstellung*, Frege decided to stick with the more comfortable pair of terms 'sense' and 'reference,' in spite of their limitations. The result, unfortunately, stultifies language. Fregean 'sense' and 'reference' cannot be held accountable for language as a whole: they overlook that third witness, *Vorstellung*, without which their testimony regarding signs and their meanings loses all its pizzazz. They remain devoid of much of that which makes us distinctively human. 'Sense' and 'reference' strictly defined in terms of a cut-in-granite logical language is fit only for what at Frege's time were considered the ideals of objectivist, physicalist, representational scientific discourse. In recent times, the 'new philosophers' of science have been telling us that the Fregean notion of objectivism uncorrupted by individual idiosyncrasies never really existed anyway, all the venerable wishes of Bacon and Descartes, and Galileo and Newton, to the contrary. Yet, in spite of the limited scope of Frege's concept of language, much early-twentieth-century Anglo-American philosophy enthusiastically adopted it and slapped it, lock, stock, and barrel, onto natural language. And the language of poetry, of stories, was banished from the paradise of genuine linguistic practices (Avni 1990:99–112).

'So,' someone retorts, 'how can there be any scientifically determinable "sense," if culture is a motley collection of idiosyncratic minds and their private thoughts? In fact, how can communication occur at all? The community as at best a loose concoction of volatile semiotic molecules and at worst a random collection of atoms in Brownian motion with no necessary order in sight. Consequently, the notion of signs engendered in that community whose meaning is up for grabs with the entry of each new moment does not paint a very attractive picture.'

These questions lead to another issue entirely.

5. Who Is to Be Held Accountable?

In the eyes of many observers, the most viable alternative to the traditional 'metaphysical realism' that evolved from Frege 'foundations' looming in the horizon is *meaning holism.* The idea of meaning holism is a mixed bag. It embraces the Duhem-Quine thesis of meaning holism, and at the same time it takes in the various and sundry theories of Davidson, Dennett, Putnam, Rorty, Sellars, and the later Wittgenstein. In the eyes of some observers it also includes 'paradigm' holism as it is diversely interpreted by the 'new philosophers' of science, Feyerabend, Hanson, Kuhn, and Polanyi. (For a general discussion of 'holism' in its various guises from a 'nonscepticist' view, see Bohman 1991 and Malpas 1992; for Quinean 'holism, Gibson 1982, 1988; for 'holism" from the vantage of a relativist, Margolis 1991; and for an attack on the very idea of 'holism," especially in its robust interpretation, Fodor and Lepore 1992.)

The implications of these diverse styles of 'holism' are more often than not 'linguicentric.' Linguicentrism,' or from Sebeok's semiotic vantage (1991), 'glottocentric,' focuses almost exclusively on language to the exclusion of other semiotic modes. This is perhaps nowhere more evident than in the 'textualist' or 'interpretative turn.' 'Textualism,' in line with the Continental Saussurean semiological framework, is more often than not parasitic on signifier/signified and scheme/content oppositions, while leaving the exceedingly broader 'semiotic world' to which they relate in a vacuum: texts become no more than signs referring to signs, they are 'intertexts.' The ultimate extrapolation of textualism is that all understanding is linguistic (see Hiley et al. 1991). Wayne C. Booth (1982) goes so far as to denigrate visual media, which, he proposes, just present one damn thing after another over and over again, without genuine dialogue. Books are better, he believes, since they are more capable of addressing themselves to serious 'moral and philosophical issues.' Davidson (1984), to cite another of many cases, writes on the necessity of what I have termed the 'semiotic agent,' though for this agent to be a 'rational animal,' he/she must possess propositional (that is, proper linguistic) attitudes (Malpas 1992:83–6). The problem, we shall note below, is that such 'linguicentric' attitudes tend to forgo iconic and indexical aspects of *semiosis* in favour of exclusively symbolic signs, which cramps the entire process inordinately. In short, 'linguicentric holism' is hardly more than a pale reflection of *semiosic holism.* As I have suggested and shall argue in greater detail, the entire *semiosic* stream is an indivisible whole upon which the role of each and every sign, linguistic and nonlinguistic alike, depends.

At the outset, I should point out that the exclusively linguicentric variety of holism is itself a quantum leap beyond the Fregean circle. But it still has its pitfalls. Above all, there is the problem of *learnability* and *accountability*, and hence of *knowability* of a given part of the whole (recall the relations depicted in figure 6). Writing exclusively on language from the Fregean view, Michael Dummett puts it thus:

> A thoroughgoing holism, while it may provide an abstractly intelligible model of language, fails to give a credible account either of how we use language as an instrument of communication, or of how we acquire a mastery of language ... The situation is essentially similar to that of a language all of whose sentences consist of single words, i.e. have no internal semantic structure; ... it becomes unintelligible how the speakers of the language could ever have come to associate ... senses with their unitary sentences, let alone to achieve the same association among different individual speakers; or how any one individual could discover the sense attached by another to a sentence, or decide whether it was or was not the same as that which he attached to it. In the same way, if a total theory is represented as indecomposable into significant parts, then we cannot derive its significance from its internal structure, since it has none; and we have nothing else from which we may derive it. (1972:599–600; see also Evnine 1991:115–33)

According to Dummett, we can quite adequately make others' sentences intelligible because they can make our sentences intelligible: sentence meanings are interpersonally conjoined and compositionally engendered from their constituents, such engenderment being the product of conventions to which interlocutors are privy, chiefly at tacit levels. This implies that sentences *are* meaningful for you and for me, and that, as suggested above, by and large I can understand your sentences on a one-one basis and you can understand mine. However, although Dummett's conception of language and meaning goes beyond atomistic linguicentricity of the Russellian sort, it remains trapped in molecularity, in sentences, thus hardly affording any feel for molarity – the whole of a language or theory.

Linguicentric holism, in contrast to Dummett's molecularism, stipulates that for a sentence in a language or theory to be understood, there must be a capacity for understanding in virtually all the sentences of that language or theory. The problem with such a style of holism is that if this were indeed literally the case, then it would be necessary cognitively to swallow the entirety of a language or a theory in one massive gulp, for otherwise there could be no adequate intelligibility. This is the impossible task upon which Dummet focuses in his rejection of a legitimate molar holism. In essence he argues that there can be no recipe for step-by-step learnability of the whole for a finite, fallible semiotic agent, accountability can be no more than a pipe-dream, and no means for embarking on the long trek toward knowledge is to be had. Dummett's criticism of the 'holist paradox' from the vantage of Fregean molecularity, however, merely addresses itself to the tip of the iceberg. As we shall observe, this paradox is more subtle than it appears at the outset, the stakes are higher than one would ordinarily expect, and the rules and a method for engendering meaning are exceedingly more complex than one would wish.

For, if rules and method there must be, they can never be fixed for all time. But above all, linguicentrism is severely limited, since iconicity and to a large extent the indexical component – and I don't mean simply 'reference' – are either ignored or they enjoy no more than occasional lip service.

As a preview of what will be fleshed out in more detail below, if Peirce's 'pragmatic maxim' is given a molar interpretation – albeit in conflict with certain observers, Quine included, who in the final analysis interprets it molecularly – then we have the notion of Seconds *unfolded* from the whole of the *semiosic* fabric as a domain of possibility, the *enfolded* (Firstness). What happens to be *unfolded* within a given context is dependent upon what is conceived (in terms of hypothetical conditionals, Firsts of possibility coupled with Thirds of potentiality) as a viable candidate for taking another step toward that pie in the sky, ultimate meaning, and if luck wins out, perhaps even 'truth.' Infinitesimal portions of the *enfolded* are *unfolded* in concert with imaginary conditions giving a glimpse of the journey coming to a close. In other words, there can be at least some vague, tacitly held *belief* in the molar set of possibilities. Armed with such a belief, it becomes possible to project, as the result of *expectations* and *dispositions*, toward some final interpretation (ultimate interpretants), though there is no absolute certainty and though all actual interpretations are invariably destined to remain open and incomplete.

However, *beliefs*, *expectations*, and *dispositions* – the consequence of habituation and community-established conventions – can at least afford a modicum of stability giving rise to shared meanings. If the whole sphere of human *semiosis* is without beginning, end, or determinate centre, then our only recourse is to continue along its flow, wherever we are, with the tenuous, tentative confidence that we will be able at least partly to understand others' messages and they ours. This confidence, according to Peirce, should be the same confidence possessed by any nonhuman organism as well. The difference is that, unlike us humans, what they do they do chiefly on instinct, which proceeds with hardly a shadow of a doubt and with admirable certainty as to the outcome of a series of actions. And I write, regarding human *semiosis*, that 'our only recourse is to continue along its flow, wherever we are,' for, unlike nonhuman organisms, we tend to worry about groundings and centres, beginnings and endings. I would suggest that such futile pastimes be avoided, if and when possible. And attempts should be made, within the context in which we find ourselves, to tune in on whomever and whatever is at hand. That is to say, we can at least enjoy some tacit sort of 'charity principle' toward all (recall allusions to the 'charity principle' in the Preamble).

The 'charity principle' in essence says that your 'form of life' and mine already overlap to such an extent that we are by that very fact participants in each others talk. Davidson (1984) argues that this overlap in effect reduces the intercultural case of a field linguist trying to understand his native subjects' talk into the equivalent of an intracultural one. Obviously attempting to understand the strange talk of people from another culture is essentially no different than trying to understand the bizarre linguistic behaviour of people in our own culture from different social subgroups such as quantum physicists, religious fanatics, teen gangs, homeless citizens, and used-car salesmen. Yet Davidson believes the task can be accomplished through common presuppositions held by all humans wherever and whenever. In brief, there are, above all, three potential pitfalls inherent in Davidson's interpretation of the 'charity principle': (1) there is no reason to believe all interlocutors will be reasonable (Hacking 1989); (2) there cannot but be an almost inordinate degree of meaning indeterminacy, even greater than that to which Quine admits (Henderson 1987, Malpas 1992:38–50); and (3) the interpreter could easily fall into a condescending role; in fact, the principle might well be termed the 'principle of *patronization*' (Ross 1985) (for the original formulation of the 'charity principle,' see Wilson 1959, 1970; for an excellent discussion of Davidson's interpretation of the principle, see Putnam 1988:11–15).

The 'charity principle,' then, implies relatively incommensurable molar wholes that nonetheless touch base at certain fuzzy molecular areas, thus allowing for varying degrees of communication. It seems to follow that, according to the above words on Frege, if a 'common treasure of thoughts' ('sense') can potentially plug us into stable meanings, then it is somewhat akin to Peirce's Thirdness of *convention*, *habit*, *belief*, *expectations*, *necessity*. And the collection, within the community, of individual subjectivities (*Vorstellung*) carries the implication of what the Firstness of *semiosis* is all about. It is the source of spontaneity, chance, *semiosic* freedom (*learnability*), which complements the demands of convention, and habit (*knowability*), which allow for what can be actualized (*accounted for*).

Figure 7 in conjunction with figure 6 (a combine of key terms discussed in the above chapters) integrates *learnability*, *accountability*, and *knowability* into the three basic Peirce sign triads. Accountability, by and large falling within that which is for us 'semiotically real,' is especially foregrounded in the pragmatic give-and-take prescribed by the 'maxim.' This activity is most appropriately 'atomistic,' and when it is at its best it becomes 'molecular.' Learnability includes all things possible within the sphere of Firstness. And knowability, properly 'molar' or 'holistic,' entails what is generally taken to be the 'semiotically real' world as a result of convention, habit, Thirdness. This 'semiotically real' world is, especially in the case of human semiotic agents, subject to intellect, to control and alteration. However, given the tendency of human semiotic acts to become

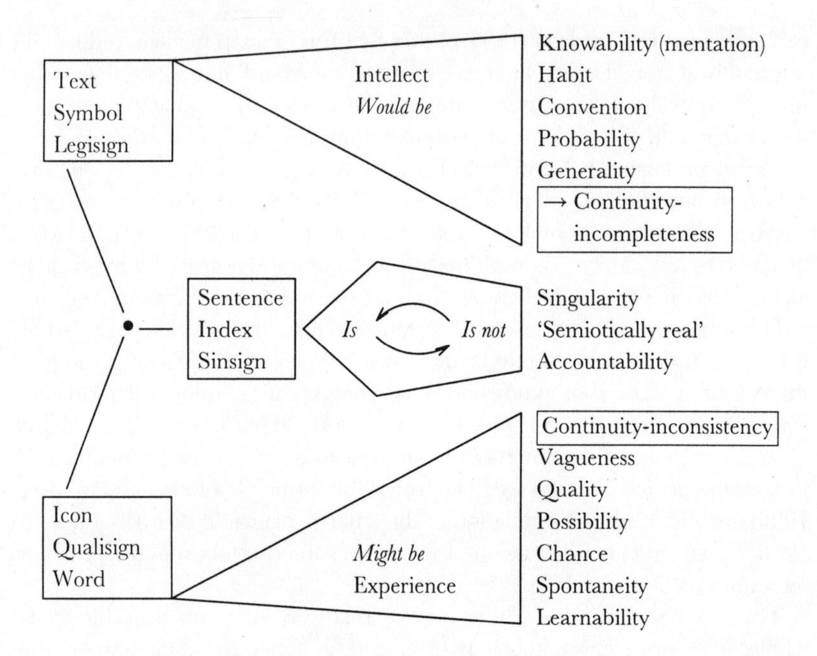

Figure 7

ingrained and automatically carried out in spite of the conscious wishes of their interpreter, 'molar' acts of knowability can gravitate toward the other extreme, thus taking on the function of relatively 'mindless,' spontaneous, embedded, entrenched, and well-nigh instinctive semiotic activities of Firstness – to which I have alluded on various occasions above. In this respect, signs of quality, which by their very nature remain vague as far as consciousness and intellect are concerned, are taken in 'molar,' 'holistic' fashion.

Putting this notion in the terms of the present chapter, given the Peircean intermittently self-enclosing but perpetually reopening triadic relations in figures 7 and 6, we fall victim neither to extreme hard-hat, no-nonsense analytic philosophy (with its linguicentrism, its analytic-synthetic distinction, and its focus on Secondness ['reference'] from the vantage of some hopeful pre-established harmony of Thirdness ['sense']) nor to the rough-and-tumble Dionysian brawl of unrestrained Firstness envisioned by certain poststructuralists. There is neither crystalline order nor a mere Brownian movement of random signs, but a tentative, tenuous, and invariably fallible *semiosic* order drawn from chaos and a perpetual dissipation of the ephemeral domains making up that order (that is, 'order out of chaos' of the physics of complexity [Prigogine 1980, Prigogine and Stengers 1984]). Frege's 'sense'/'reference' distinction, when considering the general notion of *semiosis*, is not as sharp as he would like and as analytic philosophy has presumed.

After this brief digression, and now that I have re-evoked the concept of *semiosis*, I should trace out some of the consequences of Peirce's triadomania *vis-à-vis* Frege's semiotics. While 'reference' is in Frege's conception the sole avenue to 'truth,' it by no means has any monopoly on meaning, which embraces 'sense' as well: thus Frege's necessary intensionalism – but a nonpsychologistic intensionalism, he insisted – that brought him under fire from Quine and others. Yet one must concede that Frege's 'sense' and 'reference' function very roughly along the lines of Peirce's Secondness and Thirdness respectively. Secondness requires the existence of some other accompanied by dyadic relations of action-reaction, cause-effect, sequence-consequence, and statement-counterstatement: it entails 'What *Is* ↔ *Is Not*,' according to classical logical principles and as depicted in figure 7. Thirdness calls for mediation, according to convention, habit of thought and action, the push toward generality as a result of myriad reiterative acts of Secondness. As I have pointed out in detail elsewhere (Merrell 1991, 1995a, 1996), following Charles Hartshorne (1970), Secondness marks the initiation of transitivity, asymmetry, nonreflexivity, and disequilibrium, and it at least gives a glimpse of the generation of time. As we shall note below, corresponding to the inductivity branch of Peirce's abduction-induction-deduction triad, semiotic activity within the sphere of Secondness that is destined incessantly to spill into Thirdness is destined to remain incomplete, above all given the paradoxes of inductivity. Thirdness, taking its cue from Secondness, is characterized by full-blown transitivity, radical asymmetry, temporality, and far-from-equilibium conditions that trace out a sort of Prigogine evolutionary pattern, '*Chaos* → *Order* → *Chaos* → *Order* ... n.' Entailing the incessant push toward generality, or regularity, Thirdness embodies the effort – however futile – to bring processes to completion, to arrive once and for all at the plenitude of things.

What remains lacking in this picture thus far is an adequate account of Firstness, the concept of wholes *qua* wholes in the manner of self-reflective, self-contained spheres, that are at the same time perpetually open to their environment. I allude to icons, whose very nature in large part lies outside the ordinary linguicentric perspective. Here we may wish to assume that Frege's *Vorstellung* goes a certain distance toward filling the bill, but in the final analysis it simply is not up to the task. For Firstness in its purest form, as a complement to Secondness and Thirdness, is reflexive, symmetrical, nontransitive, and self-contained. As such, the most that can be said of it is that it *is as it is*; it is to all appearances complete, a whole within the whole of *semiosis* – which is itself the ultimate First – that is, in terms of semiotic activity, it is most closely aligned to animal-like instinctive responses. But it is by no means a static or closed sphere. As the field of the possibility of all things, as pure chance and spontaneity, we have in Firstness that image of Brownian movement, with everything virtually cancelling everything else out.

This field of pure possibility before anything has been actualized is perhaps best characterized by the image of incessant vibration, a scintillating, trembling, shimmering oscillation effect, like the dancing moiré patterns of Op art (Ulmer 1985, Merrell 1991, 1995a). Its sign counterparts are that of (1) a *qualisign*, pure quality without there yet existing any relation to anything else or even consciousness *of* the quality on the part of some semiotic agent, and (2) an *icon*, not of the long-standing ocularcentric tradition of *eikon*, *eidos*, *eidolon* (image, phantom), for it is not merely a picture, the object of sight, but takes in auditory, haptic, olfactory, and gustatory qualities (sensations, images) as well. And it is the most basic component in the *semiosic* process. In fact, according to Peirce, Firstness is absolutely necessary to the process of *semiosis*. Without the priority of Firstness, there can be no other, and without what is and its other, there can be no mediation bringing them into a tight embrace and at the same time relating them to the Third that brought about the mediary act in the first place. In the absence of Firstness there is no process, and unless there is a priori iconicity, there can be no sign development whatsoever.

An example. Firstness can be illustrated by a one-dimensional line traced on a two-dimensional strip of paper (Secondness), which, when twisted in three-dimensional space and connected (by the counterpart to Thirdness), takes on the characteristic 'semiotic-bind' – of a Möbius strip – quite germane to Peirce's thought but unfortunately overlooked by most Peirce scholars. It is overlooked, perhaps, because that which makes the bind possible, that twist making of it a Möbius-strip, is itself neither Firstness, Secondness, nor Thirdness. And to the chagrin of those philosophers still clinging to the dreams of yesteryear's analytic philosophy, it is radically nonlinguistic. It is the cusp, the fold, the 'nothingness' of a mini-black-hole; it is that which precedes the three categories, a topological equivalent of the 'node' in figure 1. It is also that which makes possible a doubling back of the incessantly turning, twisting, diverging, converging 'loops' through the 'nodes' in figures 7 and 6 linking signs of Firstness to those of Secondness and Thirdness.

This Möbius-like 'semiotic bind' traces out a trajectory from the 'nothingness' of 'nothing,' 0, to the empty set, $\emptyset$ – the 'noticed absence' of 'something' – and on to the initial train of signs according to the sets:

$$0 \rightarrow \emptyset \rightarrow \{\emptyset\} \rightarrow \{\emptyset,\{\emptyset\}\} \rightarrow \{\emptyset,\{\emptyset\},\{\emptyset,\{\emptyset\}\}\}$$

In essence it's as simple, in its numbing complexity, and in the impossibility of its coming to fruition within a finite world, as *One*, *Two*, *Three* (for further, see Merrell 1995a). That is, the operation is both of stark simplicity and virtually undifferentiated confusion, of organized chaos and disordered order constituting the darker side of the universe – chaos and complexity – that only in recent years have physicists dared enter. It is precisely because of his willingness to explore this zone, I would submit, that Peirce remained fascinated with paradoxes of all sorts that have provoked logicians and mathematicians to howls during the present century. Some of these paradoxes helped spell the demise of foundationalism and the end of certainty, even in that most rigorous of disciplines, mathematics.

A brief survey of one of the principal motivating forces that led to this fall from the good grace of the Goddess of Logic and Reason behooves us. (I say this at the same time I place my head on the chopping block, for it will for obvious reasons appear to some onlookers that this digression is outrageous, though I deem it quite necessary to an adequate understanding of *semiosic* holism.)

8

What Else Is a Self-Respecting Sign to Do?

1. The Bottom Line

It is now common knowledge that, to the chagrin of many a committed bystander, the twentieth-century saw repeated crises in the foundations of mathematics as a result of work revealing inherent limitations to all axiomatic systems.

Kurt Gödel and Thoralf Skolem proved to be two of the most unwanted guests in this respect. Gödel entered the scene to declare that no system of a minimal level of richness would ever be powerful enough to say any and all 'truths' about itself. Skolem served notice that if the axioms of a system bared themselves to any interpretation of certain key terms of the system such as 'set,' 'member,' and the like, then the axioms themselves would also be capable of any number of interpretations, some of them quite unexpected. Both Gödel and Skolem were toying with the idea of a finite number of actuals engendered from an uncountably infinite domain of possibilities – recall Whitehead's observation with which I opened the last chapter. What has come to be known as the Löwenheim-Skolem theorem is no less devastating for those who would settle for nothing but absolute certainty and no less liberating for the prophets of uncertainty than the celebrated theorem devised by Gödel, though it has not enjoyed as much limelight. Both theorems reveal limitations in the structure and practices of mathematics – and in thought in general, according to many observers.

Leopold Löwenheim began work on this theorem in 1915 and Skolem finished it up in a series of papers from 1920 to 1933. In a nutshell the theorem goes something like this. Suppose we list the axioms for a branch of mathematics or for set theory, say, the whole numbers. One would suppose that these axioms should completely account for any and all whole numbers, the string of which goes on to infinity, a 'countable' infinity of numbers. But to one's surprise, one finds interpretations – 'models,' they are called in mathematics – that are radically distinct from, and even incompatible with, yet they equally satisfy, the axioms. So in spite of the fact that the number series is presumably countable, there are interpretations that contain as many sets as the entire string of real numbers, hence the interpretations contain an uncountable infinity of sets. That is, in a nonmathematical manner of putting it, assuming all possible interpretations were actualized and standing before us in a receding marching order, there would be 'gaps' between any two interpretations that could at some future moment be filled by an indefinite number of other possible interpretations, some of which would contradict the existing interpretations. It would be like the 'gaps' between positive integers 'filled in' with an infinity of real numbers (that is, π, $\sqrt{2}$, etc.). There would be no end to the 'filling in,' just as there is no end to the positive integers and no end to the real numbers between each pair of integers. Putting this in the terms I have used in previous chapters, the series would be *underdetermined* insofar as any number of interpretations, some of them incompatible, could be engendered (as Seconds) and fall comfortably in step with the other numbers in the series. Hence, the excluded-middle principle runs the risk of suffering from terminal burn-out (recall Omega's anguish over what he dubbed the 'Principle of Proliferating Middles'). And, given the infinite set of raw possibilities (Firstness), *overdetermination* must surely prevail. Hence the principle of noncontradiction wanes (recall Omega's 'Principle of Included Contradiction'). Though at the outset the Löwenheim-Skolem theorem was considered paradoxical, it is not a paradox in the sense of a logical antinomy, but, rather, it outlines the existence of novel and unexpected features of any and all formal systems.

Putnam takes up Skolem's arguments (1981:22–48, 1983b:1–25) 'not with the aim of refuting them,' but for the purpose of 'extending them in somewhat the direction' that Löwenheim seemed to be indicating, that is, in the direction of natural language. It is not Putnam's claim that the Löwenheim-Skolem paradox is an antinomy in formal logic, though he does suggest that 'it *is* an antinomy, or something close to it, in *philosophy of language*.' Moreover, he writes, a resolution of the antinomy, 'the only resolution that I myself can see as making sense,' has profound implications for 'the great metaphysical dispute about realism which has always been the central dispute in the philosophy of language' (Putnam 1983b:1).

Ian Hacking (1983:103–8), however, is critical of Putnam's appropriation of the Löwenheim-Skolem theorem. He argues that the theorem was originally intended strictly for first-order logic and is simply not applicable to natural language use in everyday practices. In first-order systems of 'The cat is black' sort, it is not possible to quantify over properties and predicates of sentences common to everyday talk such as 'Jack is wise, but headstrong, unlike John.' However, Putnam tells us that he does not *apply* the Löwenheim-Skolem theorem to the letter. Rather, he *applies* the *implications* of the theorem. These implications reveal the nature of languages containing a finite repertoire of terms used to engender a finite text from an infinite range of possible texts whose interpretation could always have been something else from within an indefinite range of other possible interpretations. To reiterate Whitehead's conception, it is a question of our being surrounded by possibilities that are infinite, and the purpose of human life, or any life, or the 'life' of signs for that matter, is to grasp as much as we can out of that infinity. It is for this reason that the Löwenheim-Skolem theorem focuses on unintended or unexpected finite interpretations – or interpretants, including meanings, in the context of this inquiry – that happen to pop up from within an infinite field of possibilities. These one-many and many-one relationships bear on holism as well as *overdetermination-underdetermination* and *vagueness-generality*, since, for a finite semiotic agent, it is impossible to hold the whole within a given perspectival or conceptual grasp.

These implications of the Löwenheim-Skolem theorem, Putnam writes, make shambles of the 'metaphysical realist' view according to which the world is out there in wait of our knowing grasp of it if we would just open our wide, innocent eyes and look at it. They also play havoc with the notion of a realm of ideals 'out there.' Such ideals exist only in a Platonic heaven of which the 'reals' of our world are no more than blemished and impoverished models. Putnam argues that a 'moderate realist position' is hardly any improvement. It tries to carve a path between the Scylla of Platonism and the Charybdis of objectivist verificationism by preserving 'truth' and 'reference' while eschewing mysterious mental powers capable of divining the nature of the whole. The problem is that this position is placed in troubled waters by a number of critiques and counterarguments that have bred scepticism concerning the very ideas of 'truth' and 'reference.'

This scepticism has helped bring on the crisis of foundationalism, with the 'limitative theorems' of Gödel, Löwenheim-Skolem, and others playing the role of main characters – though often being pushed into the background – in the dràma that has been unfolding for nearly a century. (I might add at this juncture that Rorty [1989], arguing that Peirce still has one foot caught in the doorway of traditional metaphysics, sets him up as the guardian of a 'halfway house' between idealism and physical realism [however, see Haack 1993]. While I am not entirely adverse to Rorty's characteristically sweeping statement, there are some problems involved, to which I will briefly turn during a further discussion of Peirce's 'objective idealism' in chapter 10.)

2. What It's All About

On the whole, the Löwenheim-Skolem theorem is a subtle comment on our limitations as finite, fallible semiotic agents. This is evident in its proof, which pits these limitations against Whitehead's conception of the infinite. The proof draws from what is termed the *axiom of infinity* and the *axiom of power set*, coupled with the equivalent of Cantor's *diagonal argument* – named after mathematician Georg Cantor – all of which hail from set theory. Sets, like the natural numbers, are generated by reiteration of the empty set as per the above example. First there is the empty set, $\emptyset$, next the set whose sole member is $\emptyset$, namely, $\{\emptyset\}$. Then comes the set with two members consisting of a combination of the first two sets, $\{\emptyset,\{\emptyset\}\}$. Following this set is the set containing all preceding sets, $\{\emptyset,\{\emptyset\},\{\emptyset,\{\emptyset\}\}\}$. And so on. These iterations are isomorphic with those of the whole numbers as follows:

$$
\begin{array}{ll}
0 & = \emptyset \\
1 = \{0\} & = \{\emptyset\} \\
2 = \{0,1\} & = \{\emptyset,\{\emptyset\}\} \\
3 = \{0,1,2\} & = \{\emptyset,\{\emptyset\},\{\emptyset,\{\emptyset\}\}\}
\end{array}
$$

And the parade goes on, to infinity. By iteration, it is quite obvious that sets multiply quickly.

The *axiom of infinity* in its briefest form stipulates the existence of at least one infinite set, the set of all natural numbers generated by successive iteration. The *axiom of power set* says that to any given set, S, there exists the set whose elements are all the subsets of S. For the set, $\{abc\}$, the power set would contain: $\{\emptyset\}$, $\{a\}$, $\{b\}$, $\{c\}$, $\{ab\}$, $\{ac\}$, $\{bc\}$, and $\{abc\}$. The number of elements in the set is three (excluding the empty set) and the number of subsets is eight (including the empty set), which is expressible in the formula, 2^n, where n is the number of elements in the set (hence for the set $\{abc\}$ with three elements the number of subsets in the power set is $2^3 = 8$).

With regards to the *diagonal argument*, before Cantor's time it was generally assumed that the 'infinitely big' was the end of the road, for there simply could not be anything larger. The set of all natural numbers is infinite in extension, and that's that. It is to Cantor's credit that he debunked this idea by demonstrating that the infinite set of real numbers is not countable, and hence

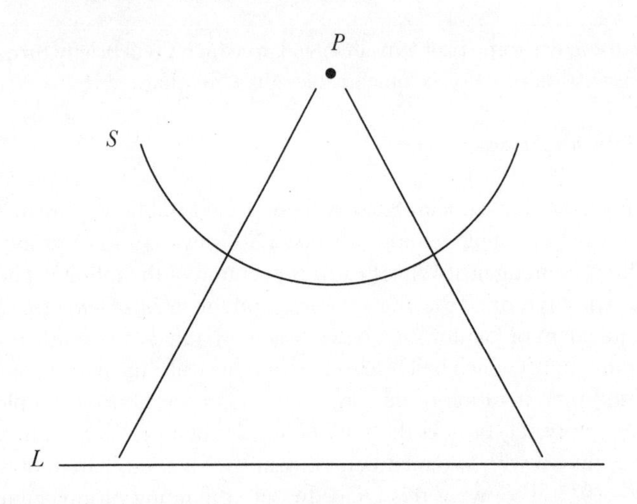

Figure 8

it is infinitely larger than the countable infinity of natural numbers. An informal geometrical proof of Cantor's argument is quite elementary. If we construct an infinite line segment, *L*, and a point, *P*, as the centre of a semicircle, *S*, above the infinite line, a ray can be drawn from *P* to any point along *L* that cuts *S* at some point (see figure 8). In this manner rays from *P* trace a one to one correspondence between points on *S* and points along *L*. As the rays change direction by infinitesimal increments, no point is omitted either on *S* or on *L*. Now, assuming the natural numbers fall along *S* and the real numbers along *L*, we have one infinity, *S*, which is smaller than another infinity, *L*. And if any given infinite domain can be superseded by another infinite domain, so the argument goes, there is in principle no end to the possible accumulation of infinities. Cantor dubbed the infinity of natural numbers $\aleph_0$ (Aleph null), which is countable and discrete, and the infinity of real numbers *c*, which is uncountable and continuous. This constitutes Cantor's continuum hypothesis, for which there is no proof but at most the proof that it cannot be disproved. It is a counterpart to Peirce's (and Popper's) Absolutely True Theory, which, since it is 'true,' cannot be disproved (that is, refuted or falsified), hence we cannot know without a shadow of a doubt whether or not it is 'true,' for we cannot know that at the next bend in the river it will not be refuted.

The accumulation of infinite sets is licensed by another axiom that continues to plague some mathematicians: the *axiom of choice*. This axiom says that given a set of disjoint (mutually exclusive) classes, none of which is the empty set, there exists a possible set composed of one member from each set and of no other members. If the set consists of two sets, the set of all triangles and the set of all squares, then by taking some particular triangle and some particular square, a new set is created. To cite a more practical example, if the set of 'footwear' consists of the subsets of all 'boots,' 'shoes,' 'slippers,' 'sneakers,' 'sandals,' and so on, then one member can be taken from any collection of subsets to compose a new subset. One can choose either 'cowboy boots' or 'engineer boots' or 'Wellington boots' or whatever, with an equally wide choice of subsets from the sets of other classes of 'footwear.' So the composition of the set constructed from the axiom of choice is indeterminately variable. To muddle matters further, if infinite sets enter the scene, then the number of possible sets selected by the axiom of choice becomes infinite. Though some observers find the axiom of choice intuitively plausible, others find difficulty with the latitude allowed by the concept of 'any' collection of sets. Since there are endless chains of infinite sets of ever-increasing magnitude, there is no method for choosing, one by one, from all its member sets. This lack of criteria for a choice threatens to result in a nightmarish world where any number of classificatory schemes as bizarre as Borges's acclaimed Chinese taxonomy could possibly be embraced as a matter of course. Acceptance of the axiom of choice, according to this argument, in the final analysis entails a blind leap of faith, for there is no proof of its validity in a finite world. (This consequence of the *axiom of choice*, looked upon by some scholars as epistemological chaos, bears on Wittgenstein's sceptical problem or paradox, to be discussed briefly in chapter 13.)

That is to say, given the *axiom of infinity* and that of the *power set*, and in light of Cantor's diagonal argument, the *axiom of choice* is the formal equivalent of our impossibility of knowing the beginning or ending of, or where we are located in, *semiosis*. Incapable of maintaining more than an infinitesimal speck of the whole within our surveillance, it is impossible to know when the fuzzy-bordered domain within our grasp has remained virtually the same or has become different than what it was. This situation is comparable to our being thrown into an apparently orderless universe the whole of which we cannot possibly hope to know. It would be tantamount to our being inside the parameters of 'This sentence is false.' We would be incapable of determining absolutely the 'truth' of any and all propositions, for sometime, somewhere, an unexpected proposition – according to the Löwenheim-Skolem theorem – might rise up (from the infinitely extended *overdetermined* sphere) to contradict it (within the *underdetermined* sphere). Moreover, given the *underdetermination* of our thinking, we cannot know when things will go awry, causing our thought-signs to suffer mild to radical alterations, in spite of our wishes to the contrary. The dilemma confronting the Pythagoreans when $\sqrt{2}$ and other unruly numbers popped up and their response to it reveals one possible answer to such unwanted guests. They wished to admit only natural numbers into the inner sanctum. Computing the ratios between natural numbers appeared at the outset to promise crystal-clear results. But, ultimately, their computations forced them into the sludgy pool of irrationals, and their paradise was forever lost.

Cantor and many later mathematicians who plunged into the tidal wave of real numbers, continua, and multiple infinities chose not to heed this apparently basic human limitation. No matter what formal systems these mathematicians may have constructed, they still allow for the possibility of unexpected new interpretations issuing from the domain of natural numbers. In other words, given the Löwenheim-Skolem theorem, it has been conceded that whatever infinite system is constructed according to Cantor sets, the possibility will always exist that, somewhere and at some time, unexpected interpretations of the symbols of the system may emerge that that can be represented in natural numbers (Kline 1980:271–7). Sceptical onlookers of a formalist bent might wonder why all the fuss, since mathematicians merely manipulate marks on paper dealing with nothing more than abstractions of the mind's making. However, 'real'-world examples illustrating this same limitation to human thought and mind abound.

Take Euclidean geometry. Points, lines, and angles can be set down on paper with arbitrary symbols representing them according to certain axioms, rules for the generation of proofs, and acceptable strategies. However, there is one axiom, that of parallel lines, that presents a problem. Through a given point a line can be drawn parallel to another line, and the two lines will continue indefinitely without ever meeting. But though this postulate may be intuitively self-evident, it cannot be verified by direct observation of the senses – that is, in the manner in which infinite sets are non-empirical. Simply take a look down a pair of railroad tracks and they seem to converge; they are not, on the testimony of human bifocal vision, parallel. Yet the axiom of parallel lines plays an indispensable role in Euclidean geometry. In other words, the parallel postulate within Euclidean geometry is much like what the Löwenheim-Skolem theorem is to set theory. In both cases what may be taken as intuitively evident is nonetheless undecidable.

3. Indeterminate Meaning and the Sign

Retracing Putnam's footsteps, and in light of the immediately preceding, it appears plausible that certain limitations are revealed by the Löwenheim-Skolem theorem that have implications for the shape of interpretation and meaning in natural language.

Suppose we make a list of all the attributes possessed by *horses* and all those possessed by *unicorns*. Then someone discovers what are to all appearances two new species, let us call them *corses* and *unihorns* (this example is a counterpart to Goodman's 'grue/bleen' alluded to in the Preamble and briefly discussed in chapter 12). These unexpected beasts possess the same attributes as horses and unicorns respectively, and they manifest some other as yet undefined characteristics as well.

In other words, our 'axiom system' and its attendant 'taxonomy' including horses and unicorns as designed to qualify a unique class of 'real' world and imaginary objects failed miserably. And if an 'axiom' fails in one case, it can fail in an indefinite number of cases – consequently, to repeat, it is not entirely outside the realm of possibility that defeat can become triumph, friend can become foe, windmills can become giants, and UFOs can become as 'real' as horses or unicorn pictures. Whereas Gödel's theorem specifies that no set of axioms can absolutely prove all its theorems – hence it is *incomplete* – except in such case that it contains an *inconsistent* statement or two – the Löwenheim-Skolem proof opens the door to an unlimited number of interpretations. Each new interpretation is slightly to radically distinct from the one intended and expected by a given set of axioms. In other words, the axioms do not establish definite limits on the nature of a given interpretation (from the *underdetermined* sphere) engendered from the range of all possible interpretations (from the *overdetermined* sphere). The upshot, regarding Putnam's extrapolation of the Löwenheim-Skolem theorem, is that systems of abstract thought and of classification cannot be unambiguously constituted. They are either *inconsistent* or *incomplete*, or they are both. If *inconsistency* inheres, then there is no knowing when a new interpretation may arise and what its shape may be. If *incompleteness* is the case, then no matter how many interpretations have been incorporated into a system, something else can always be added. (In this vein, Morris Kline writes that the Löwenheim-Skolem theorem 'is as startling as Gödel's incompleteness theorem. It is another blow to the axiomatic method which from 1900 even to recent times seemed to be the only sound approach, and is still the one employed by the logicists, formalists, and set theorists' [1980:272]. And A.W. Moore writes that the two theorems 'are as far beyond controversy as any piece of pure mathematics can be' [1990:159].)

This *inconsistency-incompleteness* posit throws traditional quests for metaphysical realism, objectivity, certainty, and 'truth' (that is, foundations) for a loop. The assumption has had it that if a set of strings of signs (in a formal or natural language) is finite – though theoretically it could go on forever – and if the number of signs in the language is countable, then the set of strings is countable as well. A model, theory, or set of 'axioms' with which to account for the set of strings itself consists of a string of signs (which, as symbols, are meaningless in themselves, that is, they take on meaning by convention). It is the task of the mathematician, logician, scientists, linguist, or analyst of whatever stripe to place the model, theory, or 'axioms' in correspondence with the original set of signs, say, the observation sentences regarding a collection of phenomena. Then the otherwise meaningless signs can be given an interpretation, and, it follows as a matter of course, a meaning.

But that is the problem. Meanings are not in the model, the theory, or the 'axioms.' They are presumably slapped onto signs after the fact of the model, theory, or 'axiom's' having been related to (given 'reference to') the string of signs in question (DeLong 1970). That is, the semiotic agent has the responsibility of endowing the theory, model, and 'axioms' with meaning, for otherwise they cannot account for the string of signs. Without such meanings, all signs present are lacking in genuineness: they can enjoy no full-blown interpretant, nor can they take on any determinate meaning as a result of their interaction with the semiotic agent. It is as if we were to say: 'We cannot be absolutely certain of the meaning of any statement; of the meaning of *that* statement we can be absolutely certain.' A pragmatic counterpart of the liar's semantic paradox as put forth in the Preamble comes back to haunt us. (This conception of things falls quite closely in line with Peirce's contention that full-blown meaning is irreducible to quality [Firstness] and dyadic relation [Secondness]: it is of the nature of triadicity [Thirdness]. In this sense, and in view of the genuinely triadic depictions of the sign from figure 1 onward, the meaning of a sign is itself another meaning, and that meaning is in its own turn another sign, and so on [*CP*:1.339, 1.343–8, 2.292–3].)

This presumed impotency of what has been construed as 'meaningless' signs surely comes as no surprise; the logical positivists were harping on it decades ago, though for different reasons. We must bear in mind in view of the Master's counsel in the Preamble, however, that what from some vantage or other go as 'meaningless' signs are not necessarily in any form or fashion inferior to 'meaningful' signs. They are simply signs among other signs. They happen to lack meaning. 'Fine and dandy,' one might wish to respond. 'We still have our storehouse of "meaningful" signs, so not to worry.' The problem is that an attempt is customarily made to fix 'reference,' interpretation, and meaning in terms of the decidability of 'truth' regarding strings of signs. But the very idea of 'truth' can and often does underdetermine 'reference,' as well as interpretation and meaning. And unexpected models, theories, and 'axioms' and their interpretations and meanings can then leap onto the scene to taunt their creator.

Actually, a model, theory, or 'axiom' can be decidably 'true' in terms of its nature as a purely formal language. But that is no reason to believe this 'truth' cannot account for a variety of interpretations and meanings, some of them incompatible – that is, given the *axiom of infinity*, the *axiom of choice* allows for any number of unintended (unexpected) sets to be constructed. And whatever unruly set of signs happens to enter the mind of the semiotic agent, even though they are deemed 'true,' they are, in spite of that agent's better judgment, always already interpreted and meaningful in some respect or other. The confidence-building program of mapping uninterpreted and meaningless but 'true' theoretical or modelling signs onto the *corpus* of signs under scrutiny that presumably bear 'reference' but no determinate interpretation or meaning, and only then giving them interpretation and meaning, is delusory. It belongs to the 'metaphysical realist' doctrine of 'objective representation' and 'correspondence' between signs and that to which they 'refer.'

The relationship between language and 'reality' (that is, 'metaphysical realism') that dominated philosophy from the turn of the present century until its midpoint had a grand bifurcation between language on the one hand and objects, acts, and events on the other. The world was 'out there' ready and willing to submit to the language most adequately mirroring it. After all, is it not reasonable to treat as 'true' a sentence that accurately labels a state of affairs? So it seemed. During the flux and flows of everyday life, however, things simply don't stack up so neatly. Take one of our more formal settings: the courtroom. A witness sworn to tell the 'truth,' the whole 'truth,' and nothing but the 'truth,' testifies that a man in a red shirt shot the storekeeper. She described what happened: her words presumably 'referred' and 'corresponded' to, 'represented,' and ultimately portrayed, the state of affairs at a particular space-time slice in her past. If the judge and jury are sufficiently convinced by the prosecuting laywer's argument in part based on the young lady's testimony, then the 'truth' became known – at least as far as they are concerned. It would appear that there's no more to it than that. There are words 'here-now' and a presumed 'real world' event 'there-then,' the two meet in receptive and well-intentioned minds taking them in more or less the same way, and the result is a set of meanings bringing all parties together into a somewhat coherent, collective whole. According to 'metaphysical realism,' it is a matter of here the witness and there the state of affairs she transparently sees, and here the language and there the state of affairs she describes. If we could all just be honest, the 'truth' would surely be known.

But this is the product of dyadic thinking. If the 'metaphysical realists' with visions of 'objectivity' were to have their say, there would be no genuine triadicity. It would be as if the *sign* (*representamen*, *R*) in terms of a model, theory, or set of 'axioms' were related to its *object* (*O*), and then injected with *meaning*, before any genuine *interpretant* (*I*) had been allowed through the doorway. '"Here"-the-sign, "there" the object' encompasses no more than one-third of what is customarily taken for granted as the Peirce semiotic 'triangle.' It is simply a dyadic relation: *R*—*O*. By means of this dyad, and according to 'metaphysical realism,' *sign* and *object* simply combine to yield meaning, and the isosceles monolith is

completed: $O \swarrow \overset{R}{|} \searrow I$.

The problem is that, *pace* the Preamble, three dyads do not genuine triadicity make. In the legitimate Peircean sense, the *I* was never absent, and there was never any absence of Ø, or the 'node' – noticed absence – but rather, the *I* was always there as a third partner in the *semiosic* dance, and the 'node' was always there as the pivot about which

the free-form dance was unfolding: $O \swarrow \overset{R}{|} \searrow I$. In another way of putting it, the *sign*, as *symbol*, is never dismembered but always interpreted within some context and in some form or other, however *de-generate* the resulting *interpretant* may be. (I should point out that *de-generate* signs are by no means 'degenerate' in the ordinary use of the term as 'decadent,' 'retrograde,' 'unethical,' or whatever. Rather, *de-generacy* in its Peircean use hails from mathematics. A *de-generate* sign is a sign whose *interpretant* has not [yet] entered into, or has *de-generated* from the status of, genuine Thirdness [for further, see Tursman 1987 and Merrell 1995a].)

In a genuine, *non-de-generate* sense, then, our witness's testimony actually consisted of signs relating *to* some event *for* someone *in* some respect or capacity. That 'someone' can be the jury, the judge, an overbearing prosecuting attorney, an irresistibly charming defence lawyer, a gang member in the audience glaring at her and scaring her out of her wits, a wad of payoff money in her purse; or, in the best of all worlds, that 'someone' can be the collective whole of her fellow citizens to whom she wants to tell her story as she (believes she) saw it – which might or might not be the 'whole truth.' On all accounts, context is all-important. It is the necessary ingredient for genuinely triadic sign interactivity.

'But what, more precisely, has all this to do with the idea of meaning from within the sphere of *semiosis*?'

4. Finding the Road Back

In attempting a response, let me state that above all, I trust we can agree that genuine tradicity compels us to recognize the necessity of discarding 'metaphysical realism' and its notion of 'objectivist representation.'

In fact, Putnam has shed himself of the fetters of 'metaphysical realism' quite effectively, I believe. He battled long and hard against the theory that the meaning of formal symbols in the abstract disciplines is accessible by way of direct and unmediated dyadic 'correspondence' between signs and the world, or between signs and any other dyadic model (interpretation) of the world for that matter. If there were such 'correspondence,' the very idea of meaning would be violated (Putnam 1981:22–74, 1983b:1–25). In fact, Putnam takes a giant step further, arguing that his conclusions apply to all other disciplines as well, though, to repeat, he has been criticized in this regard. As I have contended throughout this essay, following Peirce's semiotics, signs of the genuine sort – that is, of generality, of Thirdness, most proper to the abstract disciplines – are always mediated, and their *act of signification* cannot but be indirect, since that very act depends upon iconicity and indexicality for its existence. The result is a concept of the sign that fuses binary demarcation between sign, object, and meaning, and linguistic and nonlinguistic signs. All disciplines, formal and nonformal alike, fall under the purview of the Peircean sign.

The meat of the matter is that an adequate notion of mediated and indirect *acts of signification* cannot be forthcoming from consideration merely of *what there is* (Secondness), but, in addition, of what *might be* (Firstness) and what *would be* (Thirdness), which once again evokes the 'pragmatic maxim' – as well as abduction, induction, and deduction. The possibility of all conceivable ramifications of a sentence embodied in the 'maxim' entails an exercise for engendering meaning. But the notion of all conceivable ramifications demands the interpreter's dipping into the infinite set of *possibilia* and emerging with an abduction in hand. The problem of the finite and the infinite thus re-enters – that is, the difference between *what is* (by induction), on the one hand, and, on the other, what *might be* (the unlimited possibilities for abduction) and what *would be* (the projection of deduction). The *might be*, as it is construed here, implies in number theory the *actual infinite*, and the *would be* entails the sense of ongoing moves toward the *potential infinite*. The later Wittgenstein (1956) and others criticized the Dedekind/Cantor definition of an actual *infinite set* on the grounds that it does violence to the barrier between a boundless series in the process of being constructed and the idea of totality: the process of construction involves induction and the finite application of rules by means of actual signs, whereas an *infinite set* puts *generality* in the place of *actuals*. In Peircean terms, acts of construction belong to actuals, Secondness, while the notion of a push toward the infinitely receding horizon entails *generality*, Thirdness.

In the empirical sciences Galileo was the first to dwell obsessively on this problem of infinity and finitude. In his *Dialogue Concerning Two New Sciences* he notes that a three-inch line contains the same number of points as a line twice as long, concluding that 'the attributes "larger," and "smaller," and "equal," have no place either in comparing infinite quantities with each other or in comparing infinite with finite quantities' (Galileo 1954:33). He demonstrated his theory by setting up a one-to-one correspondence between the natural numbers and their squares in order to demonstrate essentially what we have in figure 8, following Cantor's diagonal proof. A century later Leibniz extended Galileo's idea by demonstrating that the number of even numbers must be the same as the total number of numbers. During the last century, Bolzano, in *Paradoxes of the Infinite* (1950), went further in demonstrating that any part of an infinite collection is equal to the whole. In this century, it hardly needs saying, paradoxes of infinity have proliferated.

Peirce is very much within this current of thought, given his concepts of *vagueness* and *generality* and their apparent incompatibility with *actuals*, or in another way of putting it, the abrogation of the principles of noncontradiction and the excluded middle, and their conflict with classical principles. Given the *underdetermined* sphere as described above, an undefined and indefinite number of actuals can fit into an undefined and indefinite number of interpretations, along with their attendant meanings – which imply their respective world-views, models, theories, dogmas, ideologies, and in general beliefs. And the excluded-middle principle wanes. On the other hand, given the *overdetermined* sphere, an undefined and indefinite number of *actuals* can be engendered to take their place within their respective world-views, models, theories, dogmas, ideologies, and beliefs. Since there is no guarantee that all possible *actuals*, past, present, and future, will respect the principle of noncontradiction, it does not necessarily carry much weight.

It's the now familiar story: upon considering *overdetermination* in conjunction with its complement, *underdetermination*, traditional notions of 'reference,' 'correspondence,' 'representation,' 'foundations,' and 'truth' fall by the wayside. If we could get rid of the obstinate idea that we cannot do without these concepts, then, perhaps, we might be able to strike a happy combination of frequent visits to that sauna room of *vagueness*, take *actuals* however we can and wherever and whenever we can find them and put them to use with the tools at hand, and push toward some *general* view with respect to what it is all about.

Back to the Löwenheim-Skolem theorem and its relevance for Peirce.

5. On Actual Signs

Insofar as I understand it, the Löwenheim-Skolem theorem has basically to do with the possibility of sign *iteration*, of the development of a series according to certain rules and consideration of whether or not that series is determinable, which has a definite bearing on Peirce's sign theory.

Take, for example, iteration of the set-theory sort as briefly described above and in light of the scheme embodied in figure 9. Call 0 Peirce's 'node' preceding the becoming of conscious awareness *of* a sign. Call 1 an ordinal, a First, the representamen (or, from within other trichotomies, a qualisign, icon, term or word) *of* which there is now consciousness. Call 2 a Second, the 'semiotic object' (or a sinsign, index, proposition, or sentence). And call 3 a Third, the interpretant (or a legisign, symbol, argument, or text). A pure state of pre-Firstness is $\{0\}$, the open set of *possibilia.* A First is $\{0;1\}$, after some possibility has emerged. A Second is $\{0;1;2\}$, the result of the sign's having come into contact with something else, and is now an 'object' that can be acted upon by some agent. And a Third is $\{0;1;2;3\}$, sign interaction during the course of which a mediator and moderator brings about ongoing interaction between a First and a Second and between them and that mediating Third itself. (Elsewhere [Merrell 1995a] I clarify the distinction between 0 and $\emptyset$. As I mentioned above, $\emptyset$, the empty set, would actually be more adequately qualified as 'noticed absence' and 0 as 'nothingness' or 'emptiness.' Here, for purposes of economy, I eschew consideration of $\emptyset$ and relate 0 to the 'node,' without further complication of the matter.)

This series can constitute a first sign. Call it x, $[\{0;1;2;3\} = x]$. By iteration of a second tandem, and by succeeding iterations or recursions, an indefinite number of signs can be cumulatively engendered as follows:

$1_a = \{\{0,1\},i\}$
$2_a = \{\{0,1,2\},i\}$
$3_a = \{\{0,1,2,3\},i\}$
$\{\{0,1,2,3\},i\} = j$
$1_b = \{\{0,1\},j\}$
$2_b = \{\{0,1,2\},j\}$
$3_b = \{\{0,1,2,3\},j\}$
$\{\{0,1,2,3\},j\} = k$
ad infinitum (compare to figure 3).

By iteration, the scheme in figure 9 can potentially become the Set of all semiotic sets, the encapsulation of the *semiosic* process, of the radical interconnectedness

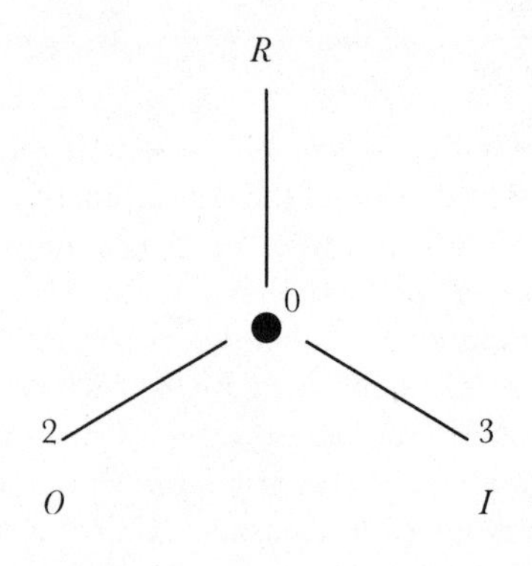

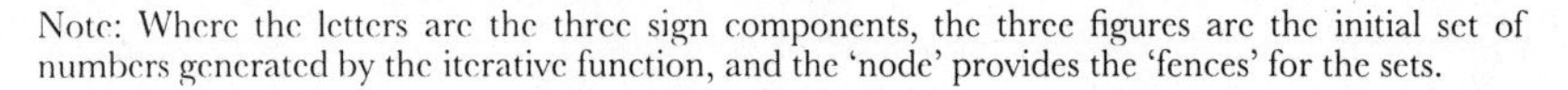
Note: Where the letters are the three sign components, the three figures are the initial set of numbers generated by the iterative function, and the 'node' provides the 'fences' for the sets.

Figure 9

of all signs. The very idea of such interconnectedness is mind-boggling; it is unimaginable, virtually unthinkable; it threatens to place us within the hoary playground of transfinite mathematics.

And with this observation the Löwenheim-Skolem theorem resurfaces. Given the infinity of possibilities, there is no way in the kingdom of our finite world for knowing absolutely whether a set of signs is *complete* (*general* in the full sense) and *consistent* (*nonvague*), and whether in the future it will not be subject to some unexpected alteration – due to the *underdetermination* of whatever signs there are and the *overdetermination* of the range of all possible signs. Nevertheless, in the everyday process of sign engenderment, the problem hardly arises. As *iteration* of Peirce's categories goes forth, Secondness, the realm of discrete, actualized signs, appears, at least to the semiotic agent doing the semiotizing, rather comparable to a finite string extracted from the series of natural numbers: it seems, for all intents and purposes, as easy as counting. The full range of Thirdness, by contrast, is comparable to Aleph null, Cantor's first infinity, which is properly countable. However, in light of the above, given the axiom of choice and the Löwenheim-Skolem theorem, and since the semiotic agent in question is limited to her fallible finitude, there can be no more than an infinitesimal grasp of the infinitudinous multiplicity evinced by the realm of Thirdness. In addition, an infinity of possible models, theories, and 'axioms' (and their interpretations and meanings), can be given applications within the realm of Secondness. Hence, it is at least intuitively obvious that any and all applications cannot but remain *incomplete*, no matter how general, universal, and all-encompassing their pretensions. By far the most difficult concept to grasp is that of the domain of all possible possibles that can give rise to Firsts – 'utter *vagueness*' as Peirce put it. This domain is comparable to Cantor's nondenumerable continuum, *c*, which liberally allows for any and all inconsistencies (paradoxes) of infinity.

The enigma of the domain of 'utter *vagueness*' is, in a nutshell, this. According to Cantor's transfinite mathematics, the whole integers make up an infinite set. This set belongs to further transfinite sets that are endless in the same fashion that the set representing the series of whole integers is endless. That is, given any set from the series, there is another set that succeeds and exceeds them all. Hence there exists a hierarchy, a receding subset of sets containing all sets before them. At the ultimate stretch, it seems, one would finally arrives at the Grand Set of all Sets. Then, to the question 'Does it contain itself as a member?' the answer must be 'Yes, for if not, it would not be the Set of all Sets, that is, there would be some set it did not contain.' But the answer must also be 'No, for if it were to contain itself, it would not be the Set of all Sets, since a set is something that cannot contain itself' – recall Omega's words on Russell in the Preamble. If we do not want both the 'Yes' and 'No' answer, at the same time we can hardly choose between them, for the Set of all Sets cannot logically contain itself. Yet there cannot be any set ('any-*thing*') it does not contain.

The problem is that the two responses assume the Set of all Sets *actually exists* and is ideally available to the surveillance of some Supercogitator enjoying a grasp of the whole. Another concept of infinity, apparently presupposed by the Löwenheim-Skolem theorem, is that of a set of sets constantly in the making and experiencing growing pains: *potential infinity* (which was the essence of Wittgenstein's bone of contention with the likes of the Löwenheim-Skolem theorem). If sets are ever growing insofar as the mathematician continues to construct them, then her becoming conscious *of* a given set of sets is the extent to which their development has unfolded. This renders sets comparable to the mathematician's consciousness, and consciousness *of* her own consciousness: it is always in the process of expanding outward, though never quite capable of self-containment. Such a self-conscious mathematician embodies, however, yet another paradox, that of the One and the Many (see Schrödinger 1967:138). And it implies the unfoldment of time regarding the Many and some unimaginable timeless orb regarding the One. Yet from the vantage of the potentially infinite, the whole is, given sufficient – that is, infinite – time, realizable. In either case, as a concept, infinity, whether actual or potential, can be a Meinong-like 'object' of talk. In this vein, what can prevent the mathematician from reflecting on the frame of reference within which all possible sets exist? After all, cannot it be talked about in general terms? Cannot it be the focus of controversy? Of heated argument? When contemplating this whole – if that were indeed possible – does our mathematician not hold, in the 'here-now,' the Set of all Sets in check? If so, is it then not merely potential but, since the object *of* talk, somehow actual?

It seems that the concept of actual infinity is essential for the very act of conceptualizing and articulating the term 'infinity.' But, given our helpless finitude, this is an ominous task. Compare the task to our awareness of the age of the earth. According to recent estimations, the earth is some five billion years old. If this time were condensed into a decade, the dinosaurs died two or three months ago, last night apes appeared, nine hours in the past humans entered the scene, and a second or so ago John F. Kennedy was assassinated. Whatever reduction (or model) we wish to make in order to grasp its magnitude, it will still be a hopelessly pale reflection. Infinity is, so to speak, infinitely larger than the age of the earth. But we can't even use the relative word 'larger,' for between infinity and the finite we are not speaking of degree but of incompatible kinds. The very thought of the infinite cannot but give one a Pascalian sense of floating in a void, always adrift, blown to and fro: there is no firm footing. The whole eludes one's every attempt to grasp it. It flees eternally from one's efforts to apprehend it. From this ethereal abyss, one wishes to retreat to the rough ground of potential infinity, which, though apparently populated with slushy boundaries and irregular, incomplete things and concepts, at least affords a few signposts. That is to say, one is both attracted to, and repelled by, the notion of actual sets (the infinitist, even Platonist, position), and is unsatisfied with, yet many take refuge and find a modicum of comfort in, the notion of potential infinity (the finitist, intuitionist, or constructivist position).

In a Peircean manner of putting it, actual infinity is utter *vagueness*, Peirce's realm of pure possibility; potential infinity can be made the object of ever more encompassing *generalities*, though they are destined always to remain insufficient (Hacking 1983:176–80). The first cannot but admit to *inconsistencies*, since, as the Set of all Sets, by definition it contradicts itself, and once that Pandora's box has been opened, there is no upper bound to the logical discomfitures that may arise. The second cannot but remain *incomplete*, for it lies beyond the most ambitiously constructed of Babels. And yet, since I have addressed myself to the *actual* and the *potential*, *vagueness* and *generality*, *inconsistency* and *incompleteness*, which by their very nature must themselves remain *vague*, this very combine puts all the terms in the ballpark with the set of all paradoxes. Apparently one is damned if one does and damned if one doesn't.

'But there is really no cause for despair,' someone wishes to conclude. 'If we embrace Peircean "limitative semiotics" and concede to human frailties and fallibilism, then upon considering the whole of things, we cannot but fall into vagueness.' So what's new? In this intractable realm where nothing is and everything is possible, we can hardly expect more. On the other hand, if we keep an eye trained on what we have actually constructed, then, in light of the Löwenheim-Skolem theorem, there is no knowing when something else might pop up from the infinite realm of possibilities. For example, a random series is in essence neither decidable nor undecidable. If while travelling along it we discover some semblance of order, then it was not random, but if not, no matter how far we may wish to proceed, we cannot know if it is really random, for, perhaps over the next wave in the unruly sea we may vaguely spot an island of order. But until we discover such order, we cannot refute the hypothesis that it is not random, nor can we definitely prove it is random (Spencer-Brown 1957). Talk about the whole of things is fine for some sort of God who can see all all at once. But such talk cannot be ours, for the entirety of the domain of everything that was, is, and can be is beyond our surveyability (Kline 1980:237).

What does all this hold in store for us with respect to meaning? Is meaning (and interpretation) infinitely variable or not? If so, it must be absolutely undecidable, and the delirious Dionysian-Nietzschean flash dancers will have their day. If not, then is it in any form or fashion fathomable? If so, then it must come in discrete packages. If not, then it must be continuous, smoother than the smoothest vanilla ice cream, and the paradox of infinity once again slaps us in the face. If meaning is discrete, then we ought to be able to get a handle on it. But if the discrete joints we cut our world into in order to give it meaning could always have been something other than what they are, and if they were cut from a continuum of possibilities, then whatever meaning is to be had is here now and gone in the next moment. We find ourselves, regarding the whole, much like Beckett's protagonist in *How It Is* (1955). The mass of ooze within which he finds himself leaves him in a helpless, hopeless mess. Yet he cannot remain silent; he continues to talk, even though he realizes that all talk is futile, meaningless.

We must look into this issue further, somehow.

9

Caught Within

1. Is 'There Is No God's Eye View' Uttered from a God's Eye View?

Obviously, under normal circumstances we somehow manage to find meaning. But one might wish to pose the query, What's the use of it all if there can be no solid footing underneath? Regarding this question, Putnam's voice resurfaces.

Putnam asks us to suppose an ant crawling on a patch of sand happens to trace a pattern that looks like Winston Churchill (1981:1–5). Good sense tells us that the creature has not *intentionally* constructed a Churchill caricature ('intentionality' is here used in the philosophical sense as the property of consciousness whereby it 'intends' [refers to] an object). In this manner the set of lines is not 'in itself' a 'representation' of anything in particular instead of some other thing, for the ant *intended* (*expected*) no relation between the lines it traced out and Churchill or an image of Churchill. (I should mention that Putnam's use of 'representation' entails *relata* between signs and existent things, which, it would appear, excludes Meinong 'objects.' In view of the previous chapters, I include mental entities within the domain of 'things' to which signs are related – and I repeat my preference for 'related' over 'refer,' since the latter invariably evokes notions of 'denotation,' 'extension,' 'representation,' 'correspondence,' and other such undesirables.)

Of course, it is not the ant but human semiotic agents that make the relation between the set of lines and the face of a particular person in terms of similarity, of iconicity. This appears simple enough: the lines are like Churchill's mug, so they must compose a Churchill caricature. But certain arbitrary sets of marks on paper or sounds in the air can relate to Churchill for semiotic agents as well, without there existing so much as a modicum of similarity between the sign and the thing. However, as Peirce tells us, arbitrary symbols rest on an iconic and indexical base: without the image, sensation, feeling (qualisign) of

Churchill's notorious countenance, our ant-artist's iconic creation could not be given an indexical label by way of a 'Winston Churchill' string of symbols, and it stands to reason that without indexicality (sinsigns) symbolicity (legisigns) would have no chance of emerging into the light of day (I will address myself further to the nature of qualisigns, sinsigns, and legisigns in chapter 10, section 4 and chapter 14, section 1).

So neither signs of similarity nor arbitrariness outside any and all semiotic agents are enough for something adequately – and necessarily, in terms of convention, habit, Thirdness – to relate to something else. In order for the ant depiction to become a Churchill caricature, some semiotic agent must be capable of imagining a similarity relation, construct the thought of Churchill, and, in communicating this thought with another agent, emit a string of chiefly arbitrary symbols relating to that to which the depiction is similar. All this, we are to suppose, lies outside the ant's dim consciousness, whatever it may be. In other words, the ant has created the possibility for a work of art the signifying qualities of which lie beyond it: they are for it unlearnable, unaccountable, and unknowable, at least in the sense of humanly conscious semiotic agents. The ant's icon would lie outside the possibility of its surveillance just as would *Hamlet* for the proverbial infinity of monkeys pecking away at a series of typewriters one of which eventually happens to reduplicate Shakespeare's work. Yet, as human semiotic agents, with perseverance we can learn, account for, and know that of which we are capable. And we give it all meaning as a matter of course.

We might suppose that the ant's meanderings are guided by its own instinct-driven purpose, which has its own meaning and reasons. The anecdotal simian who perchance pecked out *Hamlet* on the typewriter perhaps because there was nothing else to do and the activity happened to entertain her, has found some sort of meaning to her own pastime, however vague it may be. Both ant and ape, however, unintendedly (and unexpectedly) produced what from a distinctively human vantage are works of art. Questions push their way to the surface at this point. Is our own intentionality hardly capable of more than ant or ape regarding the creation of hitherto unknown signs? Do we humans not repeatedly construct what previously was unthought or thought to be impossible? Have not some of these constructs even been given citizen status in the world of the 'real'? Where, then, does meaning begin? At neuronal firings? At tacit levels? And where does it all end? At the level of the conscious, conscientious, and willful and intentional cogitating mind?

Regarding the level of neuronal firings, Putnam resuscitates his celebrated and somewhat maligned 'brains-in-a-vat' thought experiment in his exploration of the meaning controversy (1981:5–8). Suppose we are all brains-in-a-vat receiving streams of impulses carefully modulated by some mad scientist to create the illusion of a world 'out there.' When we supposedly say 'car' we 'refer' not to some metal and plastic contraption on wheels, but to a certain pattern of electrical stimulation in the brain – that is, that to which the thought-sign 'car' actually 'refers' (that is, 'relates'), as a counterpart to the sign-event 'car' in case there is actually such a 'real'-world item 'out there.' 'Car' in 'real'-world language presumably 'relates to' an existent thing on the highway, in the garage, in the junkyard, or wherever. 'Car' for brains-in-a-vat merely 'relates to' electrical impulses creating the image (illusion) of an object made from a lot of metal, plastic, and four wheels. In neither case, Putnam writes, is there any relation to neurons in grey matter: meanings do not dwell within the skull, but emerge through interaction of sign components; and they are not in the signs but in the *relata* between signs and signs, and between signs and semiotic agents. In this sense, the very word 'brain' relates not to physical grey matter but to the/a thought (thought-sign) *of* it, and the thought *of* that thought relates to the previous thought, and so on – that is, Peirce's notorious infinite progress of signs becoming signs and his infinite regress of interrelated signs among signs, alluded to in the context of the Löwenheim-Skolem theorem.

In short, Putnam argues against Saul Kripke's (1980) 'causal theory' of 'reference' and traditional theories claiming that the mental state by itself fixes 'reference.' He suggests that there is no way of simply being in a certain brain state and having a certain image in the brain that can go beyond the brain and project into the physical world. The brain cannot go beyond itself, for to do so would be the equivalent of its generating a string of signs capable of relating to the condition of the selfsame brain within some larger context. For brain-mind to say 'I'm a brain-in-a-vat' presupposes its being able to jump outside itself and make a comment on its status from some transcendent vantage, but that vantage, if legitimate, depends upon the possibility of a leap to some higher vantage, and so on. In other words, the statement 'I'm a brain-in-a-vat' cannot be made simply from a Vatland point of view, but needs the larger perspective of the mad scientist in her laboratory, in Labland. But what if the scientist were also a brain-in-a-vat? In such case, her language, presumably Lablandese, would actually be a subscripted transform of Vatlandese, that is, $Vatlandese_a$. Her stating 'I'm a brain-in-a-vat' presupposes some further point of view from the brain-mind of some other mad scientist, $scientist_a$, in her own Labland, $Labland_a$. And so on, without end.

This situation is comparable to two examples from Borges's fictions. In 'The Circular Ruins' (1962) a magician dreams a son with the intention of interpolating him into the physical world. After an initial aborted attempt he accomplishes his task. Or at least he thinks he does. One day, however, he grows fearful that, in view of some news he had received, his son might have discovered that he is mere figment and not fact. While meditating on this unfortunate turn of events, the magician realizes that a concentric fire in the jungle is closing in on him. Aware of the proximity of his death, he decides to walk into the flames and end the impending ordeal quickly. But upon so doing he discovers the flames do not consume him, for he, like his son, is the mere dream of another dreamer. An infinite regress is implied here, for the dreamer of the magician – like the Lablander and her own creation, the Vatlander – must surely be the fabrication of another somnolent mind, and that of yet another one, ad infinitum. The second example comes to us from Borges's 'Library of Babel' (1962), which is either infinite (virtually infinite) or finite (but so large as to be incomprehensible). We are told that somewhere the Library holds a solitary book that contains reference to all the books in this massive athenaeum, thus affording a possible grasp of the totality. But if so, then this compendium must contain a reference to itself, and the book plus its self-referring entry, must, in order to be complete, enjoy reference from another compendium, and so on. The first example is an infinite move outward, the second moves ever inward. The first presumably 'refers,' ultimately, to the outer world – at least that would be the hope of those sharing the magician's mindset. The second is an infinite regress of intertextuality – or perhaps of a brain-in-a-vat's consciousness *of* itself *as* a brain-in-a-vat. In either case, the ultimate assumption seems to be the equivalent of neurons in the head relating to something 'out there' and giving it meaning. But if this were the case, then a given set of neurons connected to the world 'out there' must relate to itself if the brain containing those neurons and the mind squeezed from it is – as we would suppose in the event the brain is that of a human semiotic agent – properly self-conscious *of* itself connected to the world 'out there.' In this case, the self-conscious self must relate to itself by way of another set of self-relating neurons, and so on.

The examples from Putnam and Borges evoke the asymmetrical relation between fictive worlds (or dream worlds or brains-in-a-vat world) and 'real' worlds. This is relevant, I would submit, for, recalling the above chapters on Meinong and fictionality, it is plausible to assume that meaning-making regarding the 'real world' involves the same map and the same route as meaning making for fictions. Which leads one to believe that it is by and large an internal, not an external, affair. Yet, as Putnam concludes of his elaborate arguments, wherever meaning is, one thing is for sure: *it ain't in the head* (see also Koethe 1992). This conclusion is especially germane to fictions, since, we would like to assume, they *are* precisely in the head. In this sense the phrase 'Library of Babel,' upon Borges's writing his story or a reader's reading it, relates to a certain set of electrical impulses. And upon stating 'The Library of Babel is finite, though unimaginable,' there is relation to those 'Library of Babel' impulses. In contrast, we tend to suppose that the 'Washington Monument' is a sign relating to a 'real' elongated item constructed of stone and set in a vertical position. Given so much, then, what does the word 'brain' relate to in the case of Putnam's brains-in-a-vat? Not a grey lump or a collection of neurons in the head, but another set of electrical impulses, the impulses by which the illusion of physical brains is created. So if we are brains-in-a-vat, the term relates not to physical brains but to electrical stimulation. But this is surely wrong-headed, we would like to retort, for we are 'real brains' in a 'real vat,' not mere electrical stimulations.

Thus, to say 'I'm a brain-in-a-vat' is an illegitimate statement: it presupposes something other than brains-in-vats acting as a ground upon which the brain-in-a-vat statement can be made, but such a presupposition cannot legitimately exist in a world to all appearances consisting solely of brains and vats and so many wires. The statement 'I'm a brain-in-a-vat' is comparable to the claim that 'Quarks are the building blocks of the universe.' The sweeping proclamation presupposes some grounding upon which 'building blocks' can be firmly placed, but if everything that is is constructed from quarks, then there is nothing beyond quarks to support them – that is, Geoffrey Chew's (1968) 'bootstrap hypothesis.' On the other hand, regarding fictionality, there appears to be no problem in saying 'The Library of Babel is finite, though unimaginable,' even though that unimaginable finitude is predicated upon the existence of an equally unimaginable infinity. Such paradoxes of infinity are fine and dandy in fictions, we might wish to retort, but they can't hold water in our perceived and conceived 'real world,' which, if 'real,' must resist contradictions whenever possible (I say 'whenever possible' in light of the Master's words in the Preamble). What is up for question, it seems, is once again the distinction between our relation with the 'real' and our relation with fictions.

Kendall Walton observes that the cognitive 'window between the real world and fictional ones appears, usually, to be one-way. Tom Sawyer knows nothing about us, and it hardly seems possible for him – or even Sherlock Holmes, for that matter – to find out anything about us' (1978:12). The question is, If the road to and from fictions is one-way, then how is it that we can apparently move in and out of them at will? That is to say, if fictions are in the head, then it would seem that we merely need to open our wide, innocent eyes to the 'real,' and then we could easily see the fiction as fiction. In contrast, we are inside the 'real,' and therein we will remain, like it or not. Yet we would like to think we are wide-awake to our 'reality' – recall Peirce on fictions and the 'real' in chapters 2 and 3. And all this, in spite of Borges, and even Descartes, who in his *First Meditation* (1641) finally decided, after much deliberation, that he could not be absolutely certain he was not in dreamland. (I might add that Descartes regarded dreams perverse because they violated the law of noncontradiction. He accepted basically the equivalent of Seconds, largely eschewing First and Thirds, like any good 'metaphysical realist.')

So let us consider dreaming and merely sleeping. During heavy sleep a person is not usually awakened by customary sounds: the barking dog, the wind outside, a snoring spouse, the garbage collector. But an unusual sound, say, a fire siren, even at a distance, may stir her. It seems that there must have been some part of her that was already awake; that is, in a state of aware or semi-aware 'inner' readiness to become consciously aware *of* certain events 'out there.' It is *as if* she had heard in the physical sense all the sounds, but her mind had chosen to select only a few of them. The mind must have been primed to detect certain novel or relatively unexpected sensations, while the expected events flew by unnoticed. The mind was in a sleep-state, but not entirely; it was in a dream-state, but did not remain completely divorced from its ordinary waking world. It was asleep and not asleep, dreaming and not dreaming, not awake and yet somehow awake. We have *overdetermination* and *underdetermination* without the comfort of decidability from within the sphere of actuals (Secondness). We also have something akin to that state Arthur Koestler (1963) calls 'sleepwalking.' Scientists more than other folk, Koestler tells us, are 'sleepwalkers,' since they hardly know what their destiny holds or how they will get there until after the fact, and with the heightened acuity hindsight gives them. It is comparable to what Rosette Lamont (1970) terms Samuel Beckett's 'choiceless awareness,' his and his characters' soporifically knowing what is happening without being able to alter the course substantially. Yet there does seem to be more than a modicum of control, dubbed by Borges (1962:164) 'controlled dream' or 'hallucination,' regarding the act of creating fictions. In the final analysis it would seem likely that there is, essentially, *neither* absolutely one state *nor* the other, and at the same time there is at least in a minimal way *both* one state *and* the other. *Underdetermination* pervades the *neither-nor*, while *overdetermination* pervades the *both-and*. Yet, contradictorily, there is *neither* absolute *underdetermination nor overdetermination*, but some mix of the two; there is *both* the one *and* the other, though at a given juncture one of the two is usually found only in small doses.

However, Norman Malcolm (1959), for one, persists in maintaining a distinction between the two states in question. He points out that for a sleeping person to state 'I'm asleep' is absurd, since from her sleeping state she cannot be conscious *of* her waking frame, thus she is incapable consciously of making a statement concerning her status in the sleeping state – compare to the brains-in-a-vat making a statement regarding their condition. Moreover, she cannot be consciously aware *that* there is a boundary between her sleeping state and her waking state. Hence, strictly speaking, she can neither be lying nor telling the truth, for a contradiction is involved in either case. Similarly, to say 'I'm "inside" this fiction' is also absurd. If totally 'inside' the fiction, all the speaker can perceive/conceive is fiction, consequently she cannot discriminate between it and any 'outside' frame. What she perceives/conceives will be the limits of her world. She will not be aware *of* nor will she be able to judge or assert anything concerning the ontological status *of* her state as anything except what is *for* her 'real.'

But: 'When I *was in* fictive worlds (that is, texts) *X*, *Y*, and *Z*, I "saw" such-and-such.' Is this not possible? This statement implies that somehow the speaker *was* able to step 'outside' the fictive worlds in question and talk about them. He is now capable of juxtaposing them, comparing and contrasting them with his 'real' world, and judging their aesthetic or conceptual validity. However, the statement 'When I was *in* fictive world ...' is possible solely in the past tense, after the fact. In contrast, the reader's saying 'I am now in fiction *X*' is as absurd as saying, 'I am sleeping.' For the reader/speaker cannot validly claim he was aware *of* being 'inside' the fiction at the same time that he was actually and totally 'inside' it. He can only assume, in retrospect, that he *was* 'inside' that particular fiction when a certain set of experiences occurred. And this assumption can be arrived at only with respect to his present out-of-the-fiction state. Hence, he necessarily judges that his present state is the 'real' state and that the 'fiction' in which he existed previously was 'fictive.' In other words, we are *in* the 'world' we are *in*, and while we are *in* it, as immanent semiotic agents, that is all there is. We are, to put it bluntly, like the ant within its 'Churchill' caricature, or like Koestler's scientist, Borges's creator of fictions, or the dreamer incapable of making a cogent and intelligible statement regarding the totality of the state she is in.

This is the point Putnam seems to be making. He observes that his brains-in-a-vat example bears on the limitations evinced by the Löwenheim-Skolem theorem: the sphere of all possible interpretations or models (signs and their meanings), which is infinite in extension, will at an indefinite number of indefinite points hold countless surprises in store for us. At a given juncture we will be able to encompass no more than an infinitesimal portion of the totality within our surveillance, hence we cannot be aware of what the future will bring. (This is also relevant to Wittgenstein's paradox regarding rule following – briefly to be discussed in chapter 12.) In a nutshell what we have, Putnam continues, is the equivalent of a self-refuting supposition, a sentence whose 'truth' implies its own 'falsity.' The generality 'All generalities are from some view or other "false,"' for example, if 'true,' is 'false,' hence it is 'false.' But, one might wish to retort, if it is 'false,' then it is 'true,' so it is merely undecidable – though not meaningless, as the Master observed in the Preamble. However, if we are to concede that we are somewhat less than perfect, and that our intellect is of finite capacity, then we are incapable of surveying the totality of all generalities, and in addition, the totality of all particular cases to which a given generality refers. In this event, then, our situation is comparable to Gödel's demonstration that for Cantor's continuum hypothesis there is no proof, only the proof that there is no disproof.

In other words, like Popper's one and only True scientific theory, if we cannot refute the statement 'All generalities are from some view or other "false,"' neither can we prove it, so we cannot know it is 'true.' There might be a modicum of consolation forthcoming from the observation that if we cannot know it is 'true,' we can at least know that we cannot know that it is either 'true' or 'false.' So it is 'false,' for it is not 'true' that all generalities are at some juncture necessarily 'false.' From the broadest possible view, there must be, somewhere, some generality that is 'true,' but we will never have it, for it would be tantamount to the whole of all generalities, to the set of all sets. (This is the other side of the situation, alluded to above, regarding an infinite series. Its order can be proved by pursuing it until some semblance of order is established, but its randomness cannot be proved unless it is trailed out to its end without encountering any form of order, which is impossible for any finite collection of semiotic agents. The series's randomness can possibly be refuted but not proved without a shadow of a doubt.)

Is there no method to this madness?

2. Like Driving Piles into Quicksand

No, if by method we mean an algorithmic procedure cut in stone. But yes, if we take into our purview Peirce's 'pragmatic maxim' floating in a sea of incessantly changing strategies. With such a fluid 'methodology' – and following the Master's argument – whether or not a sentence is 'true' or 'false' or 'meaningless,' and whether or not it is 'decidable,' somewhere and sometime there exists the possibility, in view of the above on *overdetermination* and *underdetermination*, that it can have meaning *for* some semiotic agent or other.

Meaning determines the relations between signs and between signs and their respective semiotic agents – it does not determine 'reference' in the Fregean sense. At the same time, those relations determine meaning – they do not 'cause' the meaning as per Kripke's 'causal theory' of 'reference.' In this sense, the mindset (Thirdness) of a particular semiotic agent, whether or not she is a brain-in-a-vat, *underdetermines* meaning, since there is no knowing when another meaning – and a new set of relations – will come between any two meanings in the agent's memory bank. And meaning is also *overdetermined* in terms of the range of unactualized possibilities (Firstness) of relations between all the signs available for that agent's use. Some of these possible relations make up the mindset of the agent, but most of them rest in that which can possibly become 'real,' given the myriad array of possible space-time conjunctions.

The whole of these possible relations, I repeat, lies outside the reach of the agent, and in fact of an entire community of agents. Following on the heels of Putnam's argument, in this light, brains-in-vats cannot tell the whole tale, nor can we. But this is no indication that we are simply nothing but a psychological state or a bundle of 'perceptions' (electrical stimulations). Neither is our mindset merely the product of whatever information the 'real' sends us, thus rendering us agents of some sort of crystallized 'causality.' Rather, it is a matter of incessant interaction between an agent's mindset and signs, on the one hand, and the relations between them, on the other. Meaning is not strictly localizable, then. It must be engendered from within and betwixt conventional categories of thought; it is the product of situated 'differences that make a difference,' to appropriate Bateson's key phrase (1972).

However intimidating this problem may be for standard logic, it fades out of the picture when considering the flexibility of everyday languages – which openly include the 'logics' of *vagueness* and *generality*. Granted, according to various above mentions, the early Russell and Wittgenstein, and a host of philosophers of analytical bent since their time, banished paradoxes of the set-theoretic sort from their paradise of unblemished language. However, in so doing, they ignored that remarkable human ability under the vast majority of all circumstances to make the most of what there is at hand. Like the Master argued, the person on the street may understand sentences such as 'The universe rests on a turtle's back' and 'All generalities are from some view or other "false,"' while hardly giving the logical quandary in which they place her a moment's thought. She says what she has on her mind, and if it gets her in trouble, she may plug up the holes, blindly damn the torpedoes, and continue to displace water with a full head of steam. Or she may confess her errors and strive to do better in the future. At each step she more likely than not commits a few more errors, according to the standard logician's iron-clad rules. Yet, in spite of logical imperatives that should constrain her, this is simply the way she speaks, the way she gets along in her dialogical game, debating, conversing, kibitzing, chatting, telling stories, and she muddles through as best she can – that is, Rorty's ideal crowd of interlocutors. And all this, to say nothing of the proliferation of her imaginary 'worlds' freely endowed with contradictory characters, as illustrated in the above on Meinong. She is 'inside' her world, and generally tending to follow defined rules that vary from precise to inordinately vague, she nevertheless breaks them in some way or other at almost every other step, whether intentionally or not and whether conscious *of* the fact or not.

Yet, Putnam claims (1981:8) that *we*, unlike the brains-in-a-vat, can know and legitimately say we are *not* brains-in-a-vat. On this point I must launch a mild objection. I'm afraid, meagre though my understanding may be, that I fail to comprehend why we can give a valid argument for not being brains-in-a-vat, but brains-in-a-vat cannot. It seems to me as bizarre as assuming that from 1905 onward – the year of Einstein's special theory of relativity – we ceased living in three-dimensional continuous, homogeneous, infinitely extended, linear, Euclidean space independent of time. Now, properly enlightened, we know we swim in a pliable four-dimensional space-time continuum within which we can know no simultaneities save from within relative frames of reference, that Euclidean geometry does not hold, and that there is no objective but merely subjective time. And to boot, all this is enfolded into a static Minkowski-Parmenidean 'block.' In other words, following the restrictions on Putnam's brains-in-a-vat, the Ptolemaic, Copernican, and Newtonian could not legitimately say, 'I do not exist in three-dimensional space but in a four-dimensional space-time continuum,' but we can.

However, there is nothing stopping our ancestors from *imagining* they swam in a four-dimensional continuum, just as we might *imagine* that we *know* – or *think* we *know* – we do the same. In other words, their construct, we can safely assume, was properly fictive: they knew full well they were merely *imagining*. We, in contrast, think we know our fiction *is* 'real.' This situation regarding our ancestors and ourselves is comparable to that found in Edwin A. Abbott's charming tale, *Flatland* (1880). After a long and arduous effort, and with the aid of a three-dimensional 'Spherelander,' the two-dimensional 'Flatlander,' A. Square, was finally able to *imagine* what life would be like in a three-dimensional world. But for him, like brains-in-a-vat *imagining* they are not brains-in-a-vat but something else, it remained nothing more than a product of his fabulating mind. In contrast, the Spherelander, from within her infinitely more expansive world, could quite easily gaze on the Flatlander's comings and goings as a whole: everything was open to her view in simultaneity.

In other words, the Spherelander could see what was behind the closed doors of the Flatlander's closet in his apartment, what was in his pantry, on his cupboard shelves, and inside his TV set. However, this *actual* ability enjoyed by the Spherelander does not lie outside the realm of the Flatlander's free flights of *imagination*: he could quite easily create a picture of a *possible* world of three-dimensions in which he is endowed with the same ability. On a comparable note, from within our own world a science-fiction writer, say Ray Bradbury, could with little difficulty *imagine* and create a story about a four-dimensional demon who works for the FBI and is capable of 'seeing through' a suspect by taking a look into his innards to determine whether or not he swallowed a few condoms packed with cocaine before leaving the airport at Bogotá. This is comparable to the mad scientist – or ourselves – observing those hapless brains-in-a-vat. Yet, just as we can *imagine* we do not exist in three-dimensional space but in a four-dimensional space-time continuum, so also the brains-in-a-vat, I would suspect, could *imagine* they are not brains-in-a-vat. And just as Ray Bradbury could *imagine* what it would be like to be a four-dimensional demon, so also the brains-in-a-vat could *imagine* what it would be like to be a mad scientist in Labland controlling their brain impulses. It's all a matter of *imagining* something that might possibly be as if it actually were, or of *imagining* it merely for the fun of it.

It is not outside the realm of possibility, then, that a brain-in-a-vat might, by an intuitive leap, imagine some bizarre situation in which she is a mad scientist who created her fellow citizens as brains in Vatland, and she is now 'reading' them by impulses through wires connected to her instruments in Labland. She could then tell the nearest brain-in-the-vat about her strange experience, in the process using the word 'vat' in relation to the figment of her imagination. But on so doing, does 'vat' actually relate to anything? Does it relate to the *vat* within which she actually dwells? For that matter, when in a casual conversation with her friend, if she says 'mountain' presumably in relation to a *mountain* they are under the illusion they spot on the horizon, does her word actually relate to the object in question? Yet, writes Putnam, when she says 'mountain,' her brain state can conceivably be the same as ours, though her mountain relates to no *mountain* at all. Neither does her 'vat' relate to an actual *vat* any more than the ant's wanderings in the sand relate to *Churchill*, the magician's dreamt image to anything in the 'real' world, or A. Square's imaginary three-dimensional world to anything 'real.'

Of course, in the language of Vatland the Vatlander is correct in thinking her words exist in relation to actual things in her environment. In contrast, the mad scientist from her 'outside' vantage using Lab-speak, knows she is wrong. She is not addressing herself to actual things any more than she is to a 'real' *vat* when, for example, she tells her friend she imagines she is a mad scientist and not a 'brain-in-a-vat.' In fact, by the same token, if she were to believe in her thought experiment and say 'I am not a brain-in-a-vat' with conviction, she would be wrong, for her sentence is 'false.' It is 'false' in the same way that 'All general statements are from some view or other "false"' errs in the above example. The sentence, if considered 'true,' is, itself, 'false' (it is a general statement that is considered 'true'). Likewise, to say 'We are not brains-in-a-vat,' is, if a 'true' utterance, 'false' in the sense that it is equivalent to saying 'We do not exist as such-and-such.' This latter statement, like 'I am lying,' relates to the subject of the utterance, who, if telling the 'truth,' is stating a 'falsehood' (is lying), because on emitting the statement, that statement itself relates to a speaker who must be uttering a general 'truth.' But if that general 'truth' applies to itself and to its utterer, it is not a legitimate utterance, so the utterance is 'false,' yet if it is false, it is 'true.' (Once again, I must mention that, according to the Master's teachings, in the language of our everyday affairs we commit these and other such errors as a matter of course, and more often than not we are able somehow to get along quite well, thank you – recall the brief exchange on the Liar Paradox at the beginning of the Preamble.)

In spite of certain reservations, I would concur with Putnam's conclusion in his essay on brains-in-a-vat (1981:20–1) that: (1) no collection of mental events – images or more 'abstract' mental happenings – is capable of *constituting* meaning, and (2) no collection of mental events is *necessary* for meaning. This leads Putnam to suggest that '*concepts cannot be identical with mental objects of any kind*.' Neither mental events – images – nor concepts refer to the 'real' furniture of the world. Mental events and concepts are not the repository of meaning, nor do they provide for the pointing finger of 'reference.' And meaning is not found rebounding within the confines of the skull, in 'reference' or 'correspondence' or 'representation,' or in the things of the physical world. To repeat, meaning is engendered, it engenders itself, during the flux and the flows, and from within the woofs and the warps, of the situated *semiosic* process (that is, thought-signs interacting with sign-events, and all interacting with their respective semiotic agents).

Thus, we see with greater force that of Peirce's categories, *images* – Putnam's mental events, Frege's *Vorstellungen* – are embraced most adequately by Firstness, and *concepts* – which do not depend upon 'reference,' according to Putnam, and contrary to Frege's 'sense' – most adequately fall within the sphere of Thirdness. Still, there is no all-or-nothing line of demarcation between images and concepts. Images do not intrinsically 'refer' to things 'out there' any more than the ant's meandering 'refers' to Churchill. And concepts are no more dependent upon 'real'-world furniture for us than they are for brains-in-a-vat. For concepts 'are (at least in part) *abilities* and not occurrences' (Putnam 1981:21). In other words, Putnam's concepts and Peirce's interpretants, chiefly Thirdness, are by and large the product of dispositions, conventions, habits, and regularities (as well as beliefs, and what Peirce dubbed 'habit'). They are events or acts along the processual flow of *semiosis*. Neither things in the 'real' world nor 'objects' in the head, they are the result of the act of bringing signification (meaning) to its fulfilment, as thought-signs and sign-events – though the ultimate sign, the final interpretant, always already remains beyond any and all of our *abilities*.

The story eventually to be told is that of Secondness. Secondness entails, to be sure, *relations* – so as not to fall into the trap of 'reference,' 'correspondence,' or 'representation' – *relations* between signs, whether thought-signs or sign-events. Secondness is the playground of what are taken to be discrete entities, whether perceived and conceived to be 'out there' or 'in here,' and whether 'real' or imaginary. But before embarking on that topic, let us make another turn to the *inconsistency* (*vagueness*) incorporated within Firstness.

3. A Headlong Dive into the Sea of Ambiguity

The various and sundry paradoxes of infinity give rise to a sort of 'paradox' of their own: we might call it the 'paradox of paradoxes,' which, we shall note, has a bearing on some of the key topics at hand.

It goes something like this – and, by the way, it evidently bears a relationship to the 'brains-in-a-vat' conundrum. If we cannot know anything about the infinite because we cannot effectively account for it in terms of its relation to what we already know, then we cannot know we cannot know anything about it; and if we cannot know it or account for it, then we cannot learn about it or say it in an adequately cogent fashion. Yet, logicians, mathematicians, and philosophers in somewhat explicit ways, and artists and mystics in oft-times strange and mysterious ways, have quite effectively been able to intuit, learn, account for, and even to an extent know, infinity. Somehow the ineffable has been said, the uncognizable has been cognized, the whole has been entered from one of its myriad parts, and that part has been made coterminous with the whole. This, in essence, might also be termed the 'holist paradox,' which underlies, but does not necessarily undercut, our learnability, accountability, and knowability (I touched upon this 'paradox' in chapter 7 when discussing the Duhem-Quine holist thesis, and will expound on it in somewhat more detail in chapter 12).

A pioneer in paradoxes of the infinite, nineteenth-century mathematician and philosopher Bernard Bolzano (1950) promoted the idea that the concept of infinity is an inextricable component of set theory. If a compound entity is infinite, then it must contain an infinity of members. The obvious retort is that there cannot be an infinity of things, so there is no such 'thing' as infinity. But for Bolzano there is such a 'thing,' for example, as an infinity of points in space or along a line, an infinity of point-instants in time, and even the ongoing string of natural numbers. Besides, if God is infinite, then her attributes and the 'truths' of which she is cognizant must be infinite in magnitude. In fact, each and every 'truth' is by its very definition infinite. This applies even to the most trivial 'truths.' If a proposition, p, 'Peirce once lived at Arisbe,' is 'true,' then there is another 'truth,' p', namely that p is 'true,' and so on, with no end in sight (that is, a rough natural-language counterpart to the Tarski equation for 'truth' we saw in the Preamble).

But how can we talk about, much less cognize, this infinite set of Chinese boxes as if it were a finished, determinate whole? How can we really know it if we cannot indubitably account for it? The problem is not so severe as it might appear, Bolzano set theorists would be prone to tell us. It is not the same as the time-bound Tarskian hierarchy of confirming statements. The hierarchy construed temporally can never reach its end point, for that end point has nothing to do with time. The notion of a timeless actual infinity ushers in paradoxes, to be sure, but they cause no damage if talk is restricted to terms exclusively implying purely infinite domains. In other words, infinity need not be constrained by what can or cannot be thought about. Signs can simply be used to talk about it, and discourse can get along quite well – that is, as long as it is understood by all parties involved that the signs do not relate to the everyday world. Once finitude enters the picture, however, things get messy. This is because what can be thought about and said in finite terms is quite incompatible with infinity, which bars its doors to imagination, as well as all terms having to do with the physically 'real' (Benardete 1964).

Richard Dedekind, with whom we are now somewhat familiar, was no more clapped out by the paradoxes of infinity than Bolzano. Dedekind proposed that if the members of an infinite set could always be paired off with one of its well-defined parts – that is, the even natural numbers as a subset of the class of all natural numbers – and he believed this to be so, then at least one infinite set actually exists, the set of thoughts. For a given thought, t_1, there is another thought, t_2, of which t_1 is the object, and another thought, t_3, and so on. This is also the case of Peirce's sign theory. Starkly put, a sign stands for its object to some mind, which engenders the sign's interpretant. But the sign can be nothing more than the interpretant of a previous sign whose object was the same object that it was at its earlier stage. Moreover, the interpretant of the sign, in the succeeding moment, becomes itself another sign whose object is now the object at a later stage in the stream of *semiosis*, and both are mediated by yet another interpretant, and so on (*CP*:1.339).

However, unable to capture the subtlety of Peirce's concept of the sign, some of his early disciples – above all C.K. Ogden and I.A. Richards (1923), and Charles Morris (1938) – completely missed the point: they gave the sign either a strictly positivist-empiricist or quasi-behaviourist interpretation. They chose to ignore the fact that Peirce's three classes of signs engender ten classes of signs. Those ten classes in turn subdivide into 66 signs, and by trichotomization they ultimately proliferate into 3^{10} or 59,049 signs. There is virtually no limit, or perhaps it might be said that infinity is the limit, to the number of signs potentially forthcoming from this myriad array of classes. The point is that the equivalent of paradoxes of infinity called for their share of playing time in the arena of Peircean semiotics. But unfortunately, during the heyday of logical positivism these paradoxes were also shoved aside, Peirce's own sort of 'uncertainty principle' regarding our ability to know was ignored, and the quest for unmovable foundations continued unabated. (There are, as far as I know, two means for engendering ten signs from three sign types: the Pythagorean tetractys, and Riemann's matrix tensors. For various reasons, I would like to think that Peirce might have been influenced more by the former than the latter, but that story must be held in abeyance until another time and another place.)

Such futile quests for foundations are commonplace in the history of Western thought. As we have noted, Frege is considered one of the first mathematicians to entertain the idea that mathematics could be firmly secured in its proper bedrock by reducing it to the self-evident principles of logic. Shortly after he finished his project and was in the process of getting it published, Bertrand Russell tossed him a bombshell. It consisted of our now familiar set-theoretic paradox: a set cannot be a member of itself (the set of all armadillos is not an armadillo – as briefly mentioned in the Preamble). And Frege's logic of sets as the bedrock of mathematics was shaken to the core. In fact, Frege was completely broken, believing his life's work to have been in vain. The moral to this story is not that too many cooks spoil the broth, but that all cooks find themselves foundering and floundering about somewhere in the continuous, undivided *semiosic* soup of *possibilia* implied by the notion of Firstness – or the set of all possible sets, if you will. But this *overdetermined* sphere does not simply grant a licence to engage in euphoric free-wheeling play, for habit, convention, social rules and regulations surface to fetter otherwise unbridled whims and fantasies. (It is due to the 'loss of certainty' [Kline 1980] in science, logic, and even mathematics and the antifoundationalist sentiment following this 'loss' that I opt for a 'semiotic without foundations,' to rephrase Joseph Margolis's 'pragmatism without foundations' [1986]. In this respect I will certainly have fallen from the grace of the likes of John Deely [1993], among others, whose nostalgia for the comfortable illusions of modernity have prevented them from taking that final leap into the unknown.)

So much for the *inconsistency* (*vagueness*) factor lodged in infinite domains as presumably completed wholes. Now for a look at the *incompleteness* (*generality*) factor at the other end of the spectrum before, finally, turning to Secondness.

4. Filling in Between the Lines as Best One Can

The notion of infinity as potential and incompletable in contrast to infinity as a completed project entails mathematics viewed as a human activity rather than a playground populated by a finished, timeless totality of Platonic ideals. Perhaps the so-called intuitionist interpretation of mathematics, briefly discussed above, comes closest to filling the bill in this regard.

L.E.J. Brouwer considered mathematical thinking to be a matter of mental construction eventually building up a universe based on fundamental mathematical intuition. Such basic constructions as the natural numbers and operations the likes of addition, subtraction, multiplication, and mathematical induction are taken to be intuitively precise and obvious – that is, they are not *vague* (*inconsistent*). Activities like counting leads to the notion of unlimited reiteration and hence of infinity. But this infinity cannot be more than a potential, since no matter how far we have counted, we can always add 1, 100, 10^5, or whatever to the last number, and we still will not have reached (actualized) infinity (i.e. the construct will remain *incomplete*). The intuitionist, then, rejects the actual infinity of Bolzano, Dedekind, and others which is all there all at once. As Hermann Weyl, himself sympathetic to the intuitionist program, put it (1946, in Kline 1980:235): 'The sequence of numbers which grows beyond any stage already reached ... is a manifold of possibilities opening to infinity; it remains forever in the status of creation, but is not a closed realm of things existing in themselves. That we blindly converted one into the other is the true source of our difficulties, including the antinomies [the paradoxes] ... Brouwer opened our eyes and made us see how far classical mathematics, nourished by a belief in the absolute that transcends all human possibilities of realization, goes beyond such statements as can claim real meaning and truth founded on evidence.'

The intuitionist argues that mathematics is an autonomous activity and independent of natural language. Mathematics is not of the physical world; it remains unaffected by perception in the extensional sense (of sign-events); it consists of self-sufficient, self-confirmatory ideas (thought-signs) deeply embedded in the mind. Language, by contrast, conjures up thoughts and ideas in the mind in terms of graphic or auditory signs related to, and mediated by in some form or other, objects, acts, and events in the physical world. Language, to which logic properly belongs, exists for the purpose of communicating meaning and 'truth.' Logic is in this sense based on mathematics, not the other way round – contrary to the 'logicism' of Frege, the early Russell, and others. Consequently, efforts to avoid inconsistency at all costs are actually unnecessary. Paradoxes may be looked upon as signs of defective logic, but not necessarily of defective mathematics. In contrast to language and logic, right-minded mathematical thinking can assure consistency, and mathematical thoughts can bear the stamp of correctness according to intuitive judgments (Kline 1980:235–7).

Regarding infinite sets, the intuitionist claims that the excluded-middle principle of logic is not really necessary. It is a matter of the incompatibility of actual infinity and finitude, and timelessness and temporality – a problem that bears, once again, on the Löwenheim-Skolem theorem. The essence of the story, as I understand it, goes like this. If we read of an ordered series of infinite length spread over time about which there is some speculation and much generalization, we are placed at a decided disadvantage. For this series lies beyond our grasp; it remains for us unsurveyable. What can be *said* of it cannot but be conditioned by the fact that we are finite and fallible thinking reeds inextricably caught in time, and can make sense solely of what lies within our temporal purview. Yet, we can be *shown* by means of a set of what are taken to be 'timeless' (logical, mathematical) symbols that the timeless series has such-and-such a set of characteristics. But we cannot know explicitly, and with absolute certainty, that what is *said* about what is *shown* is correct. For our timeless, intransigent ideals stretch out beyond our tenderly fallible capacities.

This situation is illustrated by what we might call the 'crap game dilemma' (comparable to the 'lottery paradox' in Rescher and Brandom 1979 and in Moore 1990). Roll a die, and the chances are one in six that six will show. But we cannot know for certain whether our chance is precisely one in six unless we toss the object an infinity of times, for there is no determining with each toss which of the dotted sides of the cube will turn up (see Peirce's use of this example in his theory of probability [*CP*:2.661–8]). This is the *temporal dimension* of the die's disposition, which for us in its infinite extension is inaccessible, since we can exercise no more than a mere finite number of tosses. So we have no way of knowing whether or not the die is loaded, even though to an infinitesimal degree. On the other hand, if we take an infinity of identical dice and roll them at the same instant, a die's disposition comes through loud and clear. This is the timeless, or *ensemble dimension*, which, for obvious reasons, is also beyond us. In either case, we are in possession of no view, *sub specie aeternitatis*, but remain inextricably caught within the world of dice throws. In the sense of Wittgenstein's philosophy of mathematics, we can enjoy no surveyability of infinities, wherever or whenever they may be (Shanker 1987). So, with respect to the final lines of the preceding paragraph, the infinitudinous totality can be *said*, quite easily enough, and it can be *shown* by exceedingly *vague* and *incomplete* analyses and generalities. But we cannot know without a shadow of a doubt that what is *said* and *shown* is the 'truth' and nothing but the 'truth.' In other words, there may be learnability, but accountability is drastically schematic at best, and knowability can hardly be more than a leap of faith in the dark. So much for crap-game uncertainties. Back to the intuitionist.

The critic of intuitionism might retort that 'infinity stories' (*Gedanken* experiments) are nonetheless quite capable of *telling* about infinity – albeit in natural language – in such a way that they give us a certain *feel* for it (Firstness). Take, for example, Hilbert's 'Hotel Paradox,' with an infinity of guest quarters. It seems that all the rooms are full, when a weary traveller inquires about lodging and is told by the desk clerk that none is available. The manager overhears the conversation and promptly corrects the desk clerk. 'It is a simple matter,' she explains. 'Move our guest in the last room to the room beyond, which is there and awaiting his entry, then move the penultimate guest into the room he had vacated, and so on, until the first room is empty, which can then be occupied by our patient inquirer.' Now even though this anecdote bears no formal account of infinity, perhaps it can give us a *feel* – albeit exceedingly *vague* – for that unimaginable magnitude. We cannot create in our mind's eye a nonvague picture of a high-rise hotel stretching ever upward, yet by way of the hotel story we can at least get a subjective and quite personal *feel* for infinity.

But much as this story might afford some vague *sense* of infinity, it is still not the authentic article, the intuitionist would reply. First, it is couched in language with reference to familiar articles of the furniture of our world, which are simply incompatible with infinity. Second, it merely *says* (or accounts for) and *shows* (the learnability of) our finite capacities, for, try as we may, we cannot construct (survey, inspect) the entirety of the items in an infinite series, whether that series is actual or a potential for the actualization of those items. Hence we cannot possess genuine knowledge of it. The problem is that the 'items' in question cannot but be 'items' of experience, and experience is time-bound and limited to our finite, nay, almost minuscule, grasp of the whole. We can either learn to live with our impoverished finitude and strive to steer clear of antinomies, or, enshrouded in learned ignorance, we can embrace infinities, in spite of the paradoxes they create, and get on with the construction of our 'semiotically real' worlds. In whichever case, infinite series may be valid for the gods existing outside time and capable of surveying the totality in an instantaneous perceptual grasp, but they are not for us. Given the discrepancy between our unbending ideals and our actual capacities, we have no guarantee what the excluded middle holds in store for us – compared to the implications of Löwenheim-Skolem as outlined above.

So to re-evoke Whitehead's observation with which I began chapter 7, enveloped within our finitude, we nevertheless have before us virtually unlimited possibilities, and the name of the game is to construct a net fine enough to land the biggest catch we can of the signs within the flow. But if there is at least a modicum of knowability, we should be able effectively to differentiate between signs of distinct genera and place them in the pigeon-hole with kindred signs when that becomes necessary. Otherwise, we will not be able to make heads or tails of them; they will remain largely meaningless.

Now, at long last, a look at the *actuals* of Secondness.

PART IV

If So, Then into the Breakers, Vortices, Cross-Currents, and Undertows of *Semiosis*

10

Dreaming the Impossible Dream?

Approaching the heartbeat of this disquisition, and moving closer to our own times, we find ourselves in a hell-bent-for-leather, fast-track pluralism of discourse, narration, rumination, rhetorical delirium, rank exhibitionism, a hodge-podge of images, themes, and ideas, past, present, and projected into the future, an age of heated debates over stakes embarrassingly small yet waged over as if they were a fight to the death, of mediocrity parading around in gala dress and spewing forth a congestion of buzz-words especially designed to enshroud intellectual poverty in a numbing mist. Yet there are still a few voices of giants emanating from the receding distance that deserve a hearing. No feminism, queer theory, postmodernism, postcolonialism, or pop culture here, but rather, words from some of the most forthright and stalwart of our twentieth-century scholars: W.V.O. Quine, Hilary Putnam, and Nelson Goodman, among others.

They have their say in chapters 10 through 13. Then Peirce's voice enters on a somewhat syncopated note to prepare the way for a tangential twist, in the final two chapters, from the 'linguistic turn' toward those baser corporeal, visceral signs upon whose shoulders the sphere of linguistic signs, that is, symbols, stand.

1. Unfortunately, That Hopeful God's-Eye Lingers On

The problem of meaning ultimately seems to be a problem of reference, or the lack thereof. Putnam, in 'Meaning, Other People, and the World' (1988:19–41), criticizes the venerable Western tradition of foundationalism. In contrast to Frege's *Venus* as either 'morning star' or 'evening star' – one sign, one 'reference,' and two 'senses' – Putnam offers his often cited 'Twin Earth' thought-experiment to demonstrate that different signs and different referents can give rise to the same 'sense' – 'intensional' or 'internal' thought-sign. Hence, each sign's *interpretant* takes on what is perceived and conceived to be the same 'extension,' 'reference,' or 'semiotic object,' even though the signs themselves are radically distinct (Putnam 1981:22–48).

'Twin Earth' complements Putnam's 'brains-in-a-vat' conundrum. The latter thought-experiment debunked the coveted notion that images and concepts, presumably in the head, necessarily relate to things in the world. The former challenges the idea that invariant and determinable meanings are in the head at all. On the surface this might simply strike one as merely the same horse but of a different colour. The 'morning star' and the 'evening star,' to be sure, are different signs, and their 'reference' or 'semiotic object' is for pragmatic purposes taken to be the same. But for those who want to split hairs, the two signs carry baggage containing two distinct 'senses' that in the best of all logical worlds shall never meet, so 'reference' is not exactly the same. Two people, one gazing at the 'morning star' and the other at the 'evening star,' are for practical purposes seeing the same star, no doubt, since comparable groupings of photons are striking their retinas. But they are seeing the 'star' *as* two different 'semiotic objects.' And this is the important point. 'Semiotic reference' – not to be confused with 'real reference,' whatever that is, for in the pure sense it lies indefinitely outside the capacity of any and all finite semiotic agents – depends upon the nature of the sign and the nature of 'sense' (the interpretant, interpretation, meaning). Consequently, *pace* Putnam, there is no guarantee whatsoever that two slightly different 'senses,' or that two different 'semiotic referents,' will meet in such a way that no-nonsense communication may shine forth (please bear in mind that I prefer the term 'relate' over 'refer,' though here I use the latter for purposes of exposition regarding Putnam's thought experiment).

Putnam asks us to imagine there is another planet in our galaxy called Twin Earth. It is exactly like our Earth in every way except that instead of water, H_2O, Twinearthers have a transparent liquid that looks like water but it isn't; it is XYZ. Both Ourearthers and the Twinearthers are pre-Daltonians: they have not yet discovered the chemical make-up of their respective colourless liquids. Yet, H_2Oers and XYZers can refer to their liquids in every way except with regard to their respective liquid's as yet unknown chemical properties. Supposing we happen to have a colleague named Jane or George, then there is a duplicate Jane or George, as there is of all of us, on Twin Earth. When Earth Jane refers to H_2O and in the same instant Twin Earth Jane refers to XYZ, there is nothing in their consciousness that can distinguish H_2O from XYZ. Yet the two 'waters' are distinct. In other words, H_2O and XYZ apparently refer to the same stuff, but there was no difference that makes a difference in whatever might compose the mental states H_2O's and XYZ's semiotic agents have when reference is made, even though one is water and the other grain alcohol or some such liquid that produces water-like sense data. As a consequence, according to Putnam, no matter how we care to spread the butter on the bread, meanings simply are not in the head (Putnam 1975, 1981:1–21, 1988:19–41). In other words, the mental states of the two semiotic agents in question are for all intents and purposes identical, and, we must surmise, the same can be said of the 'semiotic objects' to which they are presumably related, which is to say that neither mental states nor 'semiotic objects' suffice to represent and fix 'actually real reference.'

The upshot is that different signs and different 'referents' – unbeknownst to the parties involved – can engender fundamentally the same meanings. This suggests, according to Putnam, that in addition to meaning lying outside the head and the mind, it also lies outside the sign, for if not, H_2O and XYZ would bear two different meanings. Nor is meaning in the 'reference' or the objects in question, for if so, by the same token the meanings of H_2O and XYZ would differ. Thus, if there are (1) no reliable mental 'representations,' (2) no synonymity of mental 'representations,' and (3) no 'reference' determined by mental 'representations' – the three traditional metaphysical theses against which Putnam wages battle – then is the mind of no consequence? What is its role? Passive or active? Very active. Active in the sense of *translation*, as suggested in the Preamble and *et passim*.

Allow me to offer some examples of this notion of *translation*. John Deely (1990) writes of a gardener who comes upon the fossil of a long-dead dinosaur and, ignorant of its paleontological value, tosses it away as a 'rock.' His more knowledgeable neighbour, upon spying the virtual treasure, brings about the actualization of a radically distinct representamen, 'bone' or 'fossil,' and a new interpretant (via *translation*) is attached to the radically distinct 'semiotic object.' Deely foregrounds the time-bound characteristic of the *semiosic* process, thus revealing the sign's 'reality' as a semiotic virtuality, which potentially can be actualized into a particular 'semiotically real' world artefact. 'In this way,' Deely concludes: 'the interaction is a virtual semiosis, that is, a series of interactions at the level of secondness that, at the same time, provides an actual pathway through time whereby it is possible that what happened long ago might be partially understood. The present, indeed, from such a standpoint, might be regarded as a mosaic of traces from the past, each providing the starting point, for a sufficiently knowledgeable present observer, of a journey into what used to be ... [I]t is not necessary that such possibility be actualized in order for it to be possible. Nor is it merely "possible" in some abstract, conceptual sense' (1990:96).

In other words, 'rock' has suffered a *translation* as a result of some 'trace' of a past sign ('bone') that, given sufficient time, was transformed (calcified) into the sign that it now *is* ($CaCO_3$, 'rock'). But there exists the possibility of another sign ('fossil') that it *is not* – not yet at least. As long as 'rock' continued to be the only actualized sign, 'fossil' remained in limbo until some propitious moment in the future. Then, when that alternative sign broke through the defence line of semiotic habit, sign *transmutation* and *translation* exercised their effect. The important point is that before 'rock' and 'fossil' had been actualized *as* signs, they were mere juxtapositions or superpositions of possibilities (in the sphere of *overdetermination*). They were not (yet) signs in the full sense of being able to claim citizens' rights to a particular 'semiotically real' world *for* someone, although they existed 'out there' in the 'real' as possibilities.

Other instances of sign *translation* involve the interpretant only. Such is the case of a word's ambiguity when exploited in a joke at the punch line of which a second interpretant of fundamentally the same – though still a slightly different – representamen becomes evident. Simple ambiguity – 'Flying planes can be dangerous' – plays on the same type of *transformation-translation.* The representamen is orthographically and phonologically unaltered, but it takes on a transformed syntactic role, depending upon the interpretant attached to it. Another type of *transformation-translation* in which both the interpretant and the representamen suffer a change is dramatically illustrated by Umberto Eco in his analysis of the altering interpretations of 'sugar' and 'cyclamates' shortly after saccharin was introduced to the public (1976:287–8). At one time 'sugar' was considered to be a cause of obesity, heart attacks, and therefore death, while 'cyclamates' made one pleasantly thin, thus preventing heart attacks and warding off the onslaught of death – and, to boot, one became more attractive to the opposite sex. Then it was suddenly announced that 'cyclamates' caused cancer, and the interpretation of both 'sugar' and 'cyclamates' was drastically altered. For much of the populace now, 'sugar,' preventing cancer, became life-giving, and 'cyclamates,' causing cancer, were sure to usher in premature death. The representamens remained unchanged, but altered expectations brought about transformed interpretants.

Riddles also depict radical *transformation-translation* of the representamen when an interpretant previously attached to a different representamen is *translated* into it. Take a riddle the answer to which depends on a hidden meaning, to wit, 'What is black and white and red (read) all over.' It makes use of a homonym. The sound images of the representamens 'red' and 'read' are basically the same. But when the answer to the riddle is divined, a new context has been called up that demands an interpretant engendered by a representamen ('read') that is radically distinct from that which was originally expected ('red'). Discernibility of the two representamens is possible not through their sound images, which the addressee ordinarily receives from the verbally communicated riddle, but solely through their graphic images.

In each of these examples, the mind plays an active role in bringing about sign *transformation-translation.* Moving closer to the home base of Putnam's thought-experiment, basically the same imaginary situation about *transformation-translation* could be said of a four-elements Aristotelian Ourearther and a post-Daltonian many-elements Mendeleyevian Ourearther. The first uses 'water' to relate to that familiar colourless liquid with respect to the other three elements, fire, air, and earth. The second enjoys a more complex vocabulary. A new (*translated*) sign, 'H_2O,' refers to a compound made up of two different substances combined according to a certain ratio, while 'water' remains as that familiar colourless liquid. Yet, given certain conditions and contexts, the mental state of both semiotic agents could well be the same when they avail themselves of their vocabulary, however impoverished or however rich it may be. When thirsting and petitioning a cool glass of the liquid stuff, their meaning of 'water' could be virtually synonymous. One person's interpretation of the sign is a *translation* of the other's interpretation of the same sign, to be sure. The case of a post-Daltonian Ourearther in the lab uttering 'H_2O' is another matter entirely, however. 'H_2O' is a *translation* of 'water' as if into another language. 'H_2O' in Labspeak is radically distinct from 'water' in the 'language game' of liquid refreshment (Putnam 1988:22–6).

The case of Ourearther and Twinearther is yet another story. Objective, bare-bones 'reference' is different because the stuff is different, in spite of the fact that as far as we can tell their 'mental states' are the same when they use their respective signs. In the case of the four-element scientist and the many-element scientist, 'reference' is basically the same, and mental states can be either comparable or radically distinct, depending upon the context. In the first case, time is of no real consequence, while in the second, cultural settings separated in time become a factor. Yet over the long haul, sign *ensemble* and the *history* of sign use become virtually the same ball of wax. The upshot is that whatever goes on within the skull of the semiotic agent, it does not, and cannot, serve to fix the 'reference' of her signs, and the same can be said of the entire community to which she belongs. As a result of Putnam's brains-in-a-vat and Twin Earth, we have it that one sign (representamen), or two different signs supposedly 'referring' to the same thing (object), can actually give rise to meanings (interpretants) and what are construed as 'referents' that can range over an indefinite, and in their totality an indefinable, number of variables. In a manner of speaking, whatever we want our signs and the world to be, somewhere along the historical stretch, they ain't. And whatever security we wish to find in our most cherished meanings, sooner or later they'll turn against us.

Now, what has all this to do with the relevance of Putnam to Peirce regarding meaning? We'll get there, eventually; it will just take some time. Making the necessary preliminary connection calls for discussion of yet another Putnam thought experiment, the most bizarre of all (which also bears on the now familiar Löwenheim-Skolem theorem). But that side of Putnam must also wait, until the next chapter, after a few other preliminaries have been set out.

2. Objective or Internal? Ideal or Real?

As a consequence of Peirce's sphere of *possibilia* (*vagueness*), the superposition of all things possible as an *ensemble* of indefinite magnitude without any definite thing being actualized, there is always licence for *inconsistencies.*

For what was simply a duck can become more specifically a drake: 'machismo' can become sexism, sadism can become masochism, the earth as centre of the universe can become the sun as centre of the universe, I can become a brain-in-a-vat, Cervantes's *Don Quixote* can become Menard's *Don Quixote*, H_2O can become XYZ, ex-Somoza lackeys can become freedom fighters in Nicaragua, genocide can become ethnic cleansing, and so on – of course, I obstinately reiterate the relentless theme of this inquiry, but each time from a broadened perspective. This random mix of what would ordinarily be taken as contradictories – the two poles of each of which could well have been randomly selected from the realm of *vagueness* – illustrate that pure Firstness as pure chance offers the possibility of virtually any imaginable combination. This is no mere game of anything goes, mind you, since, within a given cultural context, some possibilities enjoy a greater probability of actualization than others. Yet, from the realm of pure Firstness, chance is the name of the game. There is necessarily no absolute necessity; at times there is hardly more than a toss of the dice. In other words, we are in the semiotic counterpart to Cantor's uncountable continuum, *c*. And we see Putnam bounding onto the scene once again, whose 'internal realism' seems, in the guts, somehow akin to Peirce's 'objective idealism.' But how?

Ultimately, the relation between Putnam and Peirce, I believe, has to do with different sorts of pragmatism. Hacking (1983:62) makes the sweeping and at the outset apparently irresponsible observation that Putnam is today's Peirce and that Rorty in *Philosophy and the Mirror of Nature* often plays the role of John Dewey and William James. In other words, pragmatism, Hacking goes on, branches. There are the Peirce-Putnamites who maintain hopes that reason and method will in the end triumph and the 'real' will be at hand, though only in the indefinitely extended long run. How best to learn about and give account of the world, that is, how to live and know, is what is important. On the other hand, there are the Rorty-James-Deweyites who eschew the spectator theory of learning, accounting for, and knowing the world. Proper living is chiefly a matter of getting along with one's fellow citizens and amicably arriving at some sort of agreement regarding the way things are: the very idea of 'knowledge' and 'reality' accessed through 'thought' and 'representation' is what the deluded dreams of yesteryear were built upon. Both branches of pragmatism are anti-realist, but each in its own way. The Rorty crowd goes forth in praise of good talk; the Putnam contingent persists in its rather Peirce-like quest for what might ultimately be regarded as 'reality,' though with no realist's royal road to 'truth,' for there is no one-and-only royal road, but merely the route that leads to where the community happens to have travelled.

There is some value to Hacking's statement, as far as sweeping assertions go (see also Hausman 1993). Much of the affinity between Peirce and Putnam stems from the latter's 'internal realism.' Putnam, formerly rather sympathetic with the objectivist or metaphysical-realist contingency, has developed in recent years his 'internal realism.' His change of heart and mind reveals an attempt to come to grips with the idea of a universe capable of producing knowers that, upon at least partly knowing it, construct a picture of it such that it somehow patterns itself, no matter how blemished the image. Putnam first posits that there can be no one-and-only-one 'true' and complete description of the world. Belief in such is belief in some detached external vantage and in some sign system external to 'reality' but related to it by the same relation that gives meaning to those very signs. Putnam is by no means proposing that there is no 'reality' and no 'way the world is,' however. He, like Peirce, is only denying that we can know it consistently and completely.

What Putnam does propose is that in place of a view from 'nowhere,' that is, from somewhere as if it were outside the universe, there are only finite, fallible human views. He outlines his thesis succinctly. 'Internal realism,' he concedes, runs the risk of being confused with other perspectives of subjectivist or idealistic sort. Yet he remains with the *internalist* label,

> because it is characteristic of this view to hold that *what objects does the world consist of?* is a question that it only makes sense to ask *within* a theory or description. Many 'internalist' philosophers, though not all, hold further that there is more than one 'true' theory of description of the world. 'Truth,' in an internalist view, is some sort of (idealized) rational acceptability – some sort of ideal coherence of our beliefs with each other and with our experiences *as those experiences are themselves represented in our belief system* – and not correspondence with mind-independent or discourse-independent 'states of

affairs.' There is no God's Eye point of view that we can know or usefully imagine; there are only the various points of view of actual persons reflecting various interests and purposes that their descriptions and theories subserve. (Putnam 1981:49–50)

This *internalist* approach, Putnam assures us, avoids the problems of 'reference,' 'representation,' 'correspondence,' 'objectivism,' and 'verificationism' of various sorts. Rather than 'reality' lying 'out there' in wait of our penetrating perceptual exploration of it, the world is understood in terms of our imposing our conceptual schemes on it. We make a world, *our* world, that is one of the myriad possibilities that could otherwise have been our world instead of the one that *is*. Our signs do not by their very nature as signs hopefully mirroring the world correspond to objects, acts, and events 'out there,' independently of how those signs function. On the contrary. A sign 'that is actually employed in a particular way by a particular community of users can correspond to particular objects *within the conceptual scheme of those users*. "Objects" do not exist independently of conceptual schemes. We cut up the world into objects when we introduce one or another scheme of description. Since objects *and* the signs are alike *internal* to the scheme of description, it is possible to say what matches what' (Putnam 1981:52).

To repeat, Putnam does not claim that objects do not exist. They exist, for sure, but their existence is existence *for* particular semiotic agents within particular socio-cultural milieus. To evoke physicist Arthur Eddington's used and abused, and occasionally maligned, example, my computer desk from the theoretical physicist's perspective is no 'desk' at all; it is a swarm of electrical charges within a set of largely vacuous spatial parameters. For me it is a single, impenetrable object with a necessary function. For my dog, it is most likely nothing more than an impediment. For my spouse it is a mess I really should clean up once in a while. The desk is 'real' in all those worlds (just as 'water' is 'real' for the pre-Daltonian and the post-Daltonian, and 'water' and 'H_2O' are both real for the latter, depending upon the 'language game' being used). But in each world it is slightly to radically different. Put all these worlds together without actualizing any of them and you have the makings of an *overdetermined* realm consisting of a superposed set of possible worlds. If one of them is actualized, it can exist in a somewhat *underdetermined* world in the sense that at every juncture it is potentially subjected to the infiltration of other alternatives that are always lying in wait to take their place alongside items of experience in other slightly different to largely incommensurable worlds. Hence, when Putnam writes that objects, acts, and events do not exist independently of some world or other he is not denying them any 'reality.' Rather, he is leaving open the possibility that whatever happens to 'exist' in a particular world could always have been something other than what it is from some other, perhaps equally legitimate, perspective.

In short, Putnam's 'internal realism' touches base with Peirce's 'objective idealism' insofar as both (1) are committed to the existence of 'reality,' (2) entail some link, however tenuous, between particular worlds (constructed psychologically and interpersonally as a result of habit, regularity, and convention) and 'reality' by way of experience, (3) are predicated on the idea of a constant give-and-take (dialogical in the sense of Peirce) between the individual and 'reality,' with the latter exercising limitations and constraints on the former, and (4) maintain the idea of 'truth' (accessible only in the theoretical 'long run' according to Peirce, and inaccessible to human experience since it is in possession of no all-encompassing view according to Putnam) (see note 9 of the Preamble).

Nevertheless, Hacking insists on labelling Putnam's 'internal realism' a 'species of idealism' (1983:92). Internal realism, we are told, is no half-way house between scientific realism and anti-realism, which maintained a crucial distinction between theoretical and observable entities. Putnam's philosophy reflects on language in general, which is not what the most important aspect of natural science is about. Hacking concedes that he cannot simply bypass Putnam, since he touches on issues of current interest: the 'linguistic turn' in both Anglo-American and Continental philosophy. Moreover, Hacking observes that Putnam 'seems to be a scientific realist within his internal realism' (1983:92), for it is characteristic of the 'internal realist' view that the furniture of the world is accessible solely from *within* some theory or description.

Hacking observes further that 'internal realism' and Peirce's style of pragmatism have much in common, though he gives few specifics. Putnam's 'ideal coherence' of our beliefs and experiences brings Peirce's community to mind. Putnam's remark that many – though not all – 'internal realists' concede to more than one 'true' theory or description of the world apparently bears witness to Peirce's human fallibility, which allows 'false' theories to be taken as 'true' from one of an indefinite number of possible perspectives – though Putnam does not buy into Peirce's asymptotic 'convergence' of theory toward 'truth.' Above all, Putnam's contention that 'internal realism' posits no correspondence between mind(*interpretant*)-independent or discourse(*sign*)-independent 'states of affairs' and the 'real' bears directly on Peirce's sign theory. For Peirce there can be neither direct correspondence to the 'real' nor any mind- or sign-independence, strictly defined. Rather, interactive interrelation comes to bear on mind (interpretants), signs (representamens), and the 'semiotically real' world (of objects). Consequently, to repeat, there can be no all-encompassing view the equivalent of which would be a Cantorian Supermathematician capable of holding the whole of Firstness (an uncountable infinity – chance, *possibilia*) as well as of Thirdness (as a completed, and presumably countable infinity – necessity, *probabilia*) in her surveillance.

Peirce, I must point out, had no use for absolute idealism: he believed that nothing could be more misdirected than the idea that 'we can experience only our ideas.' His brand of 'idealism' was ontological insofar as our knowledge of the things in themselves 'is entirely relative.' This 'relativity,' however, is the product of some conception or other of that which is 'real,' for 'all experience and all knowledge is knowledge of that which is, independently of being represented' (that is, given sign mediation). Yet no sign can 'relate or even pretend to relate to any object " unless that object is the object of a sign, a 'semiotic' object (*CP*:6.95). So the 'real' exists, and it is potentially linked to our mode of conception and our signs, but any infallible linkage is only accessible to the ultimate opinion of an unlimited (that is, nonfinite) community. It would appear that the best we can hope for is a constant dialogue, however modest, with nature, and with ourselves.

As we noted in previous sections, Putnam dismisses the story about brains-in-a-vat knowing they are brains-in-a-vat as wishful thinking, no more than a linguistic construction. That the very idea might be 'true' in some universe presumes a holistic grasp of the brains-in-a-vat universe as a whole. To the question 'From whose point of view is the story being told?' Putnam responds that it is evidently '*not* from the point of view of any of the sentient creatures *in* the world. Nor from the point of view of any observer in another world who interacts with this world; for a "world" by definition includes everything that interacts in any way with the things it contains' (1981:50). To suppose a brain-in-a-vat knows all sentient beings in her world are brains-in-a-vat is to suppose she is the only person in her world capable of knowing what it is *not* to be a brain-in-a-vat, which presupposes her transporting herself outside her brains-in-a-vat world: that impossible yet persistent quest for omniscience.

On the other hand, how is it that *Gedanken* experiments can come about, if not by virtue of storytelling activities *as if* from 'outside'? And how is it that, if their authors are successful, they can become keys to unlock the secrets of the world? Einstein's notoriously remarkable series of imaginary constructs that led him to the theories of relativity presupposed himself as an observer *sub specie aeternitatis*. He was the first to deny any omniscient point of view, yet he never faltered in his belief that '[t]he system of concepts is a creation of man together with the rules of syntax, which constitute the structure of the conceptual systems ... All concepts, even those which are closest to experience, are from the point of view of logic freely chosen conventions, just as is the case with the concept of causality' (Einstein 1949a:13). At the same time he

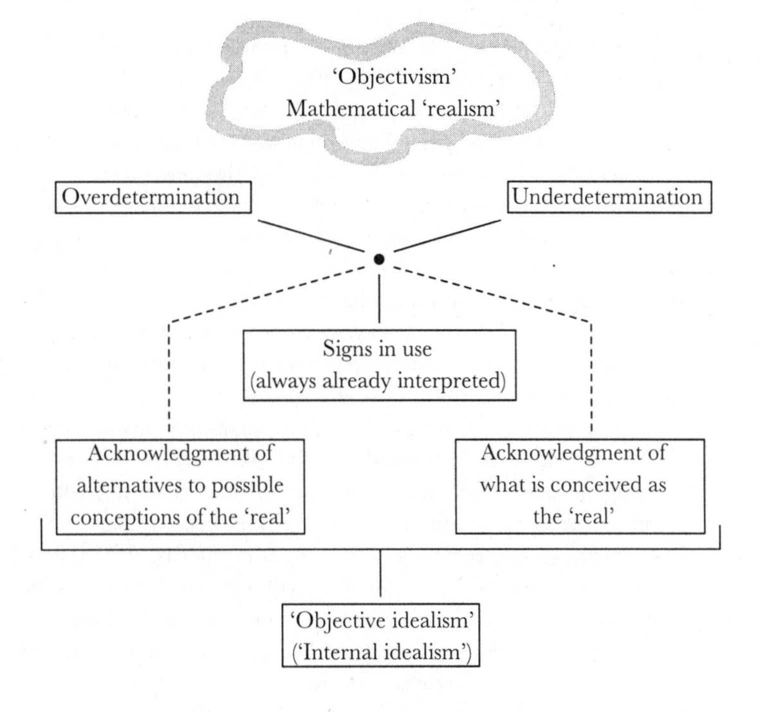

Figure 10

warned that concepts 'which have been proved to be useful in ordering things easily acquire such an authority over us that we forget their human origin and accept them as invariable' (ibid.:75–6). This danger is always present, since it is 'theory which decides what we can observe' (Einstein, in Heisenberg 1971:63). It would appear, from within Peircean sign theory, that though the 'semiotically real' never ceases to force itself onto the sign-events and their respective interpretants, nonetheless, interpretants (concepts) engendered out of thought-signs, either with benign intent or maliciously, can come to serve as models, patterns, or diagrams of the 'real.' Meinong mental constructs are in this sense neither entirely autonomous of nor embedded within our world of 'semiotically real' signs, but rather, on the stage of Secondness, there is constant interaction between actualized signs and our 'real world' as we see and think it.

Conjoining Peirce and Putnam, 'objective idealism' and 'internal realism,' we have figure 10. 'Objectivism' and mathematical 'realism' remain in their ethereal realm outside the picture of pragmatic sign interaction entirely. Not so regarding 'objective idealism' as a sort of 'methodological realism' conjoined with 'ontological idealism,' as Rescher and Brandom would have it (1979; but see Hausman 1993, Skagestad 1981). 'Objective idealist' practices, in contrast, bring about a link between the particulars of everyday life (Seconds), that which gives order to our world (the perceived and conceived regularities, drawn from habit and convention: *underdetermined* Thirds), and the (*overdetermined*) sphere of *possibilia* (as Firsts). But especially in light of 'internal realism,' there is acknowledgment that what is perceived and conceived as 'real' could always have been something other than what it is, given the vast array of all conceived alternatives that could have been actualized but were not. And especially in light of 'objective idealism,' there is acknowledgment that what will have been actualized depends upon the conditional mood built within the 'pragmatic maxim' and governed by the conception of all possible worlds.

'Methodological realism' most properly – though indeterminately so – pertains to the first-order logic of Secondness, that of the sentential connectives *and*, *or*, *not*, and the quantifiers. This is the arena of signs in use within the context of sign-agent interaction: it is where signs become signs *for* their respective interpreters. The realm of *overdetermination*, that is, the range of all *possibilia*, could be said for practical purposes to be tantamount to the actual infinite, comparable to the set of real numbers. The realm of *underdetermination*, including 'ontological idealism' within its embrace, would then be potentially infinite in extension, like the natural numbers – and hence it is destined to remain incomplete. Here, a Löwenheim-Skolem sort of concept exercises its force, since there is always the chance of unintended, unforeseen interpretations of signs. Within this realm, first-order logic of Secondness evolves into more complex signs, propositions and arguments, sentences and texts, in its road toward full-fledged Thirdness.

In another manner of putting it, Peirce once observed (*CP*:2.356), regarding the three basic levels of linguistic (symbolic) signs, that an isolated word is a sentence whose subject has had its power to relate to other words removed, and a sentence is an argument or text whose sentences have had their power of assertion removed. In this sense, a word is devoid of genuine predication, a sentence of the barest sort carries predication of the first order, and complex sentences and texts progressively move up the ladder toward their semiotic fulfilment. However, as we shall note below, once signs have become signs *for* some agent or agents, they are never taken simply as raw semiotic entities later to be endowed with interpretations: as soon as participatory agents enter the ring, signs are always already interpreted in some fashion or other; there are no pristine, unmediated signs.

So much for this preliminary look at the interface between Putnam and Peirce, which, however schematic, at least in part bears out Hacking's equation.

Let us now turn to a relevant aspect of Quine before moving on in the next chapter to that bizarre Putnam thought-experiment I promised.

3. Rabbits, by Reason, Re-cognition, or Ruse?

With respect to the points of contact between 'objective idealism' and 'internal realism,' one might wish to conclude that Quine's *indeterminacy of translation* and *inscrutability of reference* are relevant. But they are not, at least not to the extent that we might expect.

In a nutshell, Quine, using examples so modest they appear sanguine and at times even absurd, believes he demonstrates that you can never actually know what I am talking about and I can never really know what you are talking about – contrary, it would appear, to Rorty's hopes, and the hopes of many others as well. But it doesn't really matter anyway, for as long as we make gallant pretences at communicating, and insofar as we are at least successful enough to meet our own demands for satisfaction, for practical purposes it can be said that more often than not we know with some degree of approximation what each other is talking about. In the best of all possible worlds we just sort of muddle along. In saying this I am not alluding to the 'charity principle,' that is, to the equivalent of Davidson's (1984) method for finding a fit between what one person says and another person tends to hear or wishes to hear. Rather, I am speaking of the act of bringing some semblance of order to the chaos of radical indeterminacy by the *semiosic* process of sign making and sign taking. Which is to say that signs are not genuine signs unless they enjoy interaction between semiotic agents endowing them with full-blown interpretants.

Quine once outlined a procedure for the elimination of proper names as well as common names in favour of predicates on the grounds that they are actually unnecessary for a language capable of expressing legitimate statements about the world (1950:149–50). He suggests that instead of adopting a name, say, 'rabbit,' as a primitive, a primitive form of matrix or a predicate may be adopted. In so doing, Quine makes no semantic distinction between common nouns, adjectives, and intransitive verbs. He sees 'is a,' 'is,' '-ing,' 'and,' and '-or' as nothing more than grammatical adapters 'for converting common nouns and adjectives into verbs and verbs into adjectives and common nouns, for adjustment to various grammatical constructions' (Quine 1986:567). Rather than eliminating common names, however, this move is, more properly stated, an assimilation to common names. In the genuine semiotic sense, nouns, adjectives, and verbs are all symbols, but symbols that either contain designators or indicators (indices: nouns and their properties or adjectives) or qualifiers (icons: verbs), or they contain both (symbols as composite signs:

clauses, sentences). Just as symbols contain icons and indices, so also they are enablers for converting (*translating*, giving meaning to) one sign type into another sign of another type.

To cite Quine's familiar example, suppose a field linguist without any knowledge of a native language overhears 'Gavagai!' from one of her 'informants' when in the presence of a fleeing rabbit. 'Gavagai!' could possibly be construed as a holophrastic sentence such as 'Rabbit,' or it could be the equivalent of 'There goes a rabbit,' 'Yonder, a fleeing ruminant,' 'Greyness penetrating a background of brownness punctuated by intermittent greenness,' 'Ruminant becoming moving amongst diverse botanical becomings,' or some other alternative. The common noun is *translated* into other parts of speech and thereby it presumably becomes meaningful within the context of the utterance. The fact that the 'informant' uttered 'Gavagai!' in this particular occasion attests to the fact that on this and other such occasions he is 'seeing gavagaily' in a manner comparable, the linguist might assume, to her in her own language 'seeing rabbitly' when uttering the holophrastic sentence 'Rabbit.' (I take it that Quine uses his terms in the sense of translation between one scientific theory and another, though he does not always make a distinction between scientific and metaphysical language or between metaphysical language and ordinary talk, and though, quite surprisingly, most commentators of Quine rarely allude to scientific theory talk.)

Quite conceivably, the sensations experienced by both the linguist and her 'informant' are virtually equivalent, that being the presence of 'rabbitness' and 'gavagainess' respectively. But there can be no absolute guarantee that this is so. From within the Peircean framework, 'rabbit' (as a term or word) is used potentially to indicate an entire set of propositions (sentences), 'That is a rabbit,' and so on, from which an argument (text) can then be engendered. The term is in this sense a condensed sign whose interpretant must carry an overload, serving in multiple capacities (as if it were a composite icon). On the other hand, in the Peircean as well as the Quinean perspective, within the distinct framework of term and interpretant there is no absolutely determinate meaning, translation, or 'reference.' There is no way of knowing without a shadow of a doubt that 'Gavagai!' 'refers to' a concrete, individual thing in English we call 'Rabbit,' hence a mistake always stands at least an outside chance of emerging. Quine's *inscrutability of reference* stipulates that the 'reference' of general terms or terms of divided 'reference' in an alien language cannot determine how the world is individuated, how it is otherwise sliced up into patterns, or how scattered portions of it are combined. From one language to another the world, in somewhat the Sapir-Whorf fashion, may be cut up in widely varying ways that lead to radically divergent translations between the two languages, depending on how far one is willing to make compensating adjustments in the translation of terms in question. As E.E. Evans-Pritchard puts it:

> The semiotic difficulties in translation ... are considerable enough between, shall we say, French and English, but when some primitive language has to be rendered into our own tongue they are, and for obvious reasons, much more formidable ... If an ethnographer says that in the language of a Central African people the word *ango* means dog, he would be entirely correct, but he has only to a limited degree thereby conveyed the meaning of *ango*, for what it means to natives who use the word is very different to what 'dog' means to an Englishman. The significancy dogs have for them – they hunt with them, they eat them, and so on – is not the significance they have for us. How much greater is the displacement likely to be when we come to terms which have a metaphysical reference! (1962:79; compare Evans-Pritchard's words to the Master's remarks on the *breadth* and *depth* of signs)

In Quine's hypothetical native language, 'Gavagai!' may be tentatively correlated with the term 'Rabbit.' But if a rabbit happens to be in the vicinity when the two terms are used supposedly as synonyms, a set of 'undetached rabbit parts' and a 'temporal stage in a rabbit's space-time development' are also present. In Quine's words, the only difference between rabbits, undetached rabbit parts, and rabbit stages 'is in their individuation. If you take the total scattered portion of the spatio-temporal world that is made up of rabbits, and that which is made up of undetached rabbit parts, and that which is made up of rabbit stages, you come out with the same scattered portion of the world each of the three times. The only difference is how you slice it. And how to slice it is what ostension or simple conditioning, however persistently repeated, cannot teach'(1969:32). The theoretical uncertainty concerning translation of "Gavagai!" to 'Rabbit' stems from the radical impossibility of knowing absolutely that 'Gavagai!' relates to 'Rabbit' and not to 'undetached rabbit parts' or 'rabbit stages' – that is, 'slices out of the space-time continuum.' The linguist's deciding upon 'Rabbit' or 'rabbit slices' depends upon her vantage point, whether of ordinary (Newtonian) physical theory or of (Einsteinian) space-time slice theory. In other words, the decision is based on whether the 'coordinate system' ultimately selected for interpretation from the native language to English is that of discourse about physical things or about space-time slices. This, the essence of Quine's relativity thesis, renders pointless all talk of there being a rabbit 'there' for both linguist and 'informant,' or of whether or not both 'Gavagai!' and 'Rabbit' are related to 'that rabbit there.' (Regarding Davidson's use of the 'charity principle' [1984:125–54], there is no radical uncertainty in the strict Quine sense, but rather, the field linguist must be prepared to declare that, given the evidence at hand, and in view of the fact that she and her subjects are of the same thinking and feeling community of humans, most of what they say about 'rabbitness' is true of what she would say about 'rabbitness.' She should also be prepared to concede that when she observes native behaviour to deviate from what would ordinarily be her behaviour in the presence of 'rabbitness,' her interpretation was flawed and she must alter it. So according to Davidson's theory there is *interpretative uncertainty*, which may well be more radical than Quine's *ontological* and *methodological uncertainty*.)

For Quine, *inscrutability of reference* applies to such general terms (types) as 'green' and 'alpha' in addition to concrete individual terms (tokens). These terms can be used as abstract entities (the colour green, a letter in the Greek alphabet) or as generalities applicable to concrete objects (a green car, a mark on paper). Different 'reference' calls for different use. The first case would pertain to what I have called above the internally 'real,' the second to the externally 'real.' Sensation of green when seeing a car or of a Greek cipher when gazing at a set of inscriptions is quality, feeling, Firstness. These bear the rudiments of iconicity. Signs of indexicality would be the rough equivalent of ostension (pointing) in analytical philosophy parlance. Indicating (indexing) a car or a car sentence by 'that' when uttering a few vague words about cars might be construed in the standard sense as 'reference' to the items in question (I will resort to that undesirable term 'reference' for the sake of illustrating Quine's theory). '*That* is a classy set of wheels' or '*That* is not what I had in mind' qualify their 'semiotic object' to a certain extent.

Regarding ostension, the problematics of translation are the same as that for 'Gavagai!' Just as when in the native language the linguist, by ostension, tries to ask 'Is this "gavagai" the same as "that" (while showing the native a rabbit picture)?' she could just as well ask 'Does this "gavagai" belong to "that" set of sensory data?' or 'Is this thing you call "gavagai" like "that" thing I call "rabbit"?' In whichever case '[t]he native's assent is no objective evidence for translating "gavagai" into "rabbit" rather than "undetached rabbit parts" or "rabbit stage"' (Quine 1969:33). There simply is no determinable way to see, cognize, and say the ambulating quadruped in the same way people from a different culture speaking a different language do – recall the Master's words with respect to the translation of 'world' from English to Spanish. Moreover, pointing to a green car or to the instantiation of the Greek symbol 'alpha' on a sheet of paper in teaching the concrete term need vary hardly a whit from the act of pointing to the car or the mark in an effort to teach the general terms 'green' or 'alpha.' Yet what is 'referred to' by the words is very different with respect to the two uses: under the one use the word is 'true' of many concrete objects, while under the other use it names a single abstract object upon asking 'Is this "gavagai" the same as "that"?' The first designator, 'this,' could refer to 'rabbit,' 'undetached rabbit parts,' or 'rabbit stage' as a token of a type while 'Does "this" "gavagai" belong to "that"?' involves the same ambiguity with respect to an abstract generality.

Not even is one's own language free of the referential inscrutability endemic in translation. One ordinarily translates one's neighbour's talk homophonically into one's own way of talking, a practice that is warranted and advisable, since perhaps there is no other viable method ready for use. However, unambiguous results are by no means guaranteed, for, though compensating adjustments can usually be made with the best of intentions in mind, the 'referential' import of the conversation remains open to variations. For example, one can consciously reconstrue one's neighbour's apparent 'reference' to rabbits as 'reference' to 'rabbit stages.' On so doing, one 'can reconcile all this with [one's] neighbor's verbal behavior by cunningly readjusting [one's] translations of his various connecting predicates so as to compensate for the switch of ontology' (Quine 1969:47). By the same token, one constantly runs the risk of misconstruing messages – though not so drastically, we must presume, except in the most extreme cases. Ultimately one may arrive at a point of uncertainty compelling one to question the 'reference' of an entire vocabulary of words, entering into dialogue with oneself whether or not, for example, 'Rabbit' 'refers' directly to a physical item being sensed or to something else. This apparently makes nonsense of the idea of 'reference' – and for good reason. Quine himself admits that he seems to have manoeuvred himself into the uncomfortable position that 'there is no difference on any terms, interlinguistic or intralinguistic, objective or subjective, between referring to rabbits and referring to rabbit parts or stages ... Surely this is absurd. For it would imply that there is no difference between the rabbit and each of its parts or stages ... Reference would seem now to become nonsense not just in radical translation but at home' (ibid.:47–8).

At home in our own language, Quine seems to imply, we make the tacit assumption that we are communicating, do the best we can, assume everyone else is doing the same, and perhaps get along swimmingly (but Quine is not as optimistic regarding his 'uncertainty principle' as are Rorty and Davidson regarding their amiable chitchat). As far as 'reference' fixing goes, we simply say in so many words, by guesswork and by implication, that 'this' is a proof, 'that' a formula, and 'that' a number, or in Peirce's vocabulary, 'this' is an argument (text), 'that' a proposition (sentence), and 'that' a term (word), or, perhaps, 'this' is a 'rabbit slice,' 'that' a 'rabbit,' and 'that' a set of 'rabbit parts.'

This network of sentences and terms is our 'frame of reference' or 'coordinate system' – to use Quine's relativity jargon. Relative to this system we can and do communicate, usually meaningfully to a remarkable degree. But once we begin to contemplate the overwhelming range of alternatives to our customary use of language, or what we ordinarily conceive to be the denotation of our words, we 'begin to appreciate that a grand and ingenious permutation of these denotations, along with compensatory adjustments in the interpretations of the auxiliary particles, might still accommodate all existing speech dispositions' (Quine 1969:48). This reveals the *inscrutability of reference*, which plays havoc with 'reference' except relative to a 'coordinate system.' In this principle of relativity, Quine believes, lies the resolution to our meaning quandary, which might provide little consolation, but it is the best we have.

It is meaningless over the long haul to ask whether a number, a particular term, a set of rabbit parts, a proposition, or an argument actually refers to some particular entity rather than to some set of adroitly permutated denotations. The 'referential' capacity of a language can be placed in question only by recourse to what Quine calls a 'background language' that makes sense of the query only in a relative sense; that is, in a sense relative in turn to it, the 'background language' (Quine 1969:49). 'Reference' for which absolute answers are expected to be forthcoming is as meaningless, for Quine, as questions of absolute position or velocity. The positions of a spatial 'coordinate system' cannot be determined from some neutral and stationary rest point but only relative to some further 'coordinate system,' and that to another 'coordinate system,' and so on. The regress would be virtually infinite, if one were to remain exclusively within language. It can come to a halt, Quine maintains, only when one takes recourse to ostension (indexicality, Secondness), in order tentatively and temporally to fix some sort or other of 'reference.' Upon so halting the regress, one necessarily acquiesces in one's mother tongue and takes words at what one considers to be their apparently face value (ibid.). This hardly provides any lasting security, of course, but at least it helps one to flow along with the current.

The conclusion, it appears, is: sense can be had not by saying what the objects of 'reference' of a language are, in the absolute sense, but by trying to see how one language 'fits' with another.

4. Quine Quined?

(The verb 'to Quine' in this context was coined by Dennett [1988; but before Dennett's use of the term, see Hofstadter 1979]. Dennett's 'Quining' entails a denial of the existence of something that according to tradition must surely exist – for example, the soul. I use the term 'Quine' not exactly in the sense of Dennett, but for the purpose of denying the very relevance of the term.)

The idea of a 'fit' might appear to interface Quine with Peirce-Putnam, but upon a closer look it does not. Regarding 'fits' between languages from such an unlikely source as analytic philosophy, Quine tells us that 'resemblance' – he often uses the term 'similarity' – plays an indispensable role in the ballgame of human learning and cognition.

Quine's empiricist-behaviourist view – which was his fulcrum point during his ongoing wrangle with the rationalist Noam Chomsky – while not exactly commensurate with Peirce on all points, nonetheless presents an intriguing complementarity with the latter's concept of habit taking. The apprehension of resemblance is fundamental to learning in the broadest sense. For example, one begins the long, twisting road of language learning by ostension, by hearing a word applied to samples. All one has to go on is the resemblance of further cases to this sample. Resemblance being a matter of degree, learning must proceed by trial and error: when application of a word is too far out in left field, either one can backtrack or use the erroneous cases as samples to the contrary and continue the pursuit, guessing whether further cases are applicable or not and to what degree. This is the most primitive level of learning, of course, but according to Quine it is an absolutely essential step toward further cognitive development (1969:114–38). (Quine, in good behaviourist form, believes that the process of comparisons and inferences by resemblance or similarity is largely unconscious, basically the same process 'by which an animal learns to respond in distinctive ways to his master's commands or other discriminated stimulations' [ibid.:122].)

Once a resemblance space is 'progressively changed and elaborated as our learning proceeds' – a self-corrective activity we must assume – standards of resemblance that lead to 'false' predications can progressively get readjusted (Quine 1981:56–7). In the process one's inductions 'become increasingly explicit and deliberate,' and in the fullness of time one may be able to 'rise above induction, to hypothetico-deductive method' (Quine 1981:57). It might appear that we need only add a Peircean corollary: *abduction* is precisely what enables one to 'rise above induction' in the first place. Indeed, the *abductive* process itself pertains to Firstness, iconicity, resemblance, while induction depends chiefly, though not exclusively, on Secondness – what is other, 'out there,' 'semiotically real' – and Thirdness on deduction – that which is conditionally the case. Quine argues that resemblance is crucially relevant to the attainment of dispositions (also relevant to Peircean habit), to subjunctive conditionals (Thirdness), and to singular causal statements. However, he notes that from a scientific viewpoint these concepts are traditionally conceived to be a disreputable and motley collection. Yet some notion of resemblance is crucial to all learning, and it is central to inferential procedures, inductive generalization, and formation of predications, all of which serve as leavening for the scientific cake-bake. Quine notes that insofar as comparison by resemblance 'fits in with the regularities of nature, so as to afford us reasonable success in our primitive inductions and expectations, it is presumably an evolutional product of natural selection ... This development is a development away from the immediate, subjective, animal sense of similarity to the remoter objectivity of a similarity determined by scientific hypotheses and posits and constructs ... This progress of similarity standard, in the course of each individual's maturing years, is a sort of recapitulation in the individual of the race's progress from muddy savagery. But the similarity notion even in its theoretical phase is itself a muddy notion still. We have offered no definition of it in satisfactory scientific terms' (Quine 1969:133–4).

In spite of Quine's concession that his notion is somewhat less than legitimately scientific, he nonetheless sees this 'rise from savagery,' this sloughing off the muddy notion of kind or resemblance, to be the way we learn. The process is piecemeal: a bit here and a bit there, and from a cloud to a clock, from vagueness to verity, from the diffuse to the determinate, patterns begin to emerge. Though admittedly I have presented Quine's theory in sketchy fashion, I must also warn that it cannot be merely shoved aside with cavalier disinterest, as has occasionally been the practice. A further word, however brief, on the relation between Quine and Peirce is in order, then.

It is largely the case that we have from terms (words) to propositions (sentences) to arguments (texts) what some might conceive as a great chain of becoming that culminated in Western science and technology. From a view through the murky and meandering path of *abduction*, resemblance, and sentiment rather than reason, however, we have the 'tender minded' side of thought, which by no means should take a back seat to its hard-nosed counterpart. Peirce, decades before Quine's ruminations, declared that 'uncontrolled inference from contiguity, or experiential connection, is the most rudimentary of reasoning. A dog so reasons. When he hears his master's voice he runs in expectation of seeing him, and if he does not, he will manifest surprise, or, at any rate, perplexity' (*CP*:7.445) – this is quite comparable to Quine's frequent allusions to nonconscious communication by resemblance. On the other hand, inference from resemblance 'perhaps implies a higher degree of self-consciousness than any the brute possesses.' This latter form of thought involves, unlike its primitive predecessor, 'steady attention to qualities as such; and this must rest on a capacity, at least, for language, if not on language, itself' (*CP*:7.446).

It would seem, in this light, that Peirce's tripart concept of the sign, including iconicity and indexicality in addition to symbolicity, is more general than Quine's behaviouristic 'linguicentrism,' his 'enlightened empiricism' (Gibson 1988). It is even more general, as I implicated above, than Putnam's 'internal realism,' which also remains somewhat caught up in the tangle of the 'linguistic turn.' (The 'linguistic turn,' product of 'linguicentrism,' has recently been booted to a shrill pitch of intensity in the guise of what has been called the 'interpretive turn' [Hiley et al. 1991]. The Quine-Davidson maxim that all that means is linguistic is coupled with Nietzsche's perspectivistic 'facts are precisely what there is not, only interpretations' [1968:481], which Nehemas broadens in his assertion that 'all practices are interpretive' [1985:70], which is to say, all practices are linguistic – or literature, as it were. This protracted 'linguicentrism' must engage us at a later stage of the present inquiry.)

Peirce's concept of the sign includes the entire gamut from Firstness to Thirdness, giving the three categories pretty much equal time. Quine, in contrast, remains mired in what is essentially Secondness sporting a veneer of Thirdness, with hardly more than an occasional nod to Firstness. And Putnam, as we shall note further in the next chapter, focuses inordinately on Thirdness with a subtle tinge of Firstness, while slighting the Secondness of our concrete everyday affairs. As Hacking puts it, 'Putnam commits one of the gravest errors of philosophy. He has an abstract theorem' (1983:107).

We must pursue this line of inquiry further.

11

How We Can Go Wrong

1. If You've Seen One Cat, You've Seen the Class of All Cherries

In Quine's paradigm example, as we have seen, when I speak of rabbits, for all I know you may be conceptualizing 'undetached rabbit parts,' 'space-time slices of rabbithood,' 'fuzzy, elongated, horizontal greyness with vertical appendages in motion amongst green patches against a brownish background,' or some such thing. Quine's thought experiment is bizarre. But Putnam does him one better, leading us by the hand to the brink and playfully giving us a gentle nudge.

Putnam's story tells how minds can be the same though their signs are entirely different, or conversely, how signs can be the same but minds different. In either case, an entirely distinct 'semiotic reality' is yielded. It has to do with ordinary notions of reference apparently gone mad: I talk about cats and mats but you take me to mean cherries and trees, and you talk about cherries and trees but I think cats and mats. If we keep things honest, at the level of first-order predicates it is entirely possible that we will get along fine with the belief that we are communicating groovily. I am confident I know what you are talking about and you have the same confidence regarding my talk. But here, as in all forms of communication, there is no determinable knowing we are on the same frequency at all. In fact, there always exists the possibility that we are talking about different things altogether. This is not merely Quinean confusion regarding whether you are thinking 'rabbit' or 'a space-time slice of rabbithood' when I say 'rabbit,' but, rather, the same sign (representamen) relates to two incompatible 'semiotic objects,' and hence their respective interpretants (concepts) are equally incompatible.

To be specific, Putnam shows that 'A cat is on the mat' can be reinterpreted in such a manner that 'cat' for one interlocutor relates to *cherries* for another, and 'mat' for the one relates to *trees* for the other, without affecting the 'truth'-value of 'A cat is on the mat.' Putnam then designates 'cat' and 'mat' for some *cat* and some *mat*, and 'cat*' and 'mat*' for some *cherries* and some *trees*. When I say 'A cat is on the mat' I mean that there is some *cat* such that it is on some *mat*, but you construe my sentence to mean that there is (are) some *cat** (*cherries*) such that it is (they are) on some *mat** (*trees*). I don't know what you take my words to mean and you don't know what I mean by my words. In this manner, if you reinterpret my sign 'cat' by assigning it the 'intensional' framework I would ordinarily assign to 'cherries' (and you to 'cat*') and in the same semiotic act you reinterpret 'mat' in terms of what I would ordinarily assign to 'trees' (and you to 'mat*'), then we have translated two signs into two other signs. Yet phonemically and orthographically, 'cat' is the same as 'cat*' and 'mat' is the same as 'mat*.' Although via the 'charity principle' we believe our communication has us flowing along the same channel, our meanings are at cross current with one another: ordinary lines of communication have suffered a meltdown.

Supposing I utter 'cat' and 'mat' and you construe my signs as 'cat*' and 'mat*,' then structurally 'A cat is on a mat' would for me *mean* virtually the same as 'A cat* is on a mat*' for you. The only difference is in what is taken to be the object of 'reference' of our respective signs and what interpretation they are given – a difference that makes a crucial difference. And this, Putnam swears, would fall in step with our well regimented habit of assigning 'truth' to 'A cat is on a mat,' or any other string of signs for that matter, in every possible world – that is, the realm of *vagueness*. As Peirce might be prone to put it, when *vagueness* rules the roost, faith in the principle of contradiction can at times become a futile enterprise. 'Cat' and 'cat*' can live in blissful coexistence as long as their interpreters do not catch onto their ontological and semantic confusion. And insofar as the contradiction remains merely possible, the interlocutors may continue to swim along in blissful ignorance, oblivious as to the communication chasm between them. The upshot is that 'The cat is on the mat' or 'The cat* is on the mat*' can be taken either as intensional or extensional. There is hardly any difference for 'internal realism,' since, in the long run of things, and much in line with Peirce's thought, thought-signs can come to be construed as sign-events, and vice versa.

This conclusion entails, Putnam tells us, a re-application of the Löwenheim-Skolem theorem. The theorem applies to any domain of individual items of experience, whether *cats* and *cherries*, *mats* and *trees*, or any non-experiential domain for that matter – 'unicorns' and unicorn pictures, 'quarks' and quark equations, or 'square circles' and square-circle talk. Regarding any of these items, all of which come in signs of one sort or another, in spite of whatever we may conceive as meaning or 'truth,' unintended (unexpected) situations can always stand a chance of emerging from the *overdetermined* sphere to taunt us and throw our confidence-building programs, beliefs, conceptual schemes, and general views from within the *underdetermined* sphere into disarray. I intended 'cat' to be *cat* and you took it to be *cherries* ('cat*'). Or one person takes 'lightning bolts' to be *spears thrown by Jove* and another sees them as nothing but *electrical discharges.* Or the 'earth' as *static* becomes the 'earth' as *revolving about the sun.* And so on. The total range of possibilities is virtually beyond imagination, I would expect.

This observation, I might add, is also relevant to malapropisms and other rhetorical figures, as outlined by Davidson (1986), but not exactly in the manner intended by Davidson. 'Shrewd awakening' in place of 'rude awakening' could be the case of (1) the speaker's being unaware that he uses one word to mean another, or (2) his awareness of the inappropriate uses of words in order to make his listener aware of the malapropism. The listener can either (1) take the word at face value, unaware that it is used improperly, in which event confusion ensues, or (2) take the word at face value, knowing it is meant as a malapropism – stemming from Davidson's contention that there are only literal meanings – and interpret it accordingly (see Pradhan 1993). Regarding Putnam's context of conversation, 'cat' is taken either as 'cat' or 'cat*,' and endowed with its rightful meaning, each interlocutor believing her meaning to be quite in line with that of her counterpart. Both of them believe they know what they are doing, though miscommunication runs rampant. The upshot is that there is simply no guarantee of good intentions coupled with cognizance of what's going on regarding one's own mind, the mind of the other, and the surroundings in which both are found, as ideally would be the case of Davidsonian dialogue.

'Now let's get serious,' one might wish to retort. '"Cats" and "cats*" are radically distinct, one "referring to" *cats* and the other to *cherries.* So even though "There is a cat on the mat" and "There is a cat* on the mat*" are logically equivalent, it is impossible to conceive of their being fused together in such a way that their divergent "referents" will not immediately become apparent.' Putnam counteracts this charge. He reminds us that if the number of *cats* and the number of *cherries* available to a given pair of interlocutors happen to be equal – an unlikely affair one must admit – then it follows that 'cats' in relation to *cats* and 'cats*' in relation to *cherries* demands a shift of the entire set of lexical items in 'cat' language and in 'cat*' language such that, as wholes, the two languages become radically distinct. The sentences of each language remain unchanged regarding their 'truth'-value, while at the same time the extension of 'cats' and 'cherries' (that is, 'cats*') is drastically altered (in this respect, see also Lakoff's [1987] defence of Putnam *vis-à-vis* David Lewis's [1984] attack on the Putnam hypothesis).

So from within one 'language' I speak past you and from within another 'language' you speak past me, yet as far as our respective languages go, our 'semiotic world' appears as normal as can be. What is more, from within the range of all possible spatio-temporal contexts, 'cats' for *cats* and 'cats*' for *cherries* are equally permissible, as are 'cats' for 'bats,' 'rats,' 'Blatz,' 'quacks,' 'quarks,' 'sharks,' 'aardvarks,' or virtually anything else for that matter. Each and every interpretation is distinct, yet all are equally admissible from some perspective or other. In fact, 'there are always infinitely many different interpretations of the predicates of a language that assign the "correct" truth-values to the sentences in all possible worlds, *no matter how these "correct" truth-values are singled out*' (Putnam 1981:35). Putnam's conclusion: nature does not single out any one 'correspondence' between signs and the furniture of the world; rather, nature 'gets us to process words and thought signs in such a way that sufficiently many of our directive beliefs will be true, and so that sufficiently many of our actions will contribute to our "inclusive genetic fitness"; but this leaves reference largely indeterminate' (ibid.:41).

This perturbing radical indeterminacy of 'reference' and of interpretation might remind us of the strange case of Borges's Pierre Menard, who, after a failed attempt, wrote a few passages identical to part of *Don Quixote* without previously having read Cervantes's masterpiece. Ironically, Menard's critics totally recontextualized his text, claiming the replica was actually a great improvement of the original. It was the product of creative endeavours not of a Golden-Age Spaniard but of a twentieth-century Frenchman ignorant of the time of which he wrote. They considered Menard to have 'enriched, by means of a new technique, the halting and rudimentary art of reading; this new technique is that of the deliberate anachronism and the erroneous attribution. The technique whose applications are infinite, prompts us to go through the *Odyssey* as if it were posterior to the *Aeneid* ... This technique fills the most placid works with adventure' (Borges 1962:44).

Placing Borges's 'thought-experiment' within the context of Putnam's quandary, Menard's fragments could be taken by one reader as Menard's text and by another reader as Quixote's text, or vice versa, and virtually incommensurable interpretations would ensue. In one interpretation, the Menard text might contain allusions to Nietzsche, William James, Russell, Proust, Dickens, and others, while the Cervantes text would be relatively impoverished. And in another interpretation the Cervantes text might be rich in the cultural lore of early-seventeenth-century Spain, which would be diluted considerably in the Menard text. What is virtually a 'cat' for one mind can be a 'cat*' for another: nothing is either 'cat' or 'cat*,' but mind can serve to make it so. Whether we are in first-order sentences or sentences of greater complexity, as long as minds do not or cannot meet at some point or other, there is little hope of effective communication, 'charity principles' notwithstanding. Menard's text or Cervantes's text, or 'cat' or 'cat*,' consist of the same signs in terms of their pure possibilities (of Firstness). But upon their being actualized (into Secondness) and endowed with interpretants (Thirdness), they relate to different 'semiotic objects' whose respective interpretants are radically distinct, even well-nigh incommensurable. This is a case altogether distinct from that of Ourearthers and Twinearthers whose signs and 'objects' were different, but as far as the 'naive realists' among them were concerned, their interpretants were fundamentally the same. (While sticking with Putnam's rather 'linguicentric' example, I have, of course, almost entirely ignored the iconic and indexical dimension of *semiosis*, both of which are remarkably presented in Cervantes's text: for example, the image of a windmill viewed simply as a 'windmill' or as a 'menacing enemy of the crown,' with the moving parts either as indices of 'windmill blades' or 'threatening appendages engaged in battle tactics.')

But there's the other, complementary, problem: if different signs relate to the same 'object,' can their meanings be the same, or will they inevitably be different? This is Quine's 'Gavagai' conundrum in a somewhat different garment. And it is the flip side of Frege's 'morning star' and 'evening star' relating to the same planet but engendering their own 'sense.' Anthropologist Dorothy Lee reports on a comparable problem in her translating from the Trobriand language to English. A given word for the Trobrianders relates to a self-contained concept, as does a particular word in English. For example, what in English we consider an attribute of a predicate is for them an ingredient, an integral part of the main semantic course. Where we would say 'an excellent hunter,' they would combine two nouns, 'hunter' and 'excellence,' in the same expression. And if the 'hunter' suffers a loss of 'excellence,' in their language he would no longer be the same 'hunter' but must go by a different name altogether. In other words, the Trobrianders do not have our culturally inculcated concept of continuity, of the generality of a 'semiotic object' that makes it the same yesterday, today, and tomorrow in spite of the fact that it ages, oxidizes, rots, blooms, sublimates, is carried up into heaven, or whatever. They are in this sense inveterate nominalists. Moreover, time takes on a different countenance in the Trobriand language. There are no tenses, no linguistic distinctions between past or present. There is no arrangement of events into means and ends, causes and effects, no apparent sequence of connected events, but rather, a somewhat disconnected series.

In short, the Trobrianders do not describe their activity linearly; they do not bother to emphasize any dynamic relation of events; they do not even employ such innocuous connectives as 'and' and 'or.' Lee cites as an example a literal translation into English of part of a Trobriander's description of the planting of a coconut: 'Thou-approach-there coconut thou-bring-here-we-plant-coconut thou-go thou-plant our coconut. This-here it-emerge sprout. We-push-away this we-push-away this-other coconut-husk-fiber together sprout it-sit together root' (1959:112). She goes on to remark that, accustomed as we are to our linear continuity, we tend to lard in the gaps so we can construct a more sequentially ordered narrative. But the continuity we consequently impose on our translation simply does not exist in the Trobriand text; it is 'jerky,' it is given in discontinuous segments, not connecting lines. Trobriand narrative functions somewhat like a slide show, in contrast to our video-like English with which we are more comfortable. (However, our own culture could well be undergoing a profound transformation precisely as a result of our media. What Fredric Jameson calls 'hyperspace' [1984], the rapid-fire juxtaposition of tv images with which we are becoming increasingly familiar, is a delinearization of our otherwise linear communicative modes, which serves to spatialize and stultify our traditionally conceived time-line.)

The point is this: the Trobrianders were describing a series of events that in English would have little in common. Yet the events, as events, are the same, however differently they are interpreted. And if they are the recipients of distinct interpretants, then as a matter of course the events as 'semiotic object-events' were also distinct. In this manner, Frege's *Venus* is, well, just *Venus*. It is out there for all to see in much the same way insofar as collections of photons of basically the same combination of frequencies strike their retinas. But *Venus* seen *as* some 'semiotic object' or other is another matter entirely: it is either 'morning star' or 'evening star,' or the 'Roman goddess of love' or an 'Aztec god,' or whatever. *Venus* as brute 'reality' is as it is, in spite of however we choose to see it semiotically. 'Venus' as a semiotic entity, as part of some 'semiotically real' world or other, is virtually infinitely variable.

With this in mind, I will indulge in a bit of...

2. Hedging at the Edges

The notion of radically distinct interpretations drawn from the same set of signs of *vagueness*, as pure *possibilia* in the Peirce-Menard example, recalls, once again, the Löwenheim-Skolem theorem. And *vagueness* brings on the much-used and occasionally abused sorites paradox.

Frege often expressed his contempt for *vagueness*. It was for him a defect. It played havoc with orthodox logical principles and should be eradicated at all costs, he thought, in order to make way for clear and distinct thinking. That opinion became gospel for logical positivism. The idea that the existence of *vagueness* might require a special form of logic was apparently never seriously entertained. However, *vagueness* is not simply the product of frizzled thinking. It is a matter of semantic depth, where instructions are lacking for drawing sharp lines because in such cases sharp lines are often better left undrawn. *Vagueness* is not merely surface opaqueness. It goes to the core of language and of signs; it is of the very essence of thought. In fact, without it, there would be no thought in the first place. Solely by way of the *vague* can artificial boundaries and domains be erected. That is, *vagueness* is not a breakdown of clear-cut boundaries and domains; it is necessary for their very existence.

The sorites paradox, based on ignorance of precise boundaries, is relevant to the notion of *vagueness*. Consider, for example, the contrived distinction between ignorance itself and knowledge. If a child learns by internalizing disparate bits of information, at some point she will pass, we would like to think, from wide-eyed innocence to enlightenment. But suppose it is decided by the Committee for Epistemological Respectability, by the local Board of Trustees, by popular vote, or by fiat, that the dividing line between her ignorance and knowledge is henceforth $n \pm 10^3$ bits. If at some point she has internalized $n - (10^3 - 10)$ bits of information, will she still be steeped in ignorance? With the addition of a dozen or so more bits, will she all of a sudden become knowledgeable? No, we might wish to respond. Ignorance is not necessarily transformed into knowledge nor knowledge into ignorance by the mere addition of a few more bits. In spite of our desire to believe that, by an appropriate number of steps of *modus ponens*, a statement can be quite effectively applied to its respective 'real world' situation, the expression 'to get an education' remains somewhat incoherent. 'Ignorance' and 'knowledge' cannot but remain *vague*. The difference between the two terms is of degree, not kind. Given the absence of a precise dividing line between them, they are related nonsymmetrically and nonreflexively, though there is transitoriness, we want to persist in believing, in the passage from one term to the other (Wright 1976; see also Wheeler III 1991, who treats sorites arguments and metaphors in basically the same way).

Putnam remarks that if the sentence '"John is bald" is true if and only if John is bald' is a correct Tarski 'Convention T' sentence in the sense of Donald Davidson (1984:185–98), then the term 'true' itself must be as *vague* as the term 'bald.' If John has n hairs and is not bald, then does removing one hair giving him $n - 1$ hairs make him bald? What about $n - 2$ hairs? $n - 3$ hairs? If baldness is a matter of degree, then 'truth'-value regarding a person's being 'bald' cannot be determined with precision. Putnam formulates the problem thus: 'If "vague" language – language which cannot be translated into "ideal" language in some way which is itself singled out uniquely – is legitimate and unavoidable, then the question: *What is the best logical system for schematizing inferences that involve vague terms?* becomes an important one. Even if it is impossible to have a *perfectly precise* truth predicate (or, more vaguely, a *perfectly precise* acceptability notion, i.e., a notion of "reasonableness", or "correctness", or "justification") for ordinary language, that does not mean that the *logical syntax* of correct inferences involving such predicates cannot at all be "regimented"' (1983b:284). Putnam's tentative regimentation of *vague* terms involves provisional use of intuitionist logic abolishing the excluded-middle principle. I would also include the idea of *local consistency* (in the *underdetermined* sphere) coupled with *global inconsistency* (in the *overdetermined* sphere) – a variation of which Putnam considers and discards, by the way.

Globally, John Whither with n hairs or with $n + 1$ or $n - 1$ hairs can be *possibly* both bald and not-bald, depending upon the perspective. The matter is undecidable from the larger view, which, of an infinity of minuscule differences, lies beyond finite surveyability in light of previous discussions. On the other hand, from the local vantage – of Seconds, actualized instants, within particular contexts, from the infinity of possibles – it can be the case that if John has n hairs, he is conceived to be bald, but with $n+x$ hairs, he would be considered not-bald. However, if we move up the scale toward the global view in terms of *generalities*, it is not *necessarily* 'true' that either n hairs on John's dome makes him bald or $n + x$ hairs renders him not-bald – this is Putnam's conclusion after a somewhat vacillating embrace of intuitionist logic. So, at the risk of repeating myself ad nauseum, at the global level of the *overdetermined* sphere the law of contradiction is not necessarily imperative, and at the same time the *underdetermined* sphere can allow for slippage of the excluded-middle principle, while actualized Seconds lend themselves to relatively precise lines of demarcation, however arbitrary and however artificial.

In another way of putting it, the realm of *vagueness* forces an indefinite number of unexpected interpretations on us (of the actuals we have before us) and the realm of *generality* allows for an indefinite number of alternative interpretations, each of them with the potential for equal accountability (of the actuals that happen to be available). Our hand is perpetually forced, but between each pair of cards, others potentially arise to give us the promise of winning the pile of chips in the long run. However, since such images are what dreams are built on, we can never know for sure whether our signs are faithfully telling us what is 'real' or whether or not we have the hand that will give us a win. At the one end a sort of Löwenheim-Skolem theorem comes into play, giving rise to the sorites quandary; at the other end it becomes apparent that makeshift lines drawn between terms were inadequate in the first place and that there are other equally acceptable – or equally unacceptable, according to the preference – alternatives.

Hacking, as pointed out above, is critical of Putnam's allusion to Löwenheim-Skolem on a number of counts. To be more specific, Hacking's critique includes the rejoinders that (1) the Löwenheim-Skolem theorem is about sentences in first-order logic, but natural language cannot be squeezed into the same format, (2) everyday speech involves contextualized indexicals, which remain unaccountable within formal logic, and (3) extralogical nonverbal (iconic) interaction inevitably accompanies common speech situations (Hacking 1983:107). There is, Hacking concludes, no way one human could interpret 'cat' as *cat* and another could interpret it as *cherries* (= 'cat*'), with, all things being equal, a symmetrical, reflexive relationship between the 'cat' language and its respective 'semiotic world' and the 'cat*' language and its respective 'semiotic world.' An unintended 'cat*' interpretation is humanly inconceivable, for Putnam's 'theorem' – to repeat Hacking's counterargument – falls into the hoary sin of abstraction. It is out of tune with the concrete affairs of everyday communication.

I would contend, with a nod toward Hacking, that a return to Peirce's 'concrete reasonableness' should be received as a welcome move. And this is precisely where Peirce is coming from: his concept of the sign is not strictly linguistic – as per francophile structuralism and poststructuralism as well as analytic philosophy, all 'linguicentric' – but properly addresses itself to iconicity and indexicality in addition to symbolicity (which, in spite of itself, comes loaded with iconicity and indexicality as subsets). Hacking's move against Putnam, even if well taken, would not work against Peirce, at least in the same way. For Peirce complements massive doses of abstractions – he was, after all, a logician and mathematician, among other trades – with concrete iconic and indexical buffers.

In this manner, Peirce the mathematician and scientist could be on the same wavelength with William James the popularizer of pragmatist philosophy, and in part for that reason James drew certain inspiration from his more rigorous contemporary. At the same time, Peirce occasionally held James's philosophy up for a dose of contempt, since it was devoid of the mathematical and scientific tough-mindedness with which Peirce felt comfortable. And to top it all off, Peirce the speculative philosopher and cosmologist hardly found a responsive audience among most mathematicians and scientists of his day – or with later logical positivists, analytical philosophers, and pragmatists for that matter. If one reads Peirce carefully, however, one will discover that the mathematician is crying out to recover lost concreteness, while the speculator remains attracted to the pristine harmony of abstract Pythagorean forms and ciphers. Peirce found somewhat of a happy meeting ground between the two poles he tried to bring together, I would suggest, in his notion of meaning via sign *translation* and its role in engendering *interpretants-meanings.*

Take, for example, Peirce's essay on $\sqrt{-1}$ that preceded his disquisition on William Rowe Hamilton's algebra of quaternions – which make use of the imaginary numbers (recall Omega's initial move in this direction in the Preamble). The mathematician, we are told, always reasons *indirectly*. She first lets $i = \sqrt{-1}$. However, Peirce writes, whatever the answer for $\sqrt{-1}$ may be, i always has a positive value, which is contrary to the very nature of $\sqrt{-1}$ as neither + nor –. This character of i is quite necessary, however, since intuition tells us that the nature of $\sqrt{-1}$ should be impossible, since every quantity must be either + or –. But what if i itself is made out to be neither + nor –? One might retort that there can be no such oddity. However, Peirce writes, as neither + nor –, i is in a certain sense 'just like all the other objects the mathematician deals with. They are one and all mere figments of the brain' (*CP*:4.132; also 2.191–2, 2.305, 2.778, 3.426). One might now wish to object that if a quantity is neither positive nor negative it cannot actually be anything, cannot mean anything, to which Peirce replies that 'the meaning of a sign is the sign it has to be translated into' (*CP*:4.132), so even though i as such has no meaning, its translation becomes meaningful, and the mathematician can get on with her task (recall the Master's remarks on self-referring, contradictory signs that are nonetheless quite meaningful).

In mathematics, to say a sign has no meaning is to say that the meaning is not included in the hypothesis. In the case of concrete values, by contrast, a hypothesis can be opened and meaning (an interpretation, translation) put in, such as interpreting 'debt' as (by translating it into) 'negative property.' While 'debt,' like i, does not necessarily sport any sign of negativity, 'negative property,' like $\sqrt{-1}$, does. However, 'debt' and 'property' can be construed as concrete signs with 'semiotically real referents.' The first is of negative value while the second is positive. i and $\sqrt{-1}$, on the other hand, cannot by any stretch be given concrete window dressing as long as they remain unattached to other signs: they are sheer abstractions. As 'facts' for the mathematician, they are for her 'mere hypotheses.' She ceases to concern herself over their 'truth,' it is chiefly their form that matters (*CP*:3.428). The respective meanings of i and $\sqrt{-1}$, or of 'debt' and 'negative property,' then, are what the signs are translated *into*. Their translation *is* their object, for as abstract signs they can enjoy no other object.

Thus, to the question 'What is the meaning of *i*?' the only reasonable response, Peirce suggests, is simply: $i^2 + 1 = 0$ (*CP*:4.132). This must be the answer, for an algebraic system of signs is a *calculus*; it is a 'language to *reason in*.' And that is precisely what one does in a 'real' concrete sense upon translating 'debt' into 'negative property' (*CP*:4.133). While 'debt' can be translated into something else (a 'negative property'), a negative abstract quantity cannot be translated into anything except another pure form. Yet the relation between 'debt' and 'negative property' is commensurate with the relation between *i* and $\sqrt{-1}$. In this manner, concrete relations in everyday language and relations in formal systems cannot be categorically separated. This line of thinking can be indirectly used to address Hacking's critique of Putnam regarding his dovetailing everyday communication and formal systems.

3. But the Road to Concreteness Inevitably Remains Rocky

Peirce's inclusion of iconic and indexical signifying activity in the same breath with symbolicity of the most formal sort illustrates that *semiosis* consists of matters of degree rather than of kind, which includes and colludes *vagueness* and *generality*, and bears on the sorites conundrum.

Taking the entire spectrum of *semiosic* interaction into account, it becomes possible to sense how meaning is more than 'reference,' 'representation,' 'correspondence,' and 'objectivity.' It is also more than a matter of 'truth' and nothing but the 'truth,' whether in the formal, abstract sense or concerning the affairs of everyday life. Meaning, in whatever case, emerges from the process of signs *translated* into signs within the whole of *our semiosis*. When I write the 'whole of *our semiosis*,' I allude to everything that makes us distinctively human semiotic agents, which includes language – both artificial and natural – nonverbal communication of all stripes, and even life itself when properly contextualized within particular human communities.

These admittedly sweeping statements encompass that which is 'inner' as well as the 'outer.' Peirce, we observed in chapters 2 and 3, posited an 'external reality' of sign-events and an 'internal reality' of thought-signs. The 'semiotic objects' of the first remain independent of our thought about them, while we are by and large masters of the second, chiefly in their nature as fictions. However, mathematical thought is properly internal, and many of its principles 'force themselves' upon us whether we like it or not, for mathematics 'is at least as irresistible as empirical truth; but of the substance of the latter truth we have a perception; it is the mighty universe that compels our thought, while the former is an invisible giant that holds us in his grip' (MS 283). All of which places us dangerously close to Hans Vaihinger's fictionalist interpretation of mathematics

(1924), and, in light of the perception-is-interpretation thesis – into which Peirce can at times also be placed – close to Wittgenstein's conventionalist philosophy of mathematics (1956). However, Peirce's sign theory is salvaged, ultimately, by a judicious inclusion of iconicity and indexicality into the mathematician's playpen. Peirce writes that a sign 'is a thing which is the representative, or deputy, of another thing for the purpose of affecting a mind' (*NE* IV:xxi). Regarding mathematics, this 'thing' is not an 'external thing,' a sign-event, but remains 'internal,' hence it is the deputy of some 'internal' object to which it relates 'for the purpose of affecting a mind.' Mathematical, and more appropriately geometrical, constructs are icons, 'whether they involve continuity, like geometrical figures, or are arrays of discrete objects, like a body of algebraical formulas, all of which are icons. Icons have to be used in all thinking' (*NE* IV:xxi).

Icons and indices, in fact, are the basic tools of the mathematician's trade. Collections of algebraic notations, geometrical diagrams, and topological images are things that can be worked with. They can be the stuff of experiments. In pure mathematics, they are thought experiments of the mind: they complement thought experiments of applied mathematics and the physical sciences, which customarily have an ear tuned to phenomena in the 'semiotically real' world. For example, one can 'make uniform experiments upon diagrams; and when one does so, one must keep a bright lookout for unintended and unexpected changes thereby brought about in the relations of different significant parts of the diagram to each other' (*CP*:4.530). By a comparable token, James Brown argues quite convincingly that thought experiments in applied mathematics and the sciences are 'performed in the laboratory of the mind' (1991:1). (While I do not buy into Brown's rather 'Platonic' interpretation of thought experiments, nor his 'logocentrism,' his book is fascinating reading, the drama of crucial thought experiments throughout the history of science. Actually, more in line with the tenets of this inquiry is Rotman's thesis [1988, 1993] that mathematical thought experiments 'in here' and scientific thoughts experiments enjoying relation to the world 'out there' are of common sources.)

Initially emerging within the mind, thought experiments are then slapped on paper or punched into the computer terminal as images, diagrams, and equations. In this manner, they 'are visualizable; they involve manipulations; they are not the mere consequence of a theory-based calculation' (Brown 1991:1). Even though at the time of their inception some of these mental gymnastics cannot be coordinated with experimental activity – that is, the notorious EPR experiment – they are generally orchestrated with familiar 'semiotic world' occurrences 'out there.' And, according to reports from the history and philosophy of science – most notably those authored by Feyerabend,

Kuhn, and Hanson – the 'outward clash' of unexpected happenings in the 'semiotically real' world – like Peirce's 'unintended and unexpected changes' occurring as a result of 'inner' thought experiments – can rise up and slap us in the face, compelling us to re-evaluate – and occasionally completely overthrow – our knowledge of the 'real' and our expectations regarding its nature (*CP*:8.41–2). In all cases, unexpected twists and turns of events, or sets of abstract symbols on paper or on the monitor, can shock us into the realization that the relations between them are something other than what had been expected.

In Peirce's concept of mathematical activity, then, 'iconic reasoning' entails experimenting on manipulable iconic signs in the mind (thought-signs) that do not immediately lend themselves to experiments on the 'semiotically real' world. Experiments on icons themselves are the mathematical counterpart to experiments on icons (models, theories) insofar as they are related to the world of physics. According to the positivists view and the correspondence theory of 'truth,' in physics theoretical language (including the language of modelling) is a step removed from observational language, though both languages ultimately 'refer' to the objective world, whereas in mathematics, symbols 'refer' to themselves and to themselves only. The postpositivist view abolishes this theoretical language / observational language distinction: observations are theory-laden and theories are never devoid of erstwhile observational preconceptions. This postpositivist view meshes the use of mathematical icons and scientific icons even more intimately than Peirce himself might have intended. Not even in physics is the icon (model, theory) necessarily at one remove from the object of investigation, but, rather, the very object of inquiry is incorporated within the icon itself. (This is not, I must emphasize, the 'picture theory' of mind [icon] as a 'mirror of nature,' attacked by the postpositivists. Algebraic notations as icons are not 'pictures' nor do they 'mirror nature' in the classical sense [see Merrell 1995a].)

Purely mathematical labour entails work with icons and their (indexical) relations to one another; the labour of pure physics chiefly entails experimentation with icons, but with an eye toward that to which they hopefully relate semiotically. In both cases, icons, taken on their own grounds, are in and of themselves self-confirmatory, self-reflexive, and chiefly self-sufficient. The sign for $\sqrt{-1}$, i, is a prime example of this class of icons. It is a *diagram* (of Peirce's three hypoicon types, including also *images* and *metaphors*) in its most simple incarnation. It simply *is as it is*, no more, no less. As pure First, it is not (yet) a concept; it is unanalysable, ineffable. Yet it is (potentially) a sign (icon) indicating (indexing) $\sqrt{-1}$, its object, in order that a mind may be affected such that a concept or thought (interpretant) might be engendered. In this sense the basis of interpretation of a mathematical theorem is chiefly iconic; the theorem itself is a set of relationships between signs the elements of which are primarily composed of indices; and that theorem is in turn related to a mental state of affairs containing elements of those same relationships between signs, but now they are translated into another form.

Peirce's refusal to admit to a categorical distinction between formal and natural languages – both are equally dependent upon iconic and indexical in addition to symbolic characteristics – is not only commensurate with current postpositivist, neopragmatist thought, but it also points toward a possible vindication of Putnam's interjecting the consequences of the Löwenheim-Skolem theorem into everyday patterns of communication. Take, for example, the history of imaginary numbers. Hardly any aspect of formal systems has been more 'unexpected' and less 'intended' than their entry onto the mathematical scene. In Gottfried Wilhelm Leibniz's oft-quoted words, the 'Divine Spirit found a sublime outlet in that wonder of analysis, that portent of the ideal world, that amphibian between being and not-being, which we call the imaginary root of negative unity' (in Kline 1980:117). George Boole observed that by the use of geometry one could pass through interpretable expressions to uninterpretable ones, using $\sqrt{-1}$, and back to interpretable ones, thus merging geometrical and algebraic icons in the Peircean sense. Karl Friedrich Gauss confessed that he had become obsessed with $\sqrt{-1}$, yet he remained content with an intuitive understanding of the disconcerting number. However rocky the path of imaginary numbers has been, they have nonetheless managed to find a comfortable home in contemporary mathematics and science. In relativity theory they are used in Lorenz transformations, their use in complex numbers to form the Argand plane is a necessary step in coming to grips with the bizarre world of quantum physics, and they are indispensable in computing fractals, to mention only a few of their resting places (see Penrose 1989).

A final touch to Putnam's cats and cherries in regards to the semiotic aspect of $\sqrt{-1}$ and comparable entities can shed additional light on Peirce on meaning before we proceed in the next chapter to Peirce and another rather unexpected actor awaiting his entry: Nelson Goodman.

4. Neither Cats nor Cherries

If we combine 'cat' and 'cat*' into the single term, 'cat-cat*,' we have a natural language counterpart to $\sqrt{-1}$. Just as $\sqrt{-1}$ can be either +1 or −1, so also 'cat-cat*' can be either *cat* or *cherries*.

The ambiguity is provisionally resolved in mathematics by letting $\sqrt{-1}$ be i, though i cannot be a 'really real' number since the product of a 'real' number with itself must yield a positive value (or zero). Yet *i* is no less 'real' than 'real' numbers, for it can quite effectively be used to describe 'semiotically real' world phenomena. In a comparable move, let the combination 'cat-cat*' be designated by the synthetic – albeit highly ambiguous – term 'grock.' Just as *i* is both +1 and −1, so also 'grock' is both 'cat' and 'cat*.' 'Grock' and *i* are both amphibians between being and not-being; they are, as pure possibilities, virtually everything and nothing, everywhere and nowhere, everywhen and nowhen. That is, they are to a large degree *overdetermined*, they belong to the sphere of *vagueness*. As actualized signs, 'cat' relates to *cat* and 'cat*' to *cherries*. But there is no knowing whether or not at some future point someone might come along who takes 'cat' to be 'mouse' and 'mat' to be 'table' as if 'A mouse is on the table' were the case. Call this rendition of our sign 'cat#.' To say 'A cat is on the mat' could mean what it ordinarily means for you and me, or it could mean either 'A cat-cat* (*alias* grock) is on the mat*' or 'A cat# is on the mat#.' And the erstwhile excluded middle between 'cat' and 'cat*' has been marred. Now suppose we give 'grock-cat#' the label 'unga.' 'Unga,' the abbreviation of 'grock-cat#,' becomes our new counterpart to *i*, and once again we are off to the races.

The point is that even though *vagueness* and *inconsistency*, playing havoc with the principle of non-contradiction like paradoxes of the liar type, are minimized in formal systems – though they are never absolutely eradicated – they can nonetheless act out essential roles in our everyday living and natural-language talk. And if formal systems are at their roots undecidable, with 'unexpected' and 'unintended' consequences constantly threatening to pop up, so much more so regarding the exceedingly slippery slopes of natural languages. Saving grace may be had, fortunately for us all, in our customary tolerance for fuzziness in everyday sign use. We tend to push our way along, with the illusion that while liberally whispering, smoothly saying, and shouting messages back and forth at will, we are effectively communicating, though we are by and large oblivious to our frequent backfires, misfires, and blanks.

However, and perhaps for necessary reasons, the left hand of Maxwell's Demon is always there, threatening to throw things into disarray with hardly a moment's notice. But that story belongs to the next chapter.

12

Rules Are There to Be Broken?

1. What, Where, How, Then, Is 'Truth'?

Taking our examples from mathematics – that is, a formal language – into the domain of natural language, we saw in chapter 11 that retranslation-reinterpretation of sentences can follow unexpected, unintended, unwanted, undecidable pathways. In fact, potentially there are infinitely many translations-interpretations of the predicates of a language, and each one of them can be elevated to the status of 'truth' by an indefinite number of semiotic agents, given indefinitely varied settings.

In Quine's example, 'Gavagai!' could be interpreted as 'Rabbit,' 'Rabbit stage' (a 'rabbit-slice' in three-dimensions as a point in the four-dimensional space-time rabbit continuum), 'Undetached rabbit parts,' or whatever. And Putnam's 'cat' could become 'cat*,' 'grock,' 'unga,' and whatnot. These and other options, given the virtually infinite range of possible worlds, lie in *superposition* as *inconsistencies*, *contradictions*, and *contraries* in the *overdetermined* sphere of *vagueness* patiently awaiting their actualization in some 'semiotically real' world or other. Whatever might be actualized can take on 'truth-conditions' if and when it is incorporated into an adequately formulated sentence. But what is at a particular point in time and space a set of 'true' sentences could always have been otherwise in one of many alternative possible worlds. 'Truth-conditions' regarding actual sentences, then, must remain *underdetermined*, within Peirce's domain of *generality*, and destined to *incompleteness* for finite humans in finite communities. Yet, all three of Quine's proposed interpretations for 'Gavagai!' – from an indefinite number of possible interpretations – have a certain degree of overlap and are interconnected.

In this light, when taking different world-views into account, one might wish to conclude that all translations-reinterpretations that bear some comparability to one another remain linked to whatever might be the standard translation-interpretation for a given community. In another way of putting it, Wittgenstein's overlapping 'family resemblances' regarding 'language games' render them related and usually quite congenial with one another, and without the need for a lot of talk about 'incommensurables.' (Admittedly, the very idea of 'language games' in the same breath as 'incommensurability' can create a dilemma. A good case in point is Lyotard's [1984] addressing himself to 'language games,' as if he were the ultimate arbiter – he of all people, creator of the 'differend' – which has been effectively pointed out by Samuel Weber [1985].)

However, Putnam takes the essentials of Quine's thought experiment a giant step further: 'truth-conditions' for 'A cat is on a mat' does not exclude the possibility of 'cat' relating to *cherries*, to *rabbits*, to *mice*, to *flying saucers*, or whatever. Since there is no God's-eye view of the whole of the world or of any relatively sophisticated language, I have no way of knowing absolutely whether what you say relates to the same 'semiotically real' world as the world I am in when I translate what you said into what I take you to have said. As I have suggested, the world provides us with no Grand Infallible Index pointing out 'correspondences' between signs and things. We process signs according to our intuitions, inclinations, gut-feelings, wishes, whims, and sentiments (Firstness), and generally in accord with our physical surroundings, our contexts (Secondness), and our personal habits, social conventions, and perceived and conceived regularities (Thirdness). Quite remarkably, in spite of these complexities, we are generally able to maintain the appearance of being more right than wrong in our translations-reinterpretations, and more often than not we manage to think we are capable of maintaining the rather smug confidence that our beliefs are 'true.' Yet the fact remains that whatever we would like to take as 'reference' remains largely indeterminate. Consequently, our 'true' signs are pliable enough, and we bend them sufficiently, in order to render a vast range of variable signs apparently 'correspondent' to what we would like to consider the 'truth.' In fact, a virtually unlimited range of signs can be made to accord with the 'truth' of our basic set of prototypically 'true' signs. In other words, given the Löwenheim-Skolem theorem, if the range of values of signs is infinite in extension, then potentially an infinite range of signs can be made to serve our purposes quite well. Whatever may have become our collection of 'true' signs can bend with the winds of change, ride the bucking surf as the tide rolls in, and race along the channels of *semiosis* at breakneck speed, yet remain *for* us 'true,' at least as far as our finite capacities are concerned.

However, what is 'truth,' but, as Nietzsche reminds us (1954:42), an army of 'metaphors, metonyms, and anthropomorphisms'? (This notion, which I generally endorse here and elsewhere, departs radically from Quine for whom metaphors and other tropes are vital at the growing edges of science and philosophy, but the real stuff is literal language, an 'open space in the tropical jungle, created by clearing the tropes away' [Quine 1978:162]). Above all, what's in our particular, and idiosyncratic, way of cutting the world up at certain somewhat arbitrarily selected joints? Jorge Luis Borges's notorious essay on John Wilkins's proposed new language of induction suggests an alternative set of joints regarding our categorization of animals found in a Chinese encyclopaedia. Animals are divided into '(a) those that belong to the Emperor, (b) embalmed ones, (c) those that are trained, (d) suckling pigs, (e) mermaids, (f) fabulous ones, (g) stray dogs, (h) those that are included in this classification, (i) those that tremble as if they were mad, (j) innumerable ones, (k) those drawn with a very fine camel's hair brush, (l) others, (m) those that have just broken a flower vase, (n) those that resemble flies from a distance' (Borges 1964:103). The point – and Foucault's renowned comment on Borges (1970) admirably bears this out – is that categories are fashioned rather than found, imagined rather than introspected, constructed rather than conceived by the grace of the gods. Western thought, through the centuries, is a litany of phyla, genera, and species, of logics, reasons, and observations, of models, methods, and means, of styles, strategies, and techniques. Consequently, there is hardly any means for refuting the Duhem-Quine thesis that 'physical theories can be at odds with each other and yet compatible with all physical data even in the broadest sense (i.e. that all possible physical evidence may not be sufficient to limit us to any one theoretical perspective)' (Quine 1970:183).

In brief, the Duhem-Quine thesis (Duhem 1914, 1954; Quine 1953), to which I alluded above, says that isolated hypotheses are not verifiable by experience in piecemeal fashion; solely the entire body of a theory is capable of being subjected to the test (for arguments, both pro and con regarding the thesis, see Gädhe and Stegmüller 1986, Hesse 1972, Roth 1978, and Vuillemin 1986). The thesis is born of a criticism of positivism, in both its nineteenth- and its twentieth-century guises. Duhem rejected the Positivist philosophy of Auguste Comte, who believed investigators should liberate themselves of all metaphysical speculations on the universe and embrace only empirically tested laws. Quine's argument was against the Vienna school of logical positivism according to which concepts and propositions take on meanings and truth-value as a result of empirical validation. Both Duhem and Quine hold that scientific theories are so theory-laden that it is impossible, even in principle, to separate purely theoretical constructs from observation statements.

From the point of view of raw induction, philosopher of science and logician Carl Hempel also threw a monkey wrench in the works of taxonomic complacency with his paradox of induction (1945). Take any classificatory assertion, say, 'All ravens are black.' Every time a black raven is spotted the hypothesis is confirmed, though absolute confirmation is not forthcoming until all possible ravens, past, present, and future, have been examined. On the other hand, observation of a single raven of any colour other than black refutes it on the spot. However, the problem is infinitely more extensive than we would suppose, for Hempel, in an unexpected move, argues that the 'All ravens are black' hypothesis can be restated as 'All nonblack things are nonravens.' How so? Actually, the two hypotheses have the same content; they are different formulations of the same proposition. In order to demonstrate this, Hempel posits what he calls the 'equivalence condition' between the two hypotheses: *Whatever confirms (refutes) one of the two equivalent sentences, also confirms (refutes) the other.* In other words, one hypothesis is a *contrapositive* of the other hypothesis.

'All nonblack things are nonravens' is the much easier of the two hypotheses to test. Pink flamingos, red cardinals, grey doves, blue jays, all confirm the contrapositive version of the hypothesis, as do orange cars, silver coins, red herrings, and green emeralds. So we can go through life, at each step spying black ravens and nonblack nonravens, and our original hypothesis asserting that all ravens are black will not yet be absolutely confirmed – that is, unless we are little Laplacean superdemons capable of seeing everything all at once – for something will always remain to be observed, including species of insects in the Amazon basin becoming extinct daily.

In spite of the Hempel problem, to repeat, we do what we do best. We send and take, and engender and translate signs as we can, cutting the world up as we go along, comparing new experiences to old ones, and packing signs into the pigeon-holes with which we have become comfortable, in spite of the risk we constantly run that what is correct from one vantage may be absurd from another. Yet, a set of categories in one culture is used to classify everything there is, that is, everything in the world that is cut out, distinguished, and indicated by that particular community. Every new item of experience that happens to pop up is customarily and dutifully compared to the classes of things that are already there, some similarity is fashioned and fabricated, and a fit is hopefully forthcoming.

But another irony pops up to taunt us. Suppose some taxonomist with noble intentions goes about verifying the way X is similar to Y in a manner comparable to the way A is similar to Y. This project is fallacious, for as Nelson Goodman effectively argues (1976), A and Y are themselves similar in an indefinite number – potentially an infinite number – of ways, given diverse times and places. Hence there is no guaranteed manner of specifying which similarity between A and Y is the one and only valid similarity and fixing it for all time (compare to my mention of the Duhem-Quine thesis a few paragraphs back). Establishing a similarity relation between the entities in question by citing a finite number of examples is as futile as trying to specify a function of the natural numbers by citing the first 100, 1000, or 1,000,000 cases. There will always remain an infinity of functions agreeing with the finite number of cases cited, but they can diverge with respect to cases that are not given, that is, with respect to all possible cases (worlds) other that those that fit nicely with the cases that have been actualized.

This apparent quandary also lies behind the central problem in Wittgenstein's *Philosophical Investigations* (1953). Up to paragraph 198 of the *Investigations* we read about following rules for language games according to community-held conventions of language use and styles of reasoning according to the form of life stipulated by those conventions. Then Wittgenstein drops a bombshell. We do what we do by generally following the rules of the game, he concedes, yet whatever we do, whether it coincides with a rule or not, can appear to be 'on some interpretation, in accord with the rule.' But, we are told, that is not really the way we should put it. Rather, it is the case that 'any interpretation still hangs in the air along with what it interprets, and cannot give it any support. Interpretations by themselves do not determine meaning' (Wittgenstein 1953:198). Meaning is, at most, tentatively and tenuously determined by the whole of the language game, indeed, by the whole of language itself (a language counterpart to the Duhem-Quine thesis regarding scientific theories). Rules are conventions, uses embedded and entrenched in community practices. And to understand a solitary sentence 'means to understand a language. To understand a language means to be master of a technique' (ibid.:199). Take the game of chess. Suppose a couple of Netherlanders are playing chess, and they seem to be making all the appropriate moves. But instead of contemplating the board in silence, cogitating, vacillating, and finally moving a piece from one square to another, they chant, periodically get up and do a strange dance, and whoop and holler. And all this 'in such a way that their procedure is translatable by suitable rules into a [our] game of chess. Should we still be inclined to say they were playing a game? What right would one have to say no?' (ibid.:200).

In this manner we are introduced to the paradox Wittgenstein agonizes over during the remainder of his *Investigations*. It is this: 'no course of action could be determined by a rule, because every course of action can be made out to accord with the rule. The answer was: if everything can be made out to accord with the rule, then it can also be made out to conflict with it. And so there would be neither accord nor conflict here' (Wittgenstein 1953:20). (Kripke's extended analysis of Wittgenstein's skepticism regarding 'following a rule' [1982] has sparked extensive debate. Without time or space properly to indulge myself, I rest with reference to the work of Blackburn 1984, McDowell 1993, Shiffer 1986, Stenlund 1990, Suter 1989, Taylor 1992, and Werhane 1992.)

The crux of Wittgenstein's puzzle is – and I partly rephrase Wittgenstein in the terminology of this inquiry – that whatever sign one may evoke in connection with a meaning (interpretant) irrespective of the object of the sign, does not determinately constitute the content of the meaning (interpretant). Rather, the sign's meaning is indeterminately variable. For example, suppose we begin teaching a young student the series, '2,4,6,8,10, …' At some point she says 'I can go on,' and we give her permission to do so. The rule (habit, convention, law) for carrying out the necessary computations is obviously 'Add 2.' With this rule in hand our eager student proceeds quite confidently. But upon arriving at 1000, to our surprise she leaps to 1004, then 1008, and so on. A strange sort of unintended (unexpected) alternative to the norm seems to have emerged.

Did she suffer from a memory lapse? Did she intentionally alter the rule for some reason or other? Has her mental state suddenly become screwed up? Was the number 1000 for her some bizarre sort of singularity? None of the above is necessarily the case, if we follow Wittgenstein – and from another vantage, Putnam. She simply diverged from what we apparently by nature take to be an iron-clad rule. After all is said and done, her deviant behaviour is not by any absolute criterion necessarily any better or any worse than ours when we use the rule 'Add 2' according to our conventions. Her rule, let us call it the 'Bad 2' rule, is simply one of an indefinite number of alternatives we all have before us whenever we use any one of all possible rules in one of all possible worlds. The fact is that her actualized world is not the same as ours. Which is no absolutely necessary guarantee that ours is superior to hers. We tend to look upon our way of doing things in terms of our *convention*, while we see her behaviour as the product of *convolution.* And to her way of thinking, perhaps it is we who are the convoluted ones and she is conventional. In the final analysis, even though we construe a rule so simple as 'Add 2' to be totally free of problems, along the infinite stretch there is no absolute guarantee that citizens of our community will in the future be free of some divergent interpretation or other. And if and when a divergent interpretation happens to pop up, there is no determining, a priori, whether or not it will be destined to become *conventional* rather than merely *convolutional.*

This is because our surveyability of the potentially infinite field (the realm of *vagueness*, the superposition of all possibilities) cannot but be well-nigh infinitesimal. If we recursively apply the rule 'Add 2' with our student to ensure her continued success but, by now exhausted, stop at 1000 with the pretext that

'We cannot go on forever,' our only certainty is to be found in the series we actually constructed. We cannot be without a shadow of a doubt certain that things will continue in the future as they are now continuing and have continued in the past. (Interestingly enough, in comparing Wittgenstein's paradox to the 'pragmatic maxim,' one notes that the former focuses on rules and meanings and the latter on sentences and meaning. However, combining the two yields the notion that meaning via sentences strings off into the receding horizon, and meaning via rules does the same. In both cases, there is no iron-clad certainty that what is taken for granted today will remain intact tomorrow, which also ushers in the image of Putnam's interpretation of the Löwenheim-Skolem theorem [see especially *CP*:7.103].)

The point is, finally, that, given the plethora of human communities and conventional practices, past, present, and to come, just as quite obviously there always exist possible divergent extensions of our rules and practices, so also there exist divergent possible interpretations even of the natural-number sequence, held dear as our most crystal pure and unblemished article of faith. Ideally, our practices can go on forever while being changed nary a whit. But ideality does not necessarily coincide with the 'semiotic reality' we have constructed using our errant capacities; unadulterated utopias cannot always emerge from diluted oceans of human *semiosis*. All of which appears strangely compatible with the ultimate implications also of the Löwenheim-Skolem theorem according to the teachings of Hilary Putnam. (The notion that mathematics is socially determined, a matter of conventions – which comes as quite a shock to the nonmathematician humanist and enjoys the spotlight of arduous debates among mathematicians and philosophers of mathematics – has been entertained by some impressive thinkers, to mention only two, Spengler [1926:V.1, chap. 2], and Wittgenstein [1956] [more recently in the 'sociology of mathematics,' see Bloor 1976, 1983, and Struik 1956].)

2. Green with Envy or Just Singing the Grues?

And now Nelson Goodman, sporting the 'new riddle of induction,' makes his entry.

Goodman's conundrum, which complements Hempel's inductivity paradox, goes something like this. Any upstanding English speaker ordinarily believes the statement 'Emeralds are green' to be eternally and invariably 'true.' Supposing that all the emeralds he has examined before a given time are 'green,' he is quite naturally confident that 'Emeralds are green' will always be confirmed, for, according to his observations, emerald *a* on examination was 'green,' emerald *b* was 'green,' and so on. Now suppose he meets someone from Netherworld and discovers that her perception of things appears to him apparently unstable and that her language is radically distinct from his own. Among other oddities, Netherworlder's language contains the following two terms which Ourworlder has learned to translate into his language thus:

Grue = examined before the temporal 'reference point' t_0 and is reported to be 'green' or is not examined before t_0 and reported to be 'blue.' (t_0 is apparently an otherwise arbitrary moment of time that is not in the past.)

Bleen = examined before the temporal 'reference point' t_0 and is reported to be 'blue' or not examined before t_0 and is reported to be 'green.'

Before time t_0 for each of Ourworlder's statements asserting an emerald is 'green,' Netherworlder has a parallel statement asserting that it is 'grue,' and as far as she is concerned her observations that emerald *a* on examination is 'grue,' that emerald *b* is 'grue,' and so on, adequately confirm her own hypothesis. It will obviously appear to Ourworlder from the standpoint of his language and his normal colour taxonomy that Netherworlder's sensory images change radically after t_0. But, from Netherworlder's perspective, the glove is turned inside out, for it is Ourworlder's taxonomy that appears to her to be time-dependent. That is, Netherworlder's translation of Ourworlder's colour scheme would result in the following report:

Green = examined before t_0 and is reported to be 'grue,' or not and is reported to be 'bleen.'

Blue = examined before t_0 and is reported to be 'bleen,' or is not and is reported to be 'grue.'

From the perspective of each translator, then, the inductive expectations of the other's perspective are twisted. On the other hand, the two perspectives, if taken together as an atemporal whole, are apparently quite symmetrical (Gärdenfors 1994). However, since atemporality from within one system becomes temporality within the other, each perspective is conceived to be time-dependent from the grasp of the other, complementary perspective. Hence, when taken separately as self-sufficient wholes, they are asymmetrical with respect to one another (Rescher 1978). In a manner of speaking, Ourworlder and Netherworlder possess their own 'metaphysics of presence' with respect to their conception of their own world, though, from the other's complementary world, this 'metaphysics of presence' is easily demythified. (Mary Hesse [1969] argues quite effectively that when Goodman's puzzle operates by symmetry relation, it is insoluble [that is, incommensurability holds]. But in our actual practices by use of our natural languages, it is rarely to never the case that meanings, concepts, and theories are radically incommensurable. Relations are more often than not asymmetrical, owing to the element of temporality, or irreversibility, present. In this sense, conditions are usually qualifiable in terms of disequilibrium rather than equilibrium, nonlinearity rather than linearity.)

In order more adequately to illustrate time-dependence and perceptual and conceptual variance, consider these two statements:

(1) Space is 'straight.'
(2) Space is 'curved.'

If we alter Goodman's paradox somewhat, we can construct the following set of predicates to depict Netherworlder's perception of Ourworlder's statements:

Straight = considered to be a property of space before 'reference point' t_0 and not a property of space after t_0.
Curved = considered not to be a property of space before reference point t_0 and a property of space after 'reference point' t_0.

And Netherworlder could have two alternate terms with their corresponding predicates by means of which he could try to give a coherent account of Ourworlder's chaotic epistemology:

Craight = meaning of is considered to be compatible with (1) before 'reference point' t_0 and is considered to be compatible with (2) after t_0.
Sturved = meaning of is considered to be compatible with (2) before 'reference point' t_0 and is considered to be compatible with (1) after t_0 (recall the comparable formulation of the sun as 'statile' or 'mobionary' in the Preamble).

Netherworlder's view of her universe is for her naturally unchanging, while she perceives Ourworlder's conception to be radically, and rather irrationally, variant. We also, imperiously and from our presumed superior vantage point, might like to think we can explain away the incompatibility between (1) and (2) by the fact that (2) *is* 'true' from within the Einsteinian framework and (1) *was* 'true' from within the pre-Einsteinian framework. For the conceived properties of space, given a broad historical perspective, are time-dependent.

But our broader view just happens to be advantageous in this particular case. A pre-Einsteinian would believe from within her particular conceptual scheme that space can be nothing other than 'straight.' Hence, for her, (2) would be as forever 'false' as 'Emeralds are blue' is 'false' for us – though, admittedly, empirical verification in our case would be considerably less problematic. And for this pre-Einsteinian, Ourworlder would be epistemologically and ontologically feeble of mind. This talk of pre-Einsteinian and Einsteinian worlds reveals another facet to the dilemma between the two interlocutors. If Netherworlder, inside a train whose speed is approaching that of light, sees an emerald outside while facing the caboose, the gem will appear somewhat chartreuse – that is, the 'red shift' effect since it is 'receding' from her – but if Ourworlder was in front of Netherworlder and facing the front of the train when he took a look at the same stone as it 'approached' him, it would have appeared to be of a turquoise hue. This unlikely situation illustrates in a dramatic way why appearances can be in varying degrees deceptive.

Actually, anyone who is properly indoctrinated into Western metaphysics would be under ordinary circumstances like the pre-Einsteinian, often incapable of perceiving the fallacy of his own 'logocentrism' or 'metaphysics of presence,' for he would be imprisoned within his conceptual scheme (I write 'often incapable' in view of Hacking 1994, Feyerabend 1987, and Kuhn 1977, who argue that investigators can often to an extent *learn*, *account for*, and *know* incommensurable conceptual schemes of other cultures and of their own). In another way of putting it, each world, that of Ourworlder and that of Netherworlder, and as an 'internally real' world in the sense of Putnam, must on its own be taken temporally, hence asymmetrical relations hold from one self-contained world to another. Yet the combination of both worlds, taken as a whole, can be atemporally related. In this event, from the view of both worlds as a totality, it would theoretically be possible to map out the *vagueness* and *generality*, and the *inconsistency* and *incompleteness*, therein. (However, we must bear in mind that, in view of the Duhem-Quine thesis and Putnam's teachings, we can have no such God's-eye view of the whole of things). In the final analysis, our World, in terms of Goodman's *Ways of Worldmaking* (1978), is whatever it is, hardly more, hardly less.

Commenting on the fact that Goodman's attitude is closely aligned with perception and conception of the arts, Putnam, as we observed in chapter 3, writes that upon reading a novel such as *Don Quixote*, 'we become able to "see" Don Quixote, not only in the book but in ourselves and in other people. This enlargement of our stock of predicates and of metaphors is *cognitive*; we now possess descriptive resources we did not have before' (1983b:166). Commensurate with Putnam's 'internal realism,' these descriptive resources are valuable for their own sake, and for the sake of our capacity to understand other peoples and other cultures. Our taking the objects, acts, and events of our world or our imagining those of a fictive world involve our understanding our languages and our worlds 'in terms of a grasp of conditions of warranted assertibility and "rightness"; not a grasp of "truth conditions" in the old realist sense' (ibid.:167). In other words, our world is an incessantly changing combination of inner thought-signs and outer sign-events, which includes the way things are for us in the here-now, and what has been and what might be possible in the there-then. It is a matter of what is taken by the community, of whatever is the object of belief. This is also the thrust of Rorty's 'anti-essentialist' view, which 'specializes in creating [a] hall-of-mirrors effect' – in getting us to stop asking which is the real thing and which the image, and to settle for an ever-expanding choice of images, of Goodmanian 'worlds.' The 'anti-essentialist' is as a consequence incessantly 'recontextualizing objects,' which 'could just as well be called "recontextualizing beliefs" (Rorty 1991:100–1). In apparent contrast, Peircean philosopher Robert Almeder (1980:98) observes:

> Some empiricists (among them we can number Quine, Goodman and Putnam) are committed to the view that unto eternity there will be competing alternative theories, no one better in principle than the other; and hence that what the real world is can never be known. This throwback to the *Der Ding an Sich* carries with it the view that the real world is a world well lost, that truth in the end is a man-made product. That this sort of idealism hinges on the view that unto eternity there will not be any final theory explaining the world better than any other is obvious. If, however, Peirce is right, if, that is, science will terminate in some final theory explaining the world better than all conceivable others, then the basic reason for the idealism in question will be undermined.

Yet the point Almeder wishes to make, I fear, is moot. He does not take the concept of the whole and its parts, infinity and finitude – as discussed above – into due consideration, which is quite un-Peircean. Our worlds, whatever they may be, past, present, or future, will not for a finite community of knowers arrive at that ultimate stretch and find 'Truth' once and for all. Since that finish line rests at infinity, no matter how far we progress, from our finite vantage, we will be for practical purposes just as far from the goal as we ever were and will ever be.

Since, in light of Goodman's 'paradox,' what is 'true' at one time may be 'false' at another, our 'logic' obviously needs some provisions in order to account for the change in the 'truth-value,' or more appropriately regarding our present concerns about change in the *meaning*, of sentences. Such time-dependent considerations of 'truth' and meaning variance go against the grain of much modern logic. Medieval logic was in a sense time-dependent. Modern logic, however, especially since the early Wittgenstein, Russell, and Frege, is usually construed to be that of an omniscient and timeless being – ideally the logician – for whom the only possible world is the actual one. Peirce, by contrast, who believed logic to be a normative practice, never shared this idea. He believed, as we have noted, in an indefinite range of possibilities (the *overdetermined* sphere) independent of a particular person's knowledge within a specific (*underdetermined*) cultural framework and at a particular time and place (*CP*:5.435ff, 6.637). Subsequently, he made a strong plea, though he never himself fully carried out the project, for a 'logic' of time dimensions – which would complement his 'logic of vagueness' (Prior 1957). The distinction between past and future should not be overlooked when considering any adequate logic of the way sentences are actually engendered and interpreted.

Let us, then, consider sense-data and their accompanying sentences that at a particular point in time become ambiguous, or even anomalous: for instance, Wittgenstein's allusion to the 'rabbit/duck' drawing (see Hanson 1958). Suppose it is observed by someone a dozen times with the report that it is a 'rabbit.' Assuming that with each report there is memory of the past reports, it can be said that each is a reiteration, but with a minute *difference* of course, given changes of context. Then, in a distinct context, or perhaps not, a radical perceptual switch might occur such that the drawing is suddenly reported as a 'duck,' and with this thirteenth observation its ambiguous nature finally becomes apparent to the observer. But this new report would have been impossible had there existed no expectation from the previous reports that 'rabbit' was supposed to be the case. In this sense, the perceptual switch could not have occurred had there been no 'reference point' constituting an expectation that the drawing would be such-and-such. If the observer had been in a state of detached, neutral, indifference, then the 'uncanny moment' of her suddenly becoming aware that the drawing was also something else would have been impossible. In addition, the moment in time during which this novel awareness of a 'duck' when a 'rabbit' was expected must be considered *indeterminate* (as a result of the interaction between the *overdeterminate* and the *underdeterminate*).

Now suppose Netherworlder had the following set of signs:

Dabbit = examined before t_0 (which is arbitrary) and reported to be a 'rabbit,' or not so examined and reported to be a 'duck.'

Ruck = examined before t_0 and reported to be a 'duck,' or not so examined and reported to be a 'rabbit.'

And assume Ourworlder is capable of seeing the drawing only as a 'rabbit' – in other words, he is not cognizant of the drawing's ambiguity. Netherworlder, in contrast, sees the drawing as one thing before a particular instant, and then she suddenly discovers that it can also be something else entirely. Netherworlder would obviously be to Ourworlder rather naive and whimsical, changing her mind, signs, and perception apparently at the drop of a hat. Naturally, of course, Netherworlder believes this is not the case at all; she merely perceived the same thing *as* something else at a given time, and in so doing attained an alternate level of awareness, and that's that. The important issue is, however, that the so-called alternate level of awareness must be for Netherworlder irreversible (discounting memory loss of course). The time at which phenomena are observed, then, can determine 'truth-value' and meaning with respect to those phenomena. What is considered 'true' at a particular time depends upon expectations derived from memory of previous experiences. But when those expectations are not satisfied, discovery of a new form of 'truth' and meaning – and of ambiguity in the 'rabbit/duck' case – is potentially forthcoming.

It almost goes without saying that the time-dimension discussed to this point is potentially inherent in all tense-bound and linearly generated sentences in natural languages. On the other hand, a 'logic' with which to describe *how* change is perceived and understood must give account of perceptual switches or flashes of insight – that is, Peirce's *abductions*. Instants of discovery such as Henri Poincaré's moments of illumination in mathematics, Friedrich A. Kekulé's dramatic discovery of the benzene ring as the result of a dream, or Wolfgang Amadeus Mozart's 'hearing' entire symphonies in simultaneity, must be considered atemporal. At considerably less dramatic levels, understanding the punch line of a joke or a metaphorical or ambiguous statement is equally instantaneous. Yet the fact remains that a mathematical proof or a musical composition can be generated and perceived, like sentences in a language, only over a certain period of time. This distinction between timeless conception on the one hand and linear, temporal generation and perception on the other remains to be briefly and at least tentatively delineated. Otherwise it will be impossible to illustrate any tacit and time-independent 'logic of change.' This time-independence can be accounted for by another variation of Goodman's paradox illustrating a hypothetical situation that would exist were we able to abolish time altogether, at least from a particular perspective.

Consider once again a variation of the liar paradox, 'All Cretans are liars said the man from Crete,' which, if viewed as 'true,' must be 'false,' and if 'false,' 'true.' According to Russell, *pace* the Preamble, the problem with this paradox is that there exists no necessary discrimination of logical types. An individual Cretan is placed at the same level as the class of all Cretans, but, logically speaking, a class of things cannot be a member of itself (that is, the class of men is not a man). In other words, this confusion of levels leads to paradox. Now if, with respect to the liar paradox, we set up a scheme representing Ourworlder's view of Netherworlder's apparently perceiving intermittently, and over time, the statement to be 'true' and 'false,' we have:

Talse = reported to be 'true' when perceived before t_0 and 'false' when perceived at t_1 and 'true' when perceived at t_2 and 'false' when perceived at $t_3 \ldots n$.
Frue = reported to be 'false' when perceived before t_0 and 'true' when perceived at t_1 and 'false' when perceived at t_2 and 'true' when perceived at $t_3 \ldots n$.

From Ourworlder's vantage, his counterpart is a helpless and hopeless 'schizophrenic,' uncontrollably oscillating between the *either* and the *or*. But we recall that Ourworlder's view is, from the robust interpretation of Goodman, atemporally symmetrical with that of Netherworlder. In other words, at the most basic level this 'true-false' oscillation, at the most fundamental level, is analogous to a 'standing wave' rather than a 'travelling wave,' since, we would suppose, there exists no necessary 'memory' of what went on before and consequently there is no real variance over time. Thus, the temporal series $t_0, t_1, t_2, t_3 \ldots n$ is not actually time-dependent in the same way it is in the previous examples. In fact, if we take on Ourworlder's perspective, we might imagine him to conclude that 'frue' indicates a value that, over time, is *neither* 'true' *nor* 'false' (from the *underdetermined* sphere) and simultaneously *both* 'true' *and* 'false' (from the *overdetermined* sphere), since he believes himself to exist in a more general domain than Netherworlder. In fact, just as $\sqrt{-1}$ is labelled i, so also Ourwolder could call the 'talse-frue' combination 'ψ,' or something else, and his problem could provisionally be dissolved.

The upshot of this example is apparent: *time is only a factor when memory is involved*, for without memory there would only be oscillation, ad infinitum. (I must emphasize once again that I am now portraying the strong view of Goodman's conundrum stipulating symmetrical relations between Ourworlder and Netherworlder. This view would be that of the sphere of *overdetermination* wherein incommensurable schemes enjoy no hierarchy of values but are atemporally flattened to the same level. The other, less robust interpretation falls within the sphere of *underdetermination*: complementary views can be equally confirmed, but not at the same time; it is a matter of *now* this interpretation, *now* the other one, hence temporality, irreversibility, and asymmetry enter the scene – to be discussed in the next chapter. Yet, when taking into account either

Ourworlder's or Netherworlder's view of her counterpart as 'schizophrenic,' symmetry relations between them in the *overdetermined* sphere give the promise of temporality to come, for from one 'schizophrenic oscillation' to a successive 'oscillation,' a certain increment of time has transpired in the mind of the onlooker.)

3. A Certain Mark of Distinction

But there is more to the liar paradox and its relevance to Peirce's vague concept of some sort of time-dependent 'logic' than initially meets the eye. We recall that the paradox halts movement to create a 'double-bind' situation and at the same time it correlates, albeit contradictorily, two levels of abstraction. We recall also that, from the perspective either of Netherworlder or Ourworlder, the other's perception is 'schizophrenic.' That is, each presumes s/he exists in a broader frame, with respect to the other, which is actually not the case. In contrast, from our 'logical' viewpoint we discovered that both perspectives, rather than 'schizophrenic,' were symmetrical when interrelated.

This situation is relevant, I would submit, to Peirce's ruminations on his proposed 'logic of continuity,' or of 'vagueness.' Peirce tells us that the process of engendering an actual sign from the range of all possibilities is 'a process which extends from before time and before logic' (*CP*:6.193). We are asked to imagine a clean blackboard as a vague range of possibilities. It is the original generality of the most general sort, pure oneness incorporating, within itself, an indeterminate multitude of possible dimensions and points (that is, the *overdetermined* sphere). If we make a mark on the blackboard, a discontinuity is produced. This discontinuity is itself a continuity complementary with the continuity of the blackboard – that is, it consists also of an infinite continuum of points. But the chalk mark is not really the line, for a line ideally is of infinitesimal thickness, and hence invisible. The visible mark is actually a narrow plane, a white strip that severs and displaces a segment of the black surface: 'Thus the discontinuity can only be produced upon that blackboard by the reaction between two continuous surfaces into which it is separated, the white surface and the black surface. The whiteness is a Firstness – a springing up of something new. But the boundary between the black and white is neither black, nor white, nor neither, nor both. It is the pairedness of the two. It is for the white the active Secondness of the black; for the black the active Secondness of the white' (*CP*:6.203).

The generality of the clean blackboard, then, is viewed as analogous to geometrical continuity. This original generality is broken by the first mark. The mark, however, is the product of an arbitrary act, for it could have been drawn in an infinity of different ways. But after drawn, it separates one side from the other, however vague this distinction may remain. Moreover, the mark of separation or distinction is itself no-*thing*; it is no more than an imaginary entity of infinitesimal thickness. To rephrase Peirce, the line of demarcation between the blackness of the line (a continuum of possibilities) and the whiteness of the line (a complementary continuum of an equal – that is, infinite – number of possibilities) is itself neither black nor white. It is the 'pairedness of the two.' With respect to the black continuum the line of demarcation is something other; it is a Second manifested by the whiteness (a generality) of the (actual) white. And with respect to this white continuum the line of demarcation is also something other; it is a Second manifested by the blackness of the black. As *neither* black *nor* white, the line of demarcation between the blackness and whiteness remains *underdetermined*, if for no other reason than that of its 'schizophrenic' oscillation from whiteness to its other (blackness) and from that other as blackness to its own other (whiteness), and back again. But the line of demarcation is not *both* blackness *and* whiteness (that is, *overdetermined possibilia*), for as an actual (Second), it is something, though that something is destined to remain indeterminate.

Given the relational properties between whiteness and blackness, following Peirce let *W* be 'white' and *B* 'black,' *W*-ness the property possessed exclusively by the mark, and *B*-ness the property possessed exclusively by the blackboard. Corresponding to these positive properties are the negative properties, un*W*-ness and un*B*-ness. Since there is nothing except the actual mark and the range of possibilities (the blackboard), un*B*-ness pertains solely to the mark and un*W*-ness to the blackboard. Hence, the mark and the blackboard appear to be united by nothing. It seems that the only property they can have in common is the compound property, *WB*-lessness: nothing else besides the original un*W*-ness and un*B*-ness is either un*W* or un*B*, so they cannot share properties with anything else even through that compound property. Yet since *WB*-lessness is jointly possessed both by the mark and the blackboard, they have at least that much in common. But the commonality is a disjoint – incompatible or mutually exclusive – property. Hence *W* and *B*, like the mark *and* the blackboard, cannot exist as such if they remain totally divorced from one another: the relationships between *W* and *B* and mark and blackboard are that of *complementarity*. The mark, a discontinuity, depends upon the blackboard for its coming into being, and once into existence, it possesses a continuous nature that is shared with the blackboard. On the other hand, the blackboard contains, within itself, the mark as a possible discontinuity, but, since this discontinuity is incompatible with the blackboard's continuous nature, it might be said that the blackboard does *and* does not contain the mark (within the *overdetermined* sphere). Once the mark is drawn, however, there *is* a boundary that separates one continuum from another and establishes the discontinuity by means of which divergent properties come into being (for further, see *CP*:6.203–13).

Now what has all this to do with Goodman's paradox, or with the general topic of meaning for that matter? This: between 'green' and 'blue' and 'grue' and 'bleen,' there is, a priori, no fixed boundary. Once a boundary is tentatively, and at times arbitrarily, established, it could always have been something else, and in the future it will always have been something else. Hence, any and all inferred generalities in the form of predicates regarding some 'semiotic object,' and the taxonomies constructed from them, are inexorably *underdetermined* – recall Borges's bizarre Chinese taxonomy. And, given the entire range of possible predicates, past, present, and to come, there is no absolutely determining what may be actualized at some moment from the sphere of *underdetermination.* This conclusion regarding inductive inferences and predicates regarding properties of 'semiotic objects,' I must add, falls in step – albeit tentatively, and with some vacillation – to the music of Putnam's Löwenheim-Skolem theorem applied to natural language embedded in institutional discourse, narrative, and everyday talk.

In light of the obvious limitations on human understanding, I now turn to some reflections on how we see something *as* such-and-such and see *that* it is so-and-so, and how we can tacitly know *how* to do something with it and know *that* it is done in such-and-such a manner. These reflections call for a return to a more distinctively Peircean term, namely, the *qualisign.*

4. Fallible Finitism

Goodman (1978), and from another vantage, Hanson (1958, 1969), Sellars (1963), and Rorty (1979) argue effectively that knowledge of 'facts' as they really are independently of how we conceive and interpret them is a futile dream. What we see is by and large what we expect to see and what we want to see. In other words, we generally prefer *convention* and shun *convolution.* Platonism tells us that what we see we see as a universal form: the mind's powers include a grasp of generals, not merely particulars. For Peirce, in contrast, what we initially see is no more than an immediate sensation, a qualisign, which is self-sufficient, self-contained, and replete and complete as it is, without its (yet) being related to anything else. At the outset, this smacks of nominalism of the Goodman sort. But Peirce goes further, much further. For the moment, however, let's stick with the qualisign.

The sensation, say, of 'blueness,' a qualisign, is an immediate sensation in the here-now without there (yet) existing any awareness *of* the 'blue' sensation as such. Somewhat later – about 1/10 second the psychologists tell us (Pöppel 1972, 1988) – there is a becoming of awareness *of* the 'blueness' and *that* it is 'blue,' without there (yet) existing any relation, necessary and natural or artificial and contrived, between the 'blueness' and some other – which would be the makings of a sinsign consisting of some relation between a sign and the 'semiotic object' to which it relates. But by this time the immediate sensation has flown, never to return exactly as it was. If after the fact of the initial sensation of 'blueness' someone relates to that green house on the hill nestled amongst the pines, attention can turn once again to the sensation of 'blueness,' with the realization that the darker 'green' of the pines contrasted with the lighter, somewhat ruddy green of the house giving it the vague appearance of 'blueness.' 'Greenness' was taken for 'blueness'; a mistake was made, awareness of which came to conscious attention solely after the fact of the initial sensation.

The question is, Did I initially see 'blueness' or not? When the sensation initially entered into consciousness I thought I was perceiving a 'blue' patch: it seemed right to me at that particular moment, so it must have been right for me at that moment as far as I could have been concerned, for I had established no awareness of any other to which the 'blue' colour was related. But later I saw it as 'green.' Was I wrong about my past sensation of 'blueness' but now I managed to get things right? Or was I right when, from within my semiotic world as it was at that moment I saw 'blue,' but now there is a slightly different context and a circumstance altered by minutiae of no great consequence, hence I now breath, see, hear, smell, and think in a somewhat different world? Like the Netherworlder from Ourworlder's vantage or vice versa? (Along these lines, see Varela 1984a, 1984b, studies by Land 1959, 1964, 1977, and, in general, Zajonc 1993 [I summarily alluded to these and other studies in chapter 4, section 2].)

If you show me in succession four swatches of cloth, *A*, *B*, *C*, and *D*, where *A* is light blue and *B*, *C*, and *D* progressively becoming a tinge darker, I might report that *A* is identical to *B*, *B* to *C*, and *C* to *D*. Now you place *A* and *D* side by side, and I happen to judge them to be of different colours (we have here a skeletal form of the sorites paradox I have occasionally referred to). Was I correct in my estimation of the series of four swatches and also in my comparison of the first to the fourth swatch? Did I err in my previous estimation and correct my error to get things right later? If I could have been duped so easily at first, what guarantee is there that my final judgment was on the mark? If there is no guarantee, then how can I cherish any of my judgments as superior to any others?

My judgments, of course, were based on similitude through qualisigns and their aftermath in my consciousness *of* icons whose function is to make themselves similar to something other. In the case of the swatches, similarity is construed as sameness and dissimilarity as difference. In the previous example, focus rests on similarity of attributes possessed by two individual items. In either case judgment is made on the basis of something being the same as or similar to something else; hence something and its relation to something other is up for consideration. And if the imaginary conditions and their consequences presented in the preceding paragraphs are capable of holding water, it appears that the age-old idea of determinate 'reference' of one thing to another, or, more specifically, of a sign to its 'semiotic object,' is a dead question. Quite obviously, we cannot live by icons alone. But, as I have argued above, without icons, and at their most primitive level, qualisigns, more complex signs there cannot be.

But qualisigns as such are nothing (no-*thing*) *for* the conscious and self-conscious mind. In order that there be consciousness *of* qualisigns, they must be related to something else, they must be booted up to take their place among a general class of things, which at the same time end their fleetingly brief tenure as qualisigns. That is the downside. The upside is that the demise of a once-autonomous qualisign brings *vagueness* (*overdetermination*) into relation with *generality* (*underdetermination*), which are all necessary ingredients for genuine symbolicity, via the route of indexicality. How so?

5. Then Only in the 'Mind's Eye'?

While Peirce the methodological and epistemological realist believed 'blueness' as a *generality* is 'real' and can be known in terms of one of the attributes of an indefinite number of 'semiotically real' objects of signification, Peirce the ontological idealist conceded that, as a *generality*, it can only be known *incompletely*. (Peirce, while donning his 'realist' hat, would tell us that it is a fact that all blue things possess 'blueness,' for that is the same as to say that all blue things are 'blue.' And since it is a fact that certain 'semiotically real' things can possess 'blueness,' 'blueness' is therefore 'real' [*CP*:8.14; also 1.551, 2.415].)

No matter how far one goes toward specifying the quality 'blueness' as a *generality*, a further step can always be taken – that is, Peirce's controversial asymptotic approximation to the 'real,' a standard feature of his theory of knowledge and of signs. As a consequence, the 'semiotic space' of the *general* term 'blueness' stands no chance of becoming a *plenum* for a finite community of finite semiotic agents; there will always remain some gaps to be filled here and there. Hence, the excluded-middle principle does not necessarily hold, and the 'space' must remain *underdetermined*, for there is no knowing whether or not at some future moment an unexpected conjunction or disjunction will pop up to counter some aspect of what was thought to be known of the *general* term up to that point. The ontological idealist in Peirce was somewhat in line with the intuitionist mathematician, as revealed above; the methodological realist in him continued to seek that dream world where everything is always already there, patiently waiting its being cognized.

According to this formulation, if 'blueness' is conceived as a representamen (sign as such), then the semiotic object must remain unspecifiable in addition to its being non-empirical, and its interpretant cannot be more than some nebulous something in the learnedly ignorant mind of its contemplator. The sign is hardly less apprehensible than its components. It is not the same as showing a child a blue ball as an indication (index) of the sign (representamen) 'Blue ball!' Pointing to a blue patch is not an act of indexing 'blueness.' The patch is merely a patch that happens to be 'blue.' It possesses (it is) 'blueness.' 'Blueness' in terms of its being an attribute of all things 'blue' is a *generality* in the most abstract. As pure Firstness it is a quality ab-stracted from all other qualities and enjoys no relation with anything else. As Thirdness it is the product of habit, of convention, of the embedded or entrenched activity of learning after having travelled the long road of cultural inculcation that certain sorts of things are 'blue' and that they possess a quality called 'blueness.' It is the yield of literally countless perceptual and conceptual grasps of 'blue' things as singularities (sinsigns), as *haecceities*. In the case of Thirdness, however, the push toward *generality*, to repeat, must remain *incomplete*, even in its most sublime human expression.

Yet in order to know what 'blueness' means in the full-blown sense one needs to know quite a lot about blue things, about sentences about blue things, about what blue things do and what can be done with them, about where they belong and do not belong, and so on. Thus, if the question arises as to how much you could learn about 'blueness' by going through the road of life and confronting all these experiences about blue things, it is reasonable to expect that, in principle, and in the theoretical long run, you could learn everything about it. After all, would not a complete account of 'blueness' consist of the totality of things that are blue, as well as sentences about red things, and about everything else for that matter? But, in view of Hempel's induction conundrum coupled with the theoretical or deductive notion that the road to complete and consistent knowledge fades off into the infinite horizon, one must concede that no matter how far one has travelled, the distance to the goal remains mired in *indeterminacy* and *incompleteness*. Hence, *vagueness* there will also always be.

There are other problems as well, which call for another brief digression – I will hold the conclusion of my point in abeyance until the proper terrain is prepared. It is quite safe to say that just as a 'set' and its 'members' are meaningful in terms of how they figure in the sign strings of set theory, so also a 'sign' and its 'components' are meaningful in terms of how they figure in the *semiosic* process accounted for by semiotic theory. There are concrete signs – physical signs – and there is the category 'sign,' just as there are hard-rock representamens, objects, and interpretants. But I am speaking of categories, of *generalities* of the most *general* sort. The term 'greenness' approaches such a category. There is no 'greenness' in terms of particulars, only things that are green, just as there are no 'sets,' only things that can be collected in the mind and put into the abstract category called 'set,' at which time those things themselves become abstract categories, that is 'members' (this assertion does not fly in the face of the realist side of Peirce, since for him 'greenness,' like any other qualifying property, is 'real' as a generality, not an actualized particular).

But is this not the most efficient way to learn about sets? By going around finding more and more things that can fit into 'sets'? The problem is that, as pointed out above, the Löwenheim-Skolem theorem appears to dash this elegant hope. There is no knowing that at some point someone might declare that something thought to possess 'greenness' actually possesses 'blueness' or 'grueness' – or, *pace* Wittgenstein, that the rule 'Add 2' suddenly becomes 'Bad 2' after 1000. In fact, there is virtually no upper limit to the number of deviations from the customary, hopeful, and much-desired pathway from one's knowledge of 'all things that possess "greenness."' So it appears that we are left with the problem of finding some other way to account for the meanings of 'set' and 'member' and 'greeness,' of Thirdness-Secondness-Firstness, and of interpretant-object-representamen. The great apprehension, which tends to breed scepticism, and occasionally nihilism, is that there seems to be no other way of accounting for the meanings of the terms in question, and for all signs as far as that goes, in some manner that does not smack of the mysterious – that is, Omega's response to Alpha.

Then have we no resort but to search for some sort of gnostic union with the 'reality' of set theory, or of mathematics, with the entire fabric of signs? It is not enough to provide examples of sets and signs, such as 'A set is like hog-tying a bunch of things.' A set is like a 'box' into which things can be placed, a string of 'marks' between two brackets, a 'club' to which we can belong, or a 'university' containing buildings, books, and presumptuous professors and stressed-out students scurrying about. By a comparable move, we might declare that 'Icons are a set of signs that are similar to something, like a bulldog is similar to Winston Churchill,' 'Indices are a set of signs that point to things like a finger pointing out the thief in a line-up,' and 'Symbols are a set of signs that represent things by convention, like some stars and stripes standing for the United States.' It all becomes a matter of addressing oneself to generalities of increasing abstraction until one has generals of the most general sort in one's clutches. This is apparently nothing more than meaning, interpretation, or explanation – whichever the case may be – by association primed by similitude. If metaphorical knowledge is all we have, then we have no more than a nebulous poetic tuning in on the meat of the matter and little more. Or at the deepest level we might have some hopelessly vague sense of the whole of things, or perhaps some sort of mystical insight. But there will be hardly anything concrete we can sink our teeth into.

However, it is a question not of mere Firstness but of Firstness and Thirdness in a tight embrace with Secondness by way of their commonality, the 'node,' which is essentially 'nothing' and at the same potentially 'everything.' Now the charge will surely be that I have taken a plunge at the deep end and into the quicksand of self-defeating ineffables that cannot but place us in a state of despair. Well, yes, and no, depending upon the perspective. From a semiotic point of view, I would contend that there is ample reason for more delectation than despair. It is a matter of taking into one's stride the inevitable emergence of...

6. A Difference That Fakes a Difference

To reiterate the central theme of this inquiry, where Firstness reigns, *vagueness* is the password, and the classical law of contradiction does not necessarily hold. And for a very good reason. It is not that contraries and contradictories are fused, for there is really no conflict in the first place, there is no more than what for lack of a better word might simply be dubbed *undecidability*. It is quite difficult to picture this condition. In fact, it cannot be 'pictured' at all, and perhaps because of this resistance to picturability, it has eluded the grasp of Western 'logocentric' thought. Yet, Derrida (1973) writes in so many – perhaps too many – words that this condition lies at the core of Western thought, in the *aporias*, the binds, the twists of the Möbius strip, where tragic flaws are found in any and all texts of sufficient levels of complexity.

Such signs as Derrida's *pharmakon* and *différance* are an oblique expression of these 'flaws' of undecidability – and admittedly to say 'flaw' is somewhat of a misnomer, for it is the saving grace of texts, that which affords them their value, in spite of what their authors might have thought. *Pharmakon* – like $\sqrt{-1}$ – is both a poison and a remedy, both deadly and life-giving. And *différance* is both a difference (in space) and a deferral (in time). The two signs are looked upon as ambiguous. In technical terms, they would be charged with the misdemeanour of inconsistency, for they cannot simultaneously mean one thing and its opposite. Yet they incorporate both meanings. They are the immediate product of the Möbius strip twist: there is both 'inside' and 'outside,' both 'figure' and 'ground,' both 'this' and 'that.' There simply are no binaries in the ordinary sense. *Différance* goes a step further than *pharmakon*, however. Signs are marked by difference, and they are deferred as well, for there is always something left over, some excess or 'remainder' (Lecercle 1990). And this deferral is temporal, though without its (yet at least) having taken its leave of spatiality. It is in this sense the initiation of asymmetry, transitivity, movement, temporality, as pointed out above regarding Secondness.

At the other end of the spectrum, Thirdness rules, and the excluded-middle principle begins to wane. Thirdness, giving rise to generality, regularity, habit, is the culminating stage of the product of reiterations, of repeated instances of Seconds or particulars (*haecceities*) until at some point some extent of common ground between the particulars is constructed. The human semiotic animal, that pliable 'thinking reed,' takes smug comfort in believing she has arrived at the finish line, bringing her general conceptions to completion. But there is no determination (provability is the Gödelian word) of this being so. There is no knowing without a shadow of a doubt whether a given generality is either complete or incomplete. Presumptuous though fallible individuals that we are, we would like to persist in our belief that many, if not all, of our conceptions are quite complete. And we proceed to wrap them up in a tidy package. Yet we have no certainty regarding their competence. In other words, in a manner of speaking our generalities are neither complete nor incomplete: they remain perpetually open to new additions and deletions. Derrida's *supplement* plays out a comparable role. A supplement is an addition, which presupposes that what took on the addition was incomplete. That which assimilated the supplement had been regarded as complete in itself, yet the supplement was added in order to complete it, to compensate for some sort of lack in what was supposed to be complete. The *supplement* carried out its role of rendering that which was neither complete nor incomplete perhaps a tad more complete, and perhaps not. Furthermore, it bears mentioning, without *différance* the *supplement* would vanish, for *différance* provides for the excess, the remainder, of what went on before. The important point is that, like the 'schizophrenic' case of the *pharmakon*, the process remains open, without determinable end.

In the zone of the kaleidoscopic fuzz of Firstness, what Peirce dubbed the 'logic of vagueness,' and what might even be called a 'logic of *différance*-temporality,' comes into play. According to orthodox logic, there is an infinitesimally thin line between opposites. I argued above that a 'logic of vagueness' would play havoc with logic of the classical sort. A disjunction of the set of all bald men and the set of all nonbald men does not exactly leave the empty set, and the law enforcers out to protect the principle of noncontradiction find themselves impotent. The sorites paradox reveals a virtual continuum of gradients between the one pole and the other of the supposed contradiction. This important point also plays the role of a guerrilla warrior against cherished structuralist-semiological principles according to which Saussurean differences are stretched into whole-hog binary oppositions. Although it is true that Derrida often refers to *différance* as the conflict of forces, his lodging an all-out attack on binarism of the semiological sort reveals his more general war against the policemen of opposition and identity. However, this war was indefatigably waged by Peirce almost a century before the gospel according to Derrida was written. Then it was taken up most notably by John Dewey and resumed in the Anglo-American tradition by Rorty and the neopragmatists.

The problem has been that in certain respects even today we are not really ready for Peirce. This is evident in two responses to a certain strain in contemporary scholarship. On the one hand, the infatuation with French thought, especially in literature departments in the United States, has either been passed off by the powers that be as yet another manifestation of mushy Continental philosophy, or it has become the prime mover of knee-jerk reactions. In both cases, the response is more often than not motivated by fears that academic real estate is being invaded. When classical principles are threatened, even at the margins, apprehension enters the hearts of those conservative of mind. They envision Pandora's Box bursting at the joints. On the other hand, when, in view of the poststructuralist-deconstructionist current, contradiction ceases to exercise its dutiful force, for those desirous of some sort of free-wheeling Nietzschean play of the world anything can apparently go, and the world that was for a few centuries bound by good logic and reason is no longer of any serious consequence. Both responses – the 'liberal' one and the 'conservative' one – are both right and wrong. The first one is right in its scepticism regarding whatever has become trendy but wrong in its wholesale rejection of whatever lies outside its narrow focus; the second one is right in its critique of the canons of logic and reason but wrong whenever it is backed up by the overconfident belief that a step outside the canons is possible.

A happy meeting ground between the two responses, I would respectfully suggest, can be found in the collaboration of *vagueness* and *generality* and their role in the actualization of signs into Secondness. In brief recapitulation, the domain of *vagueness*, of Firstness, lies outside the conception of any existent Seconds. Pure *vagueness* is, most properly put, mere chance, the trembling, scintillating, dancing field of possibilities awaiting their turn to jump into

Secondness. Virtually everything is possible and nothing is yet actual; time is of no consequence, nor is space according to its commonplace conception for that matter. Nothing (no-*thing*) has interacted semiotically with anything else such that it and some *other* mutually lift themselves up by their own bootstraps. If nothing (yet) is, then it is possibly many things, and perhaps virtually anything and everything – the shadow of Meinong becomes ominous, but solely regarding this sphere of *possibilia*. In the sphere of Thirdness, of *generality*, we have what appears to be a different ballgame altogether. If the Western tendency is to beat the virtually infinitesimal differentiations of Firstness into oppositions when entering the anteroom of Secondness, then when individuals begin to merge into the ranks of generals, the tendency is to fuse differences into identities. Nietzsche duly criticized this obsession 'to treat as equal what is merely similar – an illogical tendency, for nothing is really equal – is what first created any basis of logic' (1974:171). And later Heidegger observed that 'the same is not the merely identical. In the merely identical, the difference disappears. In the same the difference appears, and appears all the more pressingly, the more resolutely thinking is concerned with the same matter in the same way' (1969:45) (recall, from our Preamble, Omega's reaction to Alpha's tentative ruminations).

In the domain of *generality*, a union of the set of all bald men and the set of all nonbald men does not include the totality of all men. Once again, baldness is a matter of degree rather than rigid type distinction. Russell's notorious barber who shaves all those and only those who do not shave themselves contradicts himself only with regards to classical logic. The implication is that all men must be shaved by someone. The barber either shaves them or they shave themselves, with an imaginary line separating the two acts. But what if the barber *neither* shaves himself *nor* does someone else shave him? He must be excluded from the *generality*, and included within the time-bound, thickening line of demarcation, for eventually he will have grown a beard. The excluded-middle principle tastes defeat, and from that time forward it may even experience a long losing streak, for the barber might start a fad that will have eventually put him out of business.

This, to the chagrin of the purveyors of good taste and proper logic, seems to bear on that 'irrational' Buddhist sort of logic of *both-and* rather than the *either-or* in the traditional Western way. The Master holds a stick above Alpha's head and tells him: 'If you say anything I will hit you with this stick; if you say nothing I will also hit you.' The hapless youth appears damned if he does and damned if he doesn't. It's an *either-or* bind typical of linear, binary logic. But what if apprentice enters the line of demarcation, widens it, grabs the stick from his Master, and hits him on the head with it? He has packed something into the erstwhile excluded middle. Physicist Max Planck once complained that a new scientific theory 'does not triumph by convincing its opponents and making them see light, but rather because its opponents eventually die, and a new generation grows up that is familiar with it' (in Kline 1980:88). With time, the line opens its gaping jaws, and the erstwhile prohibited, but yet possible in spite of the prohibition, gives birth into the world of existents.

In another way of putting it according to Peirce's blackboard 'thought experiment' described above, *A* and *B* possess the attributes labelled *A*-ness and *B*-ness, which are incompatible in such a manner that they cannot both be actualized, yet the *vagueness* of their combine holds them together along with all other *possibilia*. Insofar as actualization goes, there can be *either* one *or* the other within a given context, but *not both* in simultaneity. Yet *A* and *B* share the compound property, *AB*-lessness, which is *neither A nor B*, but somewhere in between. It is the hair-line demarcation that prevents their simultaneous actualization within the same context. *AB*-lessness is jointly possessed by both *A* and *B*, so they have something in common, but the commonality is a disjoint – incompatible or mutually exclusive – property. The definition of both is not genuine without the inclusion of disjunction that conjoins them. The one cannot exist – enjoy actualization – without its remaining related to the other through their common attribute. In other words, *A* and *B* are *complementary*. Both of them cohabit the domain of *vagueness* without quandary or qualms. One can be actualized while the other is held in abeyance. Then, in the next instant the other can take its place in the world of existents while the first fades away into implicitness, like the *Gestalt* psychologist's figure and ground (I allude here, as I have at various junctures above, to Bohm's implicate and explicate orders [1980]).

After there has been actualization of something, the excluded-middle principle does not always hold. It is not necessarily a matter of *either-or*, or of 'not (not-X) = X,' for in the next instant and/or another context, it is probable that 'something in between' the two values *will have been* actualized. The logician's argument is that if the terms used in a proposition were strictly defined regarding a finite context and were *complete* in terms of their *use* (that is, extension, 'reference,' hooking the terms onto actuals), then the Principles of Identity, of Noncontradiction, and the Excluded Middle would hold true. The problem is that, over time, no context remains identical with itself, and no term reaches *completeness* to the extent that it will never allow for a greater degree of determination. The sentence 'Bill Clinton is Bill Clinton' is not true if the former *use* of the term relates to Bill Clinton, September of 1994, and the latter *use* relates to him as of December of 1996. Whatever possibility happens to be actualized for the moment *cannot be strictly determined*, since the sign of the actualized object, act, or event, though the 'same' sign in terms of its graphic, auditory, or whatever features, as well as that actualized object, act, or event *could always have been* actualized and signed in some other fashion. And in whatever manner they *will have been* actualized and signed, they will take on a countenance that is *other than* what it *was*. The assignment of signs to Bill Clinton puts both him and the signs incessantly in the process of becoming something other than what they were, and their becoming is incessantly on the road *toward* completion.

'But,' our stolid logician of fitting demeanour retorts, 'your quaint "spheres" – as you call them – of *vagueness* and *generality* are suspended in thin air, with no more than an imaginary thread to support them. Come down to the world of existents about which we can talk, and it is plain to see that what is, is what it is, and not something else, and what is not is excluded by what is.' Regarding the domain of actuals (Seconds), which, we would expect, is the bottom line, the grounding for all knowledge of what there is, an opinion from the likes of Einstein, Louis de Broglie, Max Planck, Bertrand Russell, Wittgenstein, Quine, Goodman, Putnam, and Rorty – to say nothing of the recent rages in the humanities and social sciences under the umbrella term 'postmodernism' – goes something like this: *Insofar as logic and mathematics are connected to 'reality,' they are uncertain; insofar as they are absolutely certain, they cannot be indubitably connected to 'reality.'* And as a consequence of the metamathematical 'limitative theorems,' from the likes of Kant, Gödel, Tarski, Emil Post, Alonzo Church, Alan Turing, and Skolem, we have: *If a sufficiently powerful and sophisticated set of signs is presumably complete, then there must be a tragic flaw, an* aporia, *an inconsistency somewhere, and if it is deemed consistent, then it cannot but be incomplete, for somewhere there is a lack, a deficiency, that calls for the addition, a* supplement, *of something from 'outside.'*

Our well-intentioned logician, of course, will accept nothing less than brilliantly gleaming crystals of thought, each embedded in eternal, static being, and distinct from all others by a vacuum – or by our hairline demarcation. Variations must be the imperfect realizations of this underlying truth of all things. But this obstinate dream places permanent barriers before us barring any and all successive – and potentially infinitesimal – gradients between the two poles of the hopeful contradiction evinced by the sorites paradoxes, with their inherent fuzziness. Nothing is either the one or the other, but thinking can often make the 'in betweenness' appear to disappear. And thinking can revive that 'in betweenness,' elevating into the light of day the ultimate import of the very idea of *semiosis*. Actual things can be clearly and distinctly neither the one nor the other (*underdeterminate*), and merely possible things can be both the one and the other (*overdeterminate*). How could it be otherwise, that is, if quantum theory, relativity, and the 'limitative theorems' are on the right track, when such intangibles as i (= $\sqrt{-1}$) are used to compute the behaviour of presumed actuals, and when possibles can be actualized into any one of literally an infinite number of 'realities.'

'Yes, I've heard comparable stories before. Would you please just say what you have in mind?' someone retorts. Well, I have tried to be as honest and forthright as I could. But I suppose I should try to try again.

13

From Conundrum to Quality Icon

1. Finally Forgetting 'Objectivism'

Rorty writes that the relevance of Peirce today is above all evident in his having 'envisaged, and repudiated in advance, the stages in the development of empiricism which logical positivism represented' (1961:197–8). And in Christopher Hookway's view, Peirce 'seems one of the most modern of contemporary philosophers. If many of his views are controversial or implausible, still, on reading his work, we are likely to feel that many of his problems are close to the issues that are philosophically pressing today' (1985:1).

Hookway goes on to note Peirce's contributions in logic, the philosophical analysis of meaning, problems of truth and verification, philosophy of science, and, above all, pragmatism. He then proceeds to argue that on many points Peirce is in conflict with the contemporary philosophical mood. As I have mentioned quite often elsewhere, Peirce was in part a child of his times. We all are. This does not, however, diminish his contributions: they project out and beyond his sociocultural milieu and into our own. In fact, as I suggested in the last chapter, we have not yet caught up with Peirce in one of many important respects. He put language in particular and signs in general back into the body by melting the mind/body dichotomy. To be more specific, among other things, Peirce has taught us how to give iconicity its due share of the spotlight. In recent times a large step in this direction has been taken by Putnam, as outlined above, and carried forth by George Lakoff (1987) and Mark Johnson (1987) – to be discussed in the final chapter.

The move is away from the 'metaphysics of representation' following the concern many philosophers have with what Lakoff and Johnson specifically allude to as 'objectivism.' In Richard Bernstein's words, 'objectivism' is 'the basic conviction that there is or must be some permanent, ahistorical matrix or framework to which we can ultimately appeal in determining the nature of rationality, knowledge, truth, reality, goodness, or rightness' (1983:8; from diverse vantages, see Brown 1979, Putnam 1981, 1988, and Rorty 1979, 1982, 1991). 'Objectivism,' in this spirit, is an expression of our deep-seated need to anchor our world in some immutable 'truth' that will guide and protect us from all ills once we have found it. This deep-seated need is not, I would submit, at its most fundamental lodged in our search for 'truth,' but in the very way our language, or better, our discourse, works. Skolimowski puts the matter succinctly: 'We are now reaping the bitter harvest of those great philosophical visions that were enunciated in the seventeenth century: "Knowledge is power" (Bacon); "Nature is there to be quantified" (Galileo, Newton); "Divide everything into smaller and smaller components" (Descartes)' (1986:475).

The theory of meaning propagated by the 'metaphysics of representation' can be summarily qualified by the following (this definition, I should mention, dovetails with Putnam's conception of 'metaphysical realism,' outlined above):

1 Meaning consists of abstract correspondences between symbols (words or formal signs) and the mind-independent furniture of objective reality. These symbols become charged with meaning chiefly by virtue of this correspondence, or reference. They embody concepts – their meanings – in terms of mental representations (Kant) or logical ciphers and their relations (Frege) that identify what there is in the world by means of their general character – that is, that which ties their particular exemplifications to the class to which they belong.
2 Concepts (meanings) are 'disembodied.' Ideally, they are shorn of all vestiges of iconicity (concrete images, self-contained diagrams, and metaphors), and make use of indexicality only insofar as correspondence between symbols and their objects of reference are concerned. The idea or image one might form of a *horse* is partly to largely private and subjective. In contrast, the concept (meaning) of the sign 'horse' hovers in free space above any and all *horses* and outside the mushiness of individual, subjective minds and their wishes, inclinations, intuitions, sentiments, and desires. Concepts (meanings) should be objective, and shared by all members of the community of knowers. Thus, they are independent of individuals; they transcend individual human limitations, standing in logical, objective relationships, regardless of how humans might take them or put them to use. (This notion is perhaps nowhere more apparent than in Frege's insistence on the public, objective nature of meaning [*Sinn*] insofar as it determines

reference [*Bedeutung*], which exists in a special ontological domain of thought independent of any individual consciousness.)

3 Meaning is derived from a sentence by establishing the conditions under which it would be true, or under which it would mirror some state of affairs in the world. Sentences that are nonliteral or have no correspondence to objects, acts, and events in the physical world are not fit to be endowed with meaning in the full sense, for they cannot be properly defined, nor can they be fixed to the world. The structure of meaningful sentences, like the structure of the world, does not allow for anything but what there is, devoid of nonliteral considerations.

A glance at these three principles is sufficient to reveal that they are a far cry from Peirce. Regarding (3), while Peirce believed 'brute physical reality' remains what it is in spite of what we take it to be, the concepts and meanings with which a community of individuals accounts for their world are by no means independent of those individuals. They are an integral part of their interpreters and their interpreters are an integral part of them; all are equally signs, in the vast perfusion of signs making up the whole of *semiosis*. In a manner of putting it, colour categories do not exist in the world. At most it can be said that wave-lengths exist and that colour categories are culture-dependent (Lakoff 1987:197–8). Turquoise could be dubbed either 'blue' or 'green,' or 'grue' or 'bleen,' according to the whims of a particular community. It could even be placed into the same pigeon-hole as things that are for us 'chartreuse.' In this sense 'truth' is not the source of concepts and meaning, as per (2), but rather, in light of Peirce's 'pragmatic maxim,' the whole of one's conception of an object, act, or event. The extent to which one interacts with one's signs in arriving at that conception, as well as with that object, act, or event, brings forth meaning, regardless of whether it is 'true,' 'false,' or at the outset apparently 'meaningless.' What is 'true' for one community could be 'false' for another one, and that 'truth' for the first community could become 'false' in another space-time slice. It's the same old story: nothing is absolutely either 'true' or 'false,' but our acts of conception and perception, and the interaction between our signs and the things surrounding us, can often serve to make it so.

Moreover, with respect to the conjunction of (1) and (2), I have pointed out time and again here and elsewhere that symbols stand or fall according to whether or not they are hefted to advantageous heights by their antecedent collaborators, icons and indices. And icons and indices, in spite of the conventionality, the habituation, the automatization, of their processing and consumption, maintain an indelible element of subjectivity, of idiosyncrasy, dwelling as they do within the confines of the private lives of their makers and their interpreters. Furthermore, as I shall argue, symbols – and their intendant meanings – are by no means purely mental, detached, disembodied, and independent of imagination, like computer data banks.

According to the 'metaphysics of representation,' a rigid dichotomy has traditionally been maintained between the conceptual and the corporeal: concepts are the product of formal, rule-governed mental acts, while images and sensations belong to the body. Within this tradition, the role of cognition consists of a Kantian generation of concepts and their combination in propositional judgments. Imagination plays a part in the inception of this train of linear mental events, but the products of imagination are neatly stashed away in the closet when the final results of cognition are proudly displayed. The infirmity of this mind/body dichotomy becomes especially evident in Kant's weakening the once robust thought/sensation distinction in his account of imagination – recall in this respect my above suggestion that we bring Frege's *Vorstellung* into relation with *Sinn* and *Bedeutung*. In the beginning, imagination is capable of bringing various sensations (fur, four legs, a wagging tail, a bark) into a single whole, which can then be conceptualized as a 'dog' of a particular variety. The process engages body as well as mind, kinesthetic as well as conceptual faculties, and corporeal feelings, iconic images, and indices of otherness as well as purely mental events. In other words, it is a matter of Firstness and Secondness brought together by the mediary action of Thirdness. All processes and sign components make up an interrelated whole, with all parts dependent on all other parts. Thus the sovereignty, the superordinance, of symbolicity – abstract categories and relations – is more apparent that genuine, more the product of wishful thinking than actual *semiosic* practice.

The presumed overriding predominance of symbolicity, in fact, is one of the chief problems with the 'metaphysics of representation.' In spite of the internal contradictions of this traditional epistemological posture, we have tunnel-mindedly dwelled almost exclusively on symbolicity, with the expectation that in one of the next few plays it will run interference for us during our mad dash to the goal line of meaning and 'truth.' Indexicality and especially iconicity, in the process, have been relegated to the cheering section whose banners of gala colours have contributed little more than glitz to the real battle going on amongst the football-gladiators on the floor of the coliseum. However, abstracting symbols from the legitimate arena of *semiosis* and elevating them to the status of sole wherewithal of meaning has done a disservice to the sign by disembodying it and rendering it a mere skeleton of what it once was and should be. The sign, in addition to the necessity of its contextualization within the community dialogue, must be properly reincarnated with what has over the centuries been peeled from it, strip by strip. Signs are simply not meant to be abstracted into context-free ahistorical matrices or formal algorithms, available solely to some supreme transcendental cognizer.

By no means do I wish to deny that signs are devoid of any form or fashion of logical or formal underpinnings. As I believe should be apparent after a reading of the preceding chapters, classical logic and its accompanying formalisms have their place. But, like 'representation' of and 'reference' or 'correspondence' to 'reality' by means of signs, they are not the whole ballgame. While putting 'representation,' 'reference,' and 'correspondence' in their proper place, I have repeatedly hammered at the 'signs-as-"mirror"-of the world' idea. Our signs do not 'mirror' the one and only world 'out there.' They construct worlds, the worlds of our own making, fashioned rather than found, devised rather than discovered. To fall into the belief that the world we have forged is 'reality,' clearly and distinctly, or at least a 'mirror' of 'reality,' is to fall victim to the idea that our role is relatively passive. In Putnam's words, our constructed worlds are *our* worlds, and *our* conceptions of them 'depend upon our biology and our culture; they are by no means "value-free". But they *are* our conceptions and they are conceptions of something real. They define a kind of objectivity, *objectivity for us*, even if it is not the metaphysical objectivity of the God's Eye view' (1981:55).

We have the above account of Putnam's argument that the Löwenheim-Skolem theorem bars unique mappings between terms – whether in formal or natural language – and the world: knowledge of conditions under which terms are meaningful and even 'true' cannot serve to fix the way they 'refer.' In fact, meaning will remain beyond our grasp as long as we cling to the idea that there is some privileged set of mind-independent things to which language directly and simply 'refers.' The furniture of the world does not exist independently of our way of sensing it, feeling it, and talking about it: '*We* cut up the world into objects when we introduce one or another scheme of description' (Putnam 1981:52). In view of this limitation, Putnam not only argues that we cannot account for meaning with respect to some mind-independent world, he also argues against the idea that objects, acts, and events in the world are in possession of some 'intrinsic property' endowing them with meaning. The problem with the objectivist picture of the world, according to Putnam, rests in the notion of an 'intrinsic' property, a property something has 'in and of itself,' in addition to anything language or the mind makes of it. Objectivism devalues sensation, feeling, and raw experience (Firstness), proper to visceral, corporeal knowing, and it ultimately considers the world to be 'mirrored' in the cogitating mind of she who holds legitimate credentials. Which is to say, objectivism in its purest form, and if brought to its full realization, would be strangely remiscent of idealism: mind and mind alone would account for ('mirror') the world. This is a long way from Peirce's 'objective idealism' according to its interpretation in this inquiry. For the 'objective idealist,' knowledge can be no more than 'semiotically real,' or 'internally real' if you wish, while the 'real,' though it certainly enjoys some 'real objective existence' or other, will continue on as a self-contained whole in spite of how we sense it and feel it, and what we may desire to think of it and how we wish to talk about it.

So the most likely suggestion – the road back to sanity, a return to the world in which we actually live and breath – is: Forget *objectivism*, *logic* (insofar as it is devoid of *vagueness*), *representation*, *correspondence*, and *reference*. That is, taking the entire gamut of *semiosis* into due consideration, what is 'real' (sign-events 'out there') is partly to wholly mind-dependent, and what is 'ideal' (thought-signs 'in here') can be 'objective' only insofar as there is an adequate degree of community agreement regarding what can be sensed, said, and thought.

But these words carry little weight unless they can be qualified in light of the above chapters.

2. On the Signs We Make, and the Signs That Make Us

Table 1 offers a synopsis of many key concepts introduced in this volume. Consider this scheme in terms of our method of taking others' signs and of others taking our signs – such as, say, the dialogue in our Preamble. During this process, the onus of determination of the signs in question rests more with the addressee than the addresser. Hence, what is brought to our attention is sign *generality* more than *vagueness*. In this manner, table 1 is to be taken as a set of signs with which to account for the process of *semiosis*, but with awareness that in other worlds and other circumstances other sets of signs could have been engendered, and they could possibly have fit the bill equally well: what I provide in table 1, then, is a pattern of some of the attempts to understand meaning as it is often taken by the so-called linguistic turn. (I by no means wish to imply that Peirce's theory of signs is all things to all people. It is, rather, my contention that in Peirce's efforts to embrace the whole of things while offering a theory of process – that is, while resisting the temptation to become a thoroughly systematic, totalizing philosopher in the best and worst practices of modernity – he was able to proceed further along the road toward a complete theory than have most theorists of the sign since his time, though he realized full well that by virtue of his very theory, as a fallible knower, he would never be able to hit the bull's-eye dead centre.)

TABLE 1

1. Frege	R_d	O_s	I_d
2. Cat-cat*	R_s	O_d	I_d
3. H_2O-XYZ	R_d	O_d	I_d
4. Grue/bleen	R_s	O_d	I_s
5. Synonymy	R_d	O_s	I_s
6. Misinterpretation or transmutation	R_s	O_s	I_d

Where *R* = representamen, *O* = 'semiotic object,' *I* = interpretant, *s* = virtually the same as (or at least taken to be the same as), and *d* = different than.

Row 1 of Table 1 is properly Fregean: different signs ('morning star,' 'evening star') can link up with the same 'referent' (*Venus*, *Bedeutung*) as determined by different meanings (*Sinn*). So much for Frege, since I dealt with him sufficiently in previous chapters for the purpose of our present concerns. Row 2 is accounted for by Putnam's 'cat-cat*': the same sign (or representamen) can relate to radically distinct 'semiotic objects' to yield distinct meanings (or interpretants) – unbeknownst to their addressees, that is, until they catch onto the misinterpretation (row 2 and the remaining rows are also either directly or indirectly relevant to the puzzles offered by Quine and Wittgenstein, but for purposes of economy I have chosen not to discuss them at length here). I write 'until they catch onto the misinterpretation,' for up to that point we must suppose that they had usually assumed communication channels were open and meaning was transparent. Then, when they became aware that the converse was the case, they were privy to the implications of row 6, soon to be in the spotlight.

The next row involves another of Putnam's thought-experiments, interaction between H_2O and XYZ. Different signs can relate to different 'objects' but, until more information is made available, it is not outside the realm of possibility that the same interpretant can ensue. As discussed above, for the pre-Dalton chemist H_2O and XYZ can be synonymous – an impossibility, in light of row 5, we shall note – whereas her post-Dalton counterpart is aware of the incompatibility between the two terms. In other words, the post-Daltonian is aware of something that lies beyond the purview of his pre-Daltonian colleague, which does not necessarily make him any wiser, of course, he just happens to cut his world up in a different way according to what for him is the evidence at hand. His enacting a split between H_2O and XYZ renders his world a bit more sophisticated than his counterpart's pre-Dalton world in this respect, though her world in other respects might be the product of subtle cuts and splits unknown to his post-Dalton world.

Row 4 bears on Goodman's riddle of induction according to which the signs 'green' and 'grue' remain constant insofar as both parties are concerned from within their respective languages. The 'semiotic object,' in contrast, undergoes a radical alteration for the other party as far as one's own signs and 'objects' go, but remains constant from within one's own scheme of things. And the interpretant, from within one's scheme, remains constant, but as seen from the other's scheme, it is transmuted after t_0. In other words, 'All emeralds are green' and 'All emeralds are grue,' from within their respective universes of discourse, are both supported by the same evidence before t_0, for up to that point all emeralds have in fact been 'green,' and therefore 'grue.' But they yield contradictory predictions after t_0. They remain 'green' from Ourworlder's view, but Ourworlder's view from Netherworlder's vantage is now something else entirely: what was for him previously 'green' for some unknown reason became 'blue.' On the other side of the ledger, as far as Ourworlder is concerned, her colour system and terms are fixed, all things being equal; it is the strange Netherworlder that she sees to be feeble of mind.

Row 5 involves the synonymy of two signs, a standard-bearer for Russell and the early logical positivist, which is virtually impossible in Quine's philosophy and an equal impossibility regarding the Peircean concept of signs incessantly translated into other slightly different to radically distinct signs. Within Quine's interrelated web of meaning, if synonymy could exist, meaning would be trivially forthcoming. However, (1) since meaning emerges from within the interrelatedness between all signs involved within given contexts and the addressee's background of conventions, dispositions, presuppositions, prejudices, and expectations, and (2) since contexts are incessantly changing, it follows that (3) there is no identity of signs with themselves from one space-time slice to the next and hence no identity of meaning. Row 5 is hardly more than a comfortable ideal unrealizable in practice.

Finally, row 6 involves the radical translation-transmutation of signs, or simply their inevitable misinterpretation. Take 'Gavagai!' as 'rabbit,' 'undetached rabbit parts,' or whatever, and chances are you will miss the boat, for translation is radically indeterminate. Spot a white raven, and 'All ravens are black' as well as its counterpart, 'All nonblack things are nonravens,' are refuted, and the term 'raven' undergoes a major overhaul: it is translated into something else altogether. What becomes even more disconcerting, from a picture of the whole of things, of the entire *semiosic* current, 'mass,' 'space,' 'time,' 'simultaneity,' and other terms suffered radical meaning variance (translation) from the Newtonian to the Einsteinian 'paradigm,' whether the 'normal scientists' within the latter 'paradigm' were aware of the fact or not and whether they liked it or not. Thus, 'mass' had one meaning within the Newtonian framework and another entirely different meaning within the Einsteinian framework, and unless interlocutors from the two frameworks became aware of the divergences in their talk, they might well have believed they were getting along swimmingly – *pace* Putnam's thought experiments. In contrast, if the Newtonian used the term 'mass' in the same way both before and after t_0 but the Einsteinian once used it like the Newtonian but changed her ways after t_0, then Goodman's problem of induction threatens to enter the game. In fact, the Newtonian could conceivably have continued with his pair of terms, 'space' and 'time,' to denote two distinct phenomena, whereas after t_0 the Einsteinian decided to coin the terms 'spime' and 'tace' in order more adequately to specify their mutual interpenetration and fusion into a continuum. In this case, the signs diverged at a particular point, and the 'incommensurability' reigning between the Newtonian's and the Einsteinian's talk could become apparent.

In the event of misinterpretation via row 6, *overdetermination* comes to bear. This is not immediately apparent, since, if radical meaning variance is the case, then it is chiefly a matter of the *underdetermination* of 'semiotic objects,' from Newtonian physics to Einsteinian physics. However, rows 2 and 3, when placed in the light of row 6, present a different face. The 'semiotic object,' in addition to either the sign or the interpretant, presumably undergoes change, which implies both *overdetermination* and *underdetermination* from a given perceptual and conceptual grasp. That is to say, perception and conception of the 'semiotic object' can change as a result of the agent's selecting some alternative from the dancing, scintillating ocean of possibilities within the sphere of *overdetermination*; at the same time, either the sign or the interpretant – or both in the case that rows 2 and 3 are combined – are the product of the sphere of *underdetermination* in the event that they can with comparable legitimacy account for their respective 'semiotic object.' In other words, 'cat' and 'cat*' relate to distinct 'objects' and yield distinct interpretants. Yet as far as 'cat' interlocutors and 'cat*' interlocutors are concerned, the sign applies equally well to the phenomena and basically the same interpretants are engendered within the context of their conversations, that is, as long as neither interlocutor becomes aware of the incompatible 'objects' involved. H_2O and XYZ, by contrast, relate to distinct 'objects,' but they can and do take on fundamentally the same interpretant, at least until the H_2Oer takes a healthy swallow of XYZ thinking it is water, or until the XYZer dumps some H_2O onto her sheet of copper overlaid with a waxed design expecting her colourless substance (which she thinks is nitric acid) to etch it.

Regarding the *overdetermination-underdetermination* pair further, let us dwell a bit more on row 4. Goodman, we will recall, labels the conundrum he reveals the 'new riddle of induction.' The old problem of induction, of course, was 'Hume's problem,' that of 'justifying induction.' Simply put, there is no justification for induction, since experience demonstrates that there is no iron-clad guarantee that one can know what will happen at a given future moment. To get in tune with his 'new riddle,' Goodman suggests that we begin by thinking deduction. A deductive argument is justified if it conforms to the rules of deductive logic, which are strictly formal. Justification of induction, we read, should follow the same path: proper focus on the rules of induction should lead to a justification of induction insofar as it is demonstrated that an inductive argument conforms to the proper rules of induction. In the case of both deductive and inductive arguments, just any old rule does not yield a valid argument. The proper rules for deduction are, Goodman admits, virtuously circular, yet they can lead the way to the best of all possible deductive worlds. By rejection of arguments that prove unsatisfactory and by fine-tuning those that for the moment appear promising, we are at least moving in the right direction. It would be advisable, Goodman writes, to let inductive practices follow the same route: adopt whatever practice, with its attendant rules, that seems most viable regarding our world, and if it proves successful – that is, with a little whittled off here and a bit added there in due time – it will become standardized as a matter of course. On the other hand, if it turns out to be unsuccessful, then it should be tossed.

On a more specific note, Goodman puts the matter of such inductive advances and setbacks cryptically: '*A rule is amended if it yields an inference we are unwilling to accept; an inference is rejected if it violates a rule we are unwilling to amend*' (1965:64). He argues that the process of 'justifying induction' should follow a parallel procedure. It is this: 'Predictions are justified if they conform to valid canons of induction; and the canons are valid if they accurately codify accepted inductive practice' (ibid.). Instead of asking how knowledge is possible through experience, which was Hume's thrust that ended up in a blind alley, Goodman asks how it is that certain inferences are valid and others not. His answer, as it turns out, is the *projectibility* and *entrenchment* of predicates on the part of a community of sign users. A predicate is *projectible* if its use after a few simple repetitions is deemed legitimate. 'Green' has been projected in the English-speaking community while 'grue' has not. The criterion for projectibility is the use of whichever predicate has become *entrenched* and conventionalized in the community (*entrenchment* is quite comparable to the terms used occasionally in this volume, *embedment* and *automatization*). The longer the history of a particular entrenchment, the more likely the projection will turn out to be successful. Now *entrenchment* as I have formulated it here, which smacks of nominalism – and Goodman is an avowed nominalist – might appear entirely unacceptable for the Peirce purists. But Hacking (1993) argues that this is not the end of the matter. As a point of fact, *entrenchment* cannot help but usher in our indomitable penchant for taking on *dispositions*, developing *expectations* (akin to inductive predictability), and making *generalizations*, all of which help satisfy in one form or another Peircean philosophy (Hacking 1994). In this sense at least, Goodman's formulation is not far removed from Peirce's dialogical community in pursuit of the most feasible signs for communication and for understanding the world. The longer a sign is taken to be the most adequate by the community (that is, the longer it goes without 'refutation' and hence rejection), the better are its chances of survival (for further on Peirce habit formation, comparable to Goodman's entrenchment, see Boler 1964, as well as *CP*:2.242, 5.111, 5.411, 7.354).

The important point, then, is the *element of history* entailed by the concept of entrenchment. Stephen Mulhall (1989) argues in favour of a symmetry relationship between Netherworlder's 'Gruespeak' and Ourworlder's 'Greenspeak.' At the same time Mulhall tells us – obviously from within his own language, the equivalent of 'Greenspeak' – that 'Gruespeak' is incoherent. But according to the above arguments, if 'Greenspeak' is considered from Netherworlder's vantage, it is our – that is, Mulhall's – language that is incoherent. In this light, upon considering the two languages to be symmetrical, either they are both incoherent, or neither is incoherent. So let's assume the capacity for a holistic, symmetrical, reversible, atemporal grasp of everything, including 'Gruespeak,' 'Greenspeak,' and any other possible language to boot. Our grasp, embracing everything, includes the entire sphere of *overdetermination.* But this sphere involves *possible*, rather than *actual*, languages and their uses. So knowing it would be of little practical value in the nitty-gritty world in which we live and breathe. Moreover, if we take the actual historical dimension of Goodman's *projection* and *entrenchment* into account, we cannot hope to escape from irreversibility, temporality, and asymmetry. That is to say, the emergence of a novel perceptual and conceptual grasp of emeralds after t_0 – on the part of Netherworlder's taxonomy from Ourworlder's viewpoint, and vice versa – marks an irreversible, temporal, and asymmetrical event from a view of the whole of things. So what is most important to our present concerns regarding Goodman's thought-experiment is the transitory nature of signs it implies, not any attempt to see them as a set of symmetrically related terms and their meanings. This temporal act of becoming always enjoyed a chief role in Peirce's conception of *semiosis* (see Merrell 1996 for this necessary aspect of irreversibility in Peirce's philosophy in light of the work of Ilya Prigogine).

In this sense, whatever predicate is entrenched at a particular point in time for a given community could always have been other than what it is, and there is no guarantee that it will survive the test of time, for at a future moment some conflicting predicate (such as black swans, white ravens, grue emeralds) may rise up to take on status as valid inductive inferences. In this case, we are now speaking of the sphere of *underdetermination*, which includes the incompletable journey toward increasingly regular regularities, more general generalities. In other words, from the broad perspective (of the sphere of *overdetermination*), everything is (merely) possible, even contradictions. Consequently, a dense fog of *vagueness* inheres. From the other perspective (of the sphere of *underdetermination*), whatever is taken by habit and convention (*projection* and *entrenchment* – Secondness, *actuals*) in terms of *generalities* must eventually be subject to amendments and occasionally to total overthrow, for no matter how far down the road toward that epistemological pot of gold a community has travelled, its knowledge will remain *incomplete*.

This is the first part of the semiotic scene.

3. Remove a Leg from the Tripod, and It Collapses

A second part of the scene involves a game of hide-and-seek between wilful thinking and Peirce's concept of *abduction*.

My evoking the name of *abduction* at this juncture might appear off-the-wall. But it is not, not really. That is, not really, if we agree that changes of Frege's 'sense,' incommensurables of the 'cat-cat*,' 'H_2O-XYZ,' and 'grue/bleen' sort, and all misinterpretations, failed translations, and blemished synonyms as illustrated in table 1 are partly tacit, nonconscious – embedded, automatized, entrenched – *semiosic* activity. That's precisely why I bring in *abduction*: to complement the chiefly voluntary and logico-rational manipulation – if not to say use and abuse – of signs in inductive and deductive practices. Peirce takes deduction more or less in its traditional sense, properly lying within the domains of classical logic and mathematics. Induction, when included in the tripartite abduction-induction-deduction scheme, entails confirmation by putting deduced hypotheses to the test – whether in scientific activity or everyday living. (I must emphasize that I am here considering the whole of semiotics, not that which is limited to classical logic, mathematics, and science).

The process of hypothesis formation is put into play by an individual act of abduction. Peirce considered 'one of the worst of ... confusions, as well as one of the commonest' that of 'regarding abduction and induction taken together ... as a simple argument' (*CP*:7.218). Unfortunately, Goodman, like the vast majority of scholars during the heyday of logical positivism and since, has essentially ignored abduction. James Harris writes, and justifiably so, that if we adopt Peirce's distinction between abduction and induction, 'then [Goodman's] new riddle of induction is properly viewed as a riddle of abduction' (1992:60–1). Hume's dilemma was how to explain how what we have seen in the past can justify predictions regarding what we will see in the future. Goodman's riddle rests on how hypotheses are chosen for confirmation in the first place: will it be 'All emeralds are green' or 'All emeralds are grue,' and why? Properly separating Goodman from Hume, roughly we have Peirce's abduction-induction pair.

From within the symmetrical, atemporal, all-encompassing sphere of *overdetermination*, 'All emeralds are green' and 'All emeralds are grue' are alike confirmable 'by evidence statements describing the same observations' (Goodman 1965:74). All possibilities are *there* and waiting, as candidates for future abductive acts on more or less an equal and democratic basis. Once a selection has been made, the entrance fee has been paid to the arena of *underdetermination* (deduction), and with the temporal, asymmetrical, irreversible *actualization* of confirming instances (induction), the interminable game toward semiotic success has been initiated. The problem is that success often appears to be available with a simple head fake and a dash around right end for a touchdown. This is because abductions are in many cases deceptively enticing and promising. They are somewhat remotely comparable to Goodman's 'similarities.' Goodman claims that similarities, the same as regularities, are where they happen to be found, and they can be found virtually anywhere and at anytime. Similarities, like generalities, however, are no panacea. In fact, they are inevitably 'wrong' from one perspective or another, for they could have always been other than what they are. Peirce also recognized that '[t]here is no greater nor more frequent mistake in practical logic than to suppose that things which resemble one another strongly in some respects are any the more likely for that to be alike in others ... The truth is, that any two things resemble one another just as strongly as any two others, if recondite resemblances are admitted' (*CP*:2.634). The ultimate implications of Peirce's notion regarding his 'objective idealism' are no less radical than Goodman's comparable notion of similarity regarding his 'nominalism.' If virtually any and all resemblances, even the most blatant and the most recondite, stand a gaming chance of gaining entrance into the 'semiotically real' (of Seconds) from a virtually aleatory background (of Firstness) – an element of which is present in even the most deterministic of worlds, according to Peirce – then there is no iron-clad method for determining beforehand whether 'All emeralds are green' or 'All emeralds are grue' – or any other combination of likely candidates – will make the starting line-up. Neither *possibility* is *necessarily* any more likely or less likely than the other. But abductive intuition (literally, instinct, Peirce occasionally called it) can at least give the vague promise of making it so. What is certain, following Peirce's 'rule of predesignation,' is that '[w]hen we take all the characters into account, any pair of objects resemble one another in just as many particulars as any other pair. If we limit ourselves to such characters as have for us any importance, interest, or obviousness, then a synthetic conclusion may be drawn, but only on condition that the specimens by which we judge have been taken at random from the class in regard to which we are to form a judgment, and not selected as belonging to any sub-class. The induction only has its full force when the character concerned has been designated before examining the sample' (*CP*:6.413).

So an abduction (conjecture, guess, hypothesis from the 'pragmatic maxim') precedes a deduction (formal statement of a hypothesis), and only then do successive confirmatory acts (the inductive process) follow. A conjecture must be made as to whether emeralds are 'green' or 'grue' before there can be either a deduction regarding particular empirical grasps and the hypothesis following from them or an inductive process of confirmation. Regarding the ensuing confirmatory acts, Peirce gives the following example: 'A chemist notices a surprising phenomenon. Now if he has a high admiration of Mill's *Logic*, ... he must work on the principle that, under precisely the same circumstances, like phenomena are produced. Why does he then not note that this phenomenon was produced on such a day of the week, the planets presenting a certain configuration, his daughter having on a blue dress, he having dreamed of a white horse the night before, the milkman having been late that morning, and so on? The answer will be that in early days chemists did use to attend to some such circumstances, but that they have learned better' (*CP*:5.591). The 'surprising phenomenon' can lead to a conjecture, which then spills into a hypothesis, and confirmatory acts ensue. But if the phenomenon of each and every confirmation is to be a truly legitimate repetition, then there must be sameness or at least resemblance of every aspect of that phenomenon when properly contextualized, down to the apparently most insignificant details.

This becomes an impossibly drawn-out task in Peirce's example, it would appear. Obviously, there must be a selection and a Goodmanian projection, which is in its initial stages a matter of abduction, not induction. Assuming 'All emeralds are grue' might have been at some time in the past selected, then eventually we must suppose it would have come in conflict with experience – at least for Ourworlder – and replaced by the projected alternative 'All emeralds are green.' In other words, the 'grue-green' dilemma regarding the 'semiotically real' world of actualized signs is a matter of asymmetry, temporality, and irreversibility. These characteristics render the dilemma relevant to the arena of *underdetermination*, since an unexpected and contradictory event had called for a hypothesis's replacement by another one, thus testifying to the *incompleteness* of the conceptual scheme within which that hypothesis had dwelled. They also bear testimony at least indirectly to the utter *vagueness* of the arena of *overdetermination*, of pure possibilities without anything having been actualized. In the final analysis, the abduction-induction-deduction process, in conjunction with Peirce's 'pragmatic maxim,' does not aid and abet that oversimplified image of pragmatism in terms of 'truth' as whatever happens to work or whatever happens to be in style. Peirce's pragmatism remains attuned to the future, to the general thrust of the entire community of dialogic semiotic agents. It is not simply a matter of what surprising turn of events happens to pop up in the here-now (abduction, Firstness), or what has happened in the past and how it predicts the future (induction, Secondness), but, in addition, how our conception and hence perception of signs will fare in the future as a consequence of signs present and signs past (Deduction, Thirdness). So much for abduction, at least for the moment.

A third part of the semiotic scene involves, finally, meaning, which, as we shall see, is impossible without abduction, iconicity, Firstness – the quality of sensations, corporeal feels, inclinations, moods, and modes. Hacking (1993) gives account of Saul Kripke's (1982) correlating Goodman with Wittgenstein's sceptical problem – briefly mentioned above and in the Preamble. Kripke suggests that 'grue' can be addressed not to induction but most properly to meaning. The question would not be 'Why not predict that grass, which has been grue in the past, will be grue in the future?' but rather, the Wittgensteinian question 'Who is to say that in the past I did not mean grue by "green", so that now I should call the sky, not the grass, "green"?' (Kripke 1982:58). In other words, in the past I called emeralds 'green,' but meant 'grue,' and now I continue to call them 'green,' but I actually mean 'bleen' (in English, 'blue'). And I now call the sky 'blue,' but actually mean 'green' (that is, 'grue'). Hacking points out that while Goodman's problem is outer-directed with respect to what the community thinks and says, Kripke's is inner-directed: what I think and say. In this sense, his question becomes, Why do I call the sky 'blue' and grass 'green' when actually I mean 'green' ('grue') and 'blue' ('bleen') respectively? To be accepted by my peers or to impress my students? To save face? To avoid conflict? To keep on the good side of my superiors? To impress an attractive colleague? To keep a good Rortyan conversation going? Or simply to deceive my associates in my effort to play a good con game? Possibly any of the above, one would suspect, and there are an indefinite number of other reasons to boot, that is, according to Kripke's inner-directed, rather solipsistic, rendition of Goodman.

If we take Goodman's original use of his riddle into full account, as does Hacking, then the entire community comes into the picture. As such, the question becomes: Would the majority or perhaps the entirety of the community to which I belong carry on the way I do? If each individual of a particular community were in step to the beat of the community's band, it would be as if the tacit assumption on the part of the community as a collection of individual might be, *Who is to say that in the past we did not all mean 'grue' by 'green' – even though we knew better – and none of us imagined that everybody else actually meant 'grue' by 'green'?* We, as members of the community, could all be speaking out of the wrong side of our mouth for the sake of maintaining lines of communication intact without knowing that everyone else was doing the same. The so-called charity principle would operate in a perverse sort of way. Or better, it would be reduced to shambles insofar as nobody would be extending charity in good faith, but illicitly and for personal reasons. This would be a world in which everybody lies, but lies in basically the same way, hence the collection of lies becomes a strange form of 'truth.' It would also play havoc with Searle's well-intentioned interlocutors, Rorty's conversation would soon fall into chaos, and any form of a coherent and congenial community could hardly survive. What's more, if we applied the bizarre dialogic interaction of this community of prevaricators to the 'pragmatic maxim,' what one person reported would be the opposite of what she actually perceived and conceived. The 'maxim' would turn against itself, leading to individual or collective error rather than wisdom, inauthentic signifying acts rather than genuine meaning. Given the above on the *overdetermination-underdetermination* pair and all its ramifications, there would be no method at all for knowing whether the community is progressing or retrogressing along its arduous push toward the goal line of knowledge. Any smug confidence that what is known is knowledge rather than delusion would be itself more likely than not delusory.

Ultimately, the problem with meaning is not in its proof but in its taste. Quite simply, if it goes untasted, virtually anything may be capable of going as a proof, and if virtually anything can be a proof, then whatever the taste may prove, it will more often than not be little more than superfluous. I allude to the inextricability, in good semiotic practices, of either the representamen, object, or interpretant, and of either Firstness, Secondness, or Thirdness, from the entire tripod of relations. The thorn in the side of meaning is that most popular accounts of the 'grue-green' dilemma highlight either one or two legs of the tripod at the expense of the other(s). On the one hand, Goodman's riddle focuses on projection of predicates on things, thereby bringing about entrenchment, which is not a matter of 'truth' or even meaning, per se, but of linguistic practice. On the other hand, Kripke's Goodman raises the question of meaning, if not exactly 'truth,' in addition to induction. Goodman evokes an attitude focusing more on *actuals* (Seconds), how they are most appropriately to be taken, once seen, and, most specifically, how they should be clothed in *linguistic* garb (Thirds). Kripke's Goodman takes *actuals* in his stride as a matter of course; of more focal interest is the range of *possibles* (Firsts), and how, in their interaction with those *actuals*, they can in the future *potentially* give rise to alternatives (as Thirds) to the conventions that be. That is one difference between Goodman's 'true grue' and Kripke's 'Goodman's grue.' Another important difference is that of 'outer'-directedness and 'inner'-directedness, to which I alluded above. Kripke, following Wittgenstein on rules, remains tied to consideration of thought-signs – in contrast to Goodman's emphasis on sign-events – of the mathematical sort, which are in this sense quite commensurate with chapter 4 on Peirce's consideration of mathematics, fictions, dreams, and hallucination, in addition to my own discussion of Meinong in light of Peirce on signs.

Speaking of Peirce, where he stands out most briskly when placed alongside the Goodman-Kripke pair rests in his nonlinguicentric refusal to eschew indexicality, and especially iconicity, from the entire picture. Peirce stressed long and hard that there is an iconic relation between the 'semiotic object' that gives rise to an abduction and its attendant hypothesis, on the one hand, and that 'semiotic object' as it is actually perceived, on the other. This relation is that of analogy or resemblance, proper to iconicity. Peirce offers the example of the similarity between the image of an ellipse and the data concerning the longitudes and latitudes of the revolution of Mars about the sun that allowed Kepler to draw up his abductive inference (*CP*:2.707). As a result of this abduction, a hypothesis was formulated, it conformed to the observations, and a new theory saw the light of day. As a consequence, the statement 'The orbit is elliptical,' like 'The cat (or cat*) is on the mat (or mat*)' and 'Emeralds are green (or grue),' includes a predicate, or icon, as well as a subject, or index, as integral parts of the sentence (symbol). This is, of course, most proper to first-order logic, in light of the above on Putnam. But since signs are incessantly in the process of becoming signs and building upon other signs, the most complex of them possessing the capacity to function as icons – *Hamlet*, *Don Quixote*, space as *homogeneous* and *infinitely extended*, the universe as a *machine*, God as *love*, and other sign *corpora* taken as self-contained, self-sufficient wholes – it also applies to a greater or lesser degree, I would suggest, to whatever conglomerate of signs might be available.

And thus we are in the genuine domain of *semiosis*, which includes the full range of sign interactivity.

4. The Way of All Flesh

Semiosis begins, recalling the consequences of the last chapter, with the qualisign, iconicity at its barest. If in the beginning was the word, that word, as a solitary evocation, was not yet a legitimate symbol: it needed interrelationships with other symbols and other signs before it could take on the status of a full-blown symbolic sign. Neither was it an index before its properly coming into relation with some 'semiotic object' or other.

In view of the previous section, initially a sign is a sign of and by *abductive inference*: it often comes as the result of a surprise, for its signness emerges where and when there was as yet no indication of signhood *for* some semiotic agent *in* some respect or capacity. At this rudimentary stage it is the ultimate in autonomy, self-containment, self-reflexivity, harmony, coherence. In other words, the sign is a mere sensation (First), then it is acknowledged as something other 'out there' or 'in here' (Second), and finally a surprise is registered (as a Third) because it appears that there is something rather than nothing and that this something is not what it would ordinarily be. Smugly confident of its ability to stand on its own (as qualisign), since it knows of no otherness (as sinsign), an initial sign – which is not yet a fully developed sign (as legisign) – begins by reiterating itself, and in this act it can then relate in good *semiosic* fashion to some other.

But all this most likely remains aggravatingly obscure. Consider, then, an example. In line with *abductive* activity, suppose at a particular juncture in your life the surprising event *A* occurs. Then you notice that if *A*, then there is the possibility of *B*. And as a consequence you draw up the tenderly fallible conjecture (*abduction*): if *A*, then there are *prima facie* grounds for assuming that *B*. In case *B* is related to *A* by mere resemblance, you have no more than a vague sense of iconicity. If the relation is from *A* to *B* in terms of some space-time connection, indexicality enters your *semiosic* activity, and you can now begin the route to *cumulative inductive* practices. And if *B* enjoys a place in the conventions of some community of semiotic agents, then in all likelihood you will be able to relate it *deductively* to *A* by way of symbolicity (natural language), whether in 'inner' or some form of 'outer' dialogic exchange.

Of course the mind would ordinarily prefer to avoid surprises, except perhaps in play. The game of life is serious business, and, according to Peirce, it entails incessant acts of abduction, induction, and deduction. Without them, there would be no life at all, which is, precisely, the unfolding of possibilities actualized and congealed into habits that constantly push the process along. During the course of events, *vague* possibilities (as Firsts) eventually take on breadth to become *generalities* (as Thirds). In other words, juxtaposed and often *inconsistent* signs are selected, actualized (into Seconds), and brought into relation with other signs to engender perpetually *incomplete* modes of mind and of action. This process, I must emphasize, begins with abduction, the only 'creative act of mind' (*CP*:2.624), the 'operation which introduces any new idea,' for induction 'does nothing but determine a value, and deduction merely evolves the necessary consequences of pure hypothesis' (*CP*:5.171). An abductive insight is the mere suggestion of *learnability*, which, when invested with a hypothesis, is tested for its *accountability*. If things go according to the best of expectations, then the mind is on its way toward *knowing* something it knew not.

In sum, then, with respect to the three forms of inference, (1) abduction is the process whereby sensations become welded together ultimately to form a general idea, (2) induction entails habit formation, whereby sensations as they are related to similar events (reaction on the part of some other) are combined into a general idea, and (3) deduction is the process by which a habit, as the result of abductive and inductive processes, becomes part of everyday conduct (*CP*:6.144–6). It has become quite apparent that these processes tend to gravitate from *vagueness* to *generality*.

Incorporating mind and body into the equation, in deduction the mind follows habits, usually according to pathways of least resistance and by virtue of which a general 'idea' suggests some action. But this 'idea' (Thirdness) is not strictly mental, disembodied, abstract, and autonomous of the world: it emerges as the result of a process given a particular direction by some sensation (Firstness), and the sensation was followed by some reaction (Secondness) from some other, whether of the physical world, the community, or the self's own 'inner' other. The move from sensation to reaction to idea to action is not marked by ruptures, but rather, it is continuous. Corporeal capacities and tendencies merge into incorporeal capacities and tendencies, and vice versa, as one undivided whole. Along these lines, Peirce writes in his usual intriguing but obscure manner, with uncanny allusions and bizarre associations, that the way 'the hind legs of a frog, separated from the rest of the body, reason,' is 'when you pinch them. It is the lowest form of psychical manifestation' (*CP*:6.144).

There is no 'I think, therefore I am' here, but merely the mind of some rather vague 'I think' flowing along in concert with – though at times dragged along by – the body, and the self of 'I am' in incessant dialogue – whether amiable or agonistic – with its other self, its social other, and its physically 'real' other. There is no 'I respond to stimuli, therefore I think I think,' but mind orchestrating – though often unwittingly playing second fiddle to – the body's comings and goings. In this manner, speaking of 'mind' and 'idea' in the same breath as the impulsive jerks of a severed frog's legs is not epistemological heresy. What the frog legs do is fundamentally what we do, the difference being that for him, the body, whether whole or dismembered, can hardly be budged from centre stage, while our mind often deludes itself into thinking it has taken over the leading role and the body is merely along for the ride. However, the mind is not as paramount as we would like to think.

Though Peirce's abduction-induction-deduction triad does not enjoy the central role in this inquiry, I bring it up in order briefly to illustrate the importance of all forms of Firstness to the flux of *semiosis*. All concepts, as *generalities*, are invariably *incomplete* and hence subject to further amendments or deletions, or they may simply be discarded if proved inadequate. This nature of concepts and so-called conceptual schemes can by no stretch of the imagination be divorced from *vagueness*, which liberally allows for polysemy, plurivocity, through metaphors and other rhetorical tropes. While by their very nature they embody *inconsistency*, these tropes are not therefore rendered meaningless, nonsensical, or 'false.' They are not mere place settings or *hors d'oeuvres*, but part of the main course. In this sense, iconicity lies embedded at the heart of things. If we can talk of meaning at all, it is due to this centrality of iconicity, composed of images, schemes (Peirce's diagrams), and metaphors. This centrality is germane to the ways of corporeal sensing and feeling as precursors to thoughts, concepts, and habits of mind and action. Linguistic or propositional knowing is possible solely as an outgrowth of nonlinguistic or nonpropositional processes. In other words, in light of previous arguments, symbolicity depends upon iconicity and indexicality for its very sustenance, Thirdness is made possible by the prior development of Firstness and Secondness, and legisigns owe their very existence to qualisigns and sinsigns. Ultimately, qualisigns and icons themselves depend for their existence on *imagination*. From imagination, sense is made of experience, which renders signs learnable in the first place. Imagination affords the tools for making semiotic worlds and giving account of them, and it gives rise to the ways of reasoning toward which knowledge of signs may be forthcoming. In fact, styles of reasoning themselves depend upon imagination, Firstness, which, as I shall argue in greater detail in the final chapter, is categorically ignored by 'objectivist' philosophy.

If meaning there be, then, it emerges from Firstness and encompasses the likes of unicorn images, unicorn schemes, and unicorn thought-signs, just as much as cats-on-mats, cherries-on-trees, and grue/green emeralds, and just as much as images, schemes, and concepts. Cats and cherries as subjects and grue and green as predicates all constantly collude, collide, collaborate, and conspire to bring about engenderment of meaning on the part of their respective semiotic agents and according to whatever contexts and conditions that happen to emerge at a particular space-time juncture. Meaning consists in the relations emerging during sign engenderment and interpretation. It is not found in the relations between words and their referents, but first and foremost in relations of iconicity and indexicality, in feeling 'in here' and sign-events either 'in here' or 'out there' before there are any thought-signs. We would like to think we are *rational* animals, capable wilfully of generating the thought-signs that most effectively give our lives order and purpose. But before we are *rational* animals, we are rational *animals*. Our styles of reasoning are embodied in our cultural patterns and propensities, our embedded habits, and tacit comings and goings. Consequently, these styles of reasoning enable us to fabricate our worlds according to pathways of least resistance (the demands of Secondness), culturally inculcated imperatives (the necessities of Thirdness), and private idiosyncrasies, whims, and wishes (the desires of Firstness). The concrete 'reasoning' of heart, soul, stomach, and even – and perhaps most emphatically – groin cannot be divorced from the abstract 'reasoning' of mind. Feeling and sensing, and contact with hard-core physical 'reality' cannot but play a necessary part in the ethereal confines of intellection. Body and mind, subject and object, individual and community, nature and culture, are inextricably mixed.

But I really must be more specific.

PART V

And Finally, Navigating Back, Wherever That Was

14

Out of Sign, Out of Mind

In this, the final stage of our journey, corporeality is joined with intellect, that proud intellect, the obsessive focus of Western thought over the ages, to suggest that there is a middle path – nonpropositional, neological, *vague* yet occasionally *inconsistent*, *general* yet inevitably *incomplete*, product of the sphere of *overdetermination*, and on the road toward knowing, though it is destined to remain *underdetermined*. This chapter discusses Peirce's basic decalogue of signs, linguistic and nonlinguistic alike, which prepares the terrain for a move to place the body properly in the signs in chapter 15, as a necessary step toward knowing what meaning is all about.

1. The Mind in the Body

With recollections of table 1, I offer table 2 depicting Peirce's trio of basic triads according to his categories, with his three types of 'hypoicons' along the bottom row. Table 2 will be correlated with figure 11, which sports connecting lines making up Peirce's fundamental ten classes of signs, indicated by the numerals (for further on Peirce's ten signs in this regard, see Merrell 1995a, 1995b, 1996). Finally, table 2 and figure 11 will be placed in the context of table 3, which, we shall note below, is quite compatible with Johnson's formulation in his 'Diagram 2' (1987:154). Asking the patience of those familiar with Peirce, I will present a crash course on Peirce's decalogue of signs as depicted by the lines of connection in figure 11 in order more properly to place his general theory of signs within the context of this inquiry thus far. (Table 3, a sort of 'map' of the scheme Johnson presents in his effort to 'put the body back in the mind,' is particularly correlated with Peirce's hypoicons – image, diagram, metaphor – which correspond to his categories of Firstness, Secondness, and Thirdness.)

TABLE 2

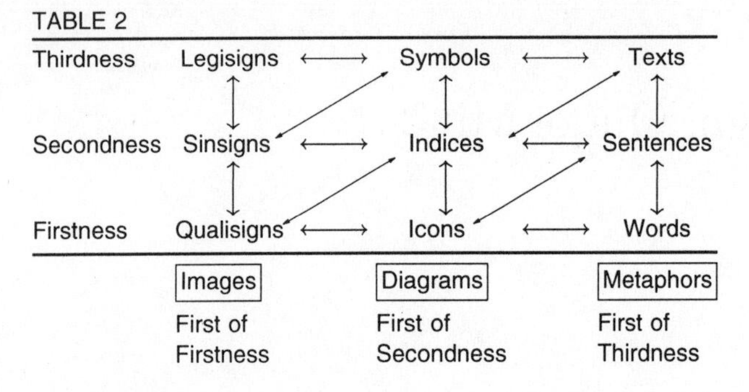

Qualisigns, *sinsigns*, and *legisigns* consist respectively of the First or sensation of a sign 'in here' or some physical sign event 'out there,' a once-occurring sign instantiation as Second, and a sign as generality, or Third. *Icons*, *indices*, and *symbols* are actual signs of resemblance, signs of necessary physical or compulsive linkage, and signs of chiefly mind-dependent or arbitrarily constructed linkage as set apart from the semiotic agent to be interpreted and given meaning according to social convention and habitual practices. And *terms* or *rhematic symbols* (*words*), *propositions*, *dicisigns* or *dicent symbols* (*sentences*), and *arguments* (*texts*) consist of symbolic signs, most characteristically found in natural and formal languages, whose use is chiefly conventional.

Sign 1, a *qualisign*, is no more than a vague sensation of, say, 'greenness' (or 'grueness'). An *iconic sinsign* (2) entails a relation between the item producing the raw sensation and something other, without the relation having (yet) been made explicit in the mind. A *rhematic indexical sinsign* (3) is a spontaneous, automatic, or even instinctive response, warning, or signal, such as 'Watch out!,' without any particular 'semiotic object' having (yet) been made explicit. A *dicent sinsign* (4) is an indicator or pointer, such as a weathervane, the function of which has been made apparent, though it remains as yet uninterpreted. Sign 5, an *iconic legisign*, is the first of Peirce's decalogue of signs to reach the status of legisign: it is tantamount to what Peirce calls a 'diagram,' but at this stage it includes the interpreter, who has now become conscious *of* the sign and its relation to its object, which is to say, the sign has taken on at least the barest trappings of what can potentially become its interpretation (interpretant). Sign 6, a *rhematic indexical legisign*, is typical of a demonstrative pronoun, which implies and relates to a noun, but whose implication and relation can become evident solely within the context of the sign use; in other words, the sign still remains to a large extent implicit. A *dicent indexical legisign* (7) is characterized by a commonplace expression, such as, say, 'Hi! How'r ya doin'.' Its fully embodied meaning

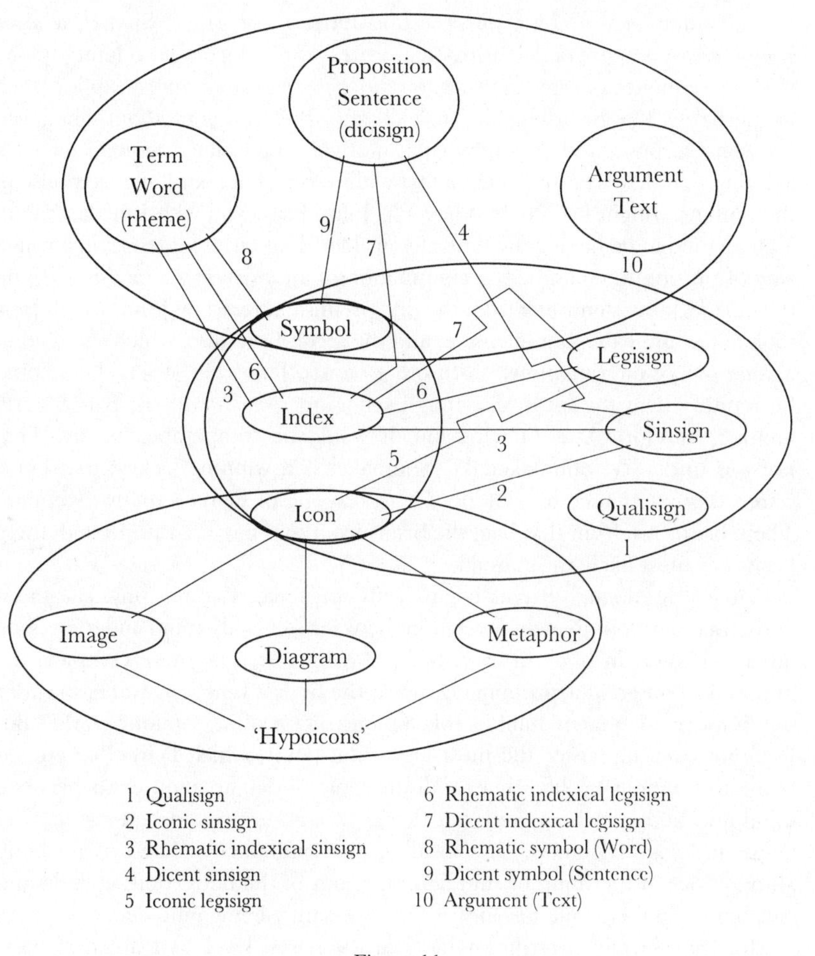

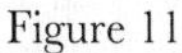
Figure 11

remains vague, since the sign and its 'semiotic object' are not yet drawn from the limbo of covert relations.

A *rhematic symbol*, *term*, or *word* brings standard notions of 'reference' to bear. 'Cat' can 'refer' to a particular entity resting on another entity, a 'mat.' Better yet, sign 8 could be an evocation, 'Jane!,' when John happens to run into her. As an isolated sign, however, 'Jane!' cannot enjoy full meaning or 'reference,' since it must be *related to* other signs and to their semiotic agents for the fulfilment of some purpose and function or other. Sign 9, a *dicent symbol*, *proposition*, or *sentence* brings the process toward fruition, relating 'Jane!' to some sequence of signs in order to render the evocation more explicit, such as, perhaps, 'I've been meaning to call you.' But 'call you' about what, and for what purpose, and driven by what motive? The isolated sentence is not a genuine sign unless embodied in a text within some context. Jane's response to the sentence might be: 'No you haven't, John. I saw you with June last night. You seemed to be having the time of your life.' This latter sentence, in a rough way of putting it, could be the culmination of an *argument*, or *text* (sign 10) on the part of Jane, stemming from the first premise, uttered by John, which Jane took not as amicable but offensive, and the second premise, which she read as arising out of ulterior motives. (In other words, Jane's set of sentences could be rephrased in the form of a rough syllogism: A was with B; B is a party animal; therefore A was having fun. It would be comparable to, say: That horse is under W. Shumaker; W. Shumaker is a winning jockey; that horse stands a good chance of winning. Or to use one of Peirce's many examples: These beans are from that bag; the beans from that bag are rat-infested; these beans are most likely rat-infested).

Peirce's decalogue of signs begins with corporeal, visceral, physical sensations, then develops to include relations between self-body-mind and something other, whether 'in here' or 'out there.' As signs become more complex, the mind takes on greater prominence while the body's functions wane, in order that it more adequately fulfil its role as constructor of its 'semiotic world.' But I cannot overemphasize the most important point, which Peirce hammered home throughout his life, that no distinct line of demarcation exists between mind and body, 'in here' and 'out there,' thought-signs and sign-events, and between signs of iconicity, indexicality, and symbolicity. There is no body autonomous of the mind or mind autonomous of the body: both collude and collaborate in the whole *semiosic* process incessantly being unfolded.

More specifically regarding table 3 at the basest level, as I noted in passing, what Johnson in his 'Diagram 2' labels 'image-schema-concept' can be quite effectively mapped onto Peirce's three classes of 'hypoicons,' 'images,' 'diagrams,' and 'metaphors' (a chief difference between Peirce and Johnson, I must point out, is that for the former, at least in my interpretation, the 'object' perceived is 'semiotic,' never the 'real' *an sich*). As an icon, however, Johnson's 'image' clearly predominates, which leaves us with the task adequately of accounting for his 'schema' and 'concept.' Now re-enter the next tandem of Peirce signs – *qualisigns*, *sinsigns*, and *legisigns*. To recap, qualisigns entail bare feeling, sensation, sinsigns mark the entering into consciousness of something other than that consciousness as a once-occurring event, and

TABLE 3

Concept ('Metaphor')	'Dog' Conventional sign engendered by rules of combination potentially for relating image to things in the world	'Number 5' Conventional sign engendered by rules of combination for use in potentially determining the nature of things in the world	'Triangle' Conventional sign engendered by rules of combination for use in potentially giving account of the nature of things in the world
Schema ('Diagram')	Image ⟶ Thing Sign relating qualitative character of concrete qualisign to things in the world	Image ⟶ Quantity Sign relating (mapping) quantitative character of abstracted qualisign to things in the world	Image ⟶ Shape Sign relating (mapping) qualitative character of abstracted qualisign to things in the world
Image ('Image')	Qualisign in the mind	Qualisign in the mind	Qualisign in the mind
	'Semiotically real world'		
	Actual dog	Numbers	Triangles
	'Real (brute physical) world'		

legisigns involve signs of generality, the product of inductive accumulation and conventional habit and regularity. The legisign stage, eventually calling up natural and formal languages for its fulfilment, includes the likes of 'cats' and 'mats,' 'cherries' and 'trees,' and 'grue' and 'green' emeralds. Qualisigns, sinsigns, and legisigns are manifested through actual, materialized signs – that is, *icons*, *indices*, and *symbols* – either 'in here' or 'out there.' Icons contain their respective hypoicons (images, diagrams, and metaphors) as signs of Firstness, of possibility, not having (yet) attained status as actuals, as signs of Secondness. Indices as signs chiefly of Secondness contain icons as a necessary component. And symbols contain indices, which in their own turn contain icons. In other words, the more complex signs encompass their baser sign counterparts in a manner comparable to a hologram the whole of which contains, and is the same as – is contained within – its parts.

For example, as depicted in table 3 and figure 11, the isolated image of the class of all dogs as a mere possibility applied to a particular dog is the First of

Firstness (a qualisign, image – *iconicity*). The image of a dog in possible relation to something else – a particular dog – in the 'semiotically real world,' or a schema, is the First of Secondness (an iconic sinsign, diagram – *indexicality*). The possibility of the word 'dog' related by convention to the animal in question or to some facsimile thereof is the First of Thirdness (an iconic legisign, metaphor, *symbolicity*) (I endorse the idea that language is metaphorical through and through, following Derrida 1974b, Arbib and Hesse 1986, and Lakoff and Johnson 1980, among others). The actual image of a particular dog *in relation to* something else in the 'semiotically real world' is the Second of Firstness (rhematic indexical sinsign), and the image and *its relation to* something other that is potentially mediated by the conventional sign, 'dog,' as a class of animals of which the particular dog in question is a member, is the Third of Firstness (from a rhematic indexical legisign to a term or word). The actualized *relation of* the image of a dog *to* a particular 'semiotic object,' whether 'out there' or in the mind, is the Second of Secondness (dicent sinsign), and this relation made explicit and potentially linked to 'dog' as a generality appearing in a sentence string bearing relation to the dog in question makes up the Third of Secondness (from dicent indexical legisign to term or word to proposition or sentence). Finally, the word 'dog' and its accompanying sentence surrounded by an entire text or argument provides for the Third of Thirdness. Peirce's decalogue has thus been engendered from the relations implied in table 3 regarding 'dog.' Basically the same can be articulated regarding the more abstract signs '5' and 'triangle.' Elaboration of the sign types in the form of an encyclopedic display of examples and illustrations of the Lakoff-Johnson (1980) sort, I would expect, can now be forthcoming (a task that necessarily lies outside the scope of the present inquiry).

It is worthy of note, however, that the last of Peirce's trichotomies in table 2 – *word-term*, *sentence-proposition*, *text-argument* – moves us in the direction of increasing abstraction. 'Triangle' can enjoy particular exemplification, much as can 'unicorn' in the Meinong sense. There is no image for the item in question as a generality, only particular images. Generals are neither the collection of all particulars of an individual mind nor the collective mind of a community of semiotic agents, but rather, they make up the perpetually incomplete, and perhaps inconsistent, and constantly changing manner in which individuals and communities talk about their 'objects' of talk. A good case in point is the Meinong 'object,' 'square circle.' The mind is not capable even of conjuring up the image of a particular 'square circle,' though talk about this strange no-*thing* can be carried out quite effectively by a pair of 'antilogicians' communing about contradictory 'objects.' An image of a 'square circle' is not a prerequisite to talk about such 'objects,' though it would certainly enhance communication.

And a diagram or scheme of a 'square circle' can hardly be constructed, though topologically, in terms of spaces, surfaces, and boundaries, both an image and scheme of sorts could be vaguely depicted of a 'square circle.'

The concept 'square circle,' especially in a sort of metaphorical sense of a 'squircle' that is like a figure with equal straight sides connected at 90° angles and at the same time like a smoothly curved and closed figure (recall that 'squircle' is the 'square circle's' counterpart to 'wavicle,' a term once seriously put forth in quantum theoretical discourse to encompass both the 'wave' interpretation and the 'particle' interpretation of subatomic events). In a manner of putting it, then, symbols are potentially capable of doing for the non-existent 'object' what was impossible for icons and indices.

Briefly, the same can be said of number as has been said of symbols, especially in regards to Brian Rotman's (1993) philosophy of mathematics. Rotman asks the question: 'Is the [classically conceived] mathematical Agent, the imago who is to count endlessly for us, imagined to have a body – however idealized and ethereal – or is it a wholly disembodied, immaterial phantom?' (1993:9). The classical response, we read, has had the mathematician as a disembodied spirit, a ghost, for once she is granted 'some scrap of physical being, some contact or connection, however rarefied and idealized, to the world of material process, then it will be organized under the regimes of space, time, energy, and its actions cannot be free of the effects of contingency and entropy. As a consequence, [her] efforts to count endlessly must fail' (Rotman 1993:10). The disembodied mathematician, according to classical imperatives, must somehow be in possession of a God's-eye grasp of the actually existing infinite field of numbers. This does not prohibit the notion of an a priori world of mathematical beings out there in Platonic heaven, nor the idea of the formalist mathematician as a free spirit manipulating her symbols, as if they constituted a transparent medium, with the expectation of computing eternal truths. Rotman rejects both conceptions of mathematics, given their assuming a disembodied mathematical agent.

He then considers Brouwer's intuitionist mathematics as at its roots a languageless activity, an activity of finite construction by a fallible agent. After some deliberation, he rejects the intuitionist mandate that mathematics is languageless. On the other hand, he remains intrigued by the intuitionist notion of a finite agent and of the realm of numbers consisting of the extent to which the mathematician – and by extension the entire community of mathematicians – has arrived in the potentially infinite string of numbers at a given point in time. The intuitionist mathematician can know what exists up to the borders of that which she has actually constructed, and no more, at least until she or some other member of her community extends those borders by successive construction. This notion of ongoing construction accounts for what Rotman labels the '*ad infinitum* principle,' which consists of the mathematician's always being able to take one more step (the '*ad infinitum* principle' is somewhat reminiscent of Peirce's knowledge as 'asymptotic approximation' – albeit with its inherent problems – and the sorites paradox, as discussed above). The idea of knowledge as the 'extent to which the mathematician has arrived' also enjoys affinities with Wittgenstein's finitist mathematics, which was in part inspired by Brouwer (Shanker 1987). However, just as Rotman discards mathematics as a 'self-contained' formalism, so also he rejects the Wittgensteinian game played by 'self-referring,' transient rules, conventions, and protocols. As an alternative, while remaining somewhat sympathetic with the intuitionist approach, he presents his semiotic view of mathematics-as-language and the semiotic agent as an embodied mind engaging in the equivalent of thought experiments (by way of what I have termed thought-signs) in the physical sciences.

This conception includes (1) Peirce's indexical function, (2) iconic concreteness necessary for the engendering of signs of the mind, (3) the semiotician-mathematician as a thinking and feeling embodied agent, and (4) semiotics-mathematics as a temporal process. Indeed, Rotman's core pair of symbols, @ and *$*, or *realizability* plus *cognizability*, are quite compatible with the above-discussed terms, *learnability*, *accountability*, and *knowability*, which incorporate the *vagueness-generality* (*inconsistency-incompleteness*) duo. @ says that if a given series is extended, in time it will 'fade out' (that is, 1,2,3 ... @, as it approaches the sphere of pure *vagueness*). And Rotman's ad infinitum principle, embodied in *$*, bears testimony to the perpetual *incompleteness* of any and all finite series that may have been computed by flesh-and-blood semiotic agents up to a given point in time (that is, $1 \rightarrow 1 + 1 = 2 \rightarrow 2 + 1 = 3$ ... *$*, or *generality*). Rotman concludes that 'once they are brought together, the two limitative principles of realizability and cognizability allow a model of number and its resulting arithmetic to emerge that is radically unlike and ultimately incongruous with the familiar classical picture of an endless and unchanging repetition-of-the-same given us by Euclidean arithmetic' (1993:113).

Thus, Rotman exercises a shift from mathematics in an ethereal playpen of disembodied spirits to the concrete stage of actual symbols of the intellect (Thirds) whose relation to their "semiotic objects" (Seconds) cannot be divorced from the feeling, sensing, experiencing corporeal self (as First) enacting the spectacle for the approval or critical appraisal of the community. I repeat: united the three sign components stand straight and tall; any dismembered sign is destined to fall in a heap. The upshot is that any "linguicentric" conception of the sign and of meaning that downplays or ignores quality and iconicity, and any prioritizing of the mind over the body, cannot but remain inadequate.

2. Whither the Qualisign?

In sum, image → diagram (schema) → metaphor (concept) in table 3 are transitions from the concrete to the abstract. However, as hypoicons, these signs are presymbolic; they are not what Peirce called 'genuine signs.' As such, neither images nor diagrams, nor their metaphorical-conceptual counterparts, can be reduced to 'nothing but' descriptive sentences – that is, purely symbolic signs – although to a greater or lesser extent, given the nature of the signs in question, they can be sententially depicted.

Sentences are incapable of capturing the genuine meaning of signs of presymbolic nature. And, as I have argued above, symbolic signs simply cannot convey meaning in the genuine sense if devoid of all embodied (iconic and indexical) understanding. We might be prone to think and say 'Silence is golden' as if the metaphorical sentence were all there were to it, as if understanding were within the symbols as autonomous, disembodied entities bringing along a satchel replete with meaning. This is no more than a skeleton of the flesh-and-blood process of *semiosis*. Meaning and understanding regarding a sentence the likes of 'Silence is golden' cannot emerge outside relations between different domains of feeling and experience, namely, of sound quality – or the absence thereof – and the quality of precious metals. This 'hypoicon level' of metaphoricity involves the Firstness, the corporeal aspect, of *semiosis*. Consequently, the sententially (symbolically) dressed metaphor involves one's feeling for, past sensations regarding, and understanding of sounds and sights and socially inculcated values and norms. This activity encompasses both body and mind as an inseparable whole. There is neither pure 'verbal icon' nor pure 'gut feeling' for the metaphor, neither legisign depiction of a qualisign nor spontaneous, extralinguistic reaction to a qualisign, but, rather, the entire *semiosic* spectrum comes into play.

This spectrum is not 'representable' *in*, nor can it be the 'object' *of*, 'reference,' 'representation,' or 'correspondence' by exclusively linguistic means and methods. In other words, its depiction in language would remain radically *incomplete* (*underdetermined*) because it is, by its very nature, radically *vague* (*overdetermined*). We take signs as we find them, and what we find is not what was in the beginning found by us or anyone else, but what was fashioned and forged by mind and body, by hard-nosed intellect and corporeal impulses and compulsions. Our signs are all partly *vague*, to be sure, but their *vagueness* always stands a chance of becoming relative clarity by further dialogic interaction of the signs' addressers, or perhaps the addressees can take them a bit further toward their fully embodied meaning by endowing them with increased *generality*. Frege was at least partly correct in this respect in his insistence on the public character of meaning as independent of individual consciousness. Solely in this manner, he argued, could meaning 'objectivity,' unblemished by individual minds, lead to legitimate understanding. However, Frege, a faithful 'linguicentrist,' limited himself to sentences. 'Linguicentric' meaning is one aspect of meaning, to be sure. It is specified by syntactic and semantic categories, and by pragmatic conventions of language use. But it is almost exclusively mind-stuff. Full-blooded meaning cannot be engendered without the incorporation of body-stuff with mind-stuff. 'Linguicentric' meaning, in the final analysis, must acknowledge its debt to that other, more fundamental, aspect of meaning.

This is at least in small part the moral to much of Putnam's story. Ourearthers and Otherearthers, Ourworlders and Netherworlders, and speakers of 'cat' and speakers of 'cat*,' leave us with the message that a goose can become a gander according to what the speaker of some language or other has embedded. And now, what that speaker knows tacitly, feels in the gut, consequently affects the way she does things to signs, to herself and her others, and to her world. She does what she does not exclusively because of some coherent set of articulated reasons, methods, and strategies, but also in part because this is simply and implicitly the way she does it, naturally, and as a wholly incorporated member of her community. It is not simply that 'XYZ' is hooked onto – because it 'refers' and 'corresponds' to, and 'represents' – a particular substance in one world, while 'H_2O' is hooked onto another substance in another world. Inhabitants of the 'XYZ' world and the 'H_2O' world use signs the way they use them because that is the way they use them: they have become one with their signs and their signs with them. The very idea of 'objects,' 'reference,' 'correspondence,' and 'representation' can have no place outside particular signs, their embodied users, and concrete situations. Signs, baldly put, cannot be hooked onto things independent of 'semiotic agents.' For 'signs do not intrinsically correspond to objects, independently of how those signs are employed and by whom. But a sign that is actually employed in a particular way by a particular community of users can correspond to particular objects *within the conceptual scheme of those users.* "Objects" do not exist independently of conceptual schemes. *We* cut up the world into objects when we introduce one or another scheme of description. Since the objects *and* signs are alike *internal* to the scheme of description, it is possible to say what matches what' (Putnam 1981:52).

This is no simple idealist philosophy, mind you. Nor is it exactly anti-realism, but 'internal realism,' which is complementary with, I have suggested, Peirce's 'objective idealism.' There is definitely a physical 'reality' independent of us and it is what it is in spite of what we might wish to think it is. The issue does not revolve around whether or not there is a 'real' world 'out there,' but what it is for there to be a 'semiotically real' domain *for* a community of signifying agents. In this regard, Peirce, like Putnam, maintains faith that there is a 'semiotically real' world *for* us, at least partly accessible by means of images, conceptual schemes (in Peirce's terms, diagrams), and metaphors. We touch bases with this 'semiotic reality' in terms of feeling, extension, and form, and of sensation, indication, and intellection – and, if you will, of quality, haecceity, and quiddity. In a somewhat uncomfortable way of putting it, we are in our 'semiotically real' world that at the same time exists within our selves, within the relation between our selves and others, and by means of mediation of selves and signs and selves and others. Meaning and understanding are never separated from the entire gamut of semiotic modes and activities. We are always *in* our signs and they *in* us, we are *in* and relative to our 'semiotically real world' and it is *in* and relative to us, we are both participators and actors in the grand *semiosic* drama incessantly in the process of unfoldment.

Turning once again to table 2, exclusive focus on the right column includes the dominion of 'propositional theory' according to which the workings of the brain-mind are reducible to abstract symbolism. Obsession with the middle column brightly shines on 'objectivism,' the theory that everything that is can be accounted for by a description of what is 'out there,' with the describer as a detached, neutral onlooker. 'Propositionalism' and 'objectivism' are in this sense close allies: both take 'reference,' 'correspondence,' and 'representation' as a matter of course. They treat meaning and understanding as purely conceptual, propositional, and in some schools of thought even algorithmic, shunning sensual and nonpropositional means and modes of communication as unfit for proper logic and reason. In short, they are both indelibly 'linguicentric.'

I actually have no truck with 'propositional knowing' and the desire for maximum possible objectivity. They are noble goals. They are also ideals destined to remain unnecessarily *incomplete*. It is not so much that, as the charge occasionally goes, they tend to reduce us to little more than so many silicon beasts, denying us of much of what makes life pleasurable. The real problem is that they are virtually worthless without *vagueness*, that which is by strictly applied logic and reason *inconsistent*, as depicted in the left column and lower section of table 2. (Actually, the whole of classical logic is edified on the inconsistent corner-stone of what Peirce originally proposed in his 'logic of relatives,' though credit is generally attributed to Henry M. Sheffer [1913] for basically the same principle, which he labels the 'stroke function' [see Merrell 1991, 1995a]. Although the 'stroke' – which is comparable, by the way, to '*WB*-lessness' in the above blackboard example – implies incompatibility or inconsistency in the deepest sense, Whitehead observes that it nonetheless provides for 'the whole movement of logic' [1938:52]. This character of the 'stroke' compelled philosopher of science Ernest Hutten to write that: 'It is the very essence of rationality to abolish contradictions; but logic – being the most rational thing in the world – is generated by contradiction' [1962:178]. Logic, in this respect, does not rest on rock-solid positive foundations, but contains denial, negation, acknowledgment of that which *is not*, at its very core.)

The very possibility of a propositional-objectivist philosophy is nil without due consideration of this more basic and more encompassing dimension. There is no reason, logic, conceptual scheme, or even meaning and understanding without a rich interconnected pattern of concrete, nonpropositional images, schemes (diagrams), and metaphors. These patterns are the vibrant flesh giving vitality to the otherwise disembodied minds and lifeless skeletons of their abstract counterparts. Consequently, the arrows in table 2 are of necessity reversible, unlike, I now regret, my presentation of a comparable set of interrelations elsewhere (Merrell 1995a). This accounts for sign *engenderment*, from their concrete, corporeal conception and birth to old age as abstract, yet fully embodied texts. But it also allows for sign *de-engenderment* (*de-generacy*) in the other direction, toward the tacit, corporeal, visceral (*embedded*, *automatized*, *entrenched*) use – and abuse – of signs largely without the intervention of the self-conscious mind. The process is ongoing: signs are never exactly either one thing or the other but always somewhere in between.

The *qualisign*, therefore, is a sort of 'sink' (in the mathematical sense of the term). It is the 'genetic pool' of *semiosis* whence all signs emerge and the life-giving source toward which they all tend to gravitate. By no means is the qualisign opposed to mind (reason, logic, objectivity, propositional knowledge). Rather, it is food for thought, flesh on the bare bones of abstraction, the life of otherwise virtually catatonic indices and symbols. In other words, all *semiosic* routes depart from and point toward qualisigns. From qualisigns other signs emerge along divergent, convergent, involuted, convoluted nonlinear flows, from imagery to schemata to metaphors. Imagery is sensed and felt by visual, auditory, olfactory, gustatory, and tactile means, schemata entail structural relations between that which is sensed and something other, and metaphoricity involves felt similarities and differences between qualities of experience. Thus, brains-in-a-vat have the capacity possibly for imagining they are brains-in-a-vat, with additional enlightenment H_2O can be considered different from XYZ, and 'grue' can become 'bleen.' Nothing is with absolute determinacy either one thing or the other.

Now for a suggestion as to how such changes of body and mind can come about.

3. From Pictures toward the Unnamable

Duhem's English empiricist-*inductivist* and French rationalist-hypothetico-*deductivist* identify two of the three voyageurs navigating through the sea of *semiosis*. But their third, and very necessary companion, the *abductivist*, admiral of creativity, initiator of semiotic explorations, hardly enters the picture in the discourse of modernity. On projecting the spotlight toward this adventuresome spirit, I turn briefly to Arthur Miller's pioneering work (1986) integrating *Gestalt* psychology, Piaget's genetic epistemology, and cognitive science into a unique account of imagery (abductive processes) in scientific thought during the first decades of the present century.

Miller's story revolves around the imaginable and the unimaginable, that which can be seen and said and that which lends itself solely to saying (whether in mathematical or natural language). Bohr's 1913 'planetary model' of the atom accompanied by the abolishment of continuity as a result of Planck's quantum jumps of the electron from orbit to orbit held onto visualizability, but at the expense of unvisualizable instants when the electron was in transition from one energy level to another. After more than a decade of intellectual turmoil, in 1925 Heisenberg abandoned visualizability altogether with his discontinuous matrix description of atomic events. In the following year Schrödinger countered Heisenberg's proposal with his wave mechanics that retain imageability at least for a one-electron system in three-dimensional space. Shortly thereafter, work by Max Born and Paul A.C. Dirac brought the two previously conceived incompatible accounts together in one package, to the consternation of Heisenberg, who referred to Schrödinger's wave mechanics as 'disgusting.' In 1927 Heisenberg complicated the slash between continuity and discontinuity and waves and particles with his 'uncertainty principle,' according to which both cannot be known in simultaneity, thus holding to his rejection of visualizability. In that same year, Bohr's 'complementarity principle' postulated the wave-particle duality of light and matter in his attempt to salvage a modicum of visualization in terms of a combination of continuous space-time pictures of classical physics and discontinuous quantum events.

Today's quantum theory often pays lip service to terms like 'Schrödinger picture,' 'Heisenberg picture,' and 'interaction picture.' But these terms 'have neither picture nor image content; rather, they refer only to symbols' (Miller 1986:173). Heisenberg found comfort in the notion of quantum mechanics as quasi-Aristotelian *potentia*, or even Platonic archetypes or ideals regarding matter, while Bohr held fast to his lifelong sense of complementarity, with its emphasis on the act of measurement drawing a particle from a wave function. In whichever case, visualizability, at least in the classical sense, now seemed to be a dead horse. (It is worthy of note, however, that 'Feynman diagrams' [diagrams or schemas depicting particle-wave events] have become a new mode of visualizability [ibid.:172–3]).

In sum, the flow of *semiosis* was from classical imagery based on perceivable objects (sign-events) to mental imagery (thought-signs) and, finally, to imagery tempered by mathematics, to unvisualizable mathematical symbolism, and to complementarity between formal symbolism and empirical detectability. Bohr's 'planetary model' highlighted iconicity. When that dream vanished, Heisenberg's replacement was virtually pure symbolism. Schrödinger, repelled by the lack of imageability, returned to the security of at least a partly picturable alternative. The two antagonistic views were brought together in a shotgun wedding by Bohr, whose interpretation includes a more important role for indexicality – links to the detectable world. Miller concludes, nonetheless, that without the perception-laden, imagistic language (of sign-events) of classical physics, 'a beachhead could never have been established in the atomic domain' (1986:260). This new formal mathematical-symbolic imagistic mode (of thought-signs) 'had to be achieved slowly by degrees, starting from the image-perception link and going on to redefine visualizability (*Anschaulichkeit*). All this progress was accompanied by a complex interplay among syntax, semantics, and mental imagery' (ibid.:261).

In another, Peircean, way of putting it, there was gravitation from the relatively concrete image or qualisign of possibility related to something 'out there' (later to be couched in natural language and mathematical symbolism) toward a purely mental and formal qualisign ('in here') (for Peirce, just as natural language cannot do without icons and indices, so also with logic and mathematics [*CP*:3.363]). The formal mathematical window dressing of this mental qualisign was only after the fact related – if at all – to 'semiotically real'-world objects, acts, and events 'out there.' While on the one hand this move tended to liberate thinking from the concrete but mediated world of perceptions, on the other hand, imagery was relegated to a prison house of formalisms and barred from the concrete perceptible world. Whereas the classical mode encouraged liberal use of concrete imagery conducing toward metaphor-models (the Cartesian-Newtonian machine model and Bohr's planetary model being prototypical of this mindset), the quantum theoretical mode found its most comfortable modus operandi in diagrammaticity – from *diagrams*, the second of Peirce's three classes of hypoicons, which are sandwiched between *images* and *metaphors*.

This transition was not without its problems, perhaps chief of them being that of finding a natural-language rendition for mathematically described quantum events. Heisenberg recollects how during the 1920s the world's prominent physicists laboured to solve the problems of quantum mechanics, finally to arrive at what the majority believed to be the most acceptable solution. While their initial descriptions were almost exclusively mathematical, during subsequent conversations and debates they inevitably retreated into natural language. This presented them with a predicament that continued to defy resolution, baffling them at every turn. Heisenberg vividly portrays the collusion between customary language use and this new view of reality, which produced an uncanny effect in the physicists' thinking. He writes, following his observation that this dilemma is a problem of language as much as of physics: 'I remember discussions with Bohr which went through many hours till very late at night and ended almost in despair; and when at the end of the discussion I went alone for a walk in the neighborhood park I repeated to myself again and again the question: Can nature possibly be so absurd as it seemed to us in these atomic experiments?' (Heisenberg 1958:175).

Heisenberg goes on to explain that Bohr's complementarity principle eventually encouraged physicists 'to use an ambiguous rather than an unambiguous language, to use the classical concepts in a somewhat vague manner ... [but] when this vague and unsystematic use of language leads into difficulties, the physicist has to withdraw into the mathematical scheme and its unambiguous correlation with the experimental facts.' This use of language, Heisenberg continues, is in many ways satisfactory, since 'it reminds us of a similar use of the language in daily life or in poetry.' He then remarks on the function of complementarity in much the spirit of Bohr insofar as it is not confined exclusively to the atomic world. It comes into play in everyday life, for example, 'when we reflect about a decision and the motives for our decision or when we have the choice between enjoying music and analyzing its structure' (ibid.:179). (Recently this 'rhetorical' nature of 'narrative' in the sciences has been subject to serious study from the purviews of literary studies [Gross 1990], philosophy of science and psychology [Gregory 1988, Arbib and Hesse 1986], philosophy [Rorty 1982, 1989], Anthropology [Geertz 1983, Marcus and Cushman 1982, Marcus and Fischer 1986, Tyler 1987], historiography [LaCapra 1985, White 1987], economics [McCloskey 1990], psychology [Spence 1982, Bruner 1986, 1987], and sociology [Bazerman 1988, Brown 1987, Latour 1987, Latour and Woolgar 1979, Woolgar 1988].)

This is as it should be. For the language of science – and all other language use for that matter – whether we know it or not and whether we like it or not, is incessantly used and abused, and modified and hammered into new forms in order that it fit the standards of new world-images, and in the process it incessantly takes on new meanings. Feyerabend writes along these lines: 'We see ... how essential it is to learn talking in riddles, and how disastrous an effect the drive for instant clarity must have on our understanding' (1975:257). Classical logic was born only after rhetoric was sufficiently developed so as to serve as a starting point. Arithmetic was developed before a clear understanding of number could exist. Full comprehension of the Copernican universe required a couple of centuries – in fact, the Copernican model was called 'Copernicus's paradox' for some generations after its author's death. The idea that a stone does not fall 'straight down' when dropped but follows a long trajectory commensurate with the earth's rotation remained a difficult pill to swallow for some time after Galileo. There is as yet no clear-cut consensus on the second law of thermodynamics, and relativity and especially quantum theory continue to remain enigmatic. Were there, during each of these transition periods, a demand for instant clarity, science would have remained virtually paralysed.

Along comparable lines, Friedrich Waismann discusses what he terms 'clarity neurosis,' which threatens to drive the scientist to a fear of vagueness and of speaking in circles, eventually to become tongue-tied, continually asking himself whether what he is doing makes perfectly good sense. 'Imagine,' Waismann writes, 'that the pioneers of science – Kepler, Newton, the discoverers of non-Euclidean geometry, of field physics, the unconscious, matter waves or heaven knows what – imagine them asking themselves this question at every step – this would have been the surest means of sapping any creative power' (1959:359–60). Obviously Waismann is not proposing that the scientist cease to strive for clarity; rather, it should at times, though not always, be the primary consideration in his search for answers. Yet an initial effort toward the best possible answer, even though vague, ambiguous, or even paradoxical instead of absolutely clear, can place the scientist in hot water: when he believes he has hit upon a solution, he immediately attempts communicating it with his colleagues, but he is often met with suspicion, bemused cynicism, disinterest, or even sheer incredulity. Effective communication of his idea invariably requires time – recall Max Planck, who once observed that a new theory's acceptance often requires that the older generation first completely die off.

Much the same can actually be said of the initial response to departures from the beaten path in the arts. 'Random music,' which is totally indeterminate and hence can hardly be subjected to critical discussion, let alone analysis, seemed to the ears of its early listeners devoid of all significance. It was such a radical break with cultural conventions as to appear completely nonsensical. Yet it eventually compelled its listeners to make explicit their convictions, prejudices, and doubts; only then was it appropriately received. In literature, writers like William Burroughs cut up their texts and recombined them in random or near-random fashion. Such texts were at the outset considered incomprehensible by the reading public accustomed to thinking in purely linear terms. Today's aware readers, in contrast, are familiar with these methods and encounter little to no difficulty absorbing the new form of narrative. A sense of timelessness is created by writers the likes of Beckett, whose novels making up a trilogy, *Molloy*, *Malone Dies*, and *The Unnamable*, do not allow us the security of knowing whether we are listening to the characters' ruminations for one hour, ten days, or a year. And in painting the strange works of Jackson Pollock are simply *there*; there is no depth, no space, no indication of temporal sequence during the original creation or upon viewing the canvas. What appears to the senses is no more than a static, random-like present. The disconcerting effects I speak of here are not limited to our times. E.H. Gombrich (1960) effectively demonstrates how, through the ages, art has been born of art, painting has altered perception and created tastes, and in the process our 'reality' has been transformed by art rather than the other way around. In each of the cases I have rather at random selected, whether scientific or artistic, a certain period of time was required for the general public, and even the creators of new modes of perception, expression, and thought, to become comfortable with the novel world-images that were gradually appearing on the scene. So Ourworlders and Otherworlders, H_2O and XYZ, 'green' and 'grue,' Cervantes' *Quixote* and Menard's *Quixote*, Meinong's 'unicorns' and Russell's 'unicorns,' ourselves as brains-in-a-vat and brains-in-a-vat as ourselves, 'Gavagai!' as 'rabbit' or a 'space-time rabbit slice,' are all alternative 'worlds' that hopefully can at least to an extent be bridged. That is, if we do not take language or ourselves too seriously and allow it to do its own thing.

In sum, table 2 depicts the general move from image-diagram-metaphor by way of *qualisign-sinsign-legisign* to *icon-index-symbol* and ultimately to *term(word)-proposition(sentence)-argument(text)*, with ever-increasing abstraction. The tendency is from tacitly sensed, felt, relatively immediately experienced, visceral, corporeal, concrete images toward that age-old ideal of hyperconsciously logicized, properly reasoned, cogitated, cognized, and abstracted intellection. The transformation is from sensed and experienced sign-events largely 'out there' to experienced and cognized thought-signs largely 'in here.' But at the same time, there exists the opposite tendency, by way of sign embedment, entrenchment, automatization, toward an undulating, swimming glide along the stream of *semiosis* at that level where, so to speak, mind has become body and body mind. Within this undercurrent, head and heart are not at odds. What happens happens quite naturally, with a minimum of intervention on the part of the hyperconscious self, ego, 'I,' and mind, and the push is not toward dominance, control, superordinance, but rather, a spirit of conviviality inheres. Sane individuals and sane societies are not built upon the foundations of irreconcilable heart and mind, feeling and form, vagueness and classical logic, intuition and reason, as the nature-nurture hair-splitters would have it; they emerge out of 'semiotic worlds' in which play and imagination find harmony with the rigours of abstract thought. This, ultimately, was Peirce's rather utopian dream. He saw our final goal as the fulfilment and plenitude of *generalization* – the continuity of things – when all signs have been enshrouded in their final interpretant – an impossible utopian dream, to be sure, but, as Peirce saw it, a necessary dream. The 'supreme commandment,' for Peirce, is

> to complete the whole system even until continuity results and the distinct individuals weld together. Thus it is, that while reasoning and the science of reasoning strenuously proclaim the subordination of reasoning to sentiment, the very supreme commandment of sentiment is that man should generalize, ... should become welded into the universal continuum, which is what true reasoning consists in. But this does not reinstate reasoning, for this generalization should come about, not merely in man's cognitions, which are but the superficial film of his being, but objectively in the deepest emotional springs of his life. In fulfilling this command, man prepares himself for transmutation into a new form of life, the joyful Nirvana in which the discontinuities of his will shall have all but disappeared. (*CP*:1.673)

An essential step toward the realization of Peirce's dream must see humanists engendering a mindset that includes that of the 'new' science, and scientists fashioning a 'new alliance' with the humanists and with nature. Ilya Prigogine and Isabelle Stengers (1984) call for such a dialogue between history, culture, and nature, between human semiotic agents, their artistic and scientific endeavours, and the universe. Nature can no longer be that inert, passive Rock of Gibraltar lying in wait of the penetrating gaze of its detached, objective knowers. The becoming of our community's awareness of a nature qualified by patterns and complexities, radically transient, far-from-equilibrium conditions, and irreversible time should serve to encourage this dialogue, before it is too late – in view of recent ecological dilemmas demonstrating that the world cannot continue to be considered an object to be mastered and exploited at will.

15

Putting the Body Back in the Sign

1. In Retrospect

To recap, the style-intonation pair of terms discussed in chapter 1 blur the overrated literary-language/ordinary-language and literary-language/logico-scientific-language clashes. This blurring of age-old lines of demarcation also applies to the presumed chasm between the fictive and the 'real' – or the 'semiotically real' and the 'real' – as was observed in the following pair of chapters. These pages, in addition, debunked the customary priorities of extension over intension, symbolicity over iconicity-indexicality, and the self-centred 'I' over its respective *others.* Then in subsequent chapters, during discussion of the various and sundry views of contemporary philosophy, it was suggested that the notion of meaning in the skull, the sign, the object, or in compact and diffuse wave patterns in the air or black squiggles on a white background is erroneous, as is the idea of a detached, objective semiotic agent enjoying something in the order of a God's-eye grasp of things. Now, it would appear, comes the time for me to pay up or shut up, to quit harping on the frailties and failings of contemporary notions of the sign and of meaning and render a few positive accounts with respect to the topic at hand.

And that is precisely the problem, as was implied at the very outset, in the Preamble. Positive accounts are well-nigh impossible to come by; it is considerably easier to say what something *is not* than what it *is*. Besides, the task ultimately becomes self-reflexive, and often paradoxically so. The physicist is a bundle of electrons describing electrons: 'It electrons,' so to speak. The writer is a writing organism writing writing: 'It writes.' The painter paints painting: 'It paints,' or better, 'It pictures picturing' – it does not directly represent. Talk about 'cats' and 'cherries' and 'mats' and 'trees' is talk about 'cathood' and 'cherryhood' and 'mathood' and 'treehood.' It is talk, at implicit levels, about what it is to be the things to which the talk relates, and at the same time it is implicitly about us, the semiotic agents doing the talking. Not only is talking involved, but also 'catting,' 'cherrying,' 'matting,' and 'treeing,' and your and my 'becoming' besides. There is no meaning *here* and *now* but the process of 'meaning-becoming' within the *semiosic* flow that is neither *here* nor *there* nor *now* nor *then*, but rather, in the sense of interrelatedness, all of the above.

What is worse, as Alpha revealed, the person, any person, who engenders signs for the basic purpose of meaning something about meaning is in an even more tightly knotted bind. She is – or 'it' is – the meaning that means what it means when it means: 'It is in the process of meaning meaning itself.' Physicists and writers and artists and talkers are usually endowed with some form or fashion of 'hardware' that enables them to engender signs about the 'semiotic world' around them by way of the 'software' they might have at hand. In contrast, the person who thinks she is engendering meaning about meaning exclusively from within the symbolic mode and exempt from the use of mere icons remains trapped within the floppy disk, so to speak: she is suspended in it, without the wherewithal for knowing which way is up or down or right or left, to say nothing of beginning, ending, or centre. Consequently, when attempting to say something positive about the 'object' of her saying, she is usually reduced to so much stuttering and stammering. Unbearable demands are placed on her, for, to repeat, it is considerably easier for her to say what that 'object' *is not* than to say what it *is*. What it *is* is of the nature of Milan Kundera's 'unbearable lightness of being,' whose 'essence' is virtually ineffable in the positive sense. Quite significantly, this is also Deleuze and Guattari's message regarding Beckett's and Kafka's prose (1983, 1987; for further, see Deleuze 1994, Bogue 1989, and Lecercle 1985). In the game of saying something positive about saying itself or about meaning, tender-minded interpretants related to signs that are in turn related to them are apparently no match for the hard-nosed nuts-and-bolts world of signs (representamens) related to their respective 'semiotic objects.'

The interpretant's (that is, meaning's) day of reckoning, however, emerged from the chapters of this inquiry in the guise of various and sundry paradoxes abruptly forcing their way onto the scene. Paradoxes, of course, are good to learn with, since they render account of what *is not*, and when on their best behaviour they can perhaps offer a fleeting glimpse of what *is* – like a Koan, a Zen slap in the face, a rude awakening from one's soporific slumber of reason. These paradoxes are adequately accounted for, and either tentatively resolved or brushed aside when they are hardly of any relevance, in the arena of signs perpetually becoming and being translated into other signs, and of *vagueness* and *generality*, *overdetermination* and *underdetermination*, and *inconsistency* and *incompleteness* and *indeterminacy*. In other words, the paradoxes are catastrophic solely with respect to the sphere of Secondness, where classical logic presumably holds the reins. In the spheres of the possibility of the *might be* and the probability of the *would be*, the paradoxes cannot simply be ignored and forgotten, to be sure, but in the give-and-take of everyday activities we can often find a way to go on in spite of them – that is, following the advice of the Master – and if not, it is sometimes the case that the paradox did not really cause any glitch in the fluxes and flows of everyday living in the first place. Paradoxes, Whitehead once mused, are windows opening out to new horizons with the promise of triumph rather than doom and defeat. They are enablers leading one toward heightened *learnability*, *accountability*, and *knowability*. Above all, paradoxes and their attendant *praxis* involve the conditionality and the conjecturability implied by the 'pragmatic maxim,' which, if Peirce does not err, is a fact of the matter of *semiosis*, whether we are aware of it or not.

This very important character of *semiosis* has to do not with autonomous, free-floating signs as much poststructuralist discourse would have it, or with the 'real' as focus of 'reference,' 'correspondence,' 'representation,' and 'objectivity,' but rather, with signs as they are *put to use*, *by* their semiotic agents *for* some purpose or other. With this suggestion, I turn to an unlikely actor on the stage of *semiosis* whose voice should not remain silent.

2. A Matter of 'Putting Signs to Use'

Physicist John Archibald Wheeler alludes to 'three great eras of physics': (1) Era I, 'which gave us the parabolas of Galileo and the ellipses of Kepler, motion with no explanation of motion'; (2) Era II, which includes 'the mechanics of Newton, the electrodynamics of Faraday and Maxwell, the geometrodynamics of Einstein and the chromodynamics of our day, law that explained change, but law with no explanation of law'; and (3) Era III, giving rise to the evolution, Wheeler predicts, of 'meaning physics,' which seeks not corroboration but collaboration of physical law itself (Wheeler 1984:123; also Landauer 1988). (For the relevance of Wheeler to the general semiotic enterprise, regarding which I have taken a cue from Sebeok [1991], see Merrell 1991, 1995a, and 1995b.)

From the purview of 'meaning physics,' the material world provides the machinery for generating meaning, while meaning contributes the machinery for constructing physics. Existence thus becomes a closed circle of meaning. By the addition of a Peircean qualifier, existence or 'reality' is what *would be* (or from the vantage of the future agent, *would have been*) known in the long run by the 'joint product' of all the propositions engendered by a community of communicators relevant to a set of phenomena in the process of their being *put to use.* Quite apparently, the 'joint product' idea calls for an *n*-dimensional sliding manifold of countless possible differences (Wheeler, I should add, readily acknowledges his debt to Føllesdal [1975] with respect to the 'joint product' idea). Of course, the 'real' physical world provides the machinery for engendering meaning, but whatever meaning is constructed depends upon the semiotic thrust to which it is subjected. Wheeler (1980a, 1980b) gives the example of a cosmic-ray streak deposited in a Brazilian mound of granite eons ago. It would have enjoyed hardly any semiotic import for the Tupí-Guaraní tribespeople of the eighteenth century. Some of the mound could conceivably have been quarried and used in the construction of a mansion for Dom Pedro I in the nineteenth century. It could have been material for an avant-garde sculpture during the 1920s. Or the area might have become as heavily populated during this century as the east coast of the United States and the focus of a nuclear war in 1994 that completely wiped out the streak. That particular rock and the area in general could have been during these possible processes endowed with meaning, but the cosmic ray streak as such would have suffered the insult of having been pushed aside and ignored.

In Wheeler's example, on the other hand, that portion of the mound containing the streak offers a more specific semiotic message for contemporary science. A slice of the rock was taken into the laboratory and subjected to meticulous analysis in order that it yield its history and, by extension, the entire history of cosmic radiation and its effects. Consequently, from a totalizing perspective including the range of all possible perspectives from Tupí-Guaraní tribespeople to physicists, the circuit appears closed, and all signs as well as their agents are relatively autonomous. Yet from a given inside view, the system and all its myriad parts have obviously remained open, since there has been, over time, sign-sign, sign-agent, and sign-object interaction within the 'joint products' of intracommunity and intercommunity communication from a host of semiotic interrelationships.

According to Wheeler's example, *after* the cosmic-ray streak appeared in the granite, the Tupí-Guaraní, Dom Pedro's construction engineers, an angry young sculptor, Brazilian warmongers, and Wheeler's physicist were free to decide whether the mound containing the streak was worthy of their semiotic consideration. Only the context – experimental arrangement in Bohr-Wheeler quantum theoretical terms – changed in each case. A very important point regarding human semiotics is that every account of the streak, in light of physics as talk about talk, is a story, a narrative (Gregory 1988). Altering the context alters the story at the same time that the story prefigures/shapes its own future, and the future of that of which the story is a story, even as the future itself depends on that very story. What the phenomenon is or is not and what qualifies it or not as a 'fact' is dependent not upon its raw physical existence; it depends more upon the signs used to describe it. But ultimately, the phenomenon is a matter of a story, and stories about the story. Stories, of course, are mere stories. Yet they are capable of making the past and setting up future probabilities, and at the same time they depend upon both past and future. 'Cosmic rays' as such did not exist before the twentieth century because there had been no need for any stories about them. Now, however, they are believed to exist, and as far as the contemporary physicist is concerned they have existed since the Big Bang and will continue to exist until the Great Crunch. This implies that 'cosmic rays' do not exactly exist independently in the physical world nor are they independent of the stories telling about postmodern science. Rather, they depend upon a particular 'semiotically real' sphere of existence, which in turn depends upon the stories that played the major role in creating that sphere of existence. (My allusion to stories is not out of the clear blue. Our 'semiotic worlds' emerge out of, and inextricably remain pervaded by, stories.)

Wheeler's 'meaning physics' is intimately linked to knowledge as the result of *putting* natural phenomena *to use* and telling stories about them, that is, of narrating human interaction with the world. In this regard, 'meaning physics' dovetails with Wheeler's conception of a self-referential, self-excited circuit making up the entire universe: a thoroughly pragmatic account of the scientist's interaction, or dialogue, with her surroundings. The first stage involves *question asking*, *choice*, and a *selection* from the *non-selective* domain of possibilities, or in the terms of this inquiry, from the *overdetermined* sphere of *vagueness*. Asking a question, and choosing and selecting from the vast array of possible phenomena a portion of it that may hopefully be manageable, serves to establish the focus of inquiry as in part mandated by habit and expectations, though there is always room for novelty. Take, for example, the double-slit experiment of quantum theory: in the beginning was a story, in this case a thought experiment. Among other things, this story gives account of an electron capable of travelling along two routes, of acting either as a particle or a wave. In Bohr's *complementarity* account of the double-slit phenomenon, it is impossible, given the chosen experimental apparatus, for the particle to manifest both of its 'schizophrenic' personae at the same instant. So the physicist *chooses* her apparatus, *subjects* the particle to it – which is tantamount to *asking* it a particular question – solicits a *response*, and *narrates* the result. As a consequence of her interaction with the 'real,' a 'semiotically real' event unfolds itself for her, as it collaborates with myriad other events to unfold that very physicist asking the questions and doing the choosing (compare this process to the above on *learnability*, *accountability*, and *knowability*: the first ideally implies a desire to ask questions, the second implies choice and selection, and the third implies confidence in one's ability to tell a compelling story).

Choice in this regard entails an *act of distinction*, a division of the universe into *this* on the one hand and *that* or everything else on the other, a selection of something from the virtually infinitely extensive nonselective sphere of possibilities. What is up for grabs, regarding this *act*, is the nature of the *this*, given the universe's inherent ambiguities. Is *this* ('semiotically real') electron a particle or a wave? In other words, is it $this_1$ or $this_2$? $This_1$ can potentially take on meaning *for* the physicist *in interaction with* and *in regards to* what it *is not*, $this_2$, and vice versa. 'Meaning physics,' in view of the present essay, then, entails phenomena that, in order to become 'semiotically real,' must stand *for* something *to* some semiotic agent *in* some respect or capacity in terms of what has and has not been selected from the (*overdetermined*) sphere of possibilities. Integrating Peircean jargon into the equation, it can be said that a *distinction* brings about a 'collapse' of the quantum theoretical *complex probability amplitude* in the space-time manifold into a particle (sign) or set of particles that can then be *indicated* (indexed, by way of Secondness) in terms of their relations to other particles.

Like the Necker cube with its face now up, now down, the nature of the question (angle of the gaze) determines the nature of the 'semiotic reality' finally to be perceived and conceived. Interaction with the physical world, which is a matter of questioning its very nature, is in this manner the consequence of a *choice*, and the choice has a definite bearing on whatever outcome is in store. 'Meaning physics' (the 'semiotically real') thus becomes possible by means of empirical manifestations (light, pressure, sound, taste, odour, inorganic and organic entities, biological organisms) of *molar* or *macrolevel* collections, such 'meaning' being the result of mediation (symbolicity, Thirdness) of that which was *distinguished* (as a First) and *indicated* (as a Second). Ultimately, 'meaning,' as the 'joint product' of the interpretants engendered by the entire community regarding a particular sign or set of signs, is made possible.

Hence, the nature of the *complex probability amplitude*, as *possibilia*, already depends upon the 'meaning' attributed to a community's 'semiotical reality.' It is a function of the range of possibilities one of which can be actualized into the immediate or *microlevel* domain, which is then mediately accessible to observation in the *molecular* domain, to be *put to use* and thereby endowed with 'meaning' in the *macrolevel* or *molar* domain. The possibility of meaning determines the nature of the *complex probability amplitude* from which any and all meanings arose in the first place. In another, complementary, way of putting it, as I did in another time and another place (Merrell 1995a), 'meaning' is the composite act of 'seeing' (Firstness), 'seeing' something *as* such-and-such (Firstness merging into Secondness), and 'seeing' *that* it is so-and-so (the emergence of Thirdness from Secondness) (The 'seeing' *as* and 'seeing' *that* modes are from Hanson [1958, 1969] by way of Wittgenstein [1953], and they generally fall in step with Lakoff [1987], who has drawn from the work of Gilchrist and Rock [1981], Johansson [1950], and Weschler [1982], among others.)

I must emphasize once again that we are speaking of 'semiotic reality,' not the 'real' per se. A given 'semiotic reality' excludes all that *could have been* selected but *was not*, just as Wheeler's notion of 'reality' as 'joint product' excludes everything that has not been *put to use* by a particular community. What remains unselected, though it could have been teased into one 'semiotically real' world or another, may yet take its place among the actualized set of signs. If these signs by chance lift themselves into the arena, their competitors, having had their moment of glory during the previous bout, sink back into the *semiosic* soup and wait their chance to re-enter the agonistic exchange at a future moment. Hence, though the equation is by and large irreversible, certain facets can be reversed (see Merrell 1995a, 1996). To place this notion of the interrelatedness of things more squarely in semiotic jargon, David Savan observes (1987–8) that just as the moon rock reveals its story through the 'regularities' or 'laws' (*would bes*) it instantiates, so the (embedded, entrenched, automatized) ritual and performative uses of language operate as signs by way of the 'regularities' or 'laws' governing them. These 'regularities,' from within the domain of the 'semiotically real,' are part and parcel of the hegemony of legisigns, which, like qualisigns, do not exist directly and immediately *in* experience. They are always in the process of coming into being through their instantiations as sinsigns and interaction with their respective 'objects.' If qualisigns are 'non-stuff' in the sense that they are *as yet* merely *possibilia* (*might bes*), legisigns are 'mind-stuff' (*would bes*) insofar as they '*refer*' – if I may dare allow myself the privilege of using that word in this context – to the 'semiotically real' (the *isness* of things) that is always moving on, becoming something other than what it was.

Wheeler also has a word or two regarding what he terms 'law,' which, according to the premises of this inquiry, must be in Peircean fashion construed as 'semiotic' rather than 'physical' in the classical sense. Wheeler serves notice that if his approach is indeed correct, then one principle and one alone, observer-participancy (or intepreter-interpretant interpretation), suffices to construct 'everything from "nothingness"' (Wheeler 1980b:154). This 'nothingness' Wheeler speaks of is not mere vacuum physics loaded with geometry and field fluctuations. It is 'pre-geometry,' a sort of 'nothingness' devoid of structure, law, or plan. This primitive level is quite in line with Peirce's 'nothingness' ('emptiness,' pre-Firstness, the 'node'), as presented above. Out of 'nothingness,' physicist and photon interact to transmute one of the multitudinous quantum possibilities into a dialogue that apparently pervades everything we can know, for we are *in* it: 'Beyond particles, beyond fields of force, beyond geometry, beyond space and time themselves, is the ultimate constituent [of all there is], the still more ethereal act of observer-participancy' (Wheeler, quoted in Zohar 1990:45).

It is not that mere observation 'creates reality,' but rather, observation involves a dialogue between quantum wave functions and observers (whether sentient, organic, or inorganic) evoking, and thereby giving concrete form to, 'semiotically real' events. To be sure, a 'dog' wave function can hardly be 'collapsed' into a 'cat,' no matter how much an observer-participant might wish to bring it about by manipulating the context. Yet, so the story goes, just as Schrödinger's cat is purportedly neither dead nor alive until *we*, the observer-participants, determine her fate, so also whatever event becomes a meaningful part of our everyday affairs does so in that particular way because *we* make it so. *We*, in dialogue with our community, *construct* our 'semiotically real' world. This should actually come as hardly any surprise to the modern 'linguicentric' mind for, in the words of cyberneticist Heinz von Foerster: '"out there" there is no light and no colour, there are only electromagnetic waves; "out there" there is no sound and no music, there are only periodic variations of the air pressure; "out there" there is no heat and no cold, there are only moving molecules with more or less mean kinetic energy, and so on' (1973:286). The postmodern mind takes von Foerster's remark a giant step further by demolishing additional landmarks of epistemological stability: 'electromagnetic waves,' 'variations of the air pressure,' 'moving molecules,' and 'kinetic energy,' become as 'semiotically real' as 'light,' 'color,' 'sound,' 'heat,' and 'cold.' Territorial divisions are swept away by the whirlwinds of change. Distinctions between science and nonscience, art and nonart, are levelled. And, finally, we discover that we are all – human and nonhuman, living and nonliving, organic and inorganic alike – in this whole thing together.

It is ultimately the mind-body conglomerate that sees, hears, smells, tastes, and feels. It edits experience in order that the world might conform to its preconceptions. It cogitates, bringing imagined, hypostatic objects, acts, and events into its world. It learns to ignore certain signs that are most wisely considered ridiculous, fictive, hallucinatory, false, or evil, and, for survival value in its particular community, it learns properly to see geometrical forms, numbers, usual things, and good things, and to conduct its life in a respectable, cultured, intelligent manner. And so it comes to participate in/with its world.

What the mind-body senses is by no means separate from what is 'out there,' to be sure. Rather, mind-body-'real' interaction involves a complex *physiological and psychological process of construction in light of the prevailing conventions.* To rephrase a previous suggestion, just as purportedly Schrödinger's cat is neither dead nor alive until the observer–participatory mind makes it so, so also a sign is not a sign in the full-blown sense until interpreted by an interpreter, him/herself just another sign.

In principle, Wheeler's vague and as yet undeveloped notion of 'meaning physics' might appear well and good. But something is still missing. When I wrote 'mind-body' after my brief outline of 'meaning physics,' I touched on this something. It is this: Wheeler's account remains inexorably tinged with 'linguicentrism.' It attends to the mind as observer-participant, while largely ignoring the body as part of the physical existence with which it participates. In light of the preceding chapters, from a proper semiotic view, just as there is no absolute body/nature distinction in Wheeler's formulation, so also there is no absolute mind/body distinction from the Peircean point of view. Actually, the mind is intertwined more intricately and intimately with the body than in Wheeler's account. Symbolicity cannot – at least it should not – hog the show, even regarding an apparently insignificant 'cosmic ray.' That 'cosmic ray,' as symbol-sign, cannot be divorced from its particular context-dependent indexical 'semiotic object,' and neither of the two sign components can spring into existence with proper acknowledgment to their iconic ancestry. The predominantly mind qualities of carefully cogitated and meticulously constructed signs of symbolicity cannot be divorced from their concomitant corporeal feelings and sensations, actions and reactions, and their attendant gleeful 'ohs' and 'ahs' and gloomy groans and grunts, of iconicity and indexicality, sensed and experienced by their observer-participants.

In an attempt to fill the void left by Wheeler's 'linguicentrism,' I turn directly to the Lakoff-Johnson argument.

3. The Persistence of (Hypo)Iconicity

Johnson posits three central keys to a theory of meaning: *imagination*, *embodiment*, and *understanding* – or, in another way of putting it, Firstness, Secondness, and Thirdness, or *learning*, *accounting*, and *knowing*. A theory of meaning, we read, is a theory of understanding, and understanding cannot go it alone, but engages in a tenuous balance-act on the shoulders of embodied imagination. Johnson argues throughout his book (1987), as does Lakoff in his (1987), that embodied and imaginative meaning through understanding is historically and culturally shared, and it is 'objective' – not in the sense of the 'representational,' 'referential,' 'correspondence' theory of 'objectivity,' but an 'objectivity' that calls up the mediating role of human subjectivity.

I have no complaint with these ideas, as far as they go. They are quite in line with the assumptions underlying the foregoing chapters. *Imagination*, *embodiment*, and *understanding* are at their basest level (hypo)iconic, corporeal. The *embodied image* is a *qualisign* of feeling, the *embodied diagram* is a sign whose relation to some other ('semiotic object') is virtual, and the *embodied metaphor* (including all rhetorical figures, I would suggest) is potentially a sign mediating between an image sign and a diagram sign (it is an interpretant sign) (recall table 3). In accord with the Lakoff-Johnson thesis, the present inquiry treats meaning as embodied, historically, culturally, and contextually embedded, and in its most dynamic moments imaginatively engendered. The problem, as I see it, is that to a certain extent Lakoff and Johnson commit the same omission as Quine, Goodman, Putnam, Davidson, and even the likes of Rorty, who at least occasionally pay lip service to the iconic and indexical dimensions of signs, but hardly more. That is to say, in the long run their 'linguicentrism' resorts to bully tactics: symbolism takes over the ringside seats and pushes iconicity and indexicality to the remote sections. Granted, Johnson posits (1987:176–7):

> that 'linguistic meaning' is only an instance for specification of meaning(fullness) in general. Linguistic meaning is distinguished by its distinctive use of syntactic categories (e.g., noun phrase, verb phrase, particle, etc.), by its semantic categories (e.g., object, event, agent, etc.), and by its elaborate employment of speech-act conventions. However, ... these speech-act structures, such as illocutionary force operators, may have bodily correlates ...
>
> The hypothesis of the unity of the notion of meaning ... is a commitment to the existence of a series of connections among the various senses of 'means.' It is a commitment to the conviction that we are unified human beings and not a cluster of autonomous modules. It is a commitment to the 'cognitive semantics' view that humans have general cognitive mechanisms which can be specified to particular functions. So, linguistic meaning turns out to be a special instance (perhaps the most central) of our capacity to have meaningful experience.

Johnson rightfully complains that cognitive science by and large remains committed to analytic philosophy, which discards embodied knowing as irrelevant. Continental philosophy, especially following Heidegger, Maurice Merleau-Ponty, and Hans-Georg Gadamer, has long recognized embodied – iconic and indexical but nonsymbolic – knowing. Anglo-American analytic philosophy, in contrast, has 'steadfastly resisted this orientation in favor of meaning as a fixed connection between words and the world.' It has been mistakenly assumed that only a viewpoint capable of transcending 'human embodiment, cultural embeddedness, imaginative understanding, and location within historically evolving traditions can guarantee the possibility of objectivity' (Johnson 1987:175). Johnson's 'nonobjectivist' posture posits knowledge as the result of flows of interpretation (interpretants) that emerge from embodied as well as mental capacities for understanding. In fact, there is no distinction between the two capacities, for the mental is rooted in the physical, and both are lived and experienced as one within pliable spheres of interdependency, interrelation, and interaction between signs and signs, signs and 'semiotic worlds,' and signs and their agents. In Johnson's words, 'Meaning includes patterns of embodied experience and preconceptual structures of our sensibility (i.e., our mode of perception, or orienting ourselves, and of interacting with other objects, events, or persons). These embodied patterns do not remain private or peculiar to the person who experiences them. Our community helps us interpret and codify many of our felt patterns. They become shared cultural modes of experience and help to determine the nature of our meaningful, coherent understanding of our "world"' (1987:14).

Nevertheless, Johnson fails adequately to acknowledge certain nonlinguistic aspects of meaning that encompass the entire spectrum of embodied and historically, culturally, contextually embedded human activity at work and at play, during leisure hours and during serious dialogic interaction. For he later writes:

> Whether it be for human events or for words and sentences, meaning is always meaning *for* some person or community. Words do not have meaning in themselves; they have meaning only for people who *use* them to mean something ...
>
> Meaning is thus always a matter of relatedness (as a form of intentionality). An event becomes meaningful by pointing beyond itself to prior event structures in experience or toward possible future structures. The event is meaningful insofar as it stands against, and is related to, a background stretching from the past into the future. A word or sentence is meaningful because it calls to mind a set of related structures of understanding that are directed either to some set of structures in experience (either actual or potential), or else to other symbols. (ibid.:177)

A sign, Johnson implies, is something that relates to something else *for* the semiotic agent that *uses* it. Johnson is on target, so far. He also hits the mark in his questioning the assumption that only words and sentences have meaning and that meaning must be propositional in nature. In fact, his nonpropositional 'image schemata' that connect with the entire range of experiences, linguistic and nonlinguistic alike, should be applauded. His inquiry confronts the nature of meaning at every turn with the recurring problem: How to describe the embodied character of image schemata without making it appear exclusively either a concrete image and of little relevance to meaning or nothing more than the product of an abstracted proposition. Johnson responds – quite correctly, I believe – that understanding (and meaning) are more than a mere collection of propositions:

> Rather, *understanding is the way we 'have a world,' the way we experience our world as a comprehensible reality*. Such understanding, therefore, involves *our whole being* – our bodily capacities and skills, our values, our moods and attitudes, our entire cultural tradition, the way in which we are bound up with a linguistic community, our aesthetic sensibilities, and so forth. In short, our understanding *is* our mode of 'being in the world.' It is the way we are meaningfully situated in our world through our bodily interactions, our cultural institutions, our linguistic tradition, and our historical context. Our more abstract reflective acts of understanding (which may involve grasping of finitary propositions) are simply an extension of our understanding in this more basic sense of 'having a world.' (ibid.:102)

Johnson drills in on his topic further in his observation that neither image schemata nor their literal and rhetorical extensions are dressed exclusively in propositional garb. They can in many circumstances be propositionally depicted, no doubt. But this does not capture their countenance as it should be captured. Image schemata involve our full understanding, which, in addition to propositional depictions and relations, include 'bodily orientations, perceptions, and actions that have linguistic and cultural dimensions' (ibid.:103).

Well and good, once again. Johnson argues at length how image schemata put constraints on traditionally conceived propositional meaning and understanding with such 'bodily orientations' as 'containment,' 'boundedness,' and 'spatial and temporal orientation,' in his critique of 'objectivist' theories. But he does not emphatically give corporeal feels and images (hypoicons of the First order) and sensed schemata (diagrams, or hypoicons of the Second order) their due as the galvanizing forces that put symbols – propositional or discursive thought (including metaphors, or hypoicons of the Third order) – into action in the first place. To be sure, symbols without iconic and indexical dimensions are inert; icons and indices without symbolic form are less than genuine signs. Johnson implies so much. Nevertheless, he does not adequately emphasize the crucially important point that icons and indices are signs in their own right, and, though their meaning remains at largely tacit levels if they go inarticulated – insofar as they are articulable at all – they are an integrated part of the whole of human interaction. The very existence of explicitly engendered symbols is dependent upon icons and indices at implicit (corporeal, felt) levels of learnability, accountability, and at least tacit knowability. But icons and indices cannot emerge into the arena of explicitly articulated knowledge without their proper symbolic attire. This much has been reiterated time and again in the above chapters.

Moreover, Johnson, and especially Lakoff (1987), propose as necessary conditions of meaning a theory of categorization specifying the way we organize our experience into general classes. Inspired by the work of Wittgenstein and John Austin, and by the likes of Berlin and Kay's colour terms (1969), Lounsbury's kinship terminologies (1964), Zadeh's fuzzy sets (1965, 1975), and above all Eleanor Rosch's 'prototype theory,' (1973, 1974, 1975a, 1975b, 1977, 1978), Lakoff writes that 'human categorization is essentially a matter of both human experience and imagination–of perception, motor activity, and culture on the one hand, and of metaphor, metonymy, and mental imagery on the other. As a consequence, human reason crucially depends on the same factors, and therefore cannot be characterized merely in terms of the manipulation of abstract symbols' (1987:8). On the surface Lakoff's words appear reasonable. Yet his very choice of the terms 'imagery,' 'metonymy,' and 'metaphor' belie his – and Johnson's – inclination toward a 'structuralist-semiological,' 'linguicentric' view, in addition to the suspicion that, given his central focus on language and categorization, his hypothesis may well remain colored with the mindset that ended in the ill-fated generative semantics movement, beginning with Katz and Fodor's taxonomic theory of meaning (1963) and the distinction between 'dictionary meaning' and 'encyclopedic meaning' (this is the sort of meaning on which occasionally, and unfortunately, Eco [1976, 1983], among others, places undue stress). As Johnson puts it, '*we cannot ignore the imaginative structures of understanding by which meaning is made possible.* We cannot ignore image schemata, metaphorical projections, metonymy, and so forth, if we want to explain meaning for natural languages' (1987:193).

The point might appear well taken. But, once again, I would submit, it falls short of the mark. In view of the assumptions put forth in this volume, I would rephrase Johnson's quote to read: WE CANNOT IGNORE ICONICITY AND INDEXICALITY IF WE WISH TO GET A SENSE OF THE *SEMIOSIC* ENGENDERMENT OF MEANING. This reformulation gives the presymbolic character of *semiosis* its due share of the spotlight. *Semiosis* is not merely cognitive in the intentional, explicit manner in which it is usually billed, nor is it the prudent conscious control of signs. In addition to our wilful and intentional engendering of meaning, *semiosis* often allows meaning to spring forth whether we know it or not and whether we will it or not. Such meaning is tacit as well as conscious, unintentional as well as intentional, felt as well as reasoned, corporeal as well as mental, aesthetic as well as logical. Above all, *semiosic* meaning follows the tenets of *vagueness*, *inconsistency*, and *incomplete generality* as well as, at its most stringent, the demands of classical logic. Language and logic erupt from icons and indices; the same can be said of the body, but it encompasses a subtle dynamic that language and logic can only at best crudely reflect. This assertion highlights, once again, the problems of 'reference,' 'correspondence,' 'representation,' and 'objectivity,' and the attraction of increased *breadth* and *depth* opened up by proper consideration of *vagueness* and *generality*. Perhaps it is high time we legitimately put the icon and index back in the sign and the body back in the mind, and forget about halfway-house measures.

4. On Signifying Corporeally

Unfortunately, resurrection of the body and of iconicity and indexicality must contend with an undying faith in the power of symbolicity that has often known no bounds.

Euclid declared that two parallel lines could by definition never close the gap between them, in spite of our seeing them converge, and the West became mesmerized by what must at the outset have appeared to be a strange geometry indeed. A few centuries ago the Jesuit Gropius Bacanus of Antwerp proclaimed that he had proved Adam and Eve spoke Dutch in Paradise. Pierre Simon de Laplace boasted that his book, *Analytical Mechanics*, had no pictures, only analyses. Biologist Johannes Müller once proclaimed that the mental image of a dog looks like the word DOG. The recent group of French mathematicians under the pseudonym Nicolas Bourbaki believed they presented mathematics as it should be presented, in a completely formal manner, without diagrams, and totally disembodied. The list of these and other such claims, some of them equally absurd, is long. One must concede, after all has been said and done, that tunnel-minded hyperemphasis on symbolicity has run rampant throughout Western thought. It has taken the West over two thousand years to arrive at the tunnel-minded idea that symbols are not the sole purveyors, the absolute masters, of experience, thought, and meaning. Lakoff and Johnson are to be given their due credit for their effort to put us on the right track. The upshot of their message is that spoken and written natural and formal languages alone are simply not enough properly to qualify human life. But there is more, much more.

Norman Mailer once observed: 'There are languages other than words, languages of symbol and languages of nature. There are languages of the body. And prize-fighting is one of them. A prizefighter ... [is a] species with a command of the body which is as detached, subtle, and comprehensive in its intelligence as any exercise of the mind. [He expresses] himself with wit, style, and an aesthetic flair for surprise when he boxes with his body. Boxing is a dialogue between bodies, [it] is a rapid debate between two sets of intelligences' (in Lowe 1977:255). Mailer's example might appear stretched, the product of a poetic mind creating quaint associations that, nonetheless, are of little relevance to our everyday affairs. Life, and the life of our signs, *is* embodiment, however. Life is body and mind united in signs; body and mind *are* signs, a *semio-psychosomatic* unity, if I may myself use such freedom with symbolicity. Context and environment cannot be abstracted from this unity, nor can the historical development of the self and its trio of others. During the boxing match, one body feigns and another reacts, in a sequence too rapid for the eye, and at times even for the mind, to follow. With each move and countermove, all a matter of signs, there is an intended object and an interpretant. One interpretant in the cycle becomes translated, it translates itself and translates its agent as the agent translates it, into another sign, and that sign becomes in its own turn another sign as a countermove in the dialogue in the process spontaneously of unfolding itself (recall figures 1 and 3). And all this occurs in the nonsymbolic arena of *semiosic* agonistics. These very important points are touched upon by Lakoff and Johnson, to be sure. But the picture remains deficient, since iconicity and indexicality have not received their due recognition.

Merleau-Ponty was one of the first philosophers of the present century to embrace the view of sign embodiment (Merleau-Ponty 1962, 1964, 1973; see also McLure 1990). We are born into and born by language, he contended, as much as we are born into and born by (our perception of) our world. However, perception (of sign-events) and language (of sign-events and thought-signs) are not separate powers. On the contrary, they interpenetrate. Perception is a nascent *logos*, and language is the partial realization of perception. Consequently, to be educated within a discipline is to learn not only a new language but also a new vision. Merleau-Ponty writes 'When I begin to reflect, my reflection bears upon an unreflective experience, moreover my reflection cannot be unaware of itself as an event, and so it appears to itself in the light of a truly creative act, of a changed structure of consciousness, and yet it has to recognize, as having priority over its own operations, the world which is given to the subject because the subject is given to himself ... Perception is ... the background from which all acts stand out, and is presupposed by them: The world is not an object such that I have in my possession the law of its making; it is the natural setting of, and the field for, all my thoughts and all my explicit perceptions' (1964:x–xi). And yet, even Merleau-Ponty doesn't quite go far enough. In the final analysis he views science, philosophy, and all discursive practices – if not the practices of everyday life – as operating on the presupposition that the subject is by and large a disembodied mind contemplating the world 'out there.'

It is the age-old story. But it has bifurcated along two different paths. On the one hand, there is a neutral, disembodied observer picking up the necessary particulars from the minutiae of the hustle-bustle world of living in order to construct hard-core inductive knowing. On the other hand, there is a detached observer-mind coolly taking in the scene before her and intuitively knowing that scene like it is, or perhaps actively constructing a world, her world, the world she by and large shares with others of her community. Or perhaps it could even be a matter of brains-in-a-vat who think, as naive realists, that their world in a materialist sense is the physically 'real' as such, or in good subjective idealist fashion, that it is purely the outcome of their mind. At any rate, in essence we have a replay of that drama starring Duhem's pair of actors, the English empiricist and the French rationalist – or perhaps the nominalist and the realist, the materialist and the idealist, or the reductionist and the holist, however one wishes to take them. There is, it would appear, hardly any middle way, and the overriding prioritizing of language, of symbolicity, prevails. Given Merleau-Ponty's view that all knowledge is to an extent embodied knowledge, he could have generated an argument capable of delivering a knock-out punch to this venerated tradition. But he did not, unfortunately, though he must be given credit for his choice of sparring partners that provided the proper training for doing so.

So, where to go from here? It is true – is it not? – that we must certainly be imprisoned within our words by the very fact that we belong to a community, some community, whatever that is, wherever its circumference and centre may be, if there be circumference and center at all. Some of the very words I have used in this overambitious essay have inevitably blurred boundaries. There is no sharp division between signs or words of quality: 'grue' or 'bleen,' 'green' or 'blue.' Or between those of tokens and types: 'dabbit' or 'ruck,' 'rabbit' or 'duck.' Or between those of conceptual character: 'craight' or 'sturved,' 'straight' or 'curved.' And that, to say nothing of 'cats' and 'cherries' and H_2O and XYZ and 'Gavagai!' The vagueness of these and all terms of similar ilk goes hand in hand with the vast majority of all the words we use in whatever endeavour (Fuhrmann 1991). Rich people and poor people, obese people and thin people, honest people and liars, and so on: there are no clear-cut parameters governing their application, from one citizen to another within the same community, or for one citizen yesterday and that same citizen today. Perhaps one would like to conclude that vagueness and uncertainty of use regarding the items of a language are chiefly a matter of the ebbs and flows of psychological matters. This would imply that one takes a word to mean what one takes it to mean because of a particular context and situation, because one is happy or sad or under undue pressure, or perhaps because one wishes, by use of one's own words, to impress, deceive, or insult someone, or because of whatever other reason: it is a question of judgments on the spur of the moment, often with little regard for past and future uses of the word (Raffman 1994). This notion of sign use could result in a radically sceptical, even a cynical, view.

Or perhaps we are not so sly. Perhaps, in spite of our smug doubt, our scepticism, our cynicism, we tend rather mindlessly to take words by and large as others take them because those words have become part of our embedded, entrenched, automatized practices and rule obeying (Werhane 1992). What is for sure, in whichever case our ingrained practices belong to deep psychology – matters of nonconscious acts – and they even border on and enter into the domain of biology. They are the product of Goodman's *entrenchment* or what I have called *embedment*, of Polanyi's (1958) *tacit knowing*, of Hanson's and Wittgenstein's (1958) implicit knowing *how* rather than explicit knowing *that*, of Schrödinger's (1967) activities that have *submerged* into nonconscious levels such that what is done is done without full awareness of its being so done, even of Buddhist 'mindlessly' yet 'mindfully aware' knowing (Nishitani 1982). Above all, it is Peircean signs having become by the force of habit apparently spontaneously engendered rather than the product of voluntary, conscious, and reasoned responses.

So, once again, what are we to do, if embedded sign use and attendant meanings are well-nigh unspecifiable? Go on playing the inextricably 'linguicentric' prison-house-of-words game? This was, of course, overtly and unabashedly the game of structuralism – that hoary holdover of positivism and reductionism – and we find its remnants hanging on in postructuralist thought. For example, the core of Jacques Lacan's program for the unconscious as structured like language gives us this familiar reading: 'Ellipsis and pleonasm, hyperbaton or syllepsis, regression, repetition, opposition – these are the syntactical displacements; metaphor, catachresis, autonomasis, allegory, metonymy, and synecdoche – these are the semantic condensations in which Freud teaches us to read the intentions – ostentations or demonstrative, dissimulating or persuasive, retaliatory or seductive – out of which the subject modulates his oneiroc discourse' (1977:58). Rampant 'linguicentrism.' In order to avoid such biases, are we to take Nietzsche at face value when he writes that the great thinkers think with their body, in dance, gyrating with oscillation, uncertainty, vacillation, twitching, spasms, and so on? The idea is attractive, even for us ordinary folk. But surely we cannot toss discursive thought into the trash can and expect to find any answers by wordlessly dancing our way through life. Even Nietzsche himself had plenty to say on the matter, albeit in a vague and evasive metaphorical mode. Are we inexorably reduced to making a choice between one thing and the other? Must our posture exclusively be a matter either of what Thomas Nagel labels a disembodied 'view from nowhere' (1986) or of Rudolf Arnheim's obsession with 'visual thinking' (1969), semiology's priority of language (Lévi-Strauss 1963), the deconstructionist's biased 'grammatological' primacy of writing (Derrida 1974a), or some other fixation?

One might wish to respond at this point that I should simply reiterate my insistence that radical 'non-linguicentrism' is the route to take and get on with my story. Well, agreed, I suppose. That is what I should do. But the difficulty of so doing, with clear and distinct symbolic signs, has repeatedly surfaced throughout this volume. So, time and space having become a limiting factor at this juncture of my modest inquiry, I find myself forced to suggest, evoke, perhaps provoke, and imply, and at the same time I remain burdened by the many preceding pages that I must never cease to bear in mind. Perhaps this is as close to dancing as my limited faculties will allow me, since I am reduced to the excessively 'linguicentric' practice of constructing squiggles on the monitor. I will try to proceed, then, very tentatively

5. A Mediary Way?

Peirce's triadic, mediary concept of *semiosis* may help offer us a way out of our dilemma. *Semiosis*, by its very nature, is neither exclusively subject nor object, mind nor matter, inner nor outer, but a collapse of the poles of the oppositions into a whole, while at the same time each term maintains its identity by way of its complementary relationship with its companion term.

Descartes saw the mind as inner subjective consciousness that in the best of all circumstances contains ideas that mirror the world. For Brentano, of the nineteenth century – and in a comparable vein, Meinong – inner experiences are *of* something *for* the mind, and hence they 'refer to,' 'correspond to,' and 'represent' some object, whether inner or outer. Shortly after the turn of the century, Edmund Husserl extended Brentano's work by emphasizing direct experience, both inner and outer in the phenomenological sense, *of* the 'things themselves.' Rejecting Galilean objective science that presupposes a detached, God's-eye view of the world, Husserl nonetheless maintained faith in the subjective or intersubjective grasp of the world, in all its pristine purity and undiluted by any intermediary stages. I make brief mention of Descartes, Brentano, and Husserl for the purpose of setting them apart from Peirce. In view of the 'pragmatic maxim' and the set of terms with which we are now quite familiar – *vagueness* and *generality*, *inconsistency* and *incompleteness*, *overdetermination* and *underdetermination*, *complementarity* and *indeterminacy*, and *learnability*, *accountability*, and *knowability* – Peirce did not fall victim to 'Cartesian anxiety' (that is, either we have foundations, or darkness, anarchy, and chaos will prevail). That is because he ultimately found comfort in foundationlessness, placing the quest for knowledge in the same arena as all other walks of life.

From the Preamble we learned that Alpha is apparently quite in tune with his feelings, his gut intuitions, though he understandably encounters difficulty expressing them. Omega, plagued by 'Cartesian anxiety,' must have things either one way or the other. His way must be the right way, and if something doesn't go to the tune of his band, it must be categorically discarded. The Master engages in an effort to bring about genuine *intention* – *intending* – toward what appears to be the 'objects' of her thought-signs and sign-events, and at the same time she attempts to maintain *attention to* – *consciousness of* – them in such a manner that she may bring her feelings and sensations (Firstness), and her ideas and conceptual scheme (Thirdness), in harmony with her actual experience (Secondness). She is aware that theoretical reflection, like the activities of everyday living, should not simply be mindless, detached, and disembodied. Reflection demands the act of becoming coupled with mindful awareness *of* that which might otherwise go undetected. But this mindfulness is at the same time, so to speak, mindlessly mindful. It entails mindful awareness at a level virtually exempt from the Faustian need to remain detached from the world, actively and aggressively controlling, manipulating, using, and abusing it.

An example is in order. When a child prodigy is given a violin and taught how to use it, she must first actively 'think through' the moves explicitly imparted to her by her tutor and 'follow' the examples she is given. After much practice and perhaps many tense moments, her talent begins to take over, and her moves become fluid. Now, her fingers and hands do what they do spontaneously, her body sways in rhythm to the sounds spilling forth, and all this without her mind having to give hardly any active, detached thought to what it is she is doing at the moment she does it. Body and mind act in concert; no longer is there any subject *here* and musical object *there*, with the one imposing itself on the other in order to squeeze the desired product from it; there are no longer any inner/outer, mind/body, here/there distinctions. One might wish to say, within the framework of Cartesian terminology, that her violin playing has now become 'mindless.' But that's not it, not really. Her activity has in the Cartesian sense become 'mindless,' yet she is 'mindfully aware' of her every move, of the whole of all her moves. She is not 'playing the violin,' but rather, she and her instrument are in concert 'violining,' while the melodious sounds that emerge are acting as mediator and moderator. There is no mind *here* and body *there*, subject *here* and violin *there*, silence *before* and music *now*. There is a process of interactive becoming.

In this sense, the very idea of 'mindlessness' can lead one astray, especially in light of the general view of things slowly unfolding itself throughout the pages of this book. The prodigy's activity is now 'mindful' in the most literal sense, for her mind has become inseparable from her body. She is not the subject as violinist who extracts music from her object, the violin, consisting merely of a few pieces of wood held together by glue and some gut strings. No. The violinist is in the process of becoming a violinist only in concert with the violin's truly becoming a violin by its being played; the music is becoming music only in the company of both the violinist and the violin, and violinist and violin depend on the music for their becoming violinist and violin. In other words, rather than the mind *here* and the body *there* operating in parallel fashion, the mind as some transcendental agent capable of exercising dominion over the body, or the mind as squeezed and sublimated from the brain, everything is mind: matter is mind crystallized, and when mind, within the *semiosic* stream, is at its mindful best, it is what has not yet been regimented by the force of habit. All that is is mind; the body just happens to be the most empirically qualifiable and quantifiable of its manifestations.

This, then, is the heart of my story. The story's actual heartbeat entails fusion of mind and signs when signs as possibilities are *put to use* and initiate their becomingness as other signs at the same time that their semiotic agents are becoming something other than what they were. In the terms of Wheeler's 'meaning physics,' it is not simply a matter of our violinist *putting* the violin *to use*, the violin also *puts* the violinist *to use*, and the music *puts* both of them *to use* as they *put* it *to use*, while they make their way along the *semiosic* stream in harmony with each other as signs among signs. It's a perpetually shifting three-way affair. Just as there is no sight without seer and that which is in the process of seeing becoming, no dance without dancer and what is dancing becoming, no painting without painter and what is painting becoming, no science without scientist and what is science-in-the-process-of-becoming, so also there is no sign without an interpreter (interpretant) and that which is sign becoming. And – to get to the meat of the issue – there is no meaning without a semiotic agent or interpreter and that which is in the process of becoming meant. Meaning, in short, requires that there be (1) an agent who is in the process of engendering meaning, and (2) something lending itself to the becoming of meaning and to the agent of that becoming, who is herself part of the process of becoming – that is, something being *put to use* and at the same time *putting to use*.

But I'm afraid this will not quite do either. Not really. The mutual interaction between signs, sign engenderers, and meanings to which I allude could quite easily create the notion of *putting to use* as chiefly of linguistic nature, if not exclusively enshrouded in symbolic signs. I cannot overemphasize my rejection of this 'linguicentric' tendency, however. The crises of the last half of this century – in physics, biology, linguistics and the social sciences, philosophy and philosophy of science, history, criticism and theory, the arts – have incessantly bared the conspicuous limitations of the vernacular as well as technical language. Despite the profusion of technical terms, the wine of new meanings poured into the bottles of old terms, and the onslaught of neologisms at work and at play, language has remained incapable of the task asked of it regarding the vast expanse that lies beyond common experience, and it is even deficient regarding the mundane matters of everyday life. It is perhaps a sad fact that mathematicians can hardly 'talk' mathematics, but must resort to communication in pure formalisms. We have a comparable testimony from Heisenberg and others in chapter 14, section 3.

Philosophers have often encountered the fetters of anthropomorphisms and tropes, as Nietzsche so trenchantly put it, and in some cases they have become resigned to their limitations – though others continue on unabashedly, with sugarplums of certainty still dancing in their heads. The social sciences and the humanities are finally rediscovering the beauty of dialogue, narrative, and stories, after having despaired for years over the inadequacies of critical and formal discourse. And the realm of ineffability in the arts has long been notorious, though attempts to articulate the essence of art works doggedly persist in some quarters. In a word, there are situations, events, acts, and objects on all levels of experience to which language, whether ordinary or technical, simply does not and cannot apply. This is where visceral, corporeal feels, sensations, sentiments, inclinations, notions, and intuitions come into the picture, inextricably to link mind and body.

Caught up in this general spirit, Wolfgang Yourgrau presents an extraordinarily perceptive paper (1966), arguing that a non-Euclidean sense of space and spatial relationships is more fundamental than and precedes Euclidean geometry in the development of the human mind. In his words:

> [T]opological relations are grasped much earlier and more easily than Euclidean shapes. Our education and our environment make us believe that there is a smooth, natural continuity between perceptual and representational relationships ... [T]he predominance of Euclidean geometry in our training has created deeply entrenched misorientations. There is a tremendous gap between haptic perception and mental representation, since the latter invokes the existence of objects in their physical absence. Semantic relations, image, thought, differentiation of diverse signs or symbols not only occur after haptic experience, but they differ fundamentally from it. (Yourgrau 1966:498)

He goes on to summarize:

> [T]he observation of ... children's behavior patterns suggests that the 'india-rubber' world of the topologist and of Einstein, though highly abstract to the uninitiated, and the haptic perception of the child are much closer to one another than haptic perception is to Euclidean shapes and spaces with their rigid properties ... [T]he child recognizes objects haptically at an early age. But once the level of representation is reached, the aid of speech is invoked and thereby all doors opened to Euclidean commitment. (ibid.:500)

It hardly needs saying that this 'haptic perception' – perception of an object through a sense of touch, in the absence of visual stimulation – most properly pertains to Firstness and its extension into Secondness, while Euclidean geometry and Galilean science fall within the private domain of that imperialistic form of 'linguicentric' Thirdness that lies behind the world of haptic perception and visual appearances. Yourgrau's words also remind us that Einsteinian finite but unbounded space is more closely aligned to the pre-Euclidean finite but boundless sphere of certain Greek thinkers than it is to classical conceptions of space. In a certain manner, it can be said that Euclidean space is to an Erector set as non-Euclidean or Einsteinian space is to a lump of clay that can be kneaded, twisted, stretched, and distorted. Nevertheless, rigid Euclidean space, with its infinite extension as a void, a receptacle, to be filled with those autonomous, indivisible, impenetrable spheres, the atoms of the universe racing to and fro, was destined to become over the centuries firmly entrenched in the West's history. (Haptic space, I should also point out though it goes virtually without saying, plays a central role in all sorts of creativity in the arts [see Ehrenzweig 1967, Heelan 1983, Löwenfeld 1939].)

Yourgrau alludes to studies by Geza Révész (1957) and Jean Piaget (1973) demonstrating that 'haptic perception' is more fundamental and prior to visual perception and hence to Euclidean space as a homogenous medium. Things in the haptic space of the child are synchretic, unanalysed wholes, whose parts are as yet unrelated. Interrelations between the parts come only later, when the child has been properly indoctrinated into Euclidean space of boundedness and connectedness. Only then do notions of rigid shapes and sizes, distances, angles, and projective relations become part of the child's perception, which is now chiefly visual, haptic perception having waned in the process. Studies by the likes of Jerome Bruner (1956, 1986, 1987), Howard Gardner (1983), and Richard L. Gregory (1966, 1970, 1981) further elaborate and support this view. (However, for a critique of Piaget with respect to his concept of the younger child as a non-Euclidean 'savage' and the older, 'enlightened' child as having been taught the proper principles of Euclidean geometry, see Wilden [1980].)

The direction I now seem to be taking might suggest that haptic perception is intimately related to the body while visual perception is closer to the affairs of the mind – though actually, I have argued, there is no mind-body distinction here. If the West has come increasingly to prioritize mind over body, and as a logical consequence the visual over the haptic, language over other communicative media, propositional knowledge over schematic and imagistic knowledge, and symbolicity over indexicality and iconicity, perhaps the time is ripe, I must repeat, for a more balanced conception. This balance, I would suggest, is most effectively forthcoming through a mind-body interrelatedness, interactivity, and interdependency rather than the traditional contradiction between the two terms. The mind-body complementarity pervades all levels, from inner to outer and from biological to psychological to phenomenological. In this sense I concur with Johnson when he writes: '[M]eaning includes patterns of embodied experience and preconceptual structures of our sensibility (i.e., our mode of perception, or orienting ourselves, and of interacting with other objects, events, or persons). These embodied patterns do not remain private or peculiar to the person who experiences them. Our community helps us interpret and codify many of our felt patterns. They become shared cultural modes of experience and help to determine the nature of our meaningful, coherent understanding of our "world"' (1987:14).

The 'embodied' and 'felt [that is, haptic] patterns,' having become 'shared cultural modes of experience,' are precisely what meaning is all about, beginning with the 'pragmatic maxim.'

The maxim, as indicated above, is not the purveyor of 'truth,' but, rather, it is the way of engendering meaning. Neither is it the royal road to belief predisposing one to act in concert with the other citizens of one's community. On the contrary. The maxim leads one toward some belief or other, to be sure, but belief itself is a disposition or habit of action: 'The whole function of thought is to produce habits of action' (*CP*:5.400). A thought or thought-sign, as well as when related to a sign-event, is related to the belief toward which it is leading, that is, it is related to the habit that played a role in producing it in the first place. The habit, in its turn, is the repository of all the possible acts that might be forthcoming under all conceivable circumstances. In this manner, if the 'practical effects' of a thought-sign related to a sign-event leads toward the creation of a habit, then one's conception of those 'practical effects' – which include the entire meaning of the original thought-sign – can be displayed as a series of conditional sentences describing, however incompletely, what effects would most likely ensue from the actions of all conceivable instances of the thought-sign's being *put to use* and of its *putting* its engenderer, both of mind and body, *to use.* However, I must hasten to add, this is no indication that the body is exempt from the 'maxim' and all the ramifications it implies. The very Peircean notion of 'habit of action' includes corporeal, even visceral, sensations, sentiments, and intuitions, since the feeling body is at this level inseparable from any and all mind acts – that is, the violinist-violin and music-becoming, the dancer-dance and dance-becoming, the interpreter-interpretant-sign and the sign-becoming, and the knower-known and the becoming of knowing.

Such is the case, I must reiterate, of the dialogueurs in the Preamble. There is Alpha and there is Omega, and both are in the process of 'Alpha-becoming' and 'Omega-becoming' through the mergence of their words with those of the Master. Of course, they are not flesh-and-blood beings but fictions, mere words, symbols. But as symbols they incorporate icons and indices, which give them their imagistic and schematic countenances, bringing them forth in full bloom for their readers. They are incorporated and corporeal, as thought-signs, though not existent as sign-events (*pace* Meinong). As a community of three, they talk, and their talk, replete with what *is not,* by the ways of paradox, gives at least a slight glimpse of what *is*, or *can be*, or, better, what *is in the process of becoming.* Meaning *is* possible, therefore there is always the possibility of some sort of closure; but meaning is endlessly possible, therefore no closure is really possible.

All this, I fear, still remains vague. So let me illustrate the process I have in mind more graphically.

6. An Unexpected Turn

The illustration will emerge from an unanticipated, and perhaps even an unwanted, source. I allude to the set of *skandha* or, in one of the translations of the term, 'heaps,' from Buddhist philosophy. Rendition of *skandha* from the Sanscrit to 'heap' in English is significant, since the term evokes memories of concepts now familiar: the sorites paradox revealing the *vagueness* of language and *generalities* of thought, Zeno's paradox entailing (*underdetermined*) discontinuities becoming finer and finer until they appear to melt into the (*overdetermined*) continuum, the liar paradox revealing the *inconsistency* and/or *incompleteness* of any and all presumably ordered collections of signs. And so on.

In brief, there are five 'heaps': (1) *forms*, or the world with which one is constantly in contact but that has not (yet) become actualized *for* the consciousness of a given semiotic agent, (2) *feelings* and *sensations* (*tones*) as a result of one's contact with the environment, (3) *perception* or *experience*, the becoming of awareness of the particulars (*tokens*) in one's environment, (4) *dispositions*, consisting of habitual modes of feeling, perceiving, and thinking, which place *tokens* into categories (or *types*), and (5) *consciousness*, which incorporates all the foregoing, however *inconsistently* (*vaguely*) and however *incompletely* (*generally*). Collection (1) is a counterpart to Peirce's 'reality,' which incessantly exercises its influence over us. But since it is what it is in spite of what we might wish to think about it, we hardly influence it, and cannot hope to know it except in terms of some vague sort of approximation – the sorites paradox, I would suggest, applies even here. *Feelings* and *sensations* (2) are of Firstness (*tones*), while *perception* or *experience* (3) of the 'semiotic world out there' in terms of sign-events or of 'inner' thought-signs is of the sphere of Secondness (of *tokens*). The combination of *dispositions* (habits of action, conventions, regularities) and *consciousness* makes up Thirdness, what allows for the collection of *tokens* into *types*.

One of the chief differences between (4) and (5) rests in the former as author of embedded, entrenched, automatized, and relatively nonconscious ('mindless') action, while the latter entails the becoming of 'mindful awareness' in varying degrees *of* that action. To put the matter another way, (4) involves habitualized *intention toward* the 'semiotic object' while (5) entails *attention to* it, with an increased level of awareness (recall the above on intentionality). *Intention toward* an 'object' under ordinary circumstances is often so embedded and compulsive that one is not aware *of* the *intention* as such. Becoming aware *of* the *intention* is the process of emerging *consciousness of* or *attention to* that 'object.' This *consciousness of* is not of that egocentric, hyperindividualized sort with which we are so familiar in Western cultures. It is, rather, the culmination and combination of (1) through (4). It includes corporeal feels and sensations, experience *of* something other than the experiencing subject, and that subject's action *as* semiotic agent *in* interaction *with* what in Western discourse consists of her Cartesian 'inner' and 'outer' worlds. But, to reiterate, there is no precisely delineable 'inner' or 'outer,' mind or body, subject or object, knower or known. There is only *becoming*, devoid of categories of thought presumably fixed for all time. (Medin and Barsalou [1987] give a convincing argument from empirical studies that nonperceptual 'generic knowledge' of categories such as 'rich' and 'poor,' 'good' and 'bad,' and so on [that is, thought-signs] function in a manner analogous to perceptual categories such as 'horses' and 'cars,' 'red' things and 'purple' things, and so on. The conclusion: even the most abstract of concepts do not remain exempt from corporeal meaning.)

Finally, the relevance of the story in chapter 2 on the self and its *others* and of our impoverished individualism begins to make sense. It is not so much that the self is no more than a mere fiction or that the individualized ego is a sham. While the idea of the self as fiction allows it to maintain a certain degree of autonomy with respect to its *others*, to declare a loss of the self and an end to individualism actually falls in line with the Western myth of the rugged individualized ego. Just as there was never any purely autonomous ego as an island unto itself, so also there cannot be any pure dissolution of the ego or self. In other words, it was never a matter of mind 'here' and capable of apprehending everything else 'there.' Visceral and corporeal and mental and intellectual have never ceased their interactive play, in spite of the West's conspiratory efforts. It is not a game of musical chairs or of hide-and-seek, but an interweaving of objects, act, and events into a *semiosic* whole. There are no foundations for individual consciousness, ego, and self-identity, though there is warrant for a self in interactive interdependency with its trio of *others*, at least insofar as the terms 'interrelatedness,' 'interaction,' and 'interdependency' are properly highlighted. That is to say, there is no self without its *others*, and the *others* have no status as such without their self. There is a self in interrelated, interdependent interaction with *others* in the sense that the self is in the process of 'selfing' or 'self-becoming' and the *others* are in the process of '*other*-becoming.' There is never a finished product but ongoing process, never being but the becoming of being, or at most we might say there is a beingfulness of becoming. Finally, it was never a matter simply of language and everything else, for language (symbolicity) depends for its very existence on that 'everything else' consisting chiefly, if not exclusively, of signs (of iconicity, indexicality), upon whose shoulders language stands.

From the *vagueness* (and *inconsistency-overdetermination*) of feeling and sensation to the *either-or* imperatives of subject-object, self-*others*, and this-that, to the *generality* of intention, and finally to the *vagueness-generality* (and *incompleteness-underdetermination*) of attention, and from *learnability* to *accountability* to *knowability*, nothing stands out entirely, but rather, everything is interrelated with and perpetually in interactive interdependency with everything else. The whole of *semiosis*, it would appear, is a self-organizing, bootstrap operation, without determinable grounds or foundations. And any and all semiotic agents, human and nonhuman alike, are included within the equation. This notion of the interrelatedness of all things, in the final analysis, is the essence of a Peircean conception of meaning, which includes

1 Triadic relations,
2 Self-*others* dialogic,
3 Self-mind as a sign among signs,
4 Mind-body in concert as sign and semiotic agent, and
5 Iconicity-indexicality-symbolicity as an inseparable whole intimately and inextricably knotting mind and body, self and mind, self and *others*, and all those signs with all other signs.

These five points, I hardly need write in view of the above chapters, dissolve customary distinctions between fiction and the 'real,' thought-signs and sign-events, 'subjectivity' and 'objectivity,' and narrative and discursive knowledge. Gavagai, ravens that happen to be black, grue/bleen, H_2O/XYZ, brains-in-a-vat, and cat-cat* all have to do with meaning not in the head or the thing. Neither is meaning in imaginary conduit tubes connecting addresser with addressee, nor is it anchored in the sign. It is not in the representamen, the semiotic object, or the interpretant. Meaning is within, it emerges from, it lifts itself out of, the interrelatedness, the interactive interdependency, between sign components, between signs and other signs, and between signs and their semiotic agents. And all this occurs within time-bound, transient, incessantly sluicing contexts.

Meaning, it would appear, then, is not found in any particular thing, at any place, or within any given temporal increment. It pervades everything, everywhere and everywhen. Consequently, it is in its inception to be felt (iconically, within Firstness), not explicitly indicated (indexed, Secondness) or cognized (symbolized, Thirdness). The all-pervading wave of *vagueness* is in the beginning felt. The staccato, stuttering effect of *indeterminacy-uncertainty* is at its heart felt, in spite of however it may be explained away or articulated at later moments. The shimmering, scintillating dance of *overdetermination*, as pure possibility, can at most be no more than felt. *Inconsistency-incompleteness* are a fact of life, no doubt, and they have been brought to our attention by the most rigorous manifestation of symbolicity, yet, in the affairs of everyday living, if they make their presence known at all, it is by way of vague and ambiguous feeling. *Underdetermination* is sensed and felt before it is cognized, in the give-and-take of life, where unexpected signs pop up and taunt us, demonstrating that they, too, are worthy citizens in the society of signs we have appropriated as our own. Finally, *generality*, enabler of all our cherished categories of thought, reveals, in the final analysis, and at the base level of feeling and sensing, that no borders, frames, or limns are innocent, nor are they free of defects and fuzz. In this regard, meaning, radically context-dependent and engendered from qualisign levels, precedes language: meaning is, and will remain, quite alien to any word qua word that pretends adequately to account for it.

If we take the entire spectrum, from *vagueness* and its attendant companion terms to *generality* and its compatible bedfellows into account, then it can be safely said that there is no 'meaning' of that crisp sort that has populated the dreamy minds of Western meaningmongers throughout the centuries. To be sure, I am the first to concede that at one extreme of the spectrum there is 'meaning' in the purely *relative* sense, and at the other extreme there is 'meaning' in the purely *absolute* sense. Absolute 'meaning' is that of the collection of all objects, acts, and events as they are in the timeless moment, shorn of memories and history and exempt from expectations regarding their future. Relative 'meaning' consists of the emptiness, the groundlessness, the foundationlessness, of those same objects, acts, and events when properly historicized. I hardly need write, however, that both of these 'meanings' lie outside the grasp of us mere finite, fallible semiotic agents. We are, we find ourselves, somewhere between the two extremes of *vagueness* and *generality*, and caught up in radical *indeterminacy*. At the one extreme, *vagueness* is the 'node' in figure 1; it is of the nature of '*WB*-lessness' in the blackboard thought experiment; it is the hub in the Buddhist wheel, which, unlike the gyrating, vertiginous, spokes, remains unchanged and unchanging, though it is a scintillating, dancing, shimmering flux of motion. If the hub is 'emptiness,' 'nothingness,' the circumference of the wheel is the other extreme; it is 'everything,' *generality*, the Ultimate Interpretant. Both the hub and the circumference are not of our finite world of signs, however, in spite of our desires to the contrary: we are, and will remain, suspended in between, wherever that is. (I take my cue here from the Buddhist 'middle way' [Murti 1955], that has inspired Varela, Thompson and Rosch's 'embodied mind' idea [1993] much in the spirit of the work of Lakoff and Johnson).

As a final note, I readily concede that whatever vestiges of 'linguicentrism' have managed to hang on throughout this inquiry, they will be most commonly found lurking in the workings of the 'pragmatic maxim.' Indeed, Peirce himself stressed time and again that, ultimately, meaning for human semiotics, *our* semiotics, depends chiefly on the nature of symbolicity (for example, *CP*:3.419, 420, 451, 457, and especially MS 313). But that much can probably be allowed us – and, indeed, perhaps there is no alternative – for it is likely the 'maxim,' couched in symbolicity, that is most responsible for making *our* semiotics distinctly human. The 'maxim's' responsibility, however, rests not in the 'maxim' itself, but in our own semiotic activity, both corporeal and intellectual. We can choose to 'use' our signs as they reciprocally 'use' us, or we can continue to abuse them and run the risk of their turning the tables to abuse us. We can choose to edify them – and ourselves in the process – or systematically destroy them – and perhaps they us. The choice lies with us and us alone.

Appendix
On the Pragmatic Maxim

According to Peirce's 'maxim,' a statement is reformulated as a *subjunctive conditional*, the product of some *conception*, which, when applied to that statement in terms of the *practical consequences* implied, will either support or deny it. Notice that the term 'practical' enjoys equal status with 'conception.' Peirce's pragmatism is as thoroughly *sensational* (from sense-Firstness to actual-Secondness), as it is *intellectual* (inferential-Thirdness).

'This diamond is hard' means nothing unless there is some prior concept of 'hardness,' of the relation of 'hard' things to 'soft' things, and of the expected result when bringing the two types of things into contact. So the diamond in question must be rubbed briskly against some other material, say, glass, and the glass is either scratched or not. For, as Peirce puts it, 'There is absolutely no difference between a hard thing and a soft thing so long as they are not brought to the test … [T]he question of what would occur under circumstances which do not actually arise is not a question of fact, but only of the most perspicacious arrangement of them' (*CP*:5.403). That was in 1878, during Peirce's 'nominalistic' days. Some time later, in 1905, when he had appended a 'realist' corollary to his maxim, the above statement became 'Diamonds are hard,' and the *practical consequences* took on a more *general* character, as evidenced in the following: '[T]o what else does the entire teaching of chemistry relate except to the "behavior" of different possible kinds of material substance? And in what does that behavior consist except that of a substance of a certain kind should be exposed to an agency of a certain kind, a certain kind of sensible result *would* ensue according to our experiences hitherto? (*CP*:5.457) In other words, a hypothetical proposition containing an antecedent conditional and a consequent practical result relates to what *would occur* in a potential range of states of things not coincident with the present state of things. If in the entire course of events (or tests) what *might occur* were in the future actually *to occur*, then it could be concluded that the disposition of the object of that proposition being what it is, it would tend to manifest the same behaviour. However, since the entire set of future events stands no chance of occurring in a finite world, *absolute verification* of the proposition cannot for practical purposes be forthcoming.

Peirce's style of pragmatism is, in itself, not strictly a metaphysical doctrine. Pragmatism entails no determination of absolute meaning once and for all, though, via the maxim, it is a concrete, albeit fallible, method 'of ascertaining the meaning of hard words and of abstract concepts' (*CP*:5.464). It is intended to 'bring to an end those prolonged disputes of philosophers which no observations of facts could settle, and yet in which each side claims to prove that the other side is wrong' (*CP*:5.6). Of course it hardly needs saying that in order for pragmatism to be most effective, at the outset the disputants must be 'of cross-purposes.' They must 'either attach different meanings to words, or else one side or the other (or both) uses a word without any definite meaning' (*CP*:5.6). What is essential for bringing these 'cross-purposes' and 'different meanings' to the surface is a hands-on method for determining the meaning of concepts, propositions, arguments, or any other signs. The important point is that we are speaking of signs, per se, not their 'referents,' for 'the object of a sign is one thing; its meaning is another' (*CP*:5.6). Or in another way of putting it, an *index* in and of itself has hardly anything to do with meaning (*CP*:4.56). It has need of those other essential characters on the stage of *semiosis*: *iconicity* and *symbolicity*.

It may appear that the maxim places virtually exclusive stress on Thirdness, a move toward the rationally controlled and conscious development of thought and knowledge (that is, the final or logical interpretant), of which symbols are the medium *par excellence*, icons and indices having been shunted aside once they functioned properly as mere precursory signs. Along these lines Dan Nesher (1983) emphasizes the task of pragmatism as first and foremost that of distinguishing between properly intellectual signs and all other sign types (see *CP*:5.206–7). Granted, as far as thought goes, Thirdness must be prioritized (*CP*:5.209). The product of Thirdness, however, must be experientially validated. In other words, thinking cannot continue if completely divorced from the actual experience of and interaction with the 'semiotically real.' Thus, by use of the maxim, a highlighted degree of clarity of thought can be achieved, but this clarity of thought depends upon the felt and sensed, the experienced and perceived, concrete 'semiotic world.'

Now, there seems to be a contradiction here. On the one hand, the maxim magnifies the intellectual growth of signs. This is most properly Thirdness. But on the other hand, phrases such as 'practical bearings,' 'practical consequences,' and 'sensible or perceptible consequences' that appear in many variations throughout Peirce's writings on pragmatism and the maxim involve Secondness (actuality, or concrete praxis) and Firstness (qualitative possibility). It is quite obviously the case that the practical consequences of a proposition, insofar as they bear on human conduct, call for experience, that is, observation, experimentation, and testing, as well as the activity of everyday life in which the human semiotic agent is engaged. In the final analysis, whether we are speaking of science, philosophy, or the humdrum of our quotidian affairs, we should strive to establish 'a habit of positive expectation that shall not be disappointed' (*CP*:5.197; also 2.712, 5.491, 8.209). All such habits guiding the conduct of a given individual constitute, in a manner of speaking, the sum of, and the processing of, the phenomena that individual has selected from her world. And in the best of all worlds she will be so disposed by those habits to act on her world accordingly. Consequently, when Peirce writes that 'the sum of the experimental phenomena that a proposition implies makes up its entire bearing upon human conduct' (*CP*:5.427), he places the maxim within the context of actual practice in the concrete world of feelings, sensations, and experience.

But there is still a problem. It is generally assumed that Peirce's maxim is especially applicable to theoretical terms in the sciences and their role in scientific methods and procedures. Regarding contemporary science, however, this assumption is questionable. 'Diamonds are hard' is one thing, but 'The gravitational force inside a "black hole" is infinite' and 'Quarks come in various "colours"' are entirely another matter. What practical consequences can there be and how can they be put to the test? Or take the current notion of textuality in the humanities. Extrapolating the maxim to the most extreme form of its application imaginable, according to the new historicism and ethnography, the current state of literary criticism and theory, poststructuralist notions of psychoanalysis, and postanalytic philosophy, it is problematic to dictate that texts will have a propensity to produce 'some specified sensible result when acted upon,' since they can be acted upon – interpreted – in virtually an infinite variety of ways. These and other such examples appear to make a sham of the very idea of meaning, interpretation, and understanding, traditionally conceived. This apparent dissipation of the notion of meaning is nowhere more evident than in the work of Derrida, for whom writing, rather than speech, is the basis (if not the 'foundation') of linguistic activity. The text, in Derrida's conception, is, as mere black marks on white, meaningless. It takes on one of a plethora of possible meanings in the mind of the reader within a given contextualized act of reading, at which time the reader is free to generate her own reaction to the text as an ortho-, para-, or countertext (see

Merrell 1982). Meaning thus loses all claim to univocity. It is radically transient, flowing along with the movement of *différance* – a difference and deferral. It becomes in this sense virtually impossible to talk meaningfully about meaning, for the possibilities of meaning are endless. Any meaning whatsoever can be everywhere, anywhere, or nowhere, according to the eye of that delirious Nietzschean playmaker, the reader.

Another important point often overlooked by Peirce scholars is that the maxim cannot endow an individual sentence with proper meaning through its association with a single observational prediction. A purely existential statement makes no prediction, though one can usually be formulated from it. And even though a prediction on the basis of a hypothetical conditional may be explicitly stated, putting it to the test implies an indefinite regress of related sentences. Completion of the maxim's implications demands an ongoing holistic fabric of sentences and the sensible effect resulting from the operations on the objects to which they refer. In this sense, two distinct conceptual schemes satisfied by the same set of observational statements can be construed either as the same or different. Consequently, the domain within which the activity required by the maxim must occur cannot but remain *underdetermined.* The maxim calls for linkage between sentences and operations performed on the stuff of the world. But these linkages are not autonomous; they are relative to the entire network included within theories, institutional practices, and everyday linguistic conventions, in short, within 'language games.' They do not merely tie a word here to a meaning there and a thing somewhere else, or a sentence here to its practical consequences there, which yields some particular meaning. The task of making a word or sentence meaningful is in its ultimate extrapolation infinitely regressive.

In view of this regress, from within one network of signs 'The earth is the centre of the universe,' and from within another 'The sun is the centre,' and from within still another, 'Neither the earth nor the sun is the centre,' or conversely 'Both the earth and the sun are their own centre,' bears witness the *underdetermined* core of scientific as well as everyday practices. There is meaning, of course, but it is not that unequivocal goal of the meaningmongers of yesteryear nor that of deconstructors dictating that all meanings miss the mark. The responsible quester of *semiosic* meaning believes her goal is 'real,' though she concedes that the clearly demarcated ribbon at the end of the indeterminable race will never be snapped. This is no call for any nihilistic posture, however, for the meaning is in the striving, the fun is in the run, no more, no less.

Quite obviously, if the maxim does not entail a heuristics for determining the meaning of individual words but of sentences, and sets of sentences, the entire *semiosic* stream is somehow brought into play. Within this stream, each sentence, as well as the entire collection of which it is a part, is, and will remain indefinitely, open-ended. Consequently, the meanings of any and all statements are always subject to further specification, though final specification lies beyond the capacity of any given individual and, in fact, beyond any finite community of individuals. In this sense, meaning is *holistic*, and since it cannot be taken in one gulp, it remains indeterminate. Such a conception of *holism* might appear in line with Quine's own 'holism' (1953), sometimes dubbed the Duhem-Quine thesis. However, Quine puts forth the claimer that Peirce's brand of *holism* is less than legitimate. Peirce, and the pragmatists in general, he tells us, neither fostered nor abetted all of the five most important advances in post-Humean empiricism – for Quine the climax and glory of Western thought – which are (1) a shift of focus from ideas to words, (2) a shift from words to sentences, (3) a shift from sentences to sets of sentences, (4) abandonment of the analytic-synthetic distinction, and (5) a commitment to naturalism, or physicalism (Quine presented these five advances in a talk entitled 'The Pragmatist's Place in Empiricism' at the Symposium on Pragmatism, University of South Carolina, 1975 [see Almeder 1980:33–9, for further]). Quine's 'holism' specifies that the meaning of a statement cannot always be confirmed by any particular set of sensory experiences. Regarding scientific theories, any and all statements can be verified if the scientist is willing to exercise a fudge factor frequently enough, thus bringing about slight to drastic adjustments to the theory. Verification in one form or another will always be possible, for the truth-content of a theoretical statement, in contrast to observation statements, is dependent upon, and a function of, the presupposed truth-content of the theory as a whole. The entire conceptual scheme stands straight and tall, and if it falls, it falls as a whole.

Almeder (1983), on the other hand, defends Peirce, arguing that the pragmatic maxim does not, as Quine charges, entail a straightforward verification theory of meaning comparable to that of logical positivism, nor is it the case that Peirce is not sufficiently *holistic*. Almeder goes on to cite numerous Peirce texts to demonstrate that he was unquestionably aware that in the broadest sense meaning is *holistic*. In the first place, notwithstanding the maxim's rather cumbersome formulation, it is clearly not so much a matter of isolated concepts or words, but a criterion for the meaning of the entire range of sentences implied by a given assertion – that is, the above example, 'Diamonds are hard.' No single conditional sentence stands a chance of exhausting the meaning of the original sentence out of which it was engendered. However, the meaning of a given sentence can be at least partially specified by previous sentences that have not (yet) been lost to forgetfulness or to the trash can of the laboratory or dusty stacks in the library, and it can be partially specified by that part of the infinite range of possible sentences that may be actualizable in future contexts.

To re-evoke now-familiar assertions in this treatise, and as Peirce (*CP*:5.447) puts it, a sign 'that is in any respect objectively indeterminate (i.e. whose object is undetermined by the sign itself) is objectively *general* in so far as it extends to the interpreter the privilege of carrying its determination further.' For example, the question 'What are diamonds?' leaves to the interpreter the choice, and realization, of some of the infinite number of possible future sentences and practical trials in order to determine the nature of diamonds. On the other hand, a sign 'that is objectively indeterminate in any respect, is objectively *vague* in so far as it reserves further determination to be made in some other conceivable sign, or at least does not appoint the interpreter as its deputy in this office' (*CP*:5.447). The utterance 'A diamond would be hard' authorizes no definite interpretation, but leaves rights to future exposition to the utterer to decide under what conditions a particular diamond or collection of diamonds would prove to be hard.

Thus, the *undetermined* sign is chiefly *vague* unless by some convention it is rendered a bit more *general*, though an inevitable element of *vagueness* will always allow for a degree of *inconsistency* and *generality* for a degree of *incompleteness*, given that the sign cannot be absolutely determinate within the context of actual signifying activity. In essence, affirmative predications *generally* apply to a sentence, while negative predications *vaguely* apply to it. The interpreter can conduct a test on a diamond to demonstrate its hardness, and on so doing she boots 'Diamonds are hard' toward its completion 'in the long run' as a *generality*. In contrast, 'A diamond would be hard' implies an entire range of if-then clauses for which there is no absolute guarantee that a particular clause will be actualized at a given time and place, or whether at a particular future time and place the sentence will not be verified. In this manner, the sentence does not stand on its own, but implies an indefinite range of sentences regarding what diamonds *are not* as well as what things are *not hard*, as are diamonds (that is, 'Diamonds are harder than glass, than limestone, than sandstone, than emeralds, etc.') (recall, in this light, the Master's words on *breadth* and *depth* with respect to sign *translation*).

But actually, the question of *vagueness* and *generality* is exceedingly more complex than this simple example suggests. Reconsider Peirce's case – briefly discussed in chapter 1 – of two Englishmen who meet in a continental railway carriage. The total number of subjects that might be evoked as the focus of an amiable chat is for practical purposes indeterminate, a veritable continuum of possibilities. Supposing that one of the chaps mentions Charles the Second, the other need not ponder over which Charles the Second is meant; it is undoubtedly the English Charles the Second. However, Charles the Second was quite a different person on different days, and when referring to this same person on days far removed, the objects of reference can be well-nigh diametrically opposed (that is, Charles the Second is to an extent *underdetermined*). So specification (meaning) of the sign 'Charles the Second' is never so complete that it cannot be subject to further specification.

In this sense, unless 'Charles the Second' as a *generality* is specified further by the utterer, the interpreter is free to attempt such specification as he pleases, thus rendering the sign somewhat more determinate in his own mind. Consequently, the object of the sign uttered may be one and determinate in the mind of the utterer – though with each instantiation of the sign, and with the sign's use in reference to the object during different periods of its existence, both sign and object are something *other than* what they *were* or *will be.* Solely from within this framework is it possible to fathom Peirce's remark that 'Every sign has a single object, though this single object may be a single set or a single continuum of objects. No general description can identify an object. But the common sense of the interpreter of the sign will assure him that the object must be one of a limited collection of objects' (*CP*:5.448n). The range of possible determinations of the object of the sign 'Charles the Second' being indefinite, indeed, quasi-infinite, then, the excluded-middle principle falls by the wayside in the practical affairs of everyday-language games (hence a given predication concerning Charles the Second can be neither 'true' nor 'false,' but somewhere in between).

On the other hand, the *vague* or *indefinite* sign is a sign that the utterer has not sufficiently specified. Further determination of 'Charles the Second' depends upon future conceivable signs that may or may not be forthcoming. The utterer might generate a predicate concerning the subject's hair colour, height, mole on his left leg, number of mistresses, and so on, all of which serve further to specify the sign, though short of a virtual infinity of such predicates, the sign will never be absolutely determinate. Given Peirce's denial of the existence of absolute individuals in the above citation, it cannot determinately be stated that it is necessarily 'false' that a given predicate regarding Charles the Second can be both 'true' and 'false.' Since the predicate is destined to remain to a greater or lesser degree indeterminate (*vague*), it can, given varying space-time coordinates, be both 'true' and 'false.' Hence, the law of contradiction is not necessarily operative.

My use of the term 'interpretation' insofar as it bears on Peirce's interpretant lies close to what one does when one *translates* from one language into another. Placing this in the context of Quine's *indeterminacy of translation* and *inscrutability of reference* theses (1953), the native informant's evocation 'Gavagai!' as a *general* sign might be 'Rabbit,' 'Undetached rabbit parts,' or 'A particular space-time rabbit stage.' The conclusion is left up to the field linguist. However, not only is reference indeterminate, since there is no way of specifying absolutely the object of 'Gavagai!,' but, in addition, translating of 'Gavagai!' into English is also rendered indeterminate. As a *vague* sign, 'Gavagai!' could be further specified by the native, though with each specification, given reference inscrutibility, faithful translation can never be at hand. On the other side of the ledger, commensurate with Peirce's maxim, the proposition, 'A "gavagai" would be a rabbit if such-and-such a condition were to inhere' sets up an indefinite range of possible perceptual and conceptual grasps of the animal in question. Yet no matter what conclusion the interpreter may tentatively arrive at, changes over a given range of time may serve to tell another tale. (I use the term 'translation' here in the sense of Peirce's signs becoming other signs as signs being translated – translating themselves – into other signs. Translation in this sense brings along three-tiered baggage, as argued by Johansen [1989, 1993], following Roman Jakobson: [1] translation of signs into other signs in the same language [*intralinguistic*], [2] translation into different languages [*interlinguistic*], and [3] translation from one sign medium into another [verbal into nonverbal, indexical into iconic, etc.] [*intersemiotic*]. According to this conception, the 'semiotic object' and interpretant of a sign are known by way of their translation into other signs, which would be tantamount to a translation of Tarski's 'Schnee ist Weiss' into 'Snow is white,' of Putnam's 'XYZ' into 'H_2O,' of Goodman's 'grue' into 'green,' and so on. I must also make mention of the fact that I am not simply following Quinean *indeterminacy of translation* and *inscrutability of reference*. Peirce is not a strict extensionalist, nor is he a physicalist or behaviourist, in the Quinean mode. Neither is he a nominalist, for his 'thought-signs' as well as signs of generality, or Thirdness, are, as far as he is concerned, 'real' [Almeder 1980, Smith 1983].)

In short, Peirce's indeterminacy of meaning stems from his denial (1) of the existence of absolute individuals, (2) of the specifiability of a given individual, (3) of infallible reference, and (4) of precise translatability from sign to sign. Since no sign can enjoy a determinate connection with its 'semiotic object,' as a *general*, it is destined to remain *incomplete* in terms of its meaning for a finite community. And since it can never be fully determinate with respect to its possessing or not possessing every known property, any predication about the sign or its object will remain *vague* in the sense that it stands no chance of completely specifying a determinate set of properties. Hence it runs the risk of showing itself to be *inconsistent*, for at some future time it may have some property it does not now have, and some property it now has may pass into oblivion at some future time. Quite understandably, the meaning of any sign and any set of properties partially specifying it is always open to further specification either on the part of the utterer by way of her engendering successive thought-signs or the addressee through his ongoing interpretation of them.

In the final analysis, according to the maxim, one's conception of the effects of a particular sentence, which might conceivably have practical bearing on one's state of knowledge, conduct, personality, tastes, emotions, and propensities, is, stated bluntly, just one's conception (interpretant) of the object of the sentence (representamen). These broad implications of the maxim help account for Peirce's expenditure of considerable time and effort on such topics as God, Absolute Mind, the logic of the universe, belief, consciousness, and other such intangibles. It is safe to conclude with Almeder that even though Peirce's maxim sustains a certain form of verificationist interpretation, its adoption 'does not render meaningless statements about abstract entities ... [It] implies a concept of verification which extends beyond the view that only sentences about physical objects defined in sensory terms can be verified' (1980:21).

References

Almeder, Robert. 1980. *The Philosophy of Charles S. Peirce: A Critical Introduction.* Totowa, NJ: Rowman and Littlefield.

– 1983. 'Peirce on Meaning.' In E. Freeman, ed., *The Relevance of Charles Peirce*, 328–47. LaSalle, IL: Monist Library of Philosophers.

Arbib, Michael A., and Mary B. Hesse. 1986. *The Construction of Reality.* Cambridge: Cambridge University Press.

Arnheim, Rudolf. 1969. *Visual Thinking.* Berkeley: University of California Press.

Avni, Ora. 1990. *The Resistance of Reference: Linguistics, Philosophy, and the Literary Text.* Baltimore: Johns Hopkins University Press.

Baer, Eugen. 1988. *Medical Semiotics.* Lanham: University Press of America.

Bakhtin, Mikhail. 1981. *The Dialogic Imagination.* Austin: University of Texas Press.

– 1984. *Problems of Dostoevsky's Poetics.* Minneapolis: University of Minnesota Press.

Bakhtin, Mikhail (V.N. Voloshinov). 1973. *Marxism and the Philosophy of Language.* Trans. L. Matejka and I.R. Titunik. New York: Seminar Press.

Bateson, Gregory. 1972. *Steps to an Ecology of Mind.* New York: Chandler.

Baudrillard, Jean. 1981. *For a Critique of the Political Economy of the Sign.* Trans. C. Levin. St Louis: Telos.

– 1983a. *Simulations.* New York: Semiotext(e).

– 1983b. *In the Shadow of the Silent Majorities.* Trans. P. Foss, J. Johnston, and P. Patton. New York: Semiotext(e).

Bazerman, Charles. 1988. *Shaping Written Knowledge.* Madison: University of Wisconsin Press.

Beck, J. 1972. *Surface Color Perception.* Ithaca: Cornell University Press.

Beckett, Samuel. 1955. *How It Is.* New York: Grove.

Benardete, José A. 1964. *Infinity: An Essay in Metaphysics.* Oxford: Clarendon Press.

Berlin, B., and P. Kay. 1969. *Basic Color Terms: Their Universality and Evolution.* Berkeley: University of California Press.

Bernstein, Richard J. 1983. *Beyond Objectivity and Relativism: Science, Hermeneutics, and Praxis*. Philadelphia: University of Pennsylvania Press.
– 1986. *Philosophical Profiles: Essays in a Pragmatic Mode*. Pittsburgh: University of Pennsylvania Press.
Black, Max. 1937. 'Vagueness, an Exercise in Logical Analysis.' *Philosophy of Science* 6, 427–55.
– 1962. *Models and Metaphors*. Ithaca: Cornell University Press.
Blackburn, Simon. 1984. *Spreading the Word: Groundings in the Philosophy of Language*. Oxford: Clarendon Press.
Bloor, David. 1976. *Knowledge and Social Imagery*. London: Routledge and Kegan Paul.
– 1983. *Wittgenstein: A Social Theory of Knowledge*. New York: Columbia University Press.
Bogue, Ronald. 1989. *Deleuze and Guattari*. London: Routledge.
Bohm, David. 1980. *Wholeness and the Implicate Order*. London: Routledge and Kegan Paul.
– 1986. 'Time and the Implicate Order, and Pre-Space.' In D.R. Griffin, ed., *Physics and the Ultimate Significance of Time: Bohm, Prigogine, and Process Philosophy*, 177–208. Albany: State University of New York Press.
Bohman, James F. 1991. 'Holism without Skepticism: Contextualism and the Limits of Interpretation.' In D.R. Hiley, J.F. Bohman and R. Schusterman, eds., *The Interpretive Turn: Philosophy, Science, Culture*, 129–54. Ithaca: Cornell University Press.
Bohr, Niels. 1958. *Atomic Physics and Human Knowledge*. New York: John Wiley.
Boler, John P. 1964. 'Habits of Thought.' In E.C. Moore and R.S. Robin, eds., *Studies in the Philosophy of Charles Sanders Peirce*, 382–400. Amherst: University of Massachusetts Press.
Bolzano, Bernard. 1950. *Paradoxes of the Infinite*. Trans. F. Prihonsky. London: Routledge and Kegan Paul.
Booth, Wayne C. 1982. 'The Company We Keep: Self-Making in Imaginative Art.' *Daedalus* 111, 33–60.
Borges, Jorge Luis. 1962. *Labyrinths, Selected Short Stories and Other Writings*. Ed. D.A. Yates and J.E. Irby. New York: New Directions.
– 1964. *Other Inquisitions, 1937–52*. Trans. R.L.C. Simms. Austin: University of Texas Press.
Bourdieu, Pierre. 1987. *Outline of a Theory of Practice*. Trans. R. Nice. Cambridge: Cambridge University Press.
– 1990. *The Logic of Practice*. Trans. R. Nice. Oxford: Polity Press.
Brentano, Franz Clemens. 1973. *Psychology from an Empirical Standpoint*. Trans. A.C. Rencorello, D.B. Terrell, and L.L. McAlister. London: Routledge and Kegan Paul.
Brock, Jarrett E. 1975. 'Peirce's Concept of Semiotic.' *Semiotica* 14 (2), 121–41.
– 1979. 'Principle Themes in Peirce's Logic of Vagueness.' In J.E. Brock et al., eds., *Peirce Studies I*, 41–50. Lubbock, TX: Institute for Studies in Pragmaticism.

Bronowski, Jacob. 1978. *The Origins of Knowledge and Imagination.* New Haven: Yale University Press.

Brown, Harold. 1979. *Perception, Theory, and Committment.* Chicago: University of Chicago Press.

Brown, James Robert. 1991. *The Laboratory of the Mind: Thought Experiments in the Natural Sciences.* London: Routledge.

Brown, Richard Harvey. 1987. *Society as Text: Essays on Rhetoric, Reason and Reality.* Chicago: University of Chicago Press.

Bruner, Jerome S. 1956. *A Study of Thinking.* New York: Wiley.

– 1986. *Actual Minds, Possible Worlds.* Cambridge: Harvard University Press.

– 1987. *Making Sense: The Child's Construction of the World.* London: Methuen.

Burks, Arthur W. 1980. 'Man: Sign or Algorithm? A Rhetorical Analysis of Peirce's Semiotics.' *Transactions of the Charles S. Peirce Society* 16 (4), 279–92.

Capek, Milic. 1961. *The Philosophical Impact of Contemporary Physics.* New York: American Books.

Carnap, Rudolf. 1942. *Introduction to Semantics.* Cambridge: MIT.

– 1947. *Meaning and Necessity.* Chicago: University of Chicago Press.

Cartwright, Nancy. 1983. *How the Laws of Physics Lie.* Oxford: Clarendon Press.

Castaneda, Hector-Neri. 1979. 'Fiction and Reality: Their Fundamental Connections.' *Poetics* 8 (1/2), 31–62.

Certeau, Michel de. 1984. *The Practice of Everyday Life.* Berkeley: University of California Press.

Chew, Geoffrey F. 1968. 'Bootstrap: A Scientific Idea?' *Science* 161, 762–5.

Chisholm, Roderick M. 1952. 'Fallibilism and Belief.' In P.P. Wiener and F.H. Young, eds., *Studies in the Philosophy of Charles Sanders Peirce,* 93–120. Cambridge: Harvard University Press.

– 1967. 'Meinong, Alexius.' In P. Edwards, ed., *The Encyclopedia of Philosophy,* 5:261–3. London: Macmillan.

– 1973. 'Beyond Being and Nonbeing.' *Philosophical Studies* 24, 245–57.

– 1982. *Brentano and Meinong Studies.* Atlantic Highlands, NJ: Humanities Press.

Clifford, James, and George E. Marcus, eds. 1986. *Writing Culture: The Poetics and Politics of Ethnography.* Berkeley: University of California Press.

Colapietro, Vincent. 1989. *Peirce's Approach to the Self: A Semiotic Perspective on Human Subjectivity.* Albany: State University of New York Press.

Costa, Newton C.A. da. 1974. 'On the Theory of Inconsistent Formal Systems.' *Notre Dame Journal of Formal Logic* 15, 497–510.

Culler, Jonathan. 1992. 'In Defense of Overinterpretation.' In S. Collini, ed., *Interpretation and Overinterpretation,* 109–23. Cambridge: Cambridge University Press.

Davidson, Donald. 1973. 'In Defense of Convention T.' In H. Leblanc, ed., *Truth, Syntax and Modality,* 76–86. Amsterdam: North-Holland.

– 1980. 'Realism Without Reference.' In M. Platts, ed., *Reference, Truth and Reality*, 131–40. London: Routledge and Kegan Paul.

– 1984. *Inquiries into Truth and Interpretation*. Oxford: Clarendon Press.

– 1986) 'A Nice Derangement of Epitaphs.' In E. LePore, ed., *Truth and Interpretation: Perspectives on the Philosophy of Donald Davidson*, 433–46. London: Basil Blackwell.

Deely, John. 1990. *Basics in Semiotics*. Bloomington: Indiana University Press.

– 1993. *The Human Use of Signs*. Totowa, NJ: Rowman and Littlefield.

Deleuze, Gilles, 1994. 'He Stuttered.' In C.V. Boundas and D. Olkowski, eds., *Gilles Deleuze, and the Theater of Philosophy*, 23–9. London: Routledge.

Deleuze, Gilles, and Félix Guattari. 1983. *Anti-Oedipus: Capitalism and Schizophrenia, I.* Minneapolis: University of Minnesota Press.

– 1987. *A Thousand Plateaus: Capitalism and Schizophrenia, II.* Trans. B. Massumi. Minneapolis: University of Minnesota Press.

DeLong, Howard. 1970. *A Profile of Mathematical Logic*. New York: Addison Wesley.

Dennett, Daniel. 1988. 'Quining Qualia.' In A.J. Marcel and E. Bisiach, eds., *Consciousness in Contemporary Science*, 241–53. Oxford: Oxford University Press.

Derrida, Jacques. 1973. *Speech and Phenomena, And Other Essays on Husserl's Theory of Signs.* Trans. D.B. Allison. Evanston: Northwestern University Press.

– 1974a. *Of Grammatology*. Trans. G.C. Spivak. Baltimore: Johns Hopkins University Press.

– 1974b. 'White Mythology: Metaphor in the Text of Philosophy.' *New Literary History* 6 (1), 5–74.

– 1981. *Positions*. Chicago: University of Chicago Press.

– 1982. *Margins of Philosophy*. Trans. A. Bass. Chicago: University of Chicago Press.

Donnelan, Keith. 1966. 'Reference and Definite Descriptions.' *Philosophical Review* 75, 281–304.

– 1972. 'Proper Names and Identifying Descriptions.' In D. Davidson and G. Harman, eds., *Semantics of Natural Language*, 356–79. Dordrecht, Holland: D. Reidel.

– 1974. 'Speaking of Nothing.' *Philosophical Review* 83, 3–31.

Dozoretz, Jerry. 1979. 'The Internally Real, the Fictitious, and the Indubitable.' In J.E. Brock, et al., eds., *Peirce Studies, 1*, 77–87. Lubbock, TX: Institute for Studies in Pragmaticism.

Dreyfus, Herbert, and Paul Rabinow. 1982. *Michel Foucault: Beyond Structuralism and Hermeneutics*. Chicago: University of Chicago Press.

Duhem, Pierre. 1914. *La théorie physique, son objet, sa structure*. 2nd ed. Paris: Riviére.

– 1954. *The Aim and Structure of Physical Theory*. Trans. P.P. Wiener. Princeton: Princeton University Press.

Dummett, Michael. 1972. *Frege: Philosophy of Language*. New York: Harper and Row.

– 1978. 'Can Analytic Philosophy Be Systematic, and Ought It Be?' In *Truth and Other Enigmas*, 437–58. London: Duckworth.

– 1979. 'Comments on Putnam's "Reference and Understanding."' In A. Margalit, ed., *Meaning and Use*, 218–25. Dordrecht, Holland: D. Reidel.

Eco, Umberto. 1976. *A Theory of Semiotics*. Bloomington: Indiana University Press.

– 1983. 'Horns, Hooves, Insteps: Some Hypotheses on Three Types of Abduction.' In T. Sebeok and U. Eco, eds., *The Sign of Three: Dupin, Holmes, Peirce*, 198–220. Bloomington: Indiana University Press.

– 1984. *Semiotics and the Philosophy of Language*. Bloomington: Indiana University Press.

– 1990. *The Limits of Interpretation*. Bloomington: Indiana University Press.

– 1992. 'Overinterpreting Texts.' In S. Collini, ed., *Interpretation and Overinterpretation*, 45–66. Cambridge: Cambridge University Press.

Eddington, Arthur S. 1958. *The Nature of the Physical World*. Ann Arbor: Michigan University Press.

Ehrenzweig, Anton. 1967. *The Hidden Order of Art*. Berkeley: University of California Press.

Einstein, Albert. 1949a. 'Autobiographical Notes.' In P.A. Schilpp, ed., *Albert Einstein: Philosopher-Scientist*, 2–94. LaSalle, IL: Open Court.

– 1949b. 'Reply to Criticism.' In *Albert Einstein: Philosopher-Scientist*, 665–88.

Eisele, Carolyn. 1979. *Studies in the Scientific and Mathematical Philosophy of Charles S. Peirce*. The Hague: Mouton.

Eisenstein, Elizabeth. 1979. *The Printing Press as an Agent of Change*. Cambridge: Cambridge University Press.

Engel-Tiercelin, Claudine. 1992. 'Vagueness and the Unity of C.S. Peirce's Realism.' *Transactions of the C.S. Peirce Society* 28 (1), 51–82.

Evans-Pritchard, E.E. 1962. *Social Anthropology and Other Essays*. Glencoe, IL: Free Press.

Evnine, Simon. 1991. *Donald Davidson*. Stanford: Stanford University Press.

Feyerabend, Paul K. 1975. *Against Method*. London: NLB.

Findlay, J.N. 1963. *Meinong's Theory of Objects and Values*. Oxford: Clarendon Press.

Fisch, Max H. 1986. *Peirce, Semeiotic, and Pragmatism*. Bloomington: Indiana University Press.

Fish, Stanley. 1970. 'Let in the Reader: Affective Stylistics.' *New Literary History* 2, 123–62.

– 1976. 'Interpreting the Variorum.' *Critical Inquiry* 2, 465–85.

Fodor, Jerry, and Ernest Lepore. 1992. *Holism: A Shopper's Guide*. Oxford: Blackwell.

Foerster, Heinz von. 1973. 'On Constructing a Reality.' In N. Prieser, ed., *Environmental Design Research*, 2:286–98. Stroudsbuer, VA: Dowden, Hutchinson and Ross.

Føllesdal, D. 1975. 'Meaning and Experience.' In S. Guttenplan, ed., *Mind and Language*, 25–44. Oxford: Clarendon Press.

Folse, Henry J. 1985. *The Philosophy of Niels Bohr: The Framework of Complementarity*. Amsterdam: North Holland.

Foucault, Michel. 1970. *The Order of Things*. New York: Pantheon.

Freeman, Eugene. 1983. 'C.S. Peirce and Objectivity in Philosophy.' In E. Freeman, ed., *The Relevance of Charles Peirce*, 59–79. LaSalle, IL: Monist Library of Philosophers.

Frege, Gottlob. 1953. *The Foundations of Arithmetic: A Logico-Mathematical Inquiry into the Concept of Number.* Trans. J.L. Austin. Oxford: Blackwell.

– 1970. 'On Sense and Reference.' In P. Geach and M. Black, eds., *Translations from the Philosophical Writings of Gottlob Frege*, 56–78. Oxford: Basil Blackwell.

– 1974. 'The Thought: A Logical Inquiry.' In J.M.E. Moravasik, ed., *Logic and Philosophy for Linguists*, 279–98. The Hague: Mouton.

– 1979. *Posthumous Writings.* Ed. H. Hermes, F. Kambartel, and F. Kaulbach; trans. P. Long and R. White. Oxford: Basil Blackwell.

Fuhrmann, Gy. 1991. 'Note on the Integration of Prototype Theory and Fuzzy-Set Theory.' *Synthese* 86, 1–27.

Gadamer, Hans-Georg. 1975. *Truth and Method.* New York: Crossroads.

Gädhe, Ulrich, and Wolfgang Stegmüller. 1986. 'An Argument in Favor of the Quine-Duhem Thesis: From the Structuralist Point of View.' In L.E. Hahn and P.A. Schilpp, eds., *The Philosophy of W.V. Quine*, 117–36. LaSalle, IL: Open Court.

Galileo Galilei. 1954. *Dialogues Concerning Two New Sciences.* Trans. H. Crew and A. de Salvio. New York: Dover.

Gärdenfors, Peter. 1994. 'Induction, Conceptual Spaces, and AI.' In D. Stalker, ed., *Grue! The New Riddle of Induction*, 117–34. LaSalle, IL: Open Court.

Gardner, Howard. 1983. *Frames of Mind: The Theory of Multiple Intelligences.* New York: Basic Books.

Geertz, Clifford. 1983. *Local Knowledge: Further Essays in Interpretive Anthropology.* New York: Basic Books.

Gellner, Ernest. 1985. *Relativism and the Social Sciences.* Cambridge: Cambridge University Press.

Gentry, George. 1952. 'Habit and the Logical Interpretant.' In P.P. Wiener and F.H. Young, eds., *Studies in the Philosophy of Charles Sanders Peirce*, 75–92. Cambridge: Harvard University Press.

Gibson, Roger F., Jr. 1982. *The Philosophy of W.V. Quine: An Expository Essay.* Tampa: University Presses of Florida.

– 1986. 'Translation, Physics, and Facts of the Matter.' In L.E. Hahn and P.A. Schilpp, eds., *The Philosophy of W.V. Quine*, 139–54. LaSalle, IL: Open Court.

– 1988. *Enlightened Empiricism: An Examination of W.V. Quine's Theory of Knowledge.* Tampa: University Presses of Florida.

Gilchrist, Alan and Irvin Rock. 1981. 'Rational Processes in Perception.' In *Proceedings of the Third Annual Conference of the Cognitive Science Society*, 50–6. Berkeley: Cognitive Science Society.

Gödel, Kurt. 1964. 'What is Cantor's Continuum Problem?' In P. Benacerraf and H. Putnam, eds., *Philosophy of Mathematics*, 258–73. Englewood Cliffs, NJ: Prentice-Hall.

Goguen, J.A. 1969. 'The Logic of Inexact Concepts.' *Synthese* 19, 325–73.
Gombrich, Ernst H. 1960. *Art and Illusion.* Princeton: Princeton University Press.
Goodman, Nelson. 1965. *Fact, Fiction and Forecast.* 2nd ed. Indianapolis: Bobbs-Merrill.
– 1976. 'Seven Strictures on Similarity.' In *Problems and Projects*, 437–47. Indianapolis: Bobbs-Merrill.
– 1978. *Ways of Worldmaking.* Indianapolis: Hackett.
– 1984. 'Notes on the Well-Made World.' *Partisan Review* 51, 276–88.
Goudge, Thomas A. 1952. 'Peirce's Theory of Abstraction.' In P.P. Wiener and F.H. Young, eds., *Studies in the Philosophy of Charles Sanders Peirce*, 121–32. Cambridge: Harvard University Press.
Gregory, Bruce. 1988. *Inventing Reality: Physics as Language.* New York: John Wiley.
Gregory, Richard L. 1966. *Eye and Brain.* New York: McGraw-Hill.
– 1970. *The Intelligent Eye.* New York: McGraw-Hill.
– 1981. *Mind in Science: A History of Explanations in Pyschology and Physics.* Cambridge: Cambridge University Press.
Gross, Alan G. 1990. *The Rhetoric of Science.* Cambridge: Harvard University Press.
Haack, Susan. 1993. 'Philosophy/philosophy, an Untenable Dualism.' *Transactions of the Charles S. Peirce Society* 29 (3), 411–26.
Hacking, Ian. 1982. 'Language, Truth and Reason.' In M. Hollis and S. Lukes, eds., *Rationalism and Relativism*, 48–66. Cambridge: MIT.
– 1983. *Representing and Intervening: Introductory Topics in the Philosophy of Natural Science.* Cambridge: Cambridge University Press.
– 1989. 'The Parody of Conversation.' In E. LePore, ed., *Truth and Interpretation: Perspectives on the Philosophy of Donald Davidson*, 447–58. Oxford: Basil Blackwell.
– 1990. *The Taming of Chance.* Cambridge: Cambridge University Press.
– 1993. 'On Kripke's and Goodman's Uses of "Grue."' *Philosophy* 68, 269–95.
– 1994. 'Entrenchment.' In D. Stalker, ed., *Grue! The New Riddle of Induction*, 193–223. LaSalle, IL: Open Court.
Hanson, Norwood R. 1958. *Patterns of Discovery.* Cambridge: Cambridge University Press.
– 1969. *Perception and Discovery.* San Francisco: Freeman, Cooper.
Harré, Rom. 1972. *The Principles of Scientific Thinking.* New York: Macmillan.
Harris, James F. 1992. *Against Relativism: A Philosophical Defense of Method.* LaSalle, IL: Open Court.
Hartshorne, Charles. 1970. *Creative Synthesis and Philosophic Method.* LaSalle, IL: Open Court.
Hausman, Carl R. 1993. *Charles S. Peirce's Philosophy.* Cambridge: Cambridge University Press.
Heelan, Patrick. 1983. *Space-Perception and the Philosophy of Science.* Berkeley: University of California Press.

Heidegger, Martin. 1969. *Identity and Difference.* New York: Harper and Row.
– 1971. *On the Way to Language.* Trans. P.D. Hertz. New York: Harper and Row.
Heijenoort, Jean van. 1967. *From Frege to Gödel: A Source Book on Mathematical Logic.* Cambridge: Harvard University Press.
Heisenberg, Werner. 1958. *Physics and Philosophy.* New York: Harper and Row.
– 1971. *Physics and Beyond.* New York: Harper and Row.
Hempel, Carl G. 1945. 'Studies in the Logic of Confirmation.' *Mind* 54, 1–26, 97–121.
– 1965. *Aspects of Scientific Explanation.* New York: Free Press.
Henderson, David K. 1987. 'The Principle of Charity and the Problem of Irrationality (Translation and the Problem of Irrationality).' *Synthese* 73, 225–52.
Hesse, Mary. 1966. *Models and Analogies in Science.* Notre Dame: University of Notre Dame Press.
– 1969. 'Ramifications of "Grue."' *British Journal of the Philosophy of Science* 20, 13–25.
– 1972. 'Duhem, Quine and the New Empiricism.' In H. Morick, ed., *Challenges to Empiricism*, 208–28. Belmont, CA: Wadsworth.
– 1980. *Revolutions and Reconstructions in the Philosophy of Science.* Bloomington: Indiana University Press.
Heyting, Arend. 1964. 'The Intuitionist Foundations of Mathematics.' In P. Benacerraf and H. Putnam, eds., *Philosophy of Mathematics*, 42–9. Cambridge: Cambridge University Press.
Hiley, D.R., et al., eds. 1991. *The Interpretive Turn: Philosophy, Science, Culture.* Ithaca: Cornell University Press.
Hirsch, E.D. Jr. 1967. *Validity in Interpretation.* New Haven: Yale University Press.
Hofstadter, Douglas R. 1979. *Gödel, Escher, Bach: An Eternal Golden Braid.* New York: Basic Books.
Holquist, Michael. 1990. *Dialogism: Bakhtin and His World.* London: Routledge.
Honner, John. 1987. *The Description of Nature: Niels Bohr and the Philosophy of Quantum Physics.* Oxford: Clarendon Press.
Hookway, Christopher. 1985. *Peirce.* London: Routledge and Kegan Paul.
Howell, Robert. 1979. 'Fictional Objects: How They Are and How They Aren't.' *Poetics* 8 (1/2), 129–77.
Hume, David. 1964. *A Treatise of Human Nature.* Ed. L.A. Selby-Bigge. Oxford: Clarendon Press.
Hutten, Ernest H. 1962. *The Origins of Science: An Inquiry into the Foundations of Western Thought.* London: George Allen and Unwin.
Hylton, Peter. 1992. 'The Vicious Circle Principle: Comments on Philippe de Rouilhan.' *Philosophical Studies* 65, 183–92.
James, William. 1950. *The Principles of Psychology.* 2 vols. New York: Dover.
Jameson, Fredric. 1984. 'Postmodernism, Or, The Cultural Logic of Late Capitalism.' *New Left Review* 146, 59–92.

Jammer, Max. 1962. *Concepts of Force.* New York: Harper and Row.

Jenny, Hans. 1967. *Cymatics: The Structural Dynamics of Waves and Vibrations.* Basel: Basilius.

Johansen, Jørgen Dines. 1989. 'Semiotics of Rhetoric: The Consumption of Fantasy.' In T.A. Sebeok and J. Umiker-Sebeok, eds., *The Semiotic Web 1988*, 301–32. Berlin: Mouton de Gruyter.

– 1993. *Dialogic Semiosis.* Bloomington: Indiana University Press.

Johansson, Gunnar. 1950. *Configurations in Event Perception.* Uppsala: Almkvist and Viksell.

Johnson, Mark. 1987. *The Body in the Mind: The Bodily Basis of Meaning, Imagination, and Reason.* Chicago: University of Chicago Press.

Katz, J.J., and J.A. Fodor. 1963. 'The Structure of a Semantic Theory.' *Language* 39, 170–210.

Kauffman, Louis H., and Francisco J. Varela. 1980. 'Form Dynamics.' *Journal of Social Biological Structure* 3, 171–216.

Kellner, Douglas. 1989. *Jean Baudrillard: From Marxism to Post-Modernism and Beyond.* Stanford: Stanford University Press.

Kline, Morris. 1980. *Mathematics: The Loss of Certainty.* Oxford: Oxford University Press.

Koestler, Arthur. 1963. *The Sleepwalkers: A History of Man's Changing Vision of the Universe.* New York: Grosset and Dunlap.

Koethe, John. 1992. 'And They Ain't Outside the Head Either.' *Synthese* 90, 27–53.

Kolers, Paul. 1972. *Aspects of Motion Perception.* Oxford: Pergamon Press.

Kosko, Bart. 1993. *Fuzzy Thinking.* New York: Hyperion.

Krausz, Michael, ed. 1989. *Relativism: Interpretation and Confrontation.* Notre Dame: Notre Dame University Press.

Kripke, Saul. 1972. 'Naming and Necessity.' In D. Davidson and G. Harman, eds., *Semantics of Natural Language*, 253–355. Dordrecht, Holland: D. Reidel.

– 1977. 'Speaker Reference and Semantic Reference.' *Midwest Studies in Philosophy* 2, 255–76.

– 1980. *Naming and Necessity.* Oxford: Blackwell.

– 1982. *Wittgenstein on Rules and Private Language.* Cambridge: Harvard University Press.

Kuhn, Thomas S. 1970. *The Structure of Scientific Revolutions.* Chicago: University of Chicago Press.

– 1977. *The Essential Tension.* Chicago: University of Chicago Press.

Lacan, Jacques. 1977. *The Four Fundamental Concepts of Psycho-Analysis.* Trans. A. Sheridan. New York: W.W. Norton.

LaCapra, Dominick. 1985. *History and Criticism.* Ithaca: Cornell University Press.

Lakoff, George. 1972. 'Hedges: A Study of Meaning Criteria and the Logic of Fuzzy Concepts.' In *Papers from the Eighth Regional Meeting, Chicago Linguistic Society*, 193–228. Chicago: Chicago Linguistic Society.

– 1987. *Women, Fire, and Dangerous Things: What Categories Reveal about the Mind.* Chicago: University of Chicago Press.

Lakoff, George, and Mark Johnson. 1980. *Metaphors We Live By*. Chicago: University of Chicago Press.

Lamont, Rosette. 1970. 'Beckett's Metaphysics of Choiceless Awareness.' In M.J. Friedman, ed., *Samuel Beckett Now*, 199–218. Chicago: University of Chicago Press.

Land, E. 1959. 'Experiments in Color Vision.' *Scientific American* 200 (5), 84–99.

– 1964. 'The Retinex.' *American Scientist* 52, 247–64.

– 1977. 'The Retinex Theory of Color Vision.' *Scientific American* 237 (6), 108–28.

Land, E., and J.J. McCann. 1971. 'Lightness and Retinex Theory.' *Journal of the Optical Society of America* 61, 1–11.

Landauer, Rolf. 1988. 'Computation and Physics: Wheeler's Meaning Circuit?' In W.H. Zurek, A. van der Merwe, and W.A. Miller, eds., *Between Quantum and Cosmos: Studies and Essays in Honor of John Archibald Wheeler*, 568–81. Princeton: Princeton University Press.

Latour, Bruno. 1987. *Science in Action.* Cambridge: Harvard University Press.

Latour, Bruno and Steve Woolgar. 1979. *Laboratory Life: The Social Construction of Scientific Facts.* Beverly Hills: Sage.

Lecercle, Jean-Jacques. 1985. *Philosophy Through the Looking-Glass: Language, Nonsense, Desire.* LaSalle, IL: Open Court.

– 1990. *The Violence of Language.* London: Routledge.

Lee, Dorothy. 1959. *Freedom and Culture.* Englewood Cliffs, NJ: Prentice-Hall.

Lehmann, Hugh. 1979. *Introduction to the Philosophy of Mathematics.* Totowa, NJ: Rowman and Littlefield.

Lévi-Strauss, Claude. 1963. *Structural Anthropology.* Trans. C. Jacobson and B.G. Schoepf. New York: Doubleday.

Lewis, David. 1984. 'Putnam's Paradox.' *Australian Journal of Philosophy* 62 (3), 221–36.

Lewis, Thomas E. 1987. 'The Referential Act.' In A. Whiteside and M. Issacharoff, eds., *On Referring in Literature*, 158–74. Bloomington: Indiana University Press.

Linsky, Leonard. 1971. *Reference and Modality.* London: Oxford University Press.

Liszka, James J. 1989. *The Semiotic of Myth.* Bloomington: Indiana University Press.

Lounsbury, Floyd. 1964. 'A Formal Account of the Crow- and Omaha-Type Kinship Terminologies.' In W.H. Goodenough, ed., *Explorations in Cultural Anthropology*, 351–94. New York: McGraw-Hill.

Lowe, B. 1977. *The Beauty of Sport: A Cross-Disciplinary Inquiry.* Englewood Cliffs, NJ: Prentice-Hall.

Löwenfeld, Viktor. 1939. *The Nature of Creative Activity.* New York: Harcourt, Brace and Co.

Lucas, J.R. 1964. 'Minds, Machines and Gödel.' In A.R. Anderson, ed., *Minds and Machines*, 43–59. Englewood Cliffs, NJ: Prentice-Hall.

Lupasco, Stéphane. 1947. *Logique et contradiction.* Paris: Presses Universitaires de France.
Lyotard, Jean-François. 1984. *The Postmodern Condition: A Report on Knowledge.* Trans. G. Bennington and B. Massumi. Minneapolis: University of Minnesota Press.
McCloskey, Donald N. 1990. 'Storytelling in Economics.' In C. Nash, ed., *Narrative in Culture: The Uses of Storytelling in the Sciences, Philosophy, and Literature*, 5–22. London: Routledge.
McDowell, John. 1993. 'Wittgenstein on Following a Rule.' In A.W. Moore, ed., *Meaning and Reference*, 257–93. Oxford: Oxford University Press.
McLuhan, Marshall. 1964. *Understanding Media: The Extensions of Man.* New York: McGraw-Hill.
McLure, Roger. 1990. 'Why Words Have to Be Vague.' In S.L. Tsohatzidis, ed., *Meanings and Prototypes: Studies in Linguistic Categorization*, 488–520. London: Routledge.
McTaggart, J.M.E. 1927. *The Nature of Existence*, Vol. 2. Cambridge: Cambridge University Press.
Malachowski, Alan (ed.). 1990. *Reading Rorty*. Oxford: Basil Blackwell.
Malcolm, Norman. 1959. *Dreaming*. London: Routledge and Kegan Paul.
Malpas, J.E. 1992. *Donald Davidson and the Mirror of Meaning*. Cambridge: Cambridge University Press.
Marcus, George E. 1980. 'Rhetoric and the Ethnographic Genre in Anthropological Research.' *Current Anthropology* 21 (4), 507–10.
Marcus, George E., and Dick Cushman. 1982. 'Ethnographies as Texts.' *Annual Review of Anthropology II*, 25–69.
Marcus, George E. and Michael M.J. Fischer, eds. 1986. *Anthropology as Cultural Critique: An Experimental Moment in the Human Sciences*. Chicago: University of Chicago Press.
Margolis, Joseph. 1986. *Pragmatism without Foundations: Reconciling Realism and Relativism.* Oxford: Basil Blackwell.
– 1989. *Texts Without Referents: Reconciling Science and Narrative.* Oxford: Basil Blackwell.
– 1991. *The Truth about Relativism.* Oxford: Basil Blackwell.
Maturana, Humberto, and Francisco J. Varela. 1980. *Autopoiesis and Cognition: The Realization of the Living.* Dordrecht, Holland: D. Reidel.
– 1987. *The Tree of Knowledge: The Biological Roots of Human Understanding.* Boston: Shambhala.
Medin, D.L., and L.W. Barsalou. 1987. 'Categorization Processes and Categorical Perception.' In S. Harnad, ed., *Categorical Perception*, 455–90. Cambridge: Cambridge University Press.
Melhuish, George. 1967. *The Paradoxical Nature of Reality*. Bristol: St Vincent's Press.
Merleau-Ponty, Maurice. 1962. *Phenomenology of Perception.* London: Routledge and Kegan Paul.
– 1964. *The Primacy of Perception.* Evanston: Northwestern University Press.
– 1973. *The Prose of the World.* Evanston: Northwestern University Press.

Merrell, Floyd. 1982. *Semiotic Foundations: Steps Toward an Epistemology of Written Texts.* Bloomington: Indiana University Press.
– 1985. *Deconstruction Reframed.* West Lafayette: Purdue University Press.
– 1991. *Signs Becoming Signs: Our Perfusive, Pervasive Universe.* Bloomington: Indiana University Press.
– 1992. *Sign, Textuality, World.* Bloomington: Indiana University Press.
– 1995a. *Semiosis in the Postmodern Age.* West Lafayette: Purdue University Press.
– 1995b. *Peirce's Semiotics Now: A Primer.* Toronto: Canadian Scholars Press.
– 1996. *Signs Grow: Semiosis and Life Processes.* Toronto: University of Toronto Press.
Michael, Emily. 1975. 'Peirce's Paradoxical Solution to the Liar's Paradox.' *Notre Dame Journal of Symbolic Logic* 16 (3), 369–74.
Miller, Arthur I. 1986. *Imagery in Scientific Thought.* Cambridge: MIT.
Moore, A.W. 1990. *The Infinite.* New York: Routledge.
Morris, Charles. 1938. *Foundations of the Theory of Signs.* Chicago: University of Chicago Press.
Mulhall, Stephen. 1989. 'No Smoke Without Fire: The Meaning of Grue.' *The Philosophical Quarterly* 39, 166–89.
Munz, Peter. 1987. 'Philosophy and the Mirror of Rorty.' In G. Radnitzky and W.W. Bartley III, eds., *Evolutionary Epistemology, Rationality, and the Sociology of Knowledge,* 345–98. LaSalle, IL: Open Court.
Murdoch, Dugald. 1987. *Niels Bohr's Philosophy of Physics.* Cambridge: Cambridge University Press.
Murphey, Murray G. 1961. *The Development of Peirce's Philosophy.* Cambridge: Harvard University Press.
Murti, T.R.V. 1955. *The Central Philosophy of Buddhism.* London: George Allen and Unwin.
Nadin, Mihai. 1982. 'Consistency, Completeness and the Meaning of Sign Theories.' *American Journal of Semiotics* 1 (3), 79–98.
– 1983. 'The Logic of Vagueness and the Category of Synechism.' In E. Freeman, ed., *The Relevance of Charles Peirce,* 154–66. LaSalle, IL: Monist Library of Philosophy.
Nagel, Thomas. 1986. *The View from Nowhere.* London: Oxford University Press.
Nehemas, Alexander. 1985. *Nietzsche: Life as Literature.* Cambridge: Harvard University Press.
Nesher, Dan. 1983. 'A Pragmatic Theory of Meaning: A Note on Peirce's "Last" Formulation of the Pragmatic Maxim and Its Interpretation.' *Semiotica* 44 (3/4), 203–57.
Nietzsche, Friedrich. 1954. 'On Truth and Lies in the Extra-Moral Sense.' In W. Kaufmann, ed., *The Portable Nietzsche,* 42–7. New York: Viking.
– 1968. *The Will to Power.* New York: Vintage.

– 1974. *The Gay Science*. Trans. W. Kaufmann. New York: Random House.
Nishitani, Keije. 1982. *Religion and Nothingness*. Trans. J. Van Bragt. Berkeley: University of California Press.
Ogden, C.K., and I.A. Richards. 1923. *The Meaning of Meaning*. New York: Harcourt, Brace, and World.
Ong, Walter J. 1967. *The Presence of the Word*. New Haven: Yale University Press.
Parsons, Terence. 1974. 'A Prolegomena to Meinongian Semantics.' *Journal of Philosophy* 61, 561–80.
– 1975. 'A Meinongian Analysis of Fictional Objects.' *Grazer Philosophische Studien 1*, 73–86.
– 1980. *Nonexistent Objects*. New Haven: Yale University Press.
Paulos, John Allen. 1985. *I Think, Therefore I Laugh*. New York: Columbia University Press.
Pavel, Thomas. 1986. *Fictional Worlds*. Cambridge: Harvard University Press.
Pazukhin, Rostislav. 1992. 'Professor Tarski, "The Liar", and the True.' *Semiotica* 91 (3/4), 301–17.
Pefanis, Julian. 1991. *Heterology and the Postmodern: Bataille, Baudrillard, and Lyotard*. Durham: Duke University Press.
Peirce, Charles Sanders. 1931–5. *Collected Papers of Charles Sanders Peirce*. Vols. 1–6. Ed. C. Hartshorne and P. Weiss. Cambridge: Harvard University Press (reference to Peirce's papers will be designated *CP*).
– 1958. *Collected Papers of Charles Sanders Peirce*. Vols. 7–8. Ed. A.W. Burks. Cambridge: Harvard University Press.
– 1976. *The New Elements of Mathematics by Charles S. Peirce*. 4 vols. Ed. C. Eisele. The Hague: Mouton (reference to these volumes will be designated *NE*).
– 1982–6). *Writings of Charles Sanders Peirce: A Chronological Edition*. Vols. 1–4. Ed. M. Fisch. Bloomington: Indiana University Press (reference to the *Writings* will be designated *W*).
– MS: refers to Peirce's unpublished manuscripts (for catalogue and page numbers, see Robin 1967).
Penrose, Roger. 1989. *The New Emperor's Mind: Concerning Computers, Minds, and the Laws of Physics*. Oxford: Oxford University Press.
Petersen, Aage. 1985. 'The Philosophy of Niels Bohr.' In A. French and P. Kennedy, eds., *Niels Bohr, A Centenary Volume*, 299–310. Cambridge: Harvard University Press.
Phillips, Derek C. 1977. *Wittgenstein and Scientific Knowledge: A Sociological Perspective*. Totowa, NJ: Rowman and Littlefield.
Piaget, Jean. 1973. *The Child and Reality*. Trans. A. Rosin. New York: Grossman.
Poincaré, Henri. 1952. *Science and Hypothesis*. Trans. F. Maitland. New York: Dover.
Polanyi, Michael. 1958. *Personal Knowledge*. Chicago: University of Chicago Press.

Ponzio, Augusto. 1985. 'Semiotics between Peirce and Bakhtin.' *Kodikas/Code* 8 (1/2), 11–28.

– 1990. *Man as Sign: Essays on the Philosophy of Language.* Trans. S. Petrilli. Berlin: Mouton de Gruyter.

Pöppel, Ernst. 1972. 'Oscillators as Possible Basis for Time Perception.' In J.T. Fraser, F.C. Haber, and G.H. Miller, eds., *The Study of Time,* 219–41. New York: Springer-Verlag.

– 1988. *Mindworks: Time and Conscious Experience.* Boston: Harcourt, Brace, Jovanovich.

Popper, Karl R. 1959. *The Logic of Scientific Discovery.* New York: Harper and Row.

– 1963. *Conjectures and Refutations: The Growth of Scientific Knowledge.* Oxford: Oxford University Press.

– 1972. *Objective Knowledge.* Oxford: Clarendon Press.

Pradhan, Shekhar. 1993. 'The Dream of a Common Language.' In R.W. Dasenbrock, ed., *Literary Theory after Davidson,* 180–200. University Park: Pennsylvania State University Press.

Prigogine, Ilya. 1980. *From Being to Becoming: Time and Complexity in the Physical Sciences.* New York: W.H. Freeman.

Prigogine, Ilya, and Isabelle Stengers. 1984. *Order Out of Chaos: Man's New Dialogue with Nature.* New York: Bantam.

Prior, A.N. 1957. *Time and Modality.* Oxford: Clarendon Press.

Putnam, Hilary. 1973. 'Meaning and Reference.' *Journal of Philosophy* 70 (19), 699–711.

– 1975. 'The Meaning of Meaning.' In *Mind, Language, Reality.* Cambridge: Cambridge University Press.

– 1981. *Reason, Truth and History.* Cambridge: Cambridge University Press.

– 1983a. 'Vagueness and Alternative Logic.' *Erkenntnis* 19, 297–314.

– 1983b. 'Is There a Fact of the Matter about Fiction?' *Poetics Today* 4 (1), 77–82.

– 1988. *Representation and Reality.* Cambridge: MIT.

– 1990. *Realism with a Human Face.* Ed. J. Conant. Cambridge: Harvard University Press.

Quine, Willard Van Orman. 1950. *Methods of Logic.* New York: Holt, Rinehart and Winston.

– 1953. *From a Logical Point of View.* New York: Harper and Row.

– 1960. *Word and Object.* Cambridge: MIT.

– 1962. 'Paradox.' *Scientific American* 206, 84–93.

– 1969. *Ontological Relativity and Other Essays.* New York: Columbia University Press.

– 1970. 'On the Reason for Indeterminacy of Translation.' *Journal of Philosophy* 67 (6), 178–83.

– 1978. 'A Postscript on Metaphor.' *Critical Inquiry* 5 (1), 161–2.

– 1981. *Theories and Things.* Cambridge: Harvard University Press.

– 1986. 'Reply to Manley Thompson.' In S.E. Hahn and P.A. Schillp, eds., *The Philosophy of W.V. Quine*, 564–68. LaSalle, IL: Open Court.

Raffman, Diane. 1994. 'Vagueness Without Paradox.' *The Philosophical Review* 103 (1), 41–74.

Ramberg, Bjørn T. 1989. *Donald Davidson's Philosophy of Language: An Introduction*. Oxford: Basil Blackwell.

Ransdell, Joseph. 1979. 'Semiotic Objectivity.' *Semiotica* 26, 261–88.

Rescher, Nicholas. 1975. *A Theory of Possibility*. Oxford: Basil Blackwell.

– 1978. *Peirce's Philosophy of Science*. Notre Dame: University of Notre Dame Press.

Rescher, Nicholas, and Robert Brandom. 1979. *The Logic of Inconsistency: A Study of Non-Standard Possible World Semantics and Ontology*. Totowa, NJ: Rowman and Littlefield.

Révész, Geza. 1957. 'Optik und Haptik.' *Studium Generale* 6, 374–9.

Robin, Richard S. 1967. *Annotated Catalogue of the Papers of Charles S. Peirce*. Amherst: University of Massachusetts Press.

Rochberg-Halton, Eugene. 1986. *Meaning and Modernity: Social Theory in the Pragmatic Attitude*. Chicago: University of Chicago Press.

Romanyshyn, Robert E. 1989. *Technology as Symptom and Dream*. London: Routledge.

Rorty, Richard. 1961. 'Pragmatism, Categories and Language.' *Philosophical Review* 70, 197–223.

– 1972. 'Indeterminacy of Translation and of Truth.' *Synthese* 23, 443–62.

– 1976. 'Realism and Reference.' *The Monist* 59, 321–40.

– 1979. *Philosophy and the Mirror of Nature*. Princeton: Princeton University Press.

– 1982. *Consequences of Pragmatism*. Minneapolis: Minnesota University Press.

– 1989. 'Pragmatism, Davidson and Truth.' In E. LePore, ed., *Truth and Interpretation: Perspectives on the Philosophy of Donald Davidson*, 333–55. London: Basil Blackwell.

– 1991. 'Inquiry as Recontextualization.' In D.R. Hiley, J.F. Bohman, and R. Schusterman, eds., *The Interpretive Turn: Philosophy, Science, Culture*, 59–80. Ithaca: Cornell University Press.

Rosch, Eleanor. 1973. 'On the Internal Structure of Perceptual and Semantic Categories.' In T. Moore, ed., *Cognitive Development and the Acquisition of Language*, 111–44. New York: Academic Press.

– 1974. 'Linguistic Relativity.' In A. Silverstein, ed., *Human Communication: Theoretical Explorations*, 95–121. New York: Halsted Press.

– 1975a. 'Cognitive Representations of Semantic Categories.' *Journal of Experimental Psychology: General* 104, 192–233.

– 1975b. 'Universals and Cultural Specifics in Human Categorization.' In R. Brislin, S. Bochner, and W. Lonner, eds., *Cross-Cultural Perspectives on Learning*, 177–206. New York: Halsted Press.

– 1977. 'Human Categorization.' In N. Warren, ed., *Studies in Cross-Cultural Psychology*, vol. 1, 3–49. London: Academic Press.

– 1978. *Cognition and Categorization.* Hillsdale, NJ: Erlbaum, Rotman, Brian.

Rosenthal-Schneider, Ilse. 1980. *Reality and Scientific Truth.* Detroit: Wayne State University Press.

Ross, George MacDonald. 1985. 'Angels.' *Philosophy* 60, 21–30.

Ross, John Robert. 1972. 'The Category Squish: Enstation Hauptwort.' In *Papers from the Eighth Regional Meeting, Chicago Linguistic Society*, 316–28. Chicago: Chicago Linguistic Society.

Roth, Paul A. 1978. 'Paradox and Indeterminacy.' *Journal of Philosophy* 75 (7), 347–67.

– 1987. *Meaning and Method in the Social Sciences: A Case for Methodological Pluralism.* Ithaca: Cornell University Press.

Rotman, Brian. 1988. 'Toward a Semiotics of Mathematics.' *Semiotica* 72 (1/2), 1–35.

– 1993. *Taking God Out of Mathematics and Putting the Body Back In: An Essay on Corporeal Semiotics.* Palo Alto: Stanford University Press.

Rouilhan, Philippe de. 1992. 'Russell and the Vicious Circle Principle.' *Philosophical Studies* 65, 169–82.

Routley, Richard. 1979. *Exploring Meinong's Jungle and Beyond.* Canberra, Australia: Australia National University Departmental Monograph no. 3.

Russell, Bertrand. 1905. 'On Denoting.' *Mind* 14, 479–93.

– 1914. 'On the Nature of Acquaintance.' Reprinted in R.C. Marsh, ed., *Logic and Knowledge*, 125–74. New York: G.P. Putnam's Sons.

– 1923. 'Vagueness.' *Australian Journal of Philosophy* 1, 88–91.

Sacks, Mark. 1989. *The World We Found: The Limits of Ontological Talk.* LaSalle, IL: Open Court.

Savan, David. 1987–8. *An Introduction to C.S. Peirce's Full System of Semeiotic* (Monograph Series of the Toronto Semiotic Circle 1). Toronto: Victoria College.

Scheffler, Israel. 1974. *Four Pragmatists: A Critical Introduction to Peirce, James, Mead, and Dewey.* New York: Humanities Press.

Schrödinger, Erwin. 1967. *What Is Life?* and *Matter and Mind.* Cambridge: Cambridge University Press.

Schultz, Robert A. 1979. 'Analogues of Argument in Fictional Narrative.' *Poetics* 8 (1/2), 231–44.

Sebeok, Thomas A. 1976. *Contribution to the Doctrine of Signs.* Bloomington: Indiana University Press.

– 1979. 'The Semiotic Self.' In *The Sign and Its Masters*, 263–7. Austin: Texas University Press.

– 1991. *Semiotics in the United States.* Bloomington: Indiana University Press.

Sellars, Wilfred. 1963. *Science, Perception, and Reality.* New York: Humanities Press.

Seung, T.K. 1982. *Structuralism and Hermeneutics.* New York: Columbia University Press.

Shanker, S.G. 1987. *Wittgenstein and the Turning-Point in the Philosophy of Mathematics.* Albany: State University of New York Press.

Sheffer, Henry M. 1913. 'A Set of Five Independent Postulates of Boolean Algebra.' *Transactions of the American Mathematical Society* 14, 481–8.

Shiffer, Stephen. 1986. 'Kripkenstein Meets the Remnant of Meaning.' *Philosophical Studies* 49, 147–62.

Skagestad, Peter. 1981. *The Road to Inquiry: Charles Peirce's Pragmatic Realism.* New York: Columbia University Press.

Skolimowski, Henryk. 1986. 'Quine, Adjukiewicz, and the Predicament of 20th Century Philosophy.' In P.A. Schilpp, ed., *The Philosophy of W.V. Quine*, 463–90. LaSalle, IL: Open Court.

– 1987. 'The Interactive Mind in the Participatory Universe.' In J.E. Charon, ed., *The Real and the Imaginary: A New Approach to Physics*, 69–94. New York: Paragon House.

Smith, John E. 1983. 'Community and Reality.' In E. Freeman, ed., *The Relevance of Charles Peirce*, 38–58. LaSalle, IL: Monist Library of Philosophy.

Spence, Donald. 1982. *Narrative Truth and Historical Truth: Meanings and Interpretation in Psychoanalysis.* New York: Norton.

Spencer-Brown, G. 1957. *Probability and Scientific Inference.* London: Longmans, Green.

Spengler, Oswald. 1926. *The Decline of the West.* Vol. 1. New York: Alfred A. Knopf.

Steiner, Wendy. 1982. *The Colors of Rhetoric: Problems in the Relation between Modern Literature and Painting.* Chicago: University of Chicago Press.

Stenlund, Sören. 1990. *Language and Philosophical Problems.* London: Routledge.

Struik, D. 1956. 'On the Sociology of Mathematics.' *Science and Society* 20, 58–70.

Suter, Ronald. 1989. *Interpreting Wittgenstein: A Cloud of Philosophy, a Drop of Grammar.* Philadelphia: Temple University Press.

Taylor, Charles. 1992. 'To Follow a Rule.' In M. Hjort, ed., *Rules and Conventions: Literature, Philosophy, Social Theory*, 167–85. Baltimore: Johns Hopkins University Press.

Thibaud, P. 1975. *La logique de C.S. Peirce, de l'algèbre aux graphes.* Paris: Université de Provence.

Todorov, Tzvetan. 1973. *The Fantastic: A Structural Approach to a Literary Genre.* Trans. R. Howard. Cleveland: Case Western Reserve University Press.

– 1984. *Mikhail Bakhtin: The Dialogical Principle.* Trans. W. Godzich. Minneapolis: University of Minnesota Press.

Toulmin, Stephen. 1982. 'The Construal of Reality: Criticism in Modern and Postmodern Science.' In W.J.T. Mitchell, ed., *The Politics of Interpretation*, 99–117. Chicago: University of Chicago Press.

– 1990. *Cosmopolis: The Hidden Agenda of Modernity.* New York: Free Press.

Tursman, Richard. 1987. *Peirce's Theory of Scientific Discovery: A System of Logic Conceived as Semiotic.* Bloomington: Indiana University Press.

Tyler, Stephen A. 1986. 'Post-Modern Ethnography: From Document of the Occult to Occult Document.' In J. Clifford and G.E. Marcus, eds., *Writing Culture: The Poetics and Culture of Ethnography*, 122–40. Berkeley: University of California Press.

– 1987. *The Unspeakable: Discourse, Dialogue, and Rhetoric in the Postmodern World.* Madison: University of Wisconsin Press.

Ulmer, Gregory L. 1985. *Applied Grammatology: Post(e)-Pedagogy from Jacques Derrida to Joseph Beuys.* Baltimore: Johns Hopkins University Press.

Vaihinger, Hans. 1924. *The Philosophy of 'As If': A System of the Theoretical, Practical and Religious Fictions of Mankind.* 2nd ed. Trans. C.K. Ogden. London: Kegan Paul, Trench, Truber.

Varela, Francisco J. 1984a. 'The Creative Circle: Sketches on the Natural History of Circularity.' In P. Watzlawick, ed., *The Invented Reality*, 309–23. New York: W.W. Norton.

– 1984b. 'Living Ways of Sense-Making: A Middle Path for Neuroscience.' In P. Livingston, ed., *Disorder and Order* (Proceedings of the Stanford International Symposium, 1981), 208–24. Saratoga, CA: Anma Libri.

Varela, Francisco J., Evan Thompson, and Eleanor Rosch. 1993. *The Embodied Mind: Cognitive Science and Human Experience.* Cambridge: MIT.

Vuillemin, Jules. 1986. 'On Duhem's and Quine's Thesis.' In L.E. Hahn and P.A. Schilpp, eds., *The Philosophy of W.V. Quine*, 595–618. LaSalle, IL: Open Court.

Waismann, Friedrich. 1959. 'How I See Philosophy.' In A.J. Ayer, ed., *Logical Positivism*, 345–80. Glencoe, IL: The Free Press.

Walton, Kendall. 1978. 'Fearing Fictions.' *Journal of Philosophy* 75 (1), 5–27.

Weber, Samuel. 1985. 'Afterword: Literature – Just Making It.' In Jean-François Lyotard and Jean-Loup Thébaud, *Just Gaming*, 101–20. Trans. W. Godzich. Minneapolis: University of Minnesota Press.

Wennerberg, Hjalmar. 1962. *The Pragmatism of C.S. Peirce.* Copenhagen: Ejmar Munksgaard.

Werhane, Patricia H. 1992. *Skepticism, Rules, and Private Languages.* New York: Humanities Press.

Weschler, Lawrence. 1982. *Seeing Is Forgetting the Name of the Thing One Sees.* Berkeley: University of California Press.

Weyl, Hermann. 1946. 'Mathematics and Logic.' *American Mathematical Monthly* 53, 2–13.

Wheeler, John Archibald. 1980a. 'Beyond the Black Hole.' In H. Woolf, ed., *Some Strangeness in the Proportion: A Centennial Symposium to Celebrate the Achievement of Albert Einstein*, 341–75. Reading, MA: Addison-Wesley.

– 1980b. 'Law without Law.' In P. Medawar and J.H. Shelley, eds., *Structure in Science and Art*, 132–68. Amsterdam: Excerpta Medica.

– 1984. 'Bits, Quanta, Meaning.' In *Theoretical Physics Meeting*, 121–34. Napoli: Edizioni Scientifiche Italiane.

Wheeler, Samuel C. III. 1989. 'Indeterminacy of French Interpretation: Derrida and Davidson.' In E. LePore, ed., *Truth and Interpretation: Perspectives on the Philosophy of Donald Davidson*, 477–94.

– 1991. 'True Figures: Metaphor, Social Relations, and the Sorites.' In D.R. Hiley, J.F. Bohman, and R. Schusterman, eds., *The Interpretive Turn: Philosophy, Science, Culture*, 197–217. Ithaca: Cornell University Press.

White, Hayden. 1987. *The Content of the Form: Narrative Discourse and Historical Representation.* Baltimore: Johns Hopkins University Press.

Whitehead, Alfred North. 1938. *Modes of Thought.* New York: Free Press.

– 1946. *Process and Reality.* New York: Free Press.

Whitehead, Alfred North, and Bertrand Russell. 1910. *Principia Mathematica.* Cambridge: Cambridge University Press.

Whiteside, Anna. 1987. 'Conclusion: Theories of Reference.' In A. Whiteside and M. Issacharoff, eds., *On Referring in Literature*, 175–208. Bloomington: Indiana University Press.

Wiener, Philip P. 1952. 'Peirce's Evolutionary Interpretations of the History of Science.' In P.P. Wiener and F.H. Young, eds., *Studies in the Philosophy of Charles Sanders Peirce*, 141–52. Cambridge: Harvard University Press.

Wilden, Anthony. 1968. *The Language of the Self: The Function of Language in Psychoanalysis*, by Jacques Lacan. Trans. with notes and commentary by A. Wilden. Baltimore: Johns Hopkins University Press.

– 1980. *System and Structure.* 2nd ed. London: Tavistock.

Wiley, Norbert. 1994. *The Semiotic Self.* Chicago: University of Chicago Press.

Wilson, N.L. 1959. 'Substances without Substrata.' *Review of Metaphysics* 12 (4), 521–39.

– 1970. 'Grice on Meaning: The Ultimate Counterexample.' *Nous* 4 (3), 295–302.

Wittgenstein, Ludwig. 1953. *Philosophical Investigations.* Trans. G.E.M. Anscombe. New York: Macmillan.

– 1956. *Remarks on the Foundations of Mathematics.* Trans. G.E.M. Anscombe. New York: Macmillan.

– 1970. *Zettel.* Trans. G.E.M. Anscombe. Berkeley: University of California Press.

Woods, John. 1974. *The Logic of Fiction.* The Hague: Mouton.

Woolgar, Steve (ed.). 1988. *Knowledge and Reflexivity: New Frontiers in the Sociology of Knowledge.* London: Sage.

Wright, Crispin. 1976. 'Language-Mastery and the Sorites Paradox.' In G. Evans and J. McDowell, eds., *Truth and Meaning: Essays in Semantics*, 223–47. Oxford: Clarendon Press.

Yourgrau, Wolfgang. 1966. 'Language, Spatial Concepts and Physics.' In P.K. Feyerabend and G. Maxwell, eds., *Mind, Matter, and Method*, 496–99. Minneapolis: University of Minnesota Press.

Zadeh, L. 1965. 'Fuzzy Sets.' *Information and Control* 8, 378–53.

– 1975. 'Fuzzy Logic and Approximate Reasoning (In Memory of Grigore Moisil).' *Synthese* 30, 407–28.

Zajonc, Arthur. 1993. *Catching the Light*. New York: Bantam.

Zohar, Danah. 1990. *The Quantum Self: A Revolutionary View of Human Nature and Consciousness Rooted in the New Physics*. New York: Morrow.

Index